Software Quality Engineering

Software Quality Engineering

Testing, Quality Assurance, and
Quantifiable Improvement

Jeff Tian

Department of Computer Science and Engineering
Southern Methodist University
Dallas, TX

A JOHN WILEY & SONS, INC., PUBLICATION

Published by John Wiley & Sons, Inc., Hoboken, New Jersey.
Published simultaneously in Canada.

For general information on our other products and services please contact our Customer Care Department within the U.S. at 877-762-2974, outside the U.S. at 317-572-3993 or fax 317-572-4002.

Wiley also publishes its books in a variety of electronic formats. Some content that appears in print, however, may not be available in electronic format.

Library of Congress Cataloging-in-Publication Data is available.

ISBN 0-471-71345-7

14 13 12 11

To Sharon, Christine, and Elizabeth

CONTENTS

10 Coverage and Usage Testing Based on Finite-State Machines and Markov Chains   147

11 Control Flow, Data Dependency, and Interaction Testing   175

LIST OF FIGURES

LIST OF TABLES

PREFACE

With the pervasive use of software systems in modern society and people's reliance on them in daily life, work, and societal functions, we need to make sure that these systems meet people's expectations for quality and reliability. This is the general subject of *Software Quality Engineering*, which is organized into three major topics:

- Software testing as a primary means to ensure software quality;

- Other alternatives for quality assurance (QA), including defect prevention, process improvement, inspection, formal verification, fault tolerance, safety assurance, and damage control;

- Measurement and analysis to close the feedback loop for quality assessment and quantifiable improvement.

These topics and related concepts are introduced in Part I, with detailed coverage for each major topic in Parts II, III, and IV, respectively.

This book evolved from class notes for the one-semester course "Software Testing and Quality Assurance" that I have taught many times at Southern Methodist University since 1995. Most of our students are full-time software professionals enrolled in SMU's MS program in Software Engineering, with a few other graduate students or undergraduate juniors/seniors in related programs. Although there are many books on software testing and some on specific software QA techniques, they are typically too specialized to be suitable as a main textbook for a course like ours. On the other hand, general books on software engineering or software management cannot and do not cover software quality topics in enough detail or depth. Consequently, a combination of class notes and multiple textbooks was used. Similar situations were also common at other universities for similar courses, such as "Software Quality Assurance" and "Software Verification and Validation". With its comprehensive coverage of all the major topics in software quality engineering in an integrated framework, this book is suitable as the main textbook for such a course.

In addition, this book could be used as a technical reference about software testing, QA, and quality engineering by other readers, particularly professionals who perform QA activities as testers, inspectors, analysts, coordinators, and so forth. It should also be useful to people involved in project planning and management, product release, and support. Similarly, this book could help prepare students for their internship assignments or future employment related to testing or QA.

For more information on this book, please visit the following website:

www.engr.smu.edu/ tian/SQEbook/

Supplementary material for instructors is available at the Wiley.com product page:

www.wiley.com/WileyCDA/WileyTitle/productCd-0471713457.html

Acknowledgments

First, I thank all my students in the SMU/CSE 5314/7314 classes since 1995, particularly, Katherine Chen, Tony Cluff, DeLeon English, Janet Farrar, Nishchal Gupta, Gina Habash, Chris Jordan, Zhao Li, Sateesh Rudrangi, Zahra Shahim, and Nathan Vong, for reading the manuscript and offering many invaluable suggestions. I also thank Tim Culver, for sharing his detailed class notes with me, and Li Ma, for checking the exercise questions.

I thank the co-authors of my technical papers and the sponsors of my research projects for the material included in this book based on related publications. Since all these publications are individually cited in the bibliography, I only single out my project sponsors and industrial collaborators here: National Science Foundation, through awards MRI-9724517, CCR-9733588, and CCR-0204345; Texas Higher Education Coordinating Board, through awards 003613-0030-1999 and 003613-0030-2001; IBM, Nortel Networks, and Lockheed-Martin.

I am grateful to SMU for granting me a sabbatical leave for the 2003/2004 academic year to work on my research and to write this book. I thank my colleagues at SMU, particularly Prof. Hesham El-Rewini, for their encouragement and help. I also appreciate the opportunity to work for the IBM Software Solutions Toronto Laboratory between 1992 and 1995, where I gained invaluable practical experience in software QA and testing.

This book would not be possible without the love and support of my wife Sharon and my daughters Christine and Elizabeth. Sharon, a professional tester for many years, also helped me greatly by offering her invaluable technical critique. Utilizing her strength in reading and writing, Christine edited the entire manuscript (and many of my previous papers too).

I also thank my editor Val Moliere, her assistant Emily Simmons, and my production editor Melissa Yanuzzi, for their professional help.

JEFF (JIANHUI) TIAN

Plano, Texas

PART I

OVERVIEW AND BASICS

Part I gives an overview of the topics covered in this book, and introduces the basic concepts and definitions related to quality, quality assurance (QA), testing, quality engineering, and so forth. This part also covers quality planning as an integral part of software quality engineering.

CHAPTER 1

OVERVIEW

Computers and software systems are becoming ubiquitous in modern society. Worldwide users rely on individual and interconnected computers, as well as the global information infrastructure, such as the Internet and the World Wide Web (WWW), to fulfill their needs for information processing, storage, search, and retrieval. All these needs are met with the support of the underlying software. This reliance requires the software to function correctly over a long time, to be easy to use, and so on. In general, such requirements for high *quality* need to be satisfied by the people involved in the development and support of these software systems through various quality assurance activities, and the claims for high quality need to be supported by evidence based on concrete measurements and analyses. This chapter introduces various concepts related to quality, quality assurance (QA), and quality engineering, and outlines the contents of this book.

1.1 MEETING PEOPLE'S QUALITY EXPECTATIONS

In general, people's quality expectations for software systems they use and rely upon are two-fold:

1. The software systems must do what they are supposed to do. In other words, they must *do the right things*.

2. They must perform these specific tasks correctly or satisfactorily. In other words, they must *do the things right*.

The former requires that the software be the "right software", or perform the right functions. For example, an airline reservation system is supposed to handle reservations, not intended to fly airplanes automatically. The focus of the related activities is to *validate* the required software functions under their intended operational environment. The latter requires that the software systems perform their intended functions without problems. In the airline reservation system example, the system should help travel agents or individual travelers make valid reservations within a pre-specified time limit, instead of making invalid ones, taking too long to make a reservation, or refusing to make reservations without proper justification. The focus of the related activities is to *verify* that the implemented software functions operate as specified.

Main tasks for software quality engineering

As the main topics of this book, the tasks for software QA and quality engineering are to ensure software quality through the related validation and verification activities. These activities need to be carried out by the people and organizations responsible for developing and supporting these software systems in an overall quality engineering process that includes:

- quality planning;

- execution of selected QA or software validation and verification activities;

- measurement and analysis to provide convincing evidence to demonstrate software quality to all parties involved.

In particular, customers and users need to have the assurance that their quality expectations are satisfied by the delivered software systems. The overall experience and lessons learned in delivering such high-quality software systems can be packaged into the software quality engineering process for quantifiable quality improvement in future development projects or to provide better product support.

When viewed from a different angle, the negative impact of software problems is also increasing, accompanying the pervasive use of and reliance on software systems in modern society. The problems could be associated with performing wrong functions, or performing intended functions incorrectly, thus causing unintended consequences. We would like to see such negative impact be eliminated, if possible. However, due to the increasing demand for automation, additional functionality and convenience by modern society to the computer and software systems, and due to the ubiquitous nature of modern computer, software, and information infrastructure, the size and complexity of modern software systems have also increased steadily. This increase in size and complexity also has unintended consequences in terms of causing quality problems.

Quality problems in large software systems

Many software systems nowadays are highly complex and contain millions of lines of source code. Examples of such large software systems can be found in virtually every product segment or every application domain, from various operating systems, such as commonly used versions of the Microsoft Windows and UNIX operations systems, to commercial software products, such as database products, to aviation and in-flight entertainment software used on Boeing 777, to defense related software systems, such as various command/communication/control (CCC) systems.

Such large and complex systems typically involve hundreds or even thousands of people in their development over months or even years, and the systems are often to be operated under diverse, and sometimes unanticipated, application environments. One may argue that some systems are unnecessarily large and complex. According to (Wirth, 1995), such "fat software" may be caused by indiscriminately adding non-essential features, poor design, improper choices of languages and methodologies, which could be addressed by disciplined methodologies and return to essentials for "lean software". Various QA techniques, including many of those covered in this book, can help produce high-quality, lean software.

However, there is no "silver bullet", or an all powerful and effective solution to the size, complexity, quality, and other software engineering problems, due to the fundamental requirements and constraints that a software system must satisfy (Brooks, 1987). Accompanying the size and complexity problems are the many chances for other problems to be introduced into the software systems. Therefore, dealing with problems that may impact customers and users negatively and trying to manage and improve software quality are a fact of life for people involved in the development, management, marketing, and operational support of most modern software systems.

Testing, quality assurance (QA), and quality engineering

The above factors make it virtually impossible or practically infeasible to achieve the complete prevention or elimination of software problems and related negative impact. Consequently, various software QA activities are carried out to prevent or eliminate certain classes of problems that lead to such negative impact, or to reduce the likelihood or severity of such negative impact when it is unavoidable. This book systematically describes topics and issues related to these software QA activities, with an emphasis on the technical aspects.

Software testing plays a central role among the software QA activities. By running the software system or executing its prescribed functions, testers can determine if the observed system behavior conforms to its specifications or requirements. If discrepancies exist between the two, follow-up actions can be carried out to locate and remove the related problems in software code, which may also include modifying the software design. Therefore, the detection and removal of defects through testing help reduce the number of defects in delivered software products, thus helping to achieve the quality goals. Even if no discrepancy is observed, the specific instances can be accumulated as evidence to demonstrate that the software performs as specified. Consequently, testing is the most frequently used means to assure and to demonstrate software quality. A substantial part of this book is devoted to software testing, with an emphasis on commonly used techniques that have proven to be effective in various practical application environments.

Beyond testing, there are many other QA alternatives supported by related techniques and activities, such as inspection, formal verification, defect prevention, and fault tolerance. Inspection is a critical examination of software code or other artifacts by human inspectors to identify and remove problems directly, without resorting to execution. Fault tolerance prevents global system failures even if local problems exist, through various redundancies strategically designed and implemented into the software systems. Other QA techniques employ specific means to assure software quality. This book also provides a comprehensive coverage of these topics.

In addition, all these QA activities need to be managed in an engineering process we call the software quality engineering process, with quality goals set early in the product

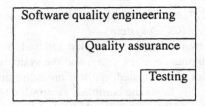

Figure 1.1   Scope and content hierarchy: Testing, quality assurance (QA), and software quality engineering

development, and strategies for QA selected, carried out, and monitored to achieve these preset quality goals. As part of this overall process, data collected during the QA activities, as well as from the overall development activities, can be analyzed to provide feedback to the software development process for decision making, project management, and quantifiable quality improvement. This book also provides a comprehensive coverage of these topics.

1.2   BOOK ORGANIZATION AND CHAPTER OVERVIEW

Figure 1.1 illustrates the general scope of the topics introduced above: Testing is an important subset of QA activities; and QA is an important subset of quality engineering activities. This diagram also explains our book title: "Software Quality Engineering: Testing, Quality Assurance, and Quantifiable Improvement". This book is organized in four major parts and 22 chapters, with the main topics outlined below.

Part I: Overview and Basics

Part I gives a general introduction and overview of the topics covered in the book, and presents the basic concepts and definitions related to quality, QA, testing, quality engineering, etc. Specific questions answered include:

- About this book: What is it? How to use it? How is it organized? In addition, what background knowledge is needed to have a thorough understanding of the technical aspects of this book? These questions are answered in Chapter 1.

- What is software quality? In particular, what are the different views of quality? Is quality a single, atomic concept, or does it consist of many different attributes or characteristics? What is the relationship between quality, correctness, and defect? Can we narrow down the definition of quality to better focus our attention on various QA activities commonly carried out during software life cycles? These questions are answered in Chapter 2.

- What is QA? The question is answered from a particular perspective in Chapter 3, representing a defect-based interpretation of quality and QA.

- What are the different QA activities and related techniques? A defect-based classification is presented, also in Chapter 3, for the major QA alternatives and techniques, such as testing, inspection, formal verification, fault tolerance, and so on.

- How to fit the different QA activities into the software development processes? What about other frameworks to classify QA activities? These questions are answered in Chapter 4.

- The QA activities are broadened in Chapter 5 into quality engineering that includes quality planning prior to specific QA activities and measurement, analysis, and feedback activities to close the loop for quality assessment and quantifiable improvement.

Part II: Software Testing

Part II deals with all the important topics related to software testing, with an emphasis on commonly used testing techniques that have proven to be effective and efficient in many practical application environments. The chapters in this part are organized into two subparts: Descriptions of specific testing techniques (Chapters 8 through 11) are surrounded by chapters on the general issues of testing (Chapters 6, 7, and 12). Individual chapters are described below:

- General questions, issues, terminology about testing, including the generic testing process and a taxonomy for testing, are discussed in Chapter 6.

- The major testing activities, people's roles and responsibilities in these activities, test management, and test automation issues are covered in Chapter 7.

- Checklist and partition-based testing: Chapter 8 starts with the simplest testing of them all, *ad hoc* testing, then progresses to more organized testing using simple models such as *lists* and *partitions*. Specific testing techniques covered in Chapter 8 include:

  – testing with different types of general checklists;

  – decision and predicate testing;

  – usage-based statistical testing using flat operational profiles.

- Boundary testing: As a special case and extension of partition testing, we cover boundary testing in Chapter 9. Application of boundary testing ideas in other testing situations is also covered.

- State-based testing: Both the finite-state machines (FSMs), which serve as the basis for state-based testing, and the augmented FSMs, which form Markov chains for more in-depth usage-based statistical testing, are covered in Chapter 10.

- Interaction testing: Instead of focusing on individual partitions or states, the testing techniques described in Chapter 11 deal with the interactions along a complete execution path or a dependency slice. Specifically, this chapter covers the following traditional testing techniques:

  – control-flow testing (CFT);

  – data-flow testing (DFT).

- Chapter 12 discusses application of specific testing techniques for specific testing tasks in different sub-phases or in specialized tasks. The integration of different testing techniques to fulfill some common purposes is also discussed.

Part III: Quality Assurance Beyond Testing

Part III covers important QA techniques other than testing, including the ones described below, and a comparison of all the QA alternatives at the end.

- Various defect prevention techniques are described in Chapter 13.

- Software inspection, or critical examination of software artifacts by human inspectors, is described in Chapter 14.

- Formal verification of program correctness with respect to its formal specifications is covered in Chapter 15.

- Fault tolerance techniques that prevent failures through some redundancy or duplication are discussed in Chapter 16. Related techniques based on similar ideas, such as failure containment to minimize failure impact, are also discussed in Chapter 16.

- Some program analysis techniques, specifically static analyses, are also covered in Chapter 14 in connection to inspection. Related topics on dynamic program analyses are briefly covered in Chapter 12 in connection to specialized testing techniques.

- Comparison of different QA alternatives and techniques, including those covered in Part III as well as testing covered in Part II, is presented in Chapter 17.

Part IV: Quantifiable Quality Improvement

Part IV covers the important activities carried out in parallel or as follow-up to the main QA activities described in Part II and Part III. The purpose of these activities is to monitor the QA activities to provide quantitative quality assessment and feedback to the quality engineering process. Such assessment and feedback can be used to help with decision making, project management, and various improvement initiatives. The main contents of the specific chapters in this part are described below:

- First, the parallel and follow-up activities, as well as the collection and usage of the raw and processed data in related analyses to provide specific feedback for various purposes, are described in Chapter 18.

- Chapter 19 describes different models and measurements for quality assessment and improvement, and classifies them according to the information provided and the specific types of data required.

- Defect classification and analysis models are described in Chapter 20, as an important sub-class of quality assessment models that focuses on the collection and analysis of detailed defect information.

- Further analysis of the discovered defects and other measurement data from QA and overall development activities can be carried out to identify high-risk or high-defect areas for focused remedial actions aimed at effective quality improvement. Various risk identification techniques and related models for doing this are presented in Chapter 21.

- As an alternative to the defect-based view of quality that is closer to the developers' perspective, reliability is a quality measure that is closer to the users' perspective and more meaningful to target customers. Chapter 22 presents software reliability models and analysis techniques to provide reliability assessments and guidance for reliability improvement.

1.3 DEPENDENCY AND SUGGESTED USAGE

The integration of the interconnected chapters is an important feature of this book. We next examine the topic and chapter dependencies, and discuss different ways that these topics can be combined for different readers with different purposes in mind.

Chapter dependency

Figure 1.2 depicts the dependencies among different chapters, as well as among different parts, with each part grouped by dotted lines. We use solid lines to depict essential dependencies and dashed lines to depict dependencies that are desirable but not essential. An example of the latter type of dependencies is the non-essential dependency between quality assessment and analysis in Part IV and QA topics in Parts II and III: The knowledge of the topics presented in Parts II and III would make most of topics covered in Part IV more meaningful. However, one can have a general understanding of Part IV without a thorough knowledge of Parts II and III. Similarly, although all the chapters in Part III except the last one can be treated as parallel ones, Chapters 13 through 16 generally follow the sequence of activities or phases in the development process. Therefore, it would be more logical to follow this sequence. Some specific dependencies are explained below:

- In addition to Chapter 17's dependency on previous chapters of Part III, it should also be preceded by chapters in Part II, at least Chapter 6, because the comparison of QA alternatives in Chapter 17 rely on the general knowledge of individual alternatives and techniques.

- The chapters on testing techniques in Part II follow the natural progression from simple models to complex ones. However, there is no essential dependency between those based on simple partitions (Chapters 8 and 9) and those based on more complex models (Chapters 10 and 11).

- The last two chapters in Part IV can be treated as parallel chapters except that part of Chapter 22, the topic on tree-based reliability models (TBRMs), uses the modeling technique called tree-based modeling covered in Chapter 21.

Suggested usage

This book is suitable as the main textbook for a one-semester course in various software engineering programs. Other people who are interested in learning all the major topics in software quality engineering should also read the whole book. However, for people who just want to get a general idea of the topics covered in this book, the following chapters are appropriate:

- *The minimal set:* Chapters 1–6, 17, and 18. This minimal set includes all five chapters in Part I and one chapter each from Parts II, III, and IV, respectively.

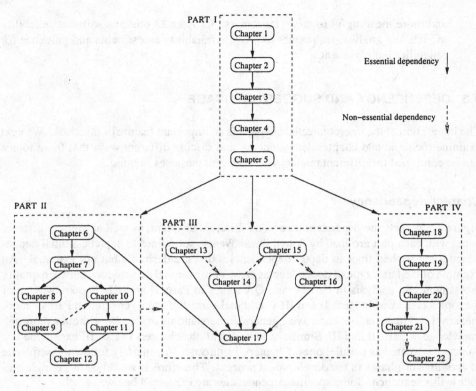

Figure 1.2 Chapter and PART dependency diagram

Between these two extremes (the minimal set and all chapters), there are also other possible usages of this book. All the following would assume the basic coverage of minimal set of chapters above and some other chapters in addition to it. Some suggested usages are given below:

- Half semester course: Cover all in selective details, with emphasis on either Part II, III, or IV.

- Short course on specialized topics: minimal set above plus one of the part from Parts II, III, and IV. Such short courses would be similar in length to about ten hours or 3–4 weeks of class lectures.

- Other combinations of chapters are also possible, but would require the reader to keep track of the cross-references in topics and related dependencies using Figure 1.2 as the guide.

In addition to its use as a textbook, or as a technical book that introduces other people to the important topics of software quality engineering, the comprehensive coverage of all the important topics and pointers to further reading should also make this book a good reference for readers in their professional career.

1.4 READER PREPARATION AND BACKGROUND KNOWLEDGE

To have a good understanding of the technical details, the readers need to have a general knowledge of mathematics, statistics, computer science, and software engineering, equivalent to that at the level of college juniors, seniors, or new graduate students in computer science, software engineering, or a related field. The following is intended as a general checklist for the readers: If you find that you lack certain background knowledge listed below, you need to study or review them on your own before proceeding to related technical discussions. This checklist will help readers link specific pieces of background knowledge to specific parts of the book.

Mathematical and statistical knowledge

Reviewing standard textbooks on mathematics and statistics covering the following topics would be useful if you are unfamiliar with some of them:

- Basic concepts of relations, algebra, and set theory: Used throughout the book, and especially in the following:
    - Sets, subsets, partitions, basic types of relations, and equivalence classes in Chapter 8 for partition-based testing.
    - Use of algebraic equations to define boundaries in Chapter 9 for boundary testing.
    - Precedence and dependency relations in Chapter 11 for control-flow and data-flow testing.
    - Cause–effect relations in Chapter 16 for hazard analysis and safety assurance, and in Chapter 20 for defect analysis.
- Logic, particularly Boolean logic, and related formalisms: Used throughout the book, and especially in the following:
    - Boolean logic for predicate and decision testing in Chapter 8.
    - Mathematical logic and formalisms in Chapter 15 for formal verification of program correctness.
- Some basic concepts of graph theory: Used throughout the book, and especially in the following:
    - Decision trees in Chapter 8 for operational profiles used in statistical testing.
    - Graph elements for finite-state machines (FSMs) and related testing in Chapter 10.
    - Flow-chart like situations for control-flow testing in Chapter 11.
    - Data dependency graphs (a tree-structured graph) for data-flow testing in Chapter 11.
    - Trees in fault-tree analysis and event-tree analysis in Chapter 16 for hazard analysis and safety assurance.
    - Tree-based models for risk identification in Chapter 21 and for reliability analysis in Chapter 22.

- Basic concepts of probability and statistics: Particularly important to the following topics:

  - Usage-based testing in Chapters 8 and 10.
  - Defect classification and distribution analysis in Chapter 20.

- Basic concepts of statistical analysis and modeling: Important to the topics in Part IV, in particular,

  - General analysis and modeling techniques in Chapter 19.
  - Various specific types of analyses for risk identification in Chapter 21.
  - Stochastic process and analysis for software reliability modeling in Chapter 22.

Computer science knowledge

Reviewing standard textbooks on computer science covering the following topics would be useful if you are unfamiliar with some of them:

- Familiarity with programming and general software development using a high-level language. However, to make the understanding of basic concepts independent of specific implementation languages, example programs in the book are given in pseudo-code form. Therefore, at a minimum, the readers need to be familiar with pseudo-code commonly used to present basic algorithms in computer science literature and sometimes to illustrate design ideas during software development.

- Fundamentals of computing, particularly:

  - Finite-state machines (FSMs), which are the basis for state-based testing in Chapter 10.
  - Execution flow and data dependencies, which are the basis for control flow and data-flow testing in Chapter 11.
  - Some formalisms about computing and programming languages used in Chapters 10, 11, and 15.
  - Some analysis techniques commonly identified with computer science and artificial intelligence, such as pattern matching, learning algorithms, and neural networks used in Chapter 21.

- Design and organization of computer and software systems such as used in parallel and redundant systems in Chapter 16.

Software engineering knowledge

Reviewing standard textbooks on software engineering covering the following topics would be useful if you are unfamiliar with some of them:

- General knowledge of software development and maintenance activities, including requirement analysis, product specification, design, coding, testing, release, support, etc.

- General awareness of different software development processes, including water-fall, spiral, incremental, iterative, extreme programming (XP), etc., and the software process capability maturity model (CMM).

- General awareness with software management and system engineering issues, including economic consequences of project decisions, tradeoffs between different objectives and concerns, feedback and improvement mechanisms, optimization, etc.

- Familiarity with at least one of the commonly used development methodologies (and related tools), such as object-oriented development (OOD), structured development (SD), Cleanroom technology, agile methods, formal methods, etc.

- Practical experience working with some industrial software projects would be extremely helpful.

Problems

1.1   Consider some of your daily activities and classify them according the role played by computers and underlying software: no role, minor role, major role, and critical role. If "no role" is your answer for all the areas/activities, STOP — this is not a book for you. Otherwise, perform an overall assessment on how important software quality is to your daily activities.

1.2   Use the dependency diagram in Figure 1.2 and related explanations in Section 1.3 to construct your individual study plan to fulfill your personal goals.

1.3   Use the checklist in Section 1.4 and your personal goals to see if you need to review any background knowledge. If so, construct your individual study plan to get yourself ready for the rest of the book.

CHAPTER 2

WHAT IS SOFTWARE QUALITY?

The question, "What is software quality?", is bound to generate many different answers, depending on whom you ask, under what circumstances, for what kind of software systems, and so on. An alternative question that is probably easier for us to get more informative answers is: "What are the characteristics for high-quality software?"

In this chapter, we attempt to define software quality by defining the expected characteristics or properties of high-quality software. In doing so, we need to examine the different perspectives and expectations of users as well as other people involved with the development, management, marketing, and maintenance of the software products. We also need to examine the individual characteristics associated with quality and their inter-relationship, and focus our attention on the critical characteristics of functional correctness. We conclude the chapter with a comparison of software quality with quality concepts for other (non-software) systems and the evolving place of quality within software engineering.

2.1 QUALITY: PERSPECTIVES AND EXPECTATIONS

We next examine the different views of quality in a systematic manner, based on the different roles, responsibilities, and quality expectations of different people, and zoom in on a small set of views and related properties to be consistently followed throughout this book. Five major views according to (Kitchenham and Pfleeger, 1996; Pfleeger et al., 2002) are: transcendental, user, manufacturing, product, and value-based views, as outlined below:

- In the *transcendental* view, quality is hard to define or describe in abstract terms, but can be recognized if it is present. It is generally associated with some intangible properties that delight users.

- In the *user* view, quality is fitness for purpose or meeting user's needs.

- In the *manufacturing* view, quality means conformance to process standards.

- In the *product* view, the focus is on inherent characteristics in the product itself in the hope that controlling these internal quality indicators (or the so-called product-internal metrics described in Chapter 18) will result in improved external product behavior (quality in use).

- In the *value-based* view, quality is the customers' willingness to pay for a software.

People's roles and responsibilities

When software quality is concerned, different people would have different views and expectations based on their roles and responsibilities. With the quality assurance (QA) and quality engineering focus of this book, we can divide the people into two broad groups:

- *Consumers* of software products or services, including customers and users, either internally or externally. Sometime we also make the distinction between the *customers*, who are responsible for the acquisition of software products or services, and the *users*, who use the software products or services for various purposes, although the dual roles of customers and users are quite common. We can also extend the concept of users to include such non-human or "invisible" users as other software, embedded hardware, and the overall operational environment that the software operates under and interacts with (Whittaker, 2001).

- *Producers* of software products, or anyone involved with the development, management, maintenance, marketing, and service of software products. We adopt a broad definition of producers, which also include third-party participants who may be involved in add-on products and services, software packaging, software certification, fulfilling independent verification and validation (IV&V) responsibilities, and so on.

Subgroups within the above groups may have different concerns, although there are many common concerns within each group. In the subsequent discussions, we use *external* view for the first group's perspective, who are more concerned with the observed or external behavior, rather than the internal details that lead to such behavior. Similarly, we use a generic label *internal* view for the second group's perspective, because they are typically familiar with or at least aware of various internal characteristic of the products. In other words, the external view mostly sees a software system as a black box, where one can observe its behavior but not see through inside; while the internal view mostly sees it as a white box, or more appropriately a clear box, where one can see what is inside and how it works.

Quality expectations on the consumer side

The basic quality expectations of a user are that a software system performs useful functions as it is specified. There are two basic elements to this expectation: First, it performs right functions as specified, which, hopefully fits the user's needs (fit for use). Second, it performs these specified functions correctly over repeated use or over a long period of time, or performs its functions *reliably*. These two elements are related to the validation and verification aspects of QA we introduced in the previous chapter, which will be expanded further in Chapter 4. Looking into the future, we can work towards meeting this basic expectation and beyond to *delight* customers and users by preventing unforeseen negative impacts and produce unexpected positive effects (Denning, 1992).

For many users of today's ubiquitous software and systems, ease of use, or usability, may be a more important quality expectation than reliability or other concerns. For example, the adoption of graphical user interfaces (GUI) in personal computers to replace text-based command interpreters often used in mainframes is primarily driven by the usability concerns for their massive user population. Similarly, ease of installation, is another major trend for software intended for the same population, to allow for painless (and nearly effortless) installation and operation, or the so-called "plug-and-play". However, different users of the same system may have different views and priorities, such as the importance of usability for novice users and the importance of reliability for sophisticated users of the web (Vatanasombut et al., 2004).

When we consider the extended definition of users beyond human users, the primary expectations for quality would be to ensure the smooth operation and interaction between the software and these non-human users in the form of better inter-operability and adaptability, so that the software can work well with others and within its surrounding environment.

The basic quality expectations of a customer are similar to that of a user, with the additional concern for the cost of the software or service. This additional concern can be reflected by the so-called value-based view of quality, that is, whether a customer is willing to pay for it. The competing interests of quality and other software engineering concerns, such as cost, schedule, functionality, and their trade-offs, are examined in Section 2.4.

Quality expectations on the producer side

For software producers, the most fundamental quality question is to fulfill their contractual obligations by producing software products that conform to product specifications or providing services that conform to service agreement. By extension, various product internal characteristics that make it easy to conform to product specifications, such as good designs that maintain conceptual integrity of product components and reduce coupling across different components, are also associated with good quality.

For product and service managers, adherence to pre-selected software process and relevant standards, proper choice of software methodologies, languages, and tools, as well as other factors, may be closely related to quality. They are also interested in managing and satisfying user's quality expectations, by translating such quality expectations into realistic quality goals that can be defined and managed internally, selecting appropriate and effective QA strategies, and seeing them through.

For other people on the producer side, their different concerns may also produce quality views and expectations different from the above. For example, usability and modifiability may be paramount for people involved with software service, maintainability for maintenance personnel, portability for third-party or software packaging service providers, and profitability and customer value for product marketing.

2.2 QUALITY FRAMEWORKS AND ISO-9126

Based on the different quality views and expectations outlined above, quality can be defined accordingly. In fact, we have already mentioned above various so-called "-ilities" connected to the term quality, such as reliability, usability, portability, maintainability, etc. Various models or frameworks have been proposed to accommodate these different quality views and expectations, and to define quality and related attributes, features, characteristics, and measurements. We next briefly describe ISO-9126 (ISO, 2001), the mostly influential one in the software engineering community today, and discuss various adaptations of such quality frameworks for specific application environments.

ISO-9126

ISO-9126 (ISO, 2001) provides a hierarchical framework for quality definition, organized into quality characteristics and sub-characteristics. There are six top-level quality characteristics, with each associated with its own exclusive (non-overlapping) sub-characteristics, as summarized below:

- Functionality: A set of attributes that bear on the existence of a set of functions and their specified properties. The functions are those that satisfy stated or implied needs. The sub-characteristics include:

    - Suitability
    - Accuracy
    - Interoperability
    - Security

- Reliability: A set of attributes that bear on the capability of software to maintain its level of performance under stated conditions for a stated period of time. The sub-characteristics include:

    - Maturity
    - Fault tolerance
    - Recoverability

- Usability: A set of attributes that bear on the effort needed for use, and on the individual assessment of such use, by a stated or implied set of users. The sub-characteristics include:

    - Understandability
    - Learnability
    - Operability

- Efficiency: A set of attributes that bear on the relationship between the level of performance of the software and the amount of resources used, under stated conditions. The sub-characteristics include:

    - Time behavior
    - Resource behavior

- Maintainability: A set of attributes that bear on the effort needed to make specified modifications. The sub-characteristics include:

    - Analyzability
    - Changeability
    - Stability
    - Testability

- Portability: A set of attributes that bear on the ability of software to be transferred from one environment to another. The sub-characteristics include:

    - Adaptability
    - Installability
    - Conformance
    - Replaceability

Alternative frameworks and focus on correctness

ISO-9126 offers a comprehensive framework to describe many attributes and properties we associate with quality. There is a strict hierarchy, where no sub-characteristics are shared among quality characteristics. However, certain product properties are linked to multiple quality characteristics or sub-characteristics (Dromey, 1995; Dromey, 1996). For example, various forms of redundancy affect both efficiency and maintainability. Consequently, various alternative quality frameworks have been proposed to allow for more flexible relations among the different quality attributes or factors, and to facilitate a smooth transition from specific quality concerns to specific product properties and metrics.

Many companies and communities associated with different application domains have adapted and customized existing quality frameworks to define quality for themselves, taking into consideration their specific business and market environment. One concrete example of this for companies is the quality attribute list CUPRIMDS (capability, usability, performance, reliability, installation, maintenance, documentation, and service) IBM used for their software products (Kan, 2002). CUPRIMDS is often used together with overall customer satisfaction (thus the acronym CUPRIMDSO) to characterize and measure software quality for IBM's software products.

Similarly, a set of quality attributes has been identified for web-based applications (Offutt, 2002), with the primary quality attributes as reliability, usability, and security, and the secondary quality attributes as availability, scalability, maintainability, and time to market. Such prioritized schemes are often used for specific application domains. For example, performance (or efficiency) and reliability would take precedence over usability and maintainability for real-time software products. On the contrary, it might be the other way round for mass market products for end users.

Among the software quality characteristics or attributes, some deal directly with the functional *correctness*, or the *conformance* to specifications as demonstrated by the absence of problems or instances of non-conformance. Other quality characteristics or attributes deal with usability, portability, etc. Correctness is typically related to several quality characteristics or sub-characteristics in quality frameworks described above. For example, in ISO-9126 it is related to both functionality, particularly its accuracy (in other words, conformance) sub-characteristics, and reliability.

Correctness is typically the most important aspect of quality for situations where daily life or business depends on the software, such as in managing corporate-wide computer networks, financial databases, and real-time control software. Even for market segments where new features and usability take priority, such as for web-based applications and software for personal use in the mass market, correctness is still a fundamental part of the users' expectations (Offutt, 2002; Prahalad and Krishnan, 1999). Therefore, we adopt the correctness-centered view of quality throughout this book. We will focus on correctness-related quality attributes and related ways to ensure and demonstrate quality defined as such.

2.3 CORRECTNESS AND DEFECTS: DEFINITIONS, PROPERTIES, AND MEASUREMENTS

When many people associate *quality* or high-quality with a software system, it is an indication that few, if any, software problems, are expected to occur during its operations. What is more, when problems do occur, the negative impact is expected to be minimal. Related issues are discussed in this section.

Definitions: Error, fault, failure, and defect

Key to the correctness aspect of software quality is the concept of defect, failure, fault, and error. The term "defect" generally refers to some problem with the software, either with its external behavior or with its internal characteristics. The IEEE Standard 610.12 (IEEE, 1990) defines the following terms related to defects:

- *Failure*: The inability of a system or component to perform its required functions within specified performance requirements.

- *Fault*: An incorrect step, process, or data definition in a computer program.

- *Error*: A human action that produces an incorrect result.

Therefore, the term *failure* refers to a behavioral deviation from the user requirement or the product specification; *fault* refers to an underlying condition within a software that causes certain failure(s) to occur; while *error* refers to a missing or incorrect human action resulting in certain fault(s) being injected into a software.

We also extend errors to include *error sources*, or the root causes for the missing or incorrect actions, such as human misconceptions, misunderstandings, etc. Failures, faults, and errors are collectively referred to as *defects* in literature. We will use the term defect in this book in this collective sense or when its derivatives are commonly used in literature, such as in defect handling.

Software problems or defects, are also commonly referred to as "bugs". However, the term bug is never precisely defined, such as the different aspects of defects defined as errors, faults, and failures above. Some people have also raised the moral or philosophical objection to the use of bug as evading responsibility for something people committed. Therefore, we try to avoid using the term "bug" in this book.

Similarly, we also try to avoid using the related terms "debug" or "debugging" for similar reasons. The term "debug" general means "get rid of the bugs". Sometimes, it also includes activities related to detecting the presence of bugs and dealing with them. In this book, we will use, in their place, the following terms:

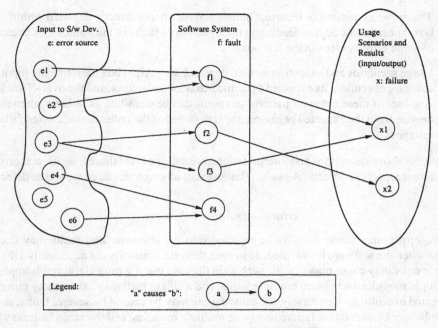

Figure 2.1 Defect related concepts and relations

- We use *defect detection and removal* for the overall concept and activities related to what many people commonly call "debugging".

- When specific activities related to "debugging" are involved, we point the specifics out using more precisely defined terms, including,

  - Specific activities related to defect discovery, including testing, inspection, etc.
  - Specific follow-up activities after defect discovery, including defect diagnosis, analysis, fixing, and re-verification.

All these specific terms will be more precisely defined in this book when they are introduced or when topics most closely related to them are covered.

Concepts and relations illustrated

The concepts of error (including error source), fault, failure, and defect can be placed into the context of software artifact, software development activities, and operational usage, as depicted in Figure 2.1. Some specific information illustrated include:

- The software system as represented by its artifacts is depicted in the middle box. The artifacts include mainly software code and sometime other artifacts such as designs, specifications, requirement documents, etc. The *faults* scattered among these artifacts are depicted as circled entities within the middle box.

- The input to the software development activities, depicted in the left box, include conceptual models and information, developers with certain knowledge and experience, reusable software components, etc. Various *error sources* are also depicted as circled entities within this left box.

- The *errors* as missing or incorrect human actions are not directly depicted within one box, but rather as actions leading to the injection of faults in the middle box because of some error sources in the left box.

- Usage scenarios and execution results, depicted in the right box, describe the input to software execution, its expected dynamic behavior and output, and the overall results. A subset of these behavior patterns or results can be classified as failures when they deviate from the expected behavior, and is depicted as the collection of circled failure instances.

With the above definitions and interpretations, we can see that failures, faults, and errors are different aspects of defects. A causal relation exists among these three aspects of defects:

$$\text{errors} \rightarrow \text{faults} \rightarrow \text{failures}$$

That is, errors may cause faults to be injected into the software, and faults may cause failures when the software is executed. However, this relationship is not necessarily 1-to-1: A single error may cause many faults, such as in the case that a wrong algorithm is applied in multiple modules and causes multiple faults, and a single fault may cause many failures in repeated executions. Conversely, the same failure may be caused by several faults, such as an interface or interaction failure involving multiple modules, and the same fault may be there due to different errors. Figure 2.1 also illustrates some of these situations, as described below:

- The error source *e3* causes multiple faults, *f2* and *f3*.

- The fault *f1* is caused by multiple error sources, *e1* and *e2*.

- Sometimes, an error source, such as *e5*, may not cause any fault injection, and a fault, such as *f4*, may not cause any failure, under the given scenarios or circumstances. Such faults are typically called *dormant* or *latent* faults, which may still cause problems under a different set of scenarios or circumstances.

Correctness-centered properties and measurements

With the correctness focus adopted in this book and the binary partition of people into consumer and producer groups, we can define quality and related properties according to these views (external views for producers vs. internal views for consumers) and attributes (correctness vs. others) in Table 2.1.

The correctness-centered quality from the external view, or from the view of consumers (users and customers) of a software product or service, can be defined and measured by various failure-related properties and measurement. To a user or a customer, the primary concern is that the software operates without failure, or with as few failures as possible. When such failures or undesirable events do occur, the impact should be as little as possible. These concerns can be captured by various properties and related measurements, as follows:

- *Failure properties and direct failure measurement*: Failure properties include information about the specific failures, what they are, how they occur, etc. These properties can be measured directly by examining failure count, distribution, density, etc. We will examine detailed failure properties and measurements in connection with defect classification and analysis in Chapter 20.

Table 2.1 Correctness-centered properties according to quality views and attributes

View	Attribute	
	Correctness	Others
Consumer/ External (user & customer)	Failure- related properties	Usability Maintainability Portability Performance Installability Readability etc. (-ilities)
Producer/ Internal (developer, manager, tester, etc.)	Fault- related properties	Design Size Change Complexity, etc.

- *Failure likelihood and reliability measurement*: How often or how likely a failure is going to occur is of critical concern to software users and customers. This likelihood is captured in various reliability measures, where *reliability* can be defined as the probability of failure-free operations for a specific time period or for a given set of input (Musa et al., 1987; Lyu, 1995a; Tian, 1998). We will discuss this topic in Chapter 22.

- *Failure severity measurement and safety assurance*: The failure impact is also a critical concern for users and customers of many software products and services, especially if the damage caused by failures could be substantial. *Accidents*, which are defined to be failures with severe consequences, need to be avoided, contained, or dealt with to ensure the safety for the personnel involved and to minimize other damages. We will discuss this topic in Chapter 16.

In contrast to the consumers' perspective of quality above, the producers of software systems see quality from a different perspectives in their interaction with software systems and related problems. They need to fix the problems or faults that caused the failures, as well as deal with the injection and activation of other faults that could potentially cause other failures that have not yet been observed.

Similar to the failure properties and related measurements discussed above, we need to examine various fault properties and related measurements from the internal view or the producers' view. We can collect and analyze information about individual faults, as well as do so collectively. Individual faults can be analyzed and examined according to their types, their relations to specific failures and accidents, their causes, the time and circumstances when they are injected, etc. Faults can be analyzed collectively according to their distribution and density over development phases and different software components. These topics will be covered in detail in Chapter 20 in connection with defect classification and analysis. Techniques to identify high-defect areas for focused quality improvement are covered in Chapter 21.

Defects in the context of QA and quality engineering

For most software development organizations, ensuring quality means dealing with defects. Three generic ways to deal with defects include: 1) defect prevention, 2) defect detection and removal, and 3) defect containment. These different ways of dealing with defects and the related activities and techniques for QA will be described in Chapter 3.

Various QA alternatives and related techniques can be used in a concerted effort to effectively and efficiently deal with defects and assure software quality. In the process of dealing with defects, various direct defect measurements and other indirect quality measurements (used as quality indicators) might be taken, often forming a multi-dimensional measurement space referred to as quality profile (Humphrey, 1998). These measurement results need to be analyzed using various models to provide quality assessment and feedback to the overall software development process. Part IV covers these topics.

By extension, quality engineering can also be viewed as defect management. In addition to the execution of the planned QA activities, quality engineering also includes:

- quality planning before specific QA activities are carried out,

- measurement, analysis, and feedback to monitor and control the QA activities.

In this respect, much of quality planning can be viewed as estimation and planning for anticipated defects. Much of the feedback is provided in terms of various defect related quality assessments and predictions. These topics are described in Chapter 5 and Part IV, respectively.

2.4 A HISTORICAL PERSPECTIVE OF QUALITY

We next examine people's views and perceptions of quality in a historical context, and trace the evolving role of software quality in software engineering.

Evolving perceptions of quality

Before software and information technology (IT) industries came into existence, quality has long been associated with physical objects or systems, such as cars, tools, radio and television receivers, etc. Under this traditional setting, QA is typically associated with the manufacturing process. The focus is on ensuring that the products conform to their specifications. What is more, these specifications often accompany the finished products, so that the buyers or users can check them for reference. For example, the user's guide for stereo equipments often lists their specifications in terms of physical dimensions, frequency responses, total harmonic distortion, and other relevant information.

Since many items in the product specifications are specified in terms of ranges and error tolerance, reducing variance in manufacturing has been the focal point of statistical quality control. Quality problems are synonymous to non-conformance to specifications or observed defects defined by the non-conformance. For example, the commonly used "initial quality" for automobiles by the industrial group J.D. Power and Associates (online at www.jdpa.com) is defined to be the average number of reported problems per 100 vehicle by owners during the first three years (they used to count only the first year) of their ownership based on actual survey results. Another commonly used quality measure for automobiles, reliability, is measured by the number of problems over a longer time for different stages of an automobile's lifetime. Therefore, it is usually treated as the most important quality measure for used vehicles.

With the development of service industries, an emerging view of quality is that business needs to adjust to the dynamically shifting expectations of customers, with the focus of quality control shifting from zero defect in products to zero defection of customers (Reichheld Jr. and Sasser, 1990). Customer loyalty due to their overall experience with the service is more important than just conforming to some prescribed specifications or standards.

According to (Prahalad and Krishnan, 1999), software industry has incorporated both the conformance and service views of quality, and high-quality software can be defined by three basic elements: conformance, adaptability, and innovation. This view generally agrees with the many facets of software quality we described so far. There are many reasons for this changing view of quality and the different QA focuses (Beizer, 1998). For example, the fundamental assumptions of physical constraints, continuity, quantifiability, composition/decomposition, etc., cannot be extended or mapped to the flexible software world. Therefore, different QA techniques covered in this book need to be used.

Quality in software engineering

Within software engineering, quality has been one of the several important factors, including cost, schedule, and functionality, which have been studied by researchers and practitioners (Blum, 1992; Humphrey, 1989; Ghezzi et al., 2003; von Mayrhauser, 1990). These factors determine the success or failure of a software product in evolving market environments, but may have varying importance for different time periods and different market segments.

In Musa and Everett (1990), these varying primary concerns were conveniently used to divide software engineering into four progressive stages:

1. In the *functional* stage, the focus was on providing the automated functions to replace what had been done manually before.

2. In the *schedule* stage, the focus was on introducing important features and new systems on a timely and orderly basis to satisfy urgent user needs.

3. In the *cost* stage, the focus was on reducing the price to stay competitive accompanied by the widespread use of personal computers.

4. In the *reliability* stage, the focus was managing users' quality expectations under the increased dependency on software and high cost or severe damages associated with software failures.

We can see a gradual increase in importance of quality within software engineering. This general characterization is in agreement with what we have discussed so far, namely, the importance of focusing on correctness-centered quality attributes in our software QA effort for modern software systems.

2.5 SO, WHAT IS SOFTWARE QUALITY?

To conclude this chapter, we can answer the opening question, "What is software quality?" as follows:

- Software quality may include many different attributes and may be defined and perceived differently based on people's different roles and responsibilities.

- We adopt in this book the correctness-centered view of quality, that is, high quality means none or few problems of limited damage to customers. These problems are encountered by software users and caused by internal software defects.

The answer to a related question, "How do you ensure quality as defined above?" include many software QA and quality engineering activities to be described in the rest of this book.

Problems

2.1   What is software quality?

2.2   What is your view of software quality? What is your company's definition of quality? What other views not mentioned in Section 2.1 can you think of?

2.3   What is the relationship between quality, correctness, defects, and other "-ilities" (quality attributes)?

2.4   Define the following terms and give some concrete examples: defect, error, fault, failure, accident. What is the relationship among them? What about (software) bugs?

2.5   What is the pre-industrial concept of quality, and what is the future concept of quality? (Notice that we started with manufacturing in our historical perspective on quality.)

2.6   What is the relationship between quality, quality assurance, and quality engineering? What about between testing and quality?

CHAPTER 3

QUALITY ASSURANCE

With the correctness-centered quality definitions adopted in the previous chapter for this book, the central activities for quality assurance (QA) can be viewed as to ensure that few, if any, defects remain in the software system when it is delivered to its customers or released to the market. Furthermore, we want to ensure that these remaining defects will cause minimal disruptions or damages. In this chapter, we survey existing QA alternatives and related techniques, and examine the specific ways they employ to deal with defects. Through this examination, we can abstract out several generic ways to deal with defects, which can then be used to classify these QA alternatives. Detailed descriptions and a general comparison of the related QA activities and techniques are presented in Part II and Part III.

3.1 CLASSIFICATION: QA AS DEALING WITH DEFECTS

A close examination of how different QA alternatives deal with defects can yield a generic classification scheme that can be used to help us better select, adapt and use different QA alternatives and related techniques for specific applications. We next describe a classification scheme initially proposed in Tian (2001) and illustrate it with examples.

A classification scheme

With the defect definitions given in the previous chapter, we can view different QA activities as attempting to prevent, eliminate, reduce, or contain various specific problems associated

27

with different aspects of defects. We can classify these QA alternatives into the following three generic categories:

- *Defect prevention through error blocking or error source removal*: These QA activities prevent certain types of faults from being injected into the software. Since errors are the missing or incorrect human actions that lead to the injection of faults into software systems, we can directly correct or block these actions, or remove the underlying causes for them. Therefore, defect prevention can be done in two generic ways:

  - *Eliminating certain error sources*, such as eliminating ambiguities or correcting human misconceptions, which are the root causes for the errors.

  - *Fault prevention or blocking* by directly correcting or blocking these missing or incorrect human actions. This group of techniques breaks the causal relation between error sources and faults through the use of certain tools and technologies, enforcement of certain process and product standards, etc.

- *Defect reduction through fault detection and removal*: These QA alternatives detect and remove certain faults once they have been injected into the software systems. In fact, most traditional QA activities fall into this category. For example,

  - Inspection directly detects and removes faults from the software code, design, etc.

  - Testing removes faults based on related failure observations during program execution.

Various other means, based on either static analyses or observations of dynamic executions, can be applied to reduce the number of faults in a software system.

- *Defect containment through failure prevention and containment*: These containment measures focus on the failures by either containing them to local areas so that there are no global failures observable to users, or limiting the damage caused by software system failures. Therefore, defect containment can be done in two generic ways:

  - Some QA alternatives, such as the use of fault-tolerance techniques, break the causal relation between faults and failures so that local faults will not cause global failures, thus "tolerating" these local faults.

  - A related extension to fault-tolerance is containment measures to avoid catastrophic consequences, such as death, personal injury, and severe property or environmental damages, in case of failures. For example, failure containment for real-time control software used in nuclear reactors may include concrete walls to encircle and contain radioactive material in case of reactor melt-down due to software failures, in order to prevent damage to environment and people's health.

Dealing with pre-/post-release defects

Different QA alternatives can be viewed as a concerted effort to deal with errors, faults, or failures, in order to achieve the common goal of quality assurance and improvement. Defect prevention and defect reduction activities directly deal with the competing processes of defect injection and removal during the software development process (Humphrey, 1995). They affect the defect contents, or the number of faults, in the finished software products by working to reduce the pre-release defect injections or to remove as many such defects as possible before product release. The faults left in the finished software products are often called "dormant defects", which may stay *dormant* for some time, but have the potential of causing problems to customers and users of the products — a situation that we would like to alleviate or avoid. Further analyses of different types of defects can be found in Chapter 20. Related techniques to identify high-risk areas for focused defect reduction and QA can be found in Chapter 21.

After product release, the failures observed and problems reported by customers and users also need to be fixed, which in turn, could lead to reduced defects and improved product quality. However, one cannot rely on these post-release problem reports and give up pre-release defect prevention and reduction activities, because the cost of fixing defects after product release is significantly higher than before product release due to the numerous installations. In addition, the damage to software vendors' reputation can be devastating. Controlled field testing, commonly referred to as "beta testing", and similar techniques discussed further in Chapter 12 have been suggested and used to complement pre-release QA activities. Related process issues are discussed in Chapter 4.

On the other hand, defect containment activities aim at minimizing the negative impact of these remaining faults during operational use after product release. However, most of the defect containment techniques involve redundancies or duplications, and require significantly more development effort to design and implement related features. Therefore, they are typically limited to the situations where in-field failures are associated with substantial damage, such as in corporate-wide database for critical data, global telecommunication networks, and various computer-controlled safety critical systems such as medical devices and nuclear reactors. The details about these issues can be found in Chapter 16.

Graphical depiction of the classification scheme

The above QA activity classification can be illustrated in Figure 3.1, forming a series of barriers represented by dotted broken lines. Each barrier removes or blocks defect sources, or prevents undesirable consequences. Specific information depicted includes:

- The barrier between the input to software development activities (left box) and the software system (middle box) represents defect prevention activities.

- The curved barrier between the software system (middle box) and the usage scenario and observed behavior (right box) represents defect or fault removal activities such as inspection and testing.

- The straight barrier to the right of and close to the above fault removal barrier represents failure prevention activities such as fault tolerance.

- The last barrier, surrounding selected failure instances, represents failure containment activities.

In Figure 3.1, faults are depicted as circled entities within the middle box for the software system. Error sources are depicted as circled entities within the left box for the input to the software development activities. Failures are depicted as the circled instances within the right box for usage scenarios and execution results. Figure 3.1 also shows the relationship

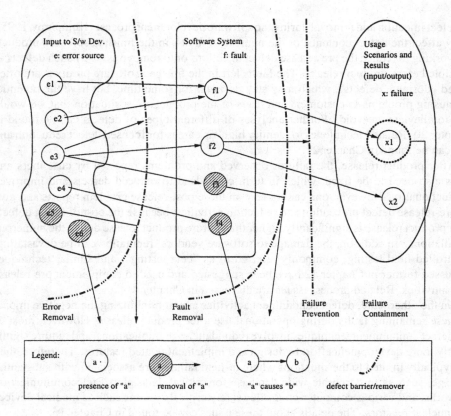

Figure 3.1 Generic ways to deal with defects

between these QA activities and related errors, faults, and failures through some specific examples, as follows:

- Some of the human conceptual errors, such as error source *e6*, are directly removed by error source removal activities, such as through better education to correct the specific human conceptual mistakes.

- Other incorrect actions or errors, such as some of those caused by error source *e3* and *e5*, are blocked. If an error source can be consistently blocked, such as *e5*, it is equivalent to being removed. On the other hand, if an error source is blocked sometimes, such as *e3*, additional or alternative defect prevention techniques need to be used, similar to the situation for other error sources such as *e1*, *e2*, and *e4*, where faults are likely to be injected into the software system because of these error sources.

- Some faults, such as *f4*, are detected directly through inspection or other static analysis and removed as a part of or as follow-up to these activities, without involving the observation of failures.

- Other faults, such as *f3*, are detected through testing or other execution-based QA alternatives by observing their dynamic behavior. If a failure is observed in these QA activities, the related faults are located by examining the execution record and removed as a part of or as follow-up to these activities. Consequently, no operational failures after product release will be caused by these faults.

- Still other faults, such as *f2*, are blocked through fault tolerance for some execution instances. However, fault-tolerance techniques typically do not identify and fix the underlying faults. Therefore, these faults could still lead to operational failures under different dynamic environments, such as *f2* leading to *x2*.

- Among the failure instances, failure containment strategy may be applied for those with severe consequences. For example, *x1* is such an instance, where failure containment is applied to it, as shown by the surrounding dotted circle.

We next survey different QA alternatives, organized in the above classification scheme, and provide pointers to related chapters where they are described in detail.

3.2 DEFECT PREVENTION

The QA alternatives commonly referred to as defect prevention activities can be used for most software systems to reduce the chance for defect injections and the subsequent cost to deal with these injected defects. Most of the defect prevention activities assume that there are known error sources or missing/incorrect actions that result in fault injections, as follows:

- If human misconceptions are the error sources, education and training can help us remove these error sources.

- If imprecise designs and implementations that deviate from product specifications or design intentions are the causes for faults, formal methods can help us prevent such deviations.

- If non-conformance to selected processes or standards is the problem that leads to fault injections, then process conformance or standard enforcement can help use prevent the injection of related faults.

- If certain tools or technologies can reduce fault injections under similar environments, they should be adopted.

Therefore, root cause analyses described in Chapter 21 are needed to establish these preconditions, or *root causes*, for injected or potential faults, so that appropriate defect prevention activities can be applied to prevent injection of similar faults in the future. Once such causal relations are established, appropriate QA activities can then be selected and applied for defect prevention.

3.2.1 Education and training

Education and training provide people-based solutions for error source elimination. It has long been observed by software practitioners that the people factor is the most important factor that determines the quality and, ultimately, the success or failure of most software projects. Education and training of software professionals can help them control, manage, and improve the way they work. Such activities can also help ensure that they have few, if any, misconceptions related to the product and the product development. The elimination of these human misconceptions will help prevent certain types of faults from being injected into software products. The education and training effort for error source elimination should focus on the following areas:

- *Product and domain specific knowledge.* If the people involved are not familiar with the product type or application domain, there is a good chance that wrong solutions will be implemented. For example, developers unfamiliar with embedded software may design software without considering its environmental constraints, thus leading to various interface and interaction problems between software and its physical surroundings.

- *Software development knowledge and expertise* plays an important role in developing high-quality software products. For example, lack of expertise with requirement analysis and product specification usually leads to many problems and rework in subsequent design, coding, and testing activities.

- *Knowledge about Development methodology, technology, and tools* also plays an important role in developing high-quality software products. For example, in an implementation of Cleanroom technology (Mills et al., 1987b), if the developers are not familiar with the key components of formal verification or statistical testing, there is little chance for producing high-quality products.

- *Development process knowledge.* If the project personnel do not have a good understanding of the development process involved, there is little chance that the process can be implemented correctly. For example, if the people involved in incremental software development do not know how the individual development efforts for different increments fit together, the uncoordinated development may lead to many interface or interaction problems.

3.2.2 Formal method

Formal methods provide a way to eliminate certain error sources and to verify the absence of related faults. Formal development methods, or formal methods in short, include formal specification and formal verification. Formal specification is concerned with producing an unambiguous set of product specifications so that customer requirements, as well as environmental constraints and design intentions, are correctly reflected, thus reducing the chances of accidental fault injections. Formal verification checks the conformance of software design or code against these formal specifications, thus ensuring that the software is fault-free with respect to its formal specifications.

Various techniques exist to specify and verify the "correctness" of software systems, namely, to answer the questions: "What is the correct behavior?", and "How to verify it?" We will describe some of these techniques in Chapter 15, with the basic ideas briefly introduced below.

- The oldest and most influential formal method is the so-call axiomatic approach (Hoare, 1969; Zelkowitz, 1993). In this approach, the "meaning" of a program element or the formal interpretation of the effect of its execution is abstracted into an axiom. Additional axioms and rules are used to connect different pieces together. A set of formal conditions describing the program state before the execution of a program is called its *pre-conditions*, and the set after program execution the *post-conditions*. This approach verifies that a given program satisfies its prescribed pre- and post-conditions.

- Other influential formal verification techniques include the predicate transformer based on weakest precondition ideas (Dijkstra, 1975; Gries, 1987), and program calculus or functional approach heavily based on mathematical functions and symbolic executions (Mills et al., 1987a). The basic ideas are similar to the axiomatic approach, but the proof procedures are somewhat different.

- Various other limited scope or semi-formal techniques also exist, which check for certain properties instead of proving the full correctness of programs. For example, model checking techniques are gaining popularity in the software engineering research community (Ghezzi et al., 2003). Various semi-formal methods based on forms or tables, such as (Parnas and Madey, 1995), instead of formal logic or mathematical functions, have found important applications as well.

So far, the biggest obstacle to formal methods is the high cost associated with the difficult task of performing these human intensive activities correctly without adequate automated support. This fact also explains, to a degree, the increasing popularity of limited scope and semi-formal approaches.

3.2.3   Other defect prevention techniques

Other defect prevention techniques, to be described in Chapter 13, including those based on technologies, tools, processes, and standards, are briefly introduced below:

- Besides the formal methods surveyed above, appropriate use of other software methodologies or technologies can also help reduce the chances of fault injections. Many of the problems with low quality "fat software" could be addressed by disciplined methodologies and return to essentials for high-quality "lean software" (Wirth, 1995). Similarly, the use of the information hiding principle (Parnas, 1972) can help reduce the complexity of program interfaces and interactions among different components, thus reducing the possibility of related problems.

- A better managed process can also eliminate many systematic problems. For example, not having a defined process or not following it for system configuration management may lead to inconsistencies or interface problems among different software components. Therefore, ensuring appropriate process definition and conformance helps eliminate some such error sources. Similarly, enforcement of selected standards for certain types of products and development activities also reduces fault injections.

- Sometimes, specific software tools can also help reduce the chances of fault injections. For example, a syntax-directed editor that automatically balances out each open parenthesis, "{", with a close parenthesis, "}", can help reduce syntactical problems in programs written in the C language.

Additional work is needed to guide the selection of appropriate processes, standards, tools, and technologies, or to tailor existing ones to fit the specific application environment. Effective monitoring and enforcement systems are also needed to ensure that the selected processes or standards are followed, or the selected tools or technologies are used properly, to reduce the chance of fault injections.

3.3 DEFECT REDUCTION

For most large software systems in use today, it is unrealistic to expect the defect prevention activities surveyed above to be 100% effective in preventing accidental fault injections. Therefore, we need effective techniques to remove as many of the injected faults as possible under project constraints.

3.3.1 Inspection: Direct fault detection and removal

Software inspections are critical examinations of software artifacts by human inspectors aimed at discovering and fixing faults in the software systems. Inspection is a well-known QA alternative familiar to most experienced software quality professionals. The earliest and most influential work in software inspection is Fagan inspection (Fagan, 1976). Various other variations have been proposed and used to effectively conduct inspection under different environments. A detailed discussion about inspection processes and techniques, applications and results, and many related topics can be found in Chapter 14. The basic ideas of inspection are outlined below:

- Inspections are critical reading and analysis of software code or other software artifacts, such as designs, product specifications, test plans, etc.

- Inspections are typically conducted by multiple human inspectors, through some coordination process. Multiple inspection phases or sessions might be used.

- Faults are detected directly in inspection by human inspectors, either during their individual inspections or various types of group sessions.

- Identified faults need to be removed as a result of the inspection process, and their removal also needs to be verified.

- The inspection processes vary, but typically include some planning and follow-up activities in addition to the core inspection activity.

- The formality and structure of inspections may vary, from very informal reviews and walkthroughs, to fairly formal variations of Fagan inspection, to correctness inspections approaching the rigor and formality of formal methods.

Inspection is most commonly applied to code, but it could also be applied to requirement specifications, designs, test plans and test cases, user manuals, and other documents or software artifacts. Therefore, inspection can be used throughout the development process, particularly early in the software development before anything can be tested. Consequently, inspection can be an effective and economical QA alternative because of the much increased cost of fixing late defects as compared to fixing early ones.

Another important potential benefit of inspection is the opportunity to conduct causal analysis during the inspection process, for example, as an added step in Gilb inspection (Gilb and Graham, 1993). These causal analysis results can be used to guide defect prevention activities by removing identified error sources or correcting identified missing/incorrect human actions. These advantages of inspection will be covered in more detail in Chapter 14 and compared to other QA alternatives in Chapter 17.

3.3.2   Testing: Failure observation and fault removal

Testing is one of the most important parts of QA and the most commonly performed QA activity. Testing involves the execution of software and the observation of the program behavior or outcome. If a failure is observed, the execution record is then analyzed to locate and fix the fault(s) that caused the failure. As a major part of this book, various issues related to testing and commonly used testing techniques are covered in Part II (Chapters 6 through 12).

Individual testing activities and techniques can be classified using various criteria and examined accordingly, as discussed below. Here we pay special attention to how they deal with defects. A more comprehensive classification scheme is presented in Chapter 6.

When can a specific testing activity be performed and related faults be detected?

Because testing is an execution-based QA activity, a prerequisite to actual testing is the existence of the implemented software units, components, or system to be tested, although preparation for testing can be carried out in earlier phases of software development. As a result, actual testing can be divided into various sub-phases starting from the coding phase up to post-release product support, including: unit testing, component testing, integration testing, system testing, acceptance testing, beta testing, etc. The observation of failures can be associated with these individual sub-phases, and the identification and removal of related faults can be associated with corresponding individual units, components, or the complete system.

If software prototypes are used, such as in the spiral process, or if a software system is developed using an incremental or iterative process, testing can usually get started much earlier. Later on, integration testing plays a much more important role in detecting inter-operability problems among different software components. This issue is discussed further in Chapter 4, in connection to the distribution of QA activities in the software processes.

What to test, and what kind of faults are found?

Black-box (or functional) testing verifies the correct handling of the external functions provided by the software, or whether the observed behavior conforms to user expectations or product specifications. White-box (or structural) testing verifies the correct implementation of internal units, structures, and relations among them. Various techniques can be used to build models and generate test cases to perform systematic black-box or white-box testing.

When black-box testing is performed, failures related to specific external functions can be observed, leading to corresponding faults being detected and removed. The emphasis is on reducing the chances of encountering functional problems by target customers. On the other hand, when white-box testing is performed, failures related to internal implementations can be observed, leading to corresponding faults being detected and removed. The emphasis is on reducing internal faults so that there is less chance for failures later on no matter what kind of application environment the software is subjected to.

When, or at what defect level, to stop testing?

Most of the traditional testing techniques and testing sub-phases use some kind of coverage information as the stopping criteria, with the implicit assumption that higher coverage means higher quality or lower levels of defects. For example, checklists are often used to make sure major functions and usage scenarios are tested before product release. Every statement or unit in a component must be covered before subsequent integration testing can proceed. More formal testing techniques include control flow testing that attempts to cover execution paths and domain testing that attempts to cover boundaries between different input sub-domains. Such formal coverage information can only be obtained by using expensive coverage analysis and testing tools. However, rough coverage measurement can be obtained easily by examining the proportion of tested items in various checklists.

On the other hand, product reliability goals can be used as a more objective criterion to stop testing. The use of this criterion requires the testing to be performed under an environment that resembles actual usage by target customers so that realistic reliability assessment can be obtained, resulting in the so-called usage-based statistical testing.

The coverage criterion ensures that certain types of faults are detected and removed, thus reducing the number of defects to a lower level, although quality is not directly assessed. The usage-based testing and the related reliability criterion ensure that the faults that are most likely to cause problems to customers are more likely to be detected and removed, and the reliability of the software reaches certain targets before testing stops.

3.3.3   Other techniques and risk identification

Inspection is the most commonly used static techniques for defect detection and removal. Various other static techniques are available, including various formal model based analyses such as algorithm analysis, decision table analysis, boundary value analysis, finite-state machine and Petri-net modeling, control and data flow analyses, software fault trees, etc.

Similarly, in addition to testing, other dynamic, execution-based, techniques also exist for fault detection and removal. For example, symbolic execution, simulation, and prototyping can help us detect and remove various defects early in the software development process, before large-scale testing becomes a viable alternative.

On the other hand, in-field measurement and related analyses, such as timing and performance analysis for real-time systems, and accident analysis and reconstruction using software fault trees and event trees for safety-critical systems, can also help us locate and remove related defects. Although these activities are an important part of product support, they are not generally considered as a part of the traditional QA activities because of the damages already done to the customers' applications and to the software vendors' reputation. As mentioned in Section 3.1, because of the benefits of dealing with problems before product release instead of after product release, the focus of these activities is to provide useful information for future QA activities.

A comprehensive survey of techniques for fault detection and removal can be found in Chapters 6 and 14, in connection with testing and inspection techniques. Related techniques for dealing with post-release defects are covered in Chapter 16 in connection with fault tolerance and failure containment techniques.

Fault distribution is highly uneven for most software products, regardless of their size, functionality, implementation language, and other characteristics. Much empirical evidence has accumulated over the years to support the so-called 80:20 rule, which states that 20% of the software components are responsible for 80% of the problems. These problematic components can generally be characterized by specific measurement properties about their design, size, complexity, change history, and other product or process characteristics. Because of the uneven fault distribution among software components, there is a great need for risk identification techniques to analyze these measurement data so that inspection, testing, and other QA activities can be more effectively focused on those potentially high-defect components.

These risk identification techniques are described in Chapter 21, including: traditional statistical analysis techniques, principal component analysis and discriminant analysis, neural networks, tree-based modeling, pattern matching techniques, and learning algorithms. These techniques are compared according to several criteria, including: accuracy, simplicity, early availability and stability, ease of result interpretation, constructive information and guidance for quality improvement, and availability of tool support. Appropriate risk identification techniques can be selected to fit specific application environments in order to identify high-risk software components for focused inspection and testing.

3.4 DEFECT CONTAINMENT

Because of the large size and high complexity of most software systems in use today, the above defect reduction activities can only reduce the number of faults to a fairly low level, but not completely eliminate them. For software systems where failure impact is substantial, such as many real-time control software sub-systems used in medical, nuclear, transportation, and other embedded systems, this low defect level and failure risk may still be inadequate. Some additional QA alternatives are needed.

On the other hand, these few remaining faults may be triggered under rare conditions or unusual dynamic scenarios, making it unrealistic to attempt to generate the huge number of test cases to cover all these conditions or to perform exhaustive inspection based on all possible scenarios. Instead, some other means need to be used to prevent failures by breaking the causal relations between these faults and the resulting failures, thus "tolerating" these faults, or to contain the failures by reducing the resulting damage.

3.4.1 Software fault tolerance

Software fault tolerance ideas originate from fault tolerance designs in traditional hardware systems that require higher levels of reliability, availability, or dependability. In such systems, spare parts and backup units are commonly used to keep the systems in operational conditions, maybe at a reduced capability, at the presence of unit or part failures. The primary software fault tolerance techniques include recovery blocks, N-version programming (NVP), and their variations (Lyu, 1995b). We will describe these techniques and examine how they deal with failures and related faults in Chapter 16, with the basic ideas summarized below:

- Recovery blocks use repeated executions (or redundancy over time) as the basic mechanism for fault tolerance. If dynamic failures in some local areas are detected, a portion of the latest execution is repeated, in the hope that this repeated execution will not lead to the same failure. Therefore, local failures will not propagate to global failures, although some time-delay may be involved.

- NVP uses parallel redundancy, where N copies, each of a different version, of programs fulfilling the same functionality are running in parallel. The decision algorithm in NVP makes sure that local failures in limited number of these parallel versions will not compromise global execution results.

One fact worth noting is that in most fault tolerance techniques, faults are not typically identified, therefore not removed, but only tolerated dynamically. This is in sharp contrast to defect detection and removal activities such as inspection and testing.

3.4.2 Safety assurance and failure containment

For safety critical systems, the primary concern is our ability to prevent accidents from happening, where an accident is a failure with a severe consequence. Even low failure probabilities for software are not tolerable in such systems if these failures may still likely lead to accidents. Therefore, in addition to the above QA techniques, various specific techniques are also used for safety critical systems based on analysis of hazards, or logical pre-conditions for accidents (Leveson, 1995). These safety assurance and improvement techniques are covered in Chapter 16. A brief analysis of how each of them deals with defects is given below:

- *Hazard elimination* through substitution, simplification, decoupling, elimination of specific human errors, and reduction of hazardous materials or conditions. These techniques reduce certain defect injections or substitute non-hazardous ones for hazardous ones. The general approach is similar to the defect prevention and defect reduction techniques surveyed earlier, but with a focus on those problems involved in hazardous situations.

- *Hazard reduction* through design for controllability (for example, automatic pressure release in boilers), use of locking devices (for example, hardware/software interlocks), and failure minimization using safety margins and redundancy. These techniques are similar to the fault tolerance techniques surveyed above, where local failures are contained without leading to system failures.

- *Hazard control* through reducing exposure, isolation and containment (for example, barriers between the system and the environment), protection systems (active protection activated in case of hazard), and fail-safe design (passive protection, fail in a safe state without causing further damages). These techniques reduce the severity of failures, therefore weakening the link between failures and accidents.

- *Damage control* through escape routes, safe abandonment of products and materials, and devices for limiting physical damages to equipments or people. These techniques reduce the severity of accidents, thus limiting the damage caused by these accidents and related software failures.

Notice that both hazard control and damage control above are post-failure activities that attempt to "contain" the failures so that they will not lead to accidents or the accident damage can be controlled or minimized. These activities are specific to safety critical systems, which are not generally covered in the QA activities for other systems. On the other hand, many techniques for defect prevention, reduction, and tolerance can also be used in safety-critical systems for hazard elimination and reductions through focused activities on safety-critical product components or features.

3.5 CONCLUDING REMARKS

According to the different ways different QA alternatives deal with defects, they can be classified into three general categories:

- *Defect prevention* through error source elimination and error blocking activities, such as education and training, formal specification and verification, and proper selection and application of appropriate technologies, tools, processes, or standards. The detailed descriptions of these specific techniques and related activities are given in Chapter 15 for formal verification techniques and in Chapter 13 for the rest.

- *Defect reduction* through inspection, testing, and other static analyses or dynamic activities, to detect and remove faults from software. As one of the most important and widely used alternatives, testing is described in Part II (Chapters 6 through 12). Related dynamic analysis is also described in Chapter 12. The other important alternative, inspection, is described in Chapter 14, where a brief description of related static analysis techniques is also included.

- *Defect containment* through fault tolerance, failure prevention, or failure impact minimization, to assure software reliability and safety. The detailed description of these specific techniques and related activities is given in Chapter 16.

Existing software quality literature generally covers defect reduction techniques such as testing and inspection in more details than defect prevention activities, while largely ignore the role of defect containment in QA. This chapter brings together information from diverse sources to offer a common starting point and information base for software quality professionals and software engineering students. Follow-up chapters describe each specific alternative in much more detail and offer a comprehensive coverage of important techniques for QA as well as integration of QA activities into the overall software development and maintenance process.

Problems

3.1 What is quality assurance?

3.2 What are the different types of QA activities? Do you know any classification other than the one described in this chapter based on how they deal with defects?

3.3 For the product your are working on, which QA strategy is used? What other QA strategies and techniques might be applicable or effective?

3.4 Can you use the QA strategies and techniques described in this chapter to deal with other problems, not necessarily defect-related problems, such as usability, performance, modifiability? In addition, can you generalize the QA activities described in this chapter to deal with defects related to things other than software?

3.5 Formal methods are related to both defect prevention and defect detection/removal. Can you think of other QA activities that cut across multiple categories in our classification of QA activities into defect prevention, reduction, and containment.

3.6 What are the similarities and differences between items in the following pairs:
  a) software testing and hardware testing
  b) software inspection and inspection of other things (for example, car inspection, house inspection, inspection for weapons-of-mass-destruction)
  c) quality assurance and safety assurance

CHAPTER 4

QUALITY ASSURANCE IN CONTEXT

With the interpretation of quality assurance (QA) as dealing with defects adopted in the previous chapter, we implicitly assumed that all discovered defects will be resolved within the software development process before product release. In this chapter, we describe defect handling during the execution of specific QA activities and examine how different QA activities fit into different software processes. In addition, we also examine the QA activities from the perspective of verification and validation (V&V), and try to reconcile this V&V view with our view of QA as different ways of dealing with defects.

4.1 HANDLING DISCOVERED DEFECT DURING QA ACTIVITIES

An important part of the normal execution of various QA activities is dealing with the discovered problems, or handling defect. At the minimum, each discovered defect needs to be resolved. To ensure its resolution, some records must be kept and tracked. The exact way used to handle defects is also influenced by the specific QA activities that led to their initial discovery, the project environment, and other factors.

Defect handling and related activities

The most important activity associated with defect handling is defect *resolution*, which ensures that each discovered defect is corrected or taken care of through appropriate actions. Each corrected or fixed defect needs to be re-verified to ensure failure-free executions under the same execution conditions.

41

In the case that a discovered defect is not corrected, all the parties involved must agree on the specific decisions or actions. For example, if a defect from testing is later re-classified as not to be a defect, a justification needs to be given and the decision agreed upon by the person who did the re-classification, the tester who reported it in the first place, and all other people involved. Similarly, if a defect is deferred because it is considered to be a minor problem that can be fixed in a future release, everyone involved must agree to this decision, and appropriate planning for future actions is needed. In addition to the planned future fix, other actions that need to be planned include relevant product support activities to deal with the possible problems.

To support defect resolution, two other important activities associated with defect handling are also needed:

- *Defect logging*, or the initial reporting and recording of a discovered defect. This ensures that a record will be kept for every discovered defect.

- *Defect tracking*, which monitors and records what happened to each defect after its initial discovery, up until its final resolution.

Various specific information about the discovered defects can be recorded and updated through the defect handling process. Details about such information and its usage in quality assessment and improvement are included in Chapter 20. To ensure proper collection and usage of defect data, we need to pay special attention to the following in the defect discovery and resolution activities:

- *Consistent defect interpretation and tracking:* We need to distinguish execution failures, internal faults, and human errors. The specific problems need to be counted and tracked consistently.

- *Timely defect reporting:* Because defect measurements are used to monitor and control software projects, we must ensure timely defect reporting to keep the information current.

Defect handling process and tools

Defect handling is an important part of QA that involves multiple parties. For example, during testing, the developers who fix discovered defects are typically not the same as the testers who observed and reported the problems in the first place. The exception is unit testing, which is usually carried out parallel to coding by the same person. However, most defects from unit testing are not formally tracked because they are considered as part of the implementation activities.

In many organizations, defect handling is implicitly assumed to be part of the project management activities, which is handled in similar ways as configuration management. A formalized defect handling process highlights important activities and associated rules, parties involved, and their responsibilities. It is typically defined by the different states associated with individual defect status and transitions among these states due to status changes. Such status changes follow certain rules defined by project management. For example, a newly reported defect has the "new" status, which may go through various different status changes, such as "working", "re-verify", etc., until it is "closed". Different defect handling processes may include different collections of defect status and other possible attributes.

The implementation of the defect handling process and enforcement of various related rules typically need the support of software tools, commonly referred to as defect tracking tools or defect handling tools. For example, during the testing of various large software systems in IBM, two defect tracking tools CMVC, an IBM product for configuration management and version control, and IDSS, an IBM internal tool, were used for defect tracking (Tian et al., 1997). Similarly, in many organizations, various software project management tools are also used for version control and defect tracking. The same trend is also carried over to the open source world. According to some recent studies (Zhao and Elbaum, 2003; Koru and Tian, 2004), tools such as Bugzilla (online at www.bugzilla.org) and Issuezilla (online at www.issuezilla.org) are typically employed to handling defects for medium and large open source projects.

Defect handling in different QA activities

Defect handling is normally implicitly assumed but not emphasized in various QA activities. For example, during testing, we typically assume that discovered defects will be fixed, re-verified, and eventually closed. However, we often do not treat this as part of the testing activities but as something carried out parallel to testing, because defect fixing is typically done by developers or "code owners" instead of testers.

Among the three classes of the QA activities described in Chapter 3, defect detection and removal activities, such as testing and inspection, are more closely associated with defect handling. For example, the inspector of a program may make an initial note about a possible problem in the program code. When it is confirmed during the inspection meeting, it is formally recorded as a defect, which needs to be fixed and re-verified later in the later stages of the inspection process.

On the other hand, various defect prevention activities do not directly deal with defects or the discovered faults, but rather deal with various ways to prevent the injection of faults into the software systems. Consequently, there are little or no discovered faults during these QA activities. As a result, defect handling is not closely associated with defect prevention.

In defect containment activities, the focus is not on the discovery of underlying faults that cause failures and possible accidents. In fact, in these techniques, such as fault tolerance, faults are not typically identified, while their dynamic impact was tolerated or corrected. Consequently, there are little or no discovered faults. As a result, defect handling is not closely associated with failure prevention and containment activities either.

4.2 QA ACTIVITIES IN SOFTWARE PROCESSES

QA activities form an integral part of the overall software process. We next examine the different ways that software QA activities can be carried out and integrated into different types of software development and maintenance processes.

QA in software development and maintenance processes

In the software maintenance process, the focus of QA is on defect handling, to make sure that each problem reported by customers from field operations is logged, analyzed, and resolved, and a complete tracking record is kept so that we can learn from past problems for future quality improvement. In addition, such defect information can be used as additional input in planning for future releases of the same product or for replacement products. Among the different QA activities, defect containment activities play an important role in post-release product operations and maintenance support. For example, fault tolerance using recovery blocks can keep systems operational even in face of problems caused by environmental disturbances. However, repeated use of recovery blocks for the same situations may be an indication of software problems instead of environmental disturbances as the primary cause of some dynamic problems. Therefore, the systems need to be taken off-line and fixed in order for recovery blocks to work consistently in the future. Even for these techniques, most of the implementation activities need to be carried out during software development, not after product release, similar to the implementation of other product functions or features.

Most of the core QA activities, including defect prevention and defect reduction, are performed during software development instead of during in-field software support after product release. Therefore, we focus on the software development processes in our examination of how different QA activities fit into software processes. In what follows, we examine different QA activities in the general context of several commonly used software development processes, including waterfall, spiral, incremental and iterative development processes. We first examine the process characteristics and the organization of different development activities, and then relate these activities in the process to specific QA activities.

QA in the waterfall process

In the most commonly used waterfall process for many large software projects, development activities are typically grouped into different sequential stages to form a waterfall, although overlaps are common among successive pairs of stages (Zelkowitz, 1988). A typical sequence includes, in chronological order: product planning, requirement analysis, specification, design, coding, testing, release, and post-release product support. As a central part of QA activities, testing is an integral part of the waterfall development process, forming an important link in the overall development chain. Other QA activities, although not explicitly stated in the process description, can be carried out throughout other phases and in the transition from one phase to another. For example, part of the criteria to move on from each phase to the next is quality, typically in the form of checking to see if certain quality plans or standards have been completed or followed, as demonstrated by the results from various forms or reviews or inspections.

Various defect prevention activities are typically concentrated in the earlier phases of software development, before actual faults have been injected into the software systems. There are several important reasons for this focus on early development phases:

- The error sources are typically associated with activities in these early phases, such as conceptual mistakes by designers and programmers, unfamiliarity with the product domain, inexperience with the specific development methodologies, etc. Therefore, error source removal, a primary method of defect preventions, is closely associated with these early development phases.

- Although some faults could be injected into the software systems during testing and other late development phases, the experience tells us that the vast majority of faults are injected in the early development phases, particularly in detailed design and implementation phases. Therefore, effective defect prevention through error blocking needs to be carried out during these phases.

Because of the possibilities of defect propagations and the increasing cost over time or successive development phases to fix defects once they are injected into the system, we need to reduce the number of faults in software systems by the combination of defect prevention and application of QA techniques that can help remove software faults early. Some defect

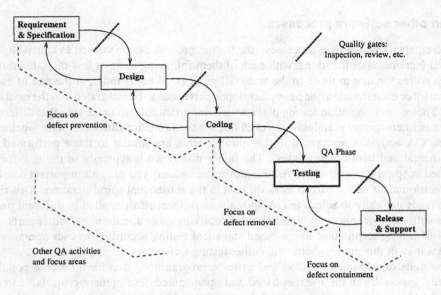

Figure 4.1 QA activities in the waterfall process

detection and removal techniques, such as inspection, can be applied to early phases, such as inspecting requirement documents, product specifications, and different levels of product designs. On the other hand, there are practical obstacles to the early fixing of injected defects. For example, dynamic problems may only become apparent during execution; and inter-dependency only becomes apparent with the implementation of related components or modules. Because of these reasons, other fault detection and removal activities, such as testing, are typically concentrated in the middle to late phases of software development.

Finally, failure prevention and containment activities, such as fault tolerance and safety assurance, are typically the focus of operational phases. However, their planning, design, and implementation need to be carried out throughout the software development process. In some sense, they are equivalent to adding some necessary functions or features into the existing product to make them safe or fault tolerant.

Figure 4.1 illustrate how the different QA activities fit into the waterfall process. Three key characteristics of this activity distribution are illustrated:

- The phase with QA as the focus: Testing phase.

- QA activities, typically inspections and reviews, carried out at the transitions from one phase to the next are shown as barriers or gates to pass. The exception to this is between testing and release, where the reviews are typically accompanied by acceptance testing.

- Other QA activities scatter over all other development phases: The general distribution scope is shown by the dotted bracket, with a focus on defect prevention in the early phases, a focus on defect removal during coding and testing phases, and a focus on defect containment in operational support.

QA in other software processes

In incremental and iterative processes, the overall process can be viewed as consisting of several increments or iterations, with each of them following more or less the same mini-stages corresponding to those in the waterfall process. What is more, at the end of each increment or each iteration, the newly developed part needs to be integrated into the existing part. Therefore, integration testing plays a very important role, to make sure that different parts can inter-operate seamlessly to fulfill the intended functionalities correctly together.

The QA activities performed in the spiral process are similar to those performed in incremental and iterative processes. The minor difference is typically in the risk focus adopted in spiral process, where risk identification and analysis play an important role on the decision as to which part to work on next in the subsequent spiral iteration. This risk focus leads naturally to selective QA with a non-uniform effort applied to different parts of the software systems, with high-risk parts receiving more attention than other parts. In terms of testing techniques, usage-based statistical testing according to user operational profiles may fit this process better than other testing techniques.

The agile development method and extreme programming that have become popular recently, especially in the Internet-based and open-source development projects, can be treated as special cases of incremental, iterative, or spiral process models where many of their elements are used or adapted. In fact, QA activities, particularly testing and inspection, play an even more important role than in the traditional software development processes. For example, test-driven development is an integral part of extreme programming (Beck, 2003), and inspection in the form of two person inspection, or programmer pairs, is extensively used (Beck, 1999).

The details about the application of different QA activities and related techniques to different software processes, phases, and activities will be covered when we describe each specific QA technique in Part II and Part III.

4.3 VERIFICATION AND VALIDATION PERSPECTIVES

As described in Chapter 1, the basic quality expectations of a user are that a software performs the right functions as specified, and performs these specified functions correctly over repeated use or over a long period of time. The related QA activities to ensure that the right functions are performed are typically grouped as *validation* activities; while the ones to ensure the correct or reliable performance of these specified functions are typically grouped as *verification* activities. The QA activity classification we used in Chapter 3 can be mapped into this binary partition of validation and verification activities using the related defects as the middle link between the two classification schemes.

Validation, failures, and QA activities

Validation activities check whether a function needed and expected by the customers is present in a software product. An absence of an expected function or feature is clearly linked to a deviation of expected behavior, or linked to a software failure. However, this is a special sub-class of failures, where an expected function is absent. By extension, when an unexpected function is present, it can be considered as a failure of this kind as well, because a customer is not likely willing to pay for something not needed. Even if it is free, the customer might be worried about possible interference with other critical needs. Therefore, various QA activities linked with such kind of failures directly observable by software users can be viewed as validation activities. Examples of QA activities that can be classified as validation activities include:

- System testing, where the focus is the overall set of system functions to be provided to users;

- Acceptance testing and beta testing, where the focus is the assessment of software acceptance or performance by users;

- Usage-based statistical testing, where the operational environment by target users is simulated during software testing before product release;

- Software fault tolerance, which focuses on providing continued service expected by customers even when local problems exist;

- Software safety assurance activities, which focus on providing the expected accident-free operations or reducing accident damage when an accident is unavoidable.

Even in the case where a specific software QA activity is not directly dealing with the above type of failures, if the intention is to detect or prevent faults that are linked to such failures, the specific activity in question can also be classified as a validation activity. For example, in inspections based on usage scenarios, faults that are likely to lead to failures under usage scenarios by target customers are the focus of the inspect effort. Therefore, this specific inspection activity can be viewed as a validation activity. In addition, if a preventive action is aimed at preventing specific problems for specific operational environments by customers, it can be classified as a validation activity as well.

Verification, conformance, and QA activities

Software verification activities check the conformance of a software system to its specifications. In performing verification activities, we assume that we have a well defined set of specifications. A deviation from the specification is either a fault or a failure, depending on whether the behavior is specified or other software related entities are specific, such as through coding standards, design patterns, etc.

When failures are involved in verification activities, we are typically dealing with internal system failures and overall system failures in the form of incorrect behavior, instead of the evidence of presence or absence of certain functions or feature directly observable by customers. For example, checking how one component works with another component is a verification activities, because it tries to eliminate internal failures related to interoperability among internal components, while customers only care if the overall functions are implemented and implemented correctly.

When a function or feature expected by the customers is present, the activity to determine whether it performs or behaves expectedly is then a verification activity. Therefore, connected to validation activities, there are almost always accompanying verification activities as well. In the above examples of various forms of testing as primarily validation activities, they all include corresponding verification components. They are also used to verify the correct implementation of various functions visible to customers. The testing environment for these activities needs to be similar to that will be subjected to by the product after it is purchased by the customers and put into operational use.

When we are checking non-behavioral specifications, non-conformance indicates the presence of faults or errors. For example, a wrong algorithm or an inappropriate data structure is used, some coding standard is violated, etc. These problems are typically associated with various types of software faults. These faults, when triggered, may cause system failures. Similarly, not following prescribed processes or selected methodologies, or misunderstanding of needed algorithms and data structures, is associated with errors or error sources that cause injection of faults. Therefore, all the QA activities we classified as dealing directly with faults, errors, or error sources can be classified as verification activities.

Verification and validation in software processes

QA activities can also be classified by the binary grouping of verification vs. validation activities. Validation checks the conformance to quality expectations of customers and users in the form of whether the expected functions or features are present or not. On the other hand, verification checks the conformance of software product implementation against its specifications to see if it is implemented correctly. Therefore, validation deals directly with users and their requirements; while verification deals with internal product specifications. In the software development process perspective, different processes may involve customers and users in different ways. Therefore, verification and validation activities may be distributed in these different processes differently.

In the waterfall process, direct involvement of users and user requirement is at the very beginning and the very end of the development process. These phases include project planning, market analysis, requirement analysis, specification, acceptance testing, product release, and post-release product support and maintenance. Therefore, these are the phases where validation activities may be the focus. For example, overall product specifications need to be validated through inspections or reviews to make sure they conform to customer requirements. Various user-oriented testing, such as system, integration, and acceptance testing focus on the validation of user requirement in the form of checking if the functions and features expected by users are present in the software product scheduled to be delivered. Similarly, beta testing and operational support make sure the software product is validated, that is, it is doing what it is supposed to do under the application environment of the target customers.

On the other hand, many development activities in the middle part of the waterfall process do not involve customers and users directly. A set of internal specifications needs to be followed or other rules or criteria need to be satisfied. For example, the product designs must satisfy the product specifications; lower-level designs must conform to the constraints imposed by the high-level designs; and the final product implementation must follow the design decisions made earlier. The satisfactory conformance of these specifications, designs, and rules is the focus of various verification activities. For example, through inspections of design documents, satisfaction of design constraints and product specifications can be verified. Program correctness with respect to its formal specifications can be formally verified using various formal verification techniques. Unit and component testing can be used to verify the unit or the component against its specifications in the form of detailed designs for them.

These verification and validation activities can be best illustrated by the V-model in Figure 4.2, a variation of the waterfall process model where the different development phases are presented in a V-shaped graph, relating specific verification or validation activities to their corresponding requirements or specifications. For example, customer requirements are *validated* by operational use; while product specification, high-level design, and low-level design are *verified* by system test, integration test, and component test, respectively. In

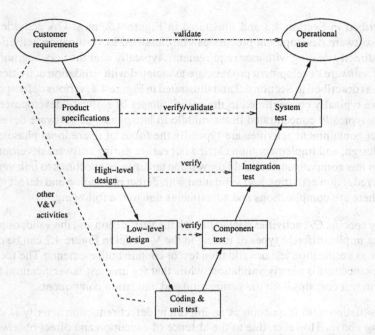

Figure 4.2 Verification and validation activities associated with the V-Model

addition, system test also *validates* the product by focusing on how the overall operations under an environment that resembles that for target customers. In a sense, the users' operational environment is captured as part of the product specification or as part of the testing model. At the bottom, coding and unit testing are typically grouped in a single phase, where the code itself specifies the expected behavior and needs to be verified through unit test. Sometimes, various other QA activities, such as inspections, reviews, walkthroughs, analyses, formal verification, etc., are also associated with the left arm of the V-model and illustrated by additional dotted lines pointed to the specific phases.

Similar to the mapping of QA activities to other process models above, validation and verification activities can be mapped into non-sequential processes such as incremental, iterative, spiral, and extreme programming processes. Typically, there is some level of user involvement in each part or iteration. Therefore, validation plays a more important role in these processes than in the waterfall process or the V-model.

4.4 RECONCILING THE TWO VIEWS

The above descriptions of verification and validation activities included examples of specific QA activities. These specific QA activities were also classified using our scheme according to the generic ways of dealing with defects. Through this connection and the inter-relations represented therein, we can establish the relationship and the mapping between the verification and validation (V&V) view on the one hand and our defect-centered (DC) view and classification on the other hand. In addition, we can use the process information as presented in Figure 4.1, Figure 4.2, and related discussions to help us with this mapping, as discussed below.

As described in Section 4.3 and illustrated in Figure 4.2, most QA activities carried within the software development process can be classified as verification activities, while only those directly dealing with user requirements, typically near the very beginning or the very end of software development process, are associated with validation activities. On the other hand, as described in Section 4.2 and illustrated in Figure 4.1, various defect prevention activities are typically concentrated in the earlier phases of software development; defect reduction is typically concentrated in the middle to late phases of software development; while defect containment activities are typically the focus of operational phases, with its planning, design, and implementation carried out earlier during software development.

Based on this comparison, we could draw some tentative connections to link verification with defect reduction activities, and validation with defect prevention and defect tolerance. However, there are complications and adjustments due to the following:

- Many specific QA activities deal with both the verification and the validation aspects. For example, different types of testing in the V-model in Figure 4.2 can be classified either as verification test or validation test or contain both elements: The focus of the acceptance test is clearly validation, while that for unit test is verification, however, system test contains both the verification and validation components.

- The situation with inspection as an important defect reduction activity is similar to testing above. However, due to the absence of execution and direct observations of failures, inspection is more closely connected to verification than to validation. For example, most of the inspection activities are performed on software code or design, which are classical verification activities. The less used requirement inspections and usage scenarios based inspections are closer to validation.

- Defect prevention deals with error source elimination and error blocking, while both verification and validation deal with failures and faults. Therefore, there is no direct connection between defect prevention and the V&V view of QA activities, but only indirectly through the target of preventive actions. For example, if the target is eliminating ambiguity in the requirement or the product domain knowledge, it is indirectly connected to validation. If the target is to block syntactic faults or other faults due to the proper selection and usage of processes, methodologies, technologies, or tools, it is indirectly connected to verification.

- Closely related to both defect prevention and formalized inspection is the use of formal method as a QA activity. The formal specification part is close to validation, but indirectly, much like the defect prevention activities above. The formal verification part naturally falls into verification activities, verifying the program or design correctness with respect to its formal specifications.

- Defect containment activities, such as through fault tolerance and safety assurance, are more closely related to validation activities than verification due to their focus on avoiding global failures or minimizing failure damages under actual operational environments. However, when such defect containment features are specific for a software system or an embedded system, the conformance to this part of the specification can be treated much the same as other verification activities to check the general conformance to specifications.

This relationship between the two views can be summarized in Table 4.1, for each of the DC view categories and related major QA activities, we point out whether it is

Table 4.1 QA activities: Mapping from defect-centered (DC) view to verification and validation (V&V) view

DC-view class	Major QA activity	V&V view
Defect prevention		both, mostly indirectly
	requirement-related	validation, indirectly
	other defect prevention	verification, indirectly
	formal specification	validation, indirectly
	formal verification	verification
Defect reduction		both, but mostly verification
	testing, unit & component	verification
	testing, integration	both, more verification
	testing, system	both
	testing, acceptance	both, more validation
	testing, beta	validation
	inspection, req. & scenario	validation
	inspection, all other	verification
	analyses, etc.	both, but mostly verification
Defect containment		both, but mostly validation
	operation	validation
	design and implementation	both, but mostly verification

related to verification, validation, or both, directly (unless specified otherwise) or indirectly. Therefore, we can follow the three-part classification outlined in Chapter 3 without losing the general perspectives of validation and verification.

4.5 CONCLUDING REMARKS

To summarize, defect handling is an integral part of QA activities, and different QA alternatives and related activities can be viewed as a concerted effort to ensure software quality. These activities can be integrated into software development and maintenance processes as an integral part of the overall process activities, typically in the following fashion:

- Testing is an integral part of any development process, forming an important link in the overall development chain.

- Quality reviews or inspections often accompany the transition from one phase or development activity to another.

- Various defect prevention activities are typically carried out in the early stages.

- Defect containment activities typically focus on the later, operational part of the development process, although their planning and implementation need to be carried out throughout the development process.

These QA activities can also be partitioned into verification and validation (V&V) activities using a bi-partite classification scheme in the so-called V&V view. Similarly, they can be partitioned by the generic way they employ to deal with errors, faults, or failures as different defect-centered (DC) activities using our tri-partite classification scheme in the so-call DC view. Both views and both classification schemes have their useful purposes and implications. Our tri-partite classification provides a balanced and systematic scheme to organize and classify existing software QA activities. It can also be easily mapped to the commonly used bi-partite scheme of validation and verification activities. Consequently, we will follow this classification in the rest of the book without losing the generality associated with the other commonly used views of QA activities.

Problems

4.1   Why is defect tracking and defect handling important in quality assurance?

4.2   In your project, do you have a defined defect handling process? If so, describe the process and compare it with the generic description in this chapter. If not, can you design one?

4.3   Define the different defect status and draw a chart/graph to depict the allowable defect status changes based on your knowledge of your actual defect handling process. You may use a hypothetical project and its defect handling process to complete this exercise if you are not working on a project or if your project does not have a defined defect handling process.

4.4   What measurements can be taken during QA activities?

4.5   Document the different QA activities and their organization/grouping in your development or maintenance process and compare them to the generic ones descried in this chapter.

4.6   What is verification and validation? How do they relate to defects? Is your organization performing more verification, more validation, or both equally?

CHAPTER 5

QUALITY ENGINEERING

In this chapter, we enlarge the scope of our discussion to include other major activities associated with quality assurance (QA) for software systems, primarily in the areas of setting quality goals, planning for QA, monitoring QA activities, and providing feedback for project management and quality improvement.

5.1 QUALITY ENGINEERING: ACTIVITIES AND PROCESS

As stated in Chapter 2, different customers and users have different quality expectations under different market environments. Therefore, we need to move beyond just performing QA activities toward quality engineering by managing these quality expectations as an engineering problem: Our goal is to meet or exceed these quality expectations through the selection and execution of appropriate QA activities while minimizing the cost and other project risks under the project constraints.

In order to ensure that these quality goals are met through the selected QA activities, various measurements need to be taken parallel to the QA activities themselves. Post-mortem data often need to be collected as well. Both in-process and post-mortem data need to be analyzed using various models to provide an objective quality assessment. Such quality assessments not only help us determine if the preset quality goals have been achieved, but also provide us with information to improve the overall product quality.

To summarize, there are three major groups of activities in the quality engineering process, as depicted in Figure 5.1. They are labeled in roughly chronological order as pre-QA activities, in-QA activities, and post-QA activities:

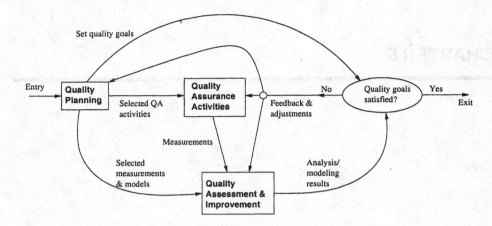

Figure 5.1   Quality engineering process

1. *Pre-QA activities: Quality planning.* These are the activities that should be carried out before carrying out the regular QA activities. There are two major types of pre-QA activities in quality planning, including:

   (a) Set specific quality goals.

   (b) Form an overall QA strategy, which includes two sub-activities:

      i. Select appropriate QA activities to perform.
      ii. Choose appropriate quality measurements and models to provide feedback, quality assessment and improvement.

   A detailed description of these pre-QA activities is presented in Section 5.2.

2. *In-QA activities: Executing planned QA activities and handling discovered defects.* In addition to performing selected QA activities, an important part of this normal execution is to deal with the discovered problems. These activities were described in the previous two chapters.

3. *Post-QA activities: Quality measurement, assessment and improvement* These are the activities that are carried out after normal QA activities have started but not as part of these normal activities. The primary purpose of these activities is to provide quality assessment and feedback so that various management decisions can be made and possible quality improvement initiatives can be carried out. These activities are described in Section 5.3.

Notice here that "post-QA" does not mean after the finish of QA activities. In fact, many of the measurement and analysis activities are carried out parallel to QA activities after they are started. In addition, pre-QA activities may overlap with the normal QA activities as well.

Pre-QA quality planning activities play a leading role in this quality engineering process, although the execution of selected QA activities usually consumes the most resources. Quality goals need to be set so that we can manage the QA activities and stop them when the quality goals are met. QA strategies need to be selected, before we can carry out specific QA activities, collect data, perform analysis, and provide feedback.

There are two kinds of feedback in this quality engineering process, both the short term direct feedback to the QA activities and the long-term feedback to the overall quality engineering process. The short term feedback to QA activities typically provides information for progress tracking, activity scheduling, and identification of areas that need special attentions. For example, various models and tools were used to provide test effort tracking, reliability monitoring, and identification of low-reliability areas for various software products developed in the IBM Software Solutions Toronto Lab to manage their testing process (Tian, 1996).

The long-term feedback to the overall quality engineering process comes in two forms:

- Feedback to quality planning so that necessary adjustment can be made to quality goals and QA strategies. For example, if the current quality goals are unachievable, alternative goals need to be negotiated. If the selected QA strategy is inappropriate, a new or modified strategy needs to be selected. Similarly, such adjustments may also be applied to future projects instead of the current project.

- Feedback to the quality assessment and improvement activities. For example, the modeling results may be highly unstable, which may well be an indication of the model inappropriateness. In this case, new or modified models need to be used, probably on screened or pre-processed data.

Quality engineering and QIP

In the TAME project and related work (Basili and Rombach, 1988; Oivo and Basili, 1992; Basili, 1995; van Solingen and Berghout, 1999), quality improvement was achieved through measurement, analysis, feedback, and organizational support. The overall framework is called QIP, or quality improvement paradigm. QIP includes three interconnected steps: understanding, assessing, and packaging, which form a feedback and improvement loop, as briefly described below:

1. The first step is to *understand* the baseline so that improvement opportunities can be identified and clear, measurable goals can be set. All future process changes are measured against this baseline.

2. The second step is to introduce process changes through experiments, pilot projects, *assess* their impact, and fine tune these process changes.

3. The last step is to *package* baseline data, experiment results, local experience, and updated process as the way to infuse the findings of the improvement program into the development organization.

QIP and related work on measurement selection and organizational support are described further in connection to defect prevention in Chapter 13 and in connection to quality assessment and improvement in Part IV.

Our approach to quality engineering can be considered as an adaptation of QIP to assure and measure quality, and to manage quality expectations of target customers. Some specific correspondences are noted below:

- Our pre-QA activities roughly correspond to the *understand* step in QIP.

- The execution of our selected QA strategies correspond to the "changes" introduced in the *assess* step in QIP. However, we are focusing on the execution of normal QA activities and the related measurement activities selected previously in our planning step, instead of specific changes.

- Our analysis and feedback (or post-QA) activities overlap with both the *assess* and *package* steps in QIP, with the analysis part roughly corresponding to the QIP-assess step and the longer term feedback roughly corresponding to the QIP-package step.

5.2 QUALITY PLANNING: GOAL SETTING AND STRATEGY FORMATION

As mentioned above, pre-QA quality planning includes setting quality goals and forming a QA strategy. The general steps include:

1. Setting quality goals by matching customer's quality expectations with what can be economically achieved by the software development organizations in the following sub-steps:

    (a) Identify quality views and attributes meaningful to target customers and users.

    (b) Select direct quality measures that can be used to measure the selected quality attributes from customer's perspective.

    (c) Quantify these quality measures to set quality goals while considering the market environment and the cost of achieving different quality goals.

2. In forming a QA strategy, we need to plan for its two basic elements:

    (a) Map the above quality views, attributes, and quantitative goals to select a specific set of QA alternatives.

    (b) Map the above external direct quality measures into internal indirect ones via selected quality models. This step selects indirect quality measures as well as usable models for quality assessment and analysis.

We next examine these steps and associated pre-QA activities in detail.

Setting quality goals

One important fact in managing customer's quality expectations is that different quality attributes may have different levels of importance to different customers and users. Relevant quality views and attributes need to be identified first. For example, reliability is typically the primary concern for various business and commercial software systems because of people's reliance on such systems and the substantial financial loss if they are malfunctioning. Similarly, if a software is used in various real-time control situations, such as air traffic control software and embedded software in automobile, medical devices, etc., accidents due to failures may be catastrophic. Therefore, safety is the major concern. On the other hand, for mass market software packages, such as various auxiliary utilities for personal computers, usability, instead of reliability or safety, is the primary concern.

Even in the narrower interpretation of quality we adopted in this book to be the correctness-centered quality attributes associated with errors, faults, failures, and accidents, there are different types of problems and defects that may mean different things to different customers. For example, for a software product that is intended for diverse operational environments, inter-operability problems may be a major concern to its customers and users; while the same problems may not be a major concern for software products with a standard operational environment. Therefore, specific quality expectations by the customers require us to identify relevant quality views and attributes prior to setting appropriate quality goals. This needs to be done in close consultation with the customers and users, or those who represents their interests, such as requirement analysts, marketing personnel, etc.

Once we obtained qualitative knowledge about customers' quality expectations, we need to quantify these quality expectations to set appropriate quality goals in two steps:

1. *We need to select or define the quality measurements and models* commonly accepted by the customers and in the software engineering community. For example, as pointed out in Chapter 2, reliability and safety are examples of correctness-centered quality measures that are meaningful to customers and users, which can be related to various internal measures of faults commonly used within software development organizations.

2. *We need to find out the expected values* or ranges of the corresponding quality measurements. For example, different market segments might have different reliability expectations. Such quality expectations are also influenced by the general market conditions and competitive pressure.

Software vendors not only compete on quality alone, but also on cost, schedule, innovation, flexibility, overall user experience, and other features and properties as well. Zero defect is not an achievable goal under most circumstances, and should not be the goal. Instead, zero defection and positive flow of new customers and users based on quality expectation management should be a goal (Reichheld Jr. and Sasser, 1990). In a sense, this activity determines to a large extent the product positioning vs. competitors in the marketplace and potential customers and users.

Another practical concern with the proper setting of quality goals is the cost associated with different levels of quality. This cost can be divided into two major components, the failure cost and the development cost. The customers typically care more about the total failure cost, C_f, which can be estimated by the average single failure cost, c_f, and failure probability, p_f, over a pre-defined duration of operation as:

$$C_f = c_f \times p_f.$$

As we will see later in Chapter 22, this failure probability can be expressed in terms of reliability, R, as $p_f = 1 - R$, where R is defined to be the probability of failure-free operations for a specific period of given set of input.

To minimize C_f, one can either try to minimize c_f or p_f. However, c_f is typically determined by the nature of software applications and the overall environment the software is used in. Consequently, not much can be done about c_f reduction without incurring substantial amount of other cost. One exception to this is in the safety critical systems, where much additional cost was incurred to establish barriers and containment in order to reduce failure impact, as described in Chapter 16. On the other hand, minimizing p_f, or improving reliability, typically requires additional development cost, in the form of additional testing time, use of additional QA techniques, etc.

Therefore, an engineering decision need to be made to match the quantified customer's quality expectations above with their willingness to pay for the quality. Such quantitative cost-of-quality analyses should help us reach a set of quality goals.

Forming a QA strategy

Once specific quality goals were set, we can select appropriate QA alternatives as part of a QA strategy to achieve these goals. Several important factors need to be considered:

- *The influence of quality perspectives and attributes:* For different kinds of customers, users, and market segments, different QA alternatives might be appropriate, because they focus on the assurance of quality attributes based on this specific perspective. For example, various usability testing techniques may be useful for ensuring the usability of a software product, but may not be effective for ensuring its functional correctness.

- *The influence of different quality levels:* Quantitative quality levels as specified in the quality goals may also affect the choice of appropriate QA techniques. For example, systems with various software fault tolerance features may incur substantially more additional cost than the ones without them. Therefore, they may be usable for highly dependable systems or safety critical systems, where large business operations and people's lives may depend on the correct operations of software systems, but may not be suitable for less critical software systems that only provide non-essential information to the users.

Notice that in dealing with both of the above factors, we assume that there is a certain relationship between these factors and specific QA alternatives. Therefore, specific QA alternatives need to be selected to fulfill specific quality goals based on the quality perspectives and attributes of concern to the customers and users.

Implicitly assumed in this selection process is a good understanding of the advantages and disadvantages of different QA alternatives under different application environments. These comparative advantages and disadvantages are the *other factors* that also need to be considered in selecting different QA alternatives and related techniques and activities. These factors include cost, applicability to different environments, effectiveness in dealing with different kinds of problems, etc. discussed in Chapter 17.

In order to achieve the quality goals, we also need to know where we are and how far away we are from the preset quality goals. To gain this knowledge, objective assessment using some quality models on collected data from the QA activities is necessary. As we will discuss in more detail in Chapter 18, there are direct quality measures and indirect quality measures. The direct quality measures need to be defined as part of the activities to set quality goals, when such goals are quantified.

Under many situations, direct quality measures cannot be obtained until it is already too late. For example, for safety critical systems, post-accident measurements provide a direct measure of safety. But due to the enormous damage associated with such accidents, we are trying to do everything to avoid such accidents. To control and monitor these safety assurance activities, various indirect measurements and indicators can be used. For all software systems there is also an increasing cost of fixing problems late instead of doing so early in general, because a hidden problem may lead to other related problems, and the longer it stays undiscovered in the system, the further removed it is from its root causes, thus making the discovery of it even more difficult. Therefore, there is a strong incentive for early indicators of quality that usually measure quality indirectly.

Indirect quality measures are those which can be used in various quality models to assess and predict quality, through their established relations to direct quality measures based on historical data or data from other sources. Therefore, we also need to choose appropriate measurements, both direct and indirect quality measurement, and models to provide quality assessment and feedback. The actual measurement and analysis activities and related usage of analysis results are discussed in Chapter 18.

5.3 QUALITY ASSESSMENT AND IMPROVEMENT

Various parallel and post-QA activities are carried out to close the quality engineering loop. The primary purpose of these activities is to provide quality assessment and feedback so that various management decisions, such as product release, can be made and possible quality and process improvement initiatives can be carried out. The major activities in this category include:

- *Measurement:* Besides defect measurements collected during defect handling, which is typically carried out as part of the normal QA activities, various other measurements are typically needed for us to track the QA activities as well as for project management and various other purposes. These measurements provide the data input to subsequent analysis and modeling activities that provide feedback and useful information to manage software project and quality.

- *Analysis and modeling:* These activities analyze measurement data from software projects and fit them to analytical models that provide quantitative assessment of selected quality characteristics or sub-characteristics. Such models can help us obtain an objective assessment of the current product quality, accurate prediction of the future quality, and some models can also help us identify problematic areas.

- *Providing feedback and identifying improvement potentials:* Results from the above analysis and modeling activities can provide feedback to the quality engineering process to help us make project scheduling, resource allocation, and other management decisions. When problematic areas are identified by related models, appropriate remedial actions can be applied for quality and process improvement.

- *Follow-up activities:* Besides the immediate use of analysis and modeling results described above, various follow-up activities can be carried out to affect the long-term quality and organizational performance. For example, if major changes are suggested for the quality engineering process or the software development process, they typically need to wait until the current process is finished to avoid unnecessary disturbance and risk to the current project.

The details about these activities are described in Part IV.

5.4 QUALITY ENGINEERING IN SOFTWARE PROCESSES

The quality engineering process forms an integral part of the overall software engineering process, where other concerns, such as cost and schedule, are also considered and managed. As described in Chapter 4, individual QA activities can be carried out and integrated into the software process. When we broaden our scope to quality engineering, it also covers pre-QA quality planning as well as the post-QA measurement and analysis activities carried out parallel to and after QA activities to provide feedback and other useful information. All these activities and the quality engineering process can be integrated into the overall software process as well, as described below.

Activity distribution and integration

Pre-QA quality planning can be an integral part of any project planning. For example, in the waterfall process, this is typically carried out in the phase for market analysis, requirement gathering, and product specification. Such activities also provide us with valuable information about quality expectations by target customers and users in the specific market segment a software vendor is prepared to compete in. Quality goals can be planned and set accordingly. Project planning typically includes decisions on languages, tools, and technologies to be used for the intended software product. It should be expanded to include 1) choices of specific QA strategies and 2) measurement and models to be used for monitoring the project progress and for providing feedback.

In alternative software processes other than waterfall, such as in incremental, iterative, spiral, and extreme programming processes,   pre-QA activities play an even more active role, because they are not only carried out at the beginning of the whole project, but also at the beginning of each subpart or iteration due to the nature that each subpart includes more or less all the elements in the waterfall phases. Therefore, we need to set specific quality goals for each subpart, and choose appropriate QA activities, techniques, measurement, and models for each subpart. The overall quality goal may evolve from these sub-goals in an iterative fashion.

For normal project monitoring and management under any process, appropriate measurement activities need to be carried out to collect or extract data from the software process and related artifacts; analyses need to be performed on these data; and management decision can be made accordingly. On the one hand, the measurement activity cannot be carried out without the involvement of the software development team, either as part of the normal defect handling and project tracking activities, or as added activity to provide specific input to related analysis and modeling. Therefore, the measurement activities have to be handled "on-line" during the software development process, with some additional activities in information or measurement extraction carried out after the data collection and recording are completed.

On the other hand, much of the analysis and modeling activities could be done "off-line", to minimize the possible disruption or disturbance to the normal software development process. However, timely feedback based on the results from such analyses and models is needed to make adjustments to the QA and to the development activities. Consequently, even such "off-line" activities need to be carried out in a timely fashion, but may be at a lower frequency. For example, in the implementation of testing tracking, measurement, reliability analysis, and feedback for IBM's software products (Tian, 1996), dedicated quality analyst performed such analyses and modeling and provided weekly feedback to the testing team, while the data measurement and recording were carried out on a daily basis.

The specific analysis, feedback, and follow-up activities in the software quality engineering process fit well into the normal software management activities. Therefore, they can be considered as an integral part of software project management. Of course, the focus of these quality engineering activities is on the quality management, as compared to the overall project management that also includes managing project features, cost, schedule, and so on.

The integration of the quality engineering process into the waterfall software development process can be illustrated by Figure 5.2. The horizontal activities roughly illustrate the timeline correspondence to software development activities. For example, quality planning starts right at the start of the requirement analysis phase, followed by the execution of the selected QA activities, and finally followed by the measurement and analysis activities.

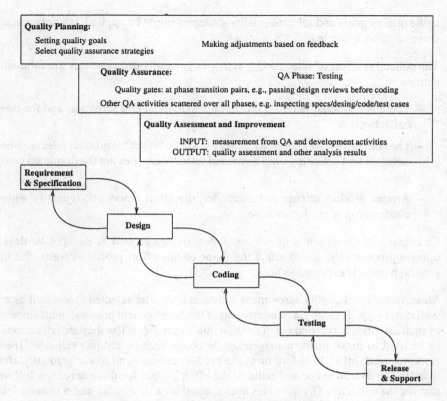

Quality Planning:

Setting quality goals
Select quality assurance strategies   Making adjustments based on feedback

Quality Assurance:
                                             QA Phase: Testing
Quality gates: at phase transition pairs, e.g., passing design reviews before coding

Other QA activities scattered over all phases, e.g. inspecting specs/desing/code/test cases

Quality Assessment and Improvement

INPUT: measurement from QA and development activities
OUTPUT: quality assessment and other analysis results

Requirement & Specification

Design

Coding

Testing

Release & Support

Figure 5.2   Quality engineering in the waterfall process

All these activities typically last over the whole development process, with different sub-activities carried out in different phases. This is particularly true for the QA activities, with testing in the test phase, various reviews or inspections at the transition from one phase to its successor phase, and other QA activities scattered over other phases.

Minor modifications are needed to integrate quality engineering activities into other development processes. However, the distribution of these activities and related effort is by no means uniform over the activities or over time, which is examined next.

Effort profile

Among the three major types of activities in the quality engineering process, the execution of specific QA activities is central to dealing with defects and assuring quality for the software products. Therefore, they should and normally do consume the most resources in terms of human effort as well as utilization of computing and other related resources. However, the effort distribution among the three is not constant over time because of the process characteristics described above and the shifting focus over time. Some key factors that affect and characterize the effort profile, or the effort distribution over time, include:

- Quality planning drives and should precede the other two groups of activities. There-fore, at the beginning part of product development, quality planning should be the dominant part of quality engineering activities. Thereafter, occasional adjustments to the quality goals and selected quality strategies might be applied, but only a small share of effort is needed.

- The collective effort of selected QA activities generally demonstrates the following pattern:

    - There is a gradual build-up process for individual QA activities, and for them collectively.

    - The collective effort normally peaks off a little bit before product release, when development activities wind down and testing activities are the dominant activities.

    - Around product release and thereafter, the effort tapers off, typically with a sudden drop at product release.

Of course, the specific mix of selected QA activities as well as the specific development process used would affect the shape of this effort profile as well. But the general pattern is expected to hold.

- Measurement and quality assessment activities start after selected QA activities are well under way. Typically, at the early part of the development process, small amounts of such activities are carried out to monitor quality progress. But they are not expected to be used to make major management decisions such as product release. These activities peak off right before or at the product release, and lower gradually after that. In the overall shape and pattern, the effort profile for these activities follows that for the collective QA activities above, but with a time delay and a heavier load at the tail-end.

One common adjustment to the above pattern is the time period after product release. Immediately after product release or after a time delay for market penetration, the initial wave of operational use by customers is typically accompanied by many user-reported problems, which include both legitimate failures and user errors. Consequently, there is typically an upswing of overall QA effort. New data and models are also called for, resulting in an upswing of measurement and analysis activities as well. The main reason for this upswing is the difference between the environment where the product is tested under and the actual operational environment the product is subjected to. The use of usage-based testing described in Chapters 8 and 10 would help make this bump smoother.

This general profile can be graphically illustrated in Figure 5.3. The overall quality engineering effort over time is divided into three parts:

- The bottom part represents the share of total effort by quality planning activities;

- The middle part represents the share of total effort for the execution of selected QA activities;

- The upper part represents the share of total effort for the measurement and quality assessment activities.

Notice that this figure is for illustration purposes only. The exact profile based on real data would not be as smooth and would naturally show large amount of variability, with many small peaks and valleys. But the general shape and pattern should preserve.

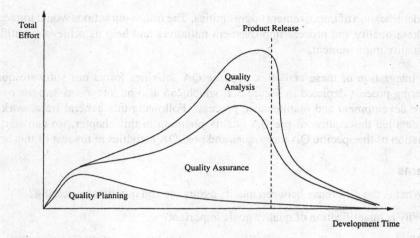

Figure 5.3   Quality engineering effort profile: The share of different activities as part of the total effort

In addition, the general shape and pattern of the profile such as in Figure 5.3 should preserve regardless of the specific development process used. Waterfall process would see more dominance of quality planning in the beginning, and dominance of testing near product release, and measurement and quality assessment activities peak right before product release.

Other development processes, such as incremental, iterative, spiral, and extreme programming processes, would be associated with curves that vary less between the peaks and valleys. QA is spread out more evenly in these processes than in the waterfall process, although it is still expected to peak a little bit before product release. Similarly, measurement and analysis activities are also spread out more evenly to monitor and assess each part or increment, with the cumulative modeling results used in product release decisions. There are also more adjustments and small-scale planning activities involved in quality planning, which also makes the corresponding profiles less variable as well.

5.5 CONCLUDING REMARKS

To manage the quality assurance (QA) activities and to provide realistic opportunities of quantifiable quality improvement, we need to go beyond QA to perform the following:

- *Quality planning* before specific QA activities are carried out, in the so-called pre-QA activities in software quality engineering. We need to set the overall quality goal by managing customer's quality expectations under the project cost and budgetary constraints. We also need to select specific QA alternatives and techniques to implement as well as measurement and models to provide project monitoring and qualitative feedback.

- *Quality quantification and improvement* through measurement, analysis, feedback, and follow-up activities. These activities need to be carried out after the start of specific QA activities, in the so-called post-QA activities in software quality engineering. The analyses would provide us with quantitative assessment of product quality, and identification of improvement opportunities. The follow-up actions would implement these quality and process improvement initiatives and help us achieve quantifiable quality improvement.

The integration of these activities with the QA activities forms our software quality engineering process depicted in Figure 5.1, which can also be integrated into the overall software development and maintenance process. Following this general framework and with a detailed description of pre-QA quality planning in this chapter, we can start our examination of the specific QA techniques and post-QA activities in the rest of this book.

Problems

5.1   What is the difference between quality assurance and quality engineering?

5.2   Why is quantification of quality goals important?

5.3   What can you do if certain quality goals are hard to quantify? Can you give some concrete examples of such situations and practical suggestions?

5.4   There are some studies on the cost-of-quality in literature, but the results are generally hard to apply to specific projects. Do you have some suggestions on how to assess the cost-of-quality for your own project? Would it be convincing enough to be relied upon in negotiating quality goals with your customers?

5.5   As mentioned in this chapter, the quality engineering effort profile would be somewhat different from that in Figure 5.3 if processes other than waterfall are used. Can you assess, qualitatively or quantitatively, the differences when other development processes are used?

5.6   Based on some project data you can access, build your own quality engineering effort profile and compare it to that in Figure 5.3. Pay special attention to development process used and the division of planning, QA, and analysis/follow-up activities.

PART II

SOFTWARE TESTING

Testing is one of the most important parts of quality assurance (QA) and the most commonly performed QA activity. Commonly used testing techniques and issues related to testing are covered in Part II. We first provide an overview of all the important issues related to testing in Chapter 6, followed by descriptions of major test activities, management, and automation in Chapter 7, specific testing techniques in Chapters 8 through 11, and practical application of testing techniques and their integration in Chapter 12.

CHAPTER 6

TESTING: CONCEPTS, ISSUES, AND TECHNIQUES

The basic idea of testing involves the execution of software and the observation of its behavior or outcome. If a failure is observed, the execution record is analyzed to locate and fix the fault(s) that caused the failure. Otherwise, we gain some confidence that the software under testing is more likely to fulfill its designated functions. We cover basic concepts, issues, and techniques related to testing in this chapter.

6.1 PURPOSES, ACTIVITIES, PROCESSES, AND CONTEXT

We first present an overview of testing in this section by examining the motivation for testing, the basic activities and process involved in testing, and how testing fits into the overall software quality assurance (QA) activities.

Testing: Why?

Similar to the situation for many physical systems and products, the purpose of software testing is to ensure that the software systems would work as expected when they are used by their target customers and users. The most natural way to show this fulfillment of expectations is to demonstrate their operation through some "dry-runs" or controlled experimentation in laboratory settings before the products are released or delivered. In the case of software products, such controlled experimentation through program execution is generally called testing.

Because of the relatively defect-free manufacturing process for software as compared to the development process, we focus on testing in the development process. We run or execute the implemented software systems or components to demonstrate that they work as expected. Therefore, "demonstration of proper behavior" is a primary purpose of testing, which can also be interpreted as providing evidence of quality in the context of software QA, or as meeting certain quality goals.

However, because of the ultimate flexibility of software, where problems can be corrected and fixed much more easily than traditional manufacturing of physical products and systems, we can benefit much more from testing by fixing the observed problems within the development process and deliver software products that are as defect-free as our budget or environment allows. As a result, testing has become a primary means to detect and fix software defects under most development environments, to the degree that "detecting and fixing defects" has eclipsed quality demonstration as the primary purpose of testing for many people and organizations.

To summarize, testing fulfills two primary purposes:

- to demonstrate quality or proper behavior;

- to detect and fix problems.

In this book, we examine testing and describe related activities and techniques with both these purposes in mind, and provide a balanced view of testing. For example, when we analyze the testing results, we focus more on the quality or reliability demonstration aspect. On the other hand, when we test the internal implementations to detect and remove faults that were injected into the software systems in the development process, we focus more on the defect detection and removal aspect.

Major activities and the generic testing process

The basic concepts of testing can be best described in the context of the major activities involved in testing. Although there are different ways to group them (Musa, 1998; Burnstein, 2003; Black, 2004), the major test activities include the following in roughly chronological order:

- *Test planning and preparation*, which set the goals for testing, select an overall testing strategy, and prepare specific test cases and the general test procedure.

- *Test execution* and related activities, which also include related observation and measurement of product behavior.

- *Analysis and follow-up*, which include result checking and analysis to determine if a failure has been observed, and if so, follow-up activities are initiated and monitored to ensure removal of the underlying causes, or faults, that led to the observed failures in the first place.

The overall organization of these activities can be described by the generic testing process illustrated in Figure 6.1. A brief comparison of it with the generic quality engineering process in Figure 5.1 reveals many similarities. In fact, we can consider this generic testing process as an instantiation of the generic quality engineering process to testing.

The major test activities are centered around test execution, or *performing* the actual tests. At a minimum, testing involves executing the software and communicating the related

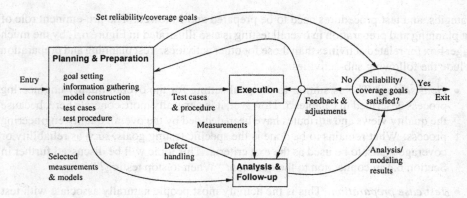

Figure 6.1   Generic testing process

observations. In fact, many forms of informal testing include just this middle group of activities related to test execution, with some informal ways to communicate the results and fix the defects, but without much planning and preparation. However, as we will see in the rest of Part II, in all forms of systematic testing, the other two activity groups, particularly test planning and preparation activities, play a much more important role in the overall testing process and activities.

The execution of a specific test case, or a sub-division of the overall test execution sequence for some systems that require continuous operation, is often referred to as a "test run". One of the key component to effective test execution is the handling of problems to ensure that failed runs will not block the executions of other test cases. This is particularly important for systems that require continuous operation. To many people, defect fixing is not considered to be a part of testing, but rather a part of the development activities. However, re-verification of problem fixes is considered as a part of testing. In this book, we consider all of these activities as a part of testing.

Data captured during execution and other related measurements can be used to locate and fix the underlying faults that led to the observed failures. After we have determined if a test run is a success or failure, appropriate actions can be initiated for failed runs to locate and fix the underlying faults. In addition, further analyses can be performed to provide valuable feedback to the testing process and to the overall development process in general. These analysis results provide us with assessments of the current status with respect to progress, effort, defect, and product quality, so that decisions, such as when to stop testing, can be made based on facts instead of on people's gut feelings. In addition, some analyses can also help us identify opportunities for long-term product quality improvement. Therefore, various other activities, such as measurement, analysis, and follow-up activities, also need to be supported.

Sub-activities in test planning and preparation

Because of the increasing size and complexity of today's software products, informal testing without much planning and preparation becomes inadequate. Important functions, features, and related software components and implementation details could be easily overlooked in such informal testing. Therefore, there is a strong need for planned, monitored, managed and optimized testing strategies based on systematic considerations for quality, formal models, and related techniques. Test cases can be planned and prepared using such testing strategies, and test procedures need to be prepared and followed. The pre-eminent role of test planning and preparation in overall testing is also illustrated in Figure 6.1, by the much bigger box for related activities than those for other activities. Test planning and preparation include the following sub-activities:

- *Goal setting*: This is similar to the goal setting for the overall quality engineering process described in Chapter 5. However, it is generally more concrete here, because the quality views and attributes have been decided by the overall quality engineering process. What remains to be done is the specific testing goals, such as reliability or coverage goals, to be used as the exit criteria. This topic will be discussed further in Section 6.4 in connection to the question: "When to stop testing?".

- *Test case preparation*: This is the activity most people naturally associate with test preparation. It includes constructing new test cases or generating them automatically, selecting from existing ones for legacy products, and organizing them in some systematic ways for easy execution and management. In most systematic testing, these test cases need to be constructed, generated, or selected based on some formal models associated with formal testing techniques covered in Chapters 8 through 11.

- *Test procedure preparation*: This is an important activity for test preparation. For systematic testing on a large scale for most of today's software products and software-intensive systems, a formal procedure is more of a necessity than a luxury. It can be defined and followed to ensure effective test execution, problem handling and resolution, and the overall test process management.

Testing as a part of QA in the overall software process

In the overall framework of software quality engineering, testing is an integral part of the QA activities. In our classification scheme based on different ways of dealing with defects in Chapter 3, testing falls into the category of defect reduction alternatives that also include inspection and various static and dynamic analyses. Unlike inspection, testing detects faults indirectly through the execution of software instead of critical examination used in inspection. However, testing and inspection often finds different kinds of problems, and may be more effective under different circumstances. Therefore, inspection and testing should be viewed more as complementary QA alternatives instead of competing ones.

Similarly, other QA alternatives introduced in Chapter 3 and described in Part III may be used to complement testing as well. For example, defect prevention may effectively reduce defect injections during software development, resulting in fewer faults to be detected and removed through testing, thus reducing the required testing effort and expenditure. Formal verification can be used to verify the correctness of some core functions in a product instead of applying exhaustive testing to them. Fault tolerance and failure containment strategies might be appropriate for critical systems where the usage environment may involve many unanticipated events that are hard or impossible to test during development. As we will examine later in Chapter 17, different QA alternatives have different strengths and weaknesses, and a concerted effort and a combined strategy involving testing and other QA techniques are usually needed for effective QA.

As an important part of QA activities, testing also fits into various software development processes as an important phase of development or as important activities accompanying other development activities. In the waterfall process, testing is concentrated in the dedicated testing phase, with some unit testing spread over to the implementation phases and some late testing spread over to the product release and support phase (Zelkowitz, 1988). However, test preparation should be started in the early phases. In addition, test result analyses and follow-up activities should be carried out in parallel to testing, and should not stop even after extensive test activities have stopped, to ensure discovered problems are all resolved and long-term improvement initiatives are planned and carried out.

Although test activities may fit into other development processes somewhat differently, they still play a similarly important role. In some specific development processes, testing plays an even more important role. For example, test-driven development plays a central role in extreme programming (Beck, 2003). Various maintenance activities also need the active support of software testing. All these issues will be examined further in Chapter 12 in connection to testing sub-phases and specialized test tasks.

6.2 QUESTIONS ABOUT TESTING

We next discuss the similarities and differences among different test activities and techniques by examining some systematic questions about testing.

Basic questions about testing

Our basic questions about testing are related to the objects being tested, perspectives and views used in testing, and overall management and organization of test activities, as described below:

- *What artifacts are tested?*

  The primary types of objects or software artifacts to be tested are software programs or code written in different programming languages. Program code is the focus of our testing effort and related testing techniques and activities. A related question, *"What other artifacts can also be tested?"*, is answered in Chapter 12 in connection to specialized testing.

- *What to test, and what kind of faults is found?*

  Black-box (or functional) testing verifies the correct handling of the external functions provided or supported by the software, or whether the observed behavior conforms to user expectations or product specifications. White-box (or structural) testing verifies the correct implementation of internal units, structures, and relations among them. When black-box testing is performed, failures related to specific external functions can be observed, leading to corresponding faults being detected and removed. The emphasis is on reducing the chances of encountering functional problems by target customers. On the other hand, when white-box testing is performed, failures related to internal implementations can be observed, leading to corresponding faults being detected and removed. The emphasis is on reducing internal faults so that there is less chance for failures later on no matter what kind of application environment the software is subjected to. Related issues are examined in Section 6.3.

- *When, or at what defect level, to stop testing?*

  Most of the traditional testing techniques and testing sub-phases use some coverage information as the stopping criterion, with the implicit assumption that higher coverage means higher quality or lower levels of defects. On the other hand, product reliability goals can be used as a more objective criterion to stop testing. The coverage criterion ensures that certain types of faults are detected and removed, thus reducing the number of defects to a lower level, although quality is not directly assessed. The usage-based testing and the related reliability criterion ensure that the faults that are most likely to cause problems to customers are detected and removed, and the reliability of the software reaches certain targets before testing stops. Related issues are examined in Section 6.4.

Questions about testing techniques

Many different testing techniques can be applied to perform testing in different sub-phases, for different types of products, and under different environments. Various questions regarding these testing techniques can help us get a better understanding of many related issues, including:

- *What is the specific testing technique used?*

   This question is answered in connection with the what-to-test and stopping-criteria in Sections 6.3 and 6.4. Many commonly used testing techniques are described in detail in Chapters 8 through 11.

- *What is the underlying model used in a specific testing technique?*

   Since most of the systematic techniques for software testing are based on some formalized models, we need to examine the types and characteristics of these models to get a better understanding of the related techniques. In fact, the coverage of major testing techniques in Chapters 8 through 11 is organized by the different testing models used, as follows:

   - There are two basic types of models: those based on simple structures such as checklists and partitions in Chapter 8, and those based on finite-state machines (FSMs) in Chapter 10.

   - The above models can be directly used for testing basic coverage defined accordingly, such as coverage of checklists and partitions in Chapter 8 and coverage of FSM states and transitions in Chapter 10.

   - For usage-based testing, minor modifications to these models are made to associate usage probabilities to partition items as in Musa's operational profiles in Chapter 8 and to make state transitions probabilistic as in Markov chain based statistical testing in Chapter 10.

   - Some specialized extensions to the two basic models can be used to support several commonly used testing techniques, such as input domain testing that extends partition ideas to input sub-domains and focuses on testing related boundary conditions in Chapter 9, and control flow and data flow testing (CFT & DFT) that extends FSMs to test complete execution paths or to test data dependencies in execution and interactions in Chapter 11.

- *Are techniques for testing in other domains applicable to software testing?*

   Examples include error/fault seeding, mutation, immunization and other techniques used in physical, biological, social, and other systems and environments. These questions are examined in Chapter 12, in connection to specialized testing.

- *If multiple testing techniques are available, can they be combined or integrated for better effectiveness or efficiency?*

  This question is the central theme of our test integration discussions in Chapter 12. Different techniques have their own advantages and disadvantages, different applicability and effectiveness under different environments. They may share many common ideas, models, and other artifacts. Therefore, it makes sense to combine or integrate different testing techniques and related activities to maximize product quality or other objectives while minimizing total cost or effort.

Questions about test activities and management

Besides the questions above, various other questions can also be used to help us analyze and classify different test activities. Some key questions are about initiators and participants of these activities, organization and management of specific activities, etc., as follows:

- *Who performs which specific activities?*

  Different people may be involved in different roles. This issue is examined in Chapter 7 in connection to the detailed description of major test activities. A related issue is the automation of some of these manual tasks performed by people, also discussed in Chapter 7.

- *When can specific test activities be performed?*

  Because testing is an execution-based QA activity, a prerequisite to actual testing is the existence of the implemented software units, components, or system to be tested, although preparation for testing can be carried out in earlier phases of software development. As a result, actual testing of large software systems is typically organized and divided into various sub-phases starting from the coding phase up to post-release product support. A related question is the possibility of specialized testing activities that are more applicable to specific products or specific situations instead of to specific sub-phases. Issues related to these questions are examined in Chapter 12.

- *What process is followed for these test activities?*

  We have answered this question in Section 6.1. Some related management issues are also discussed in Chapter 7

- *Is test automation possible?* And if so, *what kind of automated testing tools are available and usable for specific applications?*

  These questions and related issues are examined in Chapter 7 in connection with major test activities and people's roles and responsibilities in them.

- *What artifacts are used to manage the testing process and related activities?*

  This question is answered in Chapter 7 in connection with test activities management issues.

- *What is the relationship between testing and various defect-related concepts?*

  This question has been answered above and in Chapter 3.

- *What is the general hardware/software/organizational environment for testing?*

This questions is addressed in Chapter 7, in connection with major test activities management issues.

- *What is the product type or market segment for the product under testing?*

  Most of the testing techniques we describe are generally applicable to most application domains. Some testing techniques that are particularly applicable or suitable to specific application domains or specific types of products are also included in Chapter 12. We also attempt to cover diverse product domains in our examples throughout the book.

The above lists may not be all-inclusive lists of questions and issues that can be used to classify and examine testing techniques and related activities. However, they should include most of the important questions people ask regarding testing and important issues discussed in testing literature (Howden, 1980; Myers, 1979; Miller and Howden, 1981; Beizer, 1990; Burnstein, 2003; Black, 2004; Huo et al., 2003). We use the answers to these questions as the basis for test classification and examination, and to organize our chapters on testing.

6.3 FUNCTIONAL VS. STRUCTURAL TESTING: WHAT TO TEST?

The main difference between functional and structural testing is the perspective and the related focus: Functional testing focus on the external behavior of a software system or its various components, while viewing the object to be tested as a black-box that prevents us from seeing the contents inside. On the other hand, structural testing focus on the internal implementation, while viewing the object to be tested as a white-box that allows us to see the contents inside. Therefore, we start further discussion about these two basic types of testing by examining the objects to be tested and the perspectives taken to test them.

Objects and perspectives

As the primary type of objects to be tested, software programs or code exists in various forms and is written in different programming languages. They can be viewed either as individual pieces or as an integrated whole. Consequently, there are different levels of testing corresponding to different views of the code and different levels of abstraction, as follows:

- At the most detailed level, individual program elements can be tested. This includes testing of individual statements, decisions, and data items, typically in a small scale by focusing on an individual program unit or a small component. Depending on the different programming languages used, this unit may correspond to a function, a procedure, a subroutine or a method. As for the components, concepts may vary, but generally include a collection of smaller units that together accomplish something or form an object.

- At the intermediate level, various program elements or program components may be treated as an interconnected group, and tested accordingly. This could be done at component, sub-system, or system levels, with the help of some models to capture the interconnection and other relations among different elements or components.

- At the most abstract level, the whole software systems can be treated as a "black-box", while we focus on the functions or input–output relations instead of the internal implementation.

In each of the above abstraction levels, we may choose to focus on either the overall behavior or the individual elements that make up the objects of testing, resulting in the difference between functional testing and structural testing. The tendency is that at higher levels of abstraction, functional testing is more likely to be used; while at lower levels of abstraction, structural testing is more likely to be used. However, the other pairing is also possible, as we will see in some specific examples later.

Corresponding to these different levels of abstraction, actual testing for large software systems is typically organized and divided into various sub-phases starting from the coding phase up to post-release product support, including unit testing, component testing, integration testing, system testing, acceptance testing, beta testing, etc. Unit testing and component testing typically focus on individual program elements that are present in the unit or component. System testing and acceptance testing typically focus on the overall operations of the software system as a whole. These testing sub-phases are described in Chapter 12.

Functional or black-box testing (BBT)

Functional testing verifies the correct handling of the external functions provided by the software, through the observation of the program external behavior during execution. Because the software is treated as a black-box, with the external behavior observed through its input, output, and other observable characteristics, it is also commonly referred to as black-box testing (BBT). In this book, we use these two terms interchangeably.

The simplest form of BBT is to start running the software and make observations in the hope that it is easy to distinguish between expected and unexpected behavior. This form of testing is also referred to as "ad hoc" testing. Some unexpected behavior, such as a crash, is easy to detect. Once we determine that it is caused by software through repeated execution to eliminate the possibilities of hardware problems, we can pass the information to responsible parties to have the problem fixed. In fact, this is the common way through which problems experienced by actual customers are reported and fixed.

Another common form of BBT is the use of specification checklists, which list the external functions that are supposed to be present, as well as some information about the expected behavior or input–output pairing. Notice here that we used the term *input* to mean any action, artifact, or resource provided in the process of running a program, either at the beginning or at any time during the program execution. Similarly, we use the term *output* to mean any action, artifact, or result produced by the running program, either at the end or at any time during the program execution. Concrete examples of input to a calculator program might include the specific numbers entered and the action requested, such as division operation of two numbers. The output could be the actual division result, or some error message, such as when attempting to divide by zero. When problems are observed, specific follow-up actions are carried out to fix them.

More formalized and systematic BBT can be based on some formal models. These formal testing models are derived from system requirement or functional specifications. Some traditional white-box testing techniques can also be adapted to perform BBT, such as control-flow and data-flow testing for external functional units instead of for internal implementations.

BBT can follow the generic testing process described in Section 6.1 to carry out the major test activities of planning, execution, and follow-up. In test planning, the focus is on identifying the external functions to test, and deriving input conditions to test these functions. The identified external functions are usually associated with some user expectations, from which both the input and the expected output can be derived to form the test cases. For example, for a compiler, the input is source code to be compiled, and the output is the resulting object or executable code. Part of the expected behavior is system termination, that is, the compiler should produce some output within a limited amount of time. Another part of the expected behavior is that if illegal programs are provided as input, object or executable code will not be generated, and the reason should be given. Therefore, a collection of programs to be compiled constitutes the test suite, or the collection of test cases. This test suite should typically consist of both legal and illegal programs to cover the expected spectrum of input. The testing goals may be stated explicitly as exit quality levels or implicitly as the completion of planned test cases.

The focus of test execution during BBT is to observe the external behavior, to ensure orderly execution of all the test cases, and to record execution information for analysis and follow-up activities. If the observed behavior patterns cannot be immediately identified as failures, information needs to be recorded for further analysis. In the above example of the compiler, the output produced and the execution trace should be recorded, as well as the exact set-up under which the compiler operated.

Once the execution result is obtained, either individually or as a set, analyses can be carried out to compare the specific behavior and output with the expected ones. This comparison to determine if it is expected behavior or if a failure occurred is called the testing *oracle* problem. Thus BBT checks whether the observed behavior conforms to user expectations or product specifications. Failures related to specific external functions can be observed, leading to follow-up activities where corresponding faults are detected and removed. The emphasis is on reducing the chances of encountering functional problems by target customers. Information recorded at test execution is used in these follow-up activities to recreate failure scenarios, to diagnose problems, to locate failure causes and identify specific faults in software design and code, and to fix them. An important follow-up decision, when to stop testing, can be determined either using the traditional functional coverage criteria or reliability criteria, as further elaborated in Section 6.4.

Structural or white-box testing (WBT)

Structural testing verifies the correct implementation of internal units, such as program statements, data structures, blocks, etc., and relations among them. This is done through test execution by observing the program behavior related to these specific units. Because the software is treated as a white-box, or more appropriately a glass-box or a transparent-box, where one can see through to view the internal units and their interconnections, it is also commonly referred to as white-box testing (WBT) in literature. In keeping with this convention, we also label this as WBT, with the understanding that this "white-box" is really transparent so that the tester can see through it. In this book, we also use the two terms, structural testing and WBT, interchangeably.

Because the connection between execution behavior and internal units needs to be made in WBT, various software tools are typically used. The simplest form of WBT is statement coverage testing through the use of various debugging tools, or debuggers, which help us in tracing through program executions. By doing so, the tester can see if a specific statement has been executed, and if the result or behavior is expected. One of the advantages is that once a problem is detected, it is also located. However, problems of omission or design problems cannot be easily detected through WBT, because only what is present in the code is tested. Another important point worth noting is that the tester needs to be very familiar with the code under testing to trace through its executions. Consequently, WBT and related activities are typically performed by the programmers themselves because of their intimate knowledge of the specific program unit under testing. This dual role also makes defect fixing easy.

Similar to the situation for BBT, more formalized and systematic WBT can be based on some formal models. These formal testing models are typically derived from system implementation details. In fact, the majority of the traditional testing techniques is based on program analyses and program models, and therefore is white-box in nature.

WBT can also follow the generic testing process described in Section 6.1, to carry out the major test activities of planning, execution, and follow-up. However, because of the extensive amount of implementation knowledge required, and due to the possibility of combinatorial explosions to cover these implementation details, WBT is typically limited to a small scale. For small products, not much formal testing process is needed to plan and execute test cases, and to follow up on execution results. For unit testing of large products, the WBT activities are carried out in the encompassing framework where most of the planning is subject to the environment; and the environmental constraints pretty much determine what can be done. Therefore, test planning plays a much less important role in WBT than in BBT. In addition, defect fixing is made easy by the tight connection between program behavior and program units, and through the dual role played by the programmers as testers. Consequently, not much formal testing process is needed. The stopping criteria are also relatively simple: Once planned coverage has been achieved, such as exercising all statements, all paths, etc., testing can stop. Sometimes, internal quality measures, such as defect levels, can also be used as a stopping criterion.

Comparing BBT with WBT

To summarize, the key question that distinguishes black-box testing (BBT) from white-box testing (WBT) is the "perspective" question:

- *Perspective*: BBT views the objects of testing as a black-box while focusing on testing the input–output relations or external functional behavior; while WBT views the objects as a glass-box where internal implementation details are visible and tested.

BBT and WBT can also be compared by the way in which they address the following questions:

- *Objects*: Although the objects tested may overlap occasionally, WBT is generally used to test small objects, such as small software products or small units of large software products; while BBT is generally more suitable for large software systems or substantial parts of them as a whole.

- *Timeline*: WBT is used more in early sub-phases of testing for large software systems, such as unit and component testing, while BBT is used more in late sub-phases, such as system and acceptance testing.

- *Defect focus*: In BBT, failures related to specific external functions can be observed, leading to corresponding faults being detected and removed. The emphasis is on reducing the chances of encountering functional problems by target customers. In WBT, failures related to internal implementations can be observed, leading to corresponding faults being detected and removed directly. The emphasis is on reducing internal faults so that there is less chance for failures later on no matter what kind of application environment the software is subjected to.

- *Defect detection and fixing*: Defects detected through WBT are easier to fix than those through BBT because of the direct connection between the observed failures and program units and implementation details in WBT. However, WBT may miss certain types of defects, such as omission and design problems, which could be detected by BBT. In general BBT is effective in detecting and fixing problems of interfaces and interactions, while WBT is effective for problems localized within a small unit.

- *Techniques*: Various techniques can be used to build models and generate test cases to perform systematic BBT, and others can be used for WBT, with some of the same techniques being able to be used for both WBT and BBT. A specific technique is a BBT one if external functions are modeled; while the same technique can be a WBT one if internal implementations are modeled.

- *Tester*: BBT is typically performed by dedicated professional testers, and could also be performed by third-party personnel in a setting of IV&V (independent verification and validation); while WBT is often performed by developers themselves.

6.4 COVERAGE-BASED VS. USAGE-BASED TESTING: WHEN TO STOP TESTING?

For most of the testing situations, the answer to the question "when to stop testing?" depends on the completion of some pre-planned activities, coverage of certain entities, or whether a pre-set goal has been achieved. We next describe the use of different exit criteria and the corresponding testing techniques.

When to stop testing?

The question, "when to stop testing", can be refined into two different questions:

- On a small or a local scale, we can ask: "When to stop testing for a specific test activity?" This question is also commonly associated with different testing sub-phases.

- On a global scale, we can ask: "When to stop all the major test activities?" Because the testing phase is usually the last major development phase before product release, this question is equivalent to: "When to stop testing and release the product?"

These questions may yield different answers, leading us to different testing techniques and related activities. Without a formal assessment for decision making, decision to stop testing can usually be made in two general forms:

- *Resource-based criteria*, where decision is made based on resource consumptions. The most commonly used such stopping criteria are

> – "Stop when you run out of time."
>
> – "Stop when you run out of money."

Such criteria are irresponsible, as far as product quality is concerned, although they may be employed if product schedule or cost are the dominant concerns for the product in question.

- *Activity-based criteria*, commonly in the form:

  – "Stop when you complete planned test activities."

This criterion implicitly assumes the effectiveness of the test activities in ensuring the quality of the software product. However, this assumption could be questionable without strong historical evidence based on actual data from the project concerned.

Because of these shortcomings, informal decisions without using formal assessments have very limited use in managing the testing process and activities for large software systems. We next examine exit criteria based on formal analyses and assessments.

On the global level, the exit from testing is associated with product release, which determined the level of quality that a customer or a user could expect. In our overall software quality engineering process, this decision is associated with achieving quality goals, as well as achieving other project goals in the overall software development process. Therefore, the most direct and obvious way to make such product release decisions is the use of various reliability assessments. When the assessment environment is similar to the actual usage environment for customers. the resulting reliability measurement would be directly meaningful to these customers.

The basic idea in using reliability criterion is to set a reliability goal in the quality planning activity during product planning and requirement analysis, and later on to compare the reliability assessment based on testing data to see if this pre-set goal has been reached. If so, the product can be released. Otherwise, testing needs to continue and product release needs to be deferred. Various models exist today to provide reliability assessments and improvement based on data from testing, as described in Chapter 22.

One important implication of using this criterion for stopping testing is that the reliability assessments should be close to what actual users would expect, which requires that the testing right before product release resembles actual usages by target customers. This requirement resulted in the so-called usage-based testing. On the other hand, because of the large number of customers and usage situations, exhaustive coverage of all the customer usage scenarios, sequences, and patterns is infeasible. Therefore, an unbiased statistical sampling is the best that we can hope for, which results in usage-based statistical testing (UBST) that we will describe later in this section. Some specific techniques for such testing are described in Chapters 8 and 10.

For earlier sub-phases of testing, or for stopping criteria related to localized test activities, reliability definition based on customer usage scenarios and frequencies may not be meaningful. For example, many of the internal components are never directly used by actual users, and some components associated with low usage frequencies may be critical for various situations. Under these situations, the use of reliability criterion may not be meaningful or may lead to inadequate testing of some specific components. Alternative exit criteria are needed. For example, as a rule of thumb:

> "Products should not be released unless every component has been tested."

Criteria similar to this have been adopted in many organizations to test their products and related components. We call these criteria coverage criteria, which involve coverage of some specific entities, such as components, execution paths, statements, etc. The use of coverage criteria is associated with defining appropriate coverage for different testing techniques, linking what was tested with what was covered in some formal assessments.

One implicit assumption in using coverage as the stopping criterion is that everything covered is defect free with respect to this specific coverage aspect, because all defects discovered by the suite of test cases that achieved this coverage goal would have been fixed or removed before product release. This assumption is similar to the one above regarding the effectiveness of test activities, when we use the completion of planned test activities as the exit criterion. However, this assumption is more likely to be enforced because specific coverage is closely linked to specific test cases.

From the quality perspective, the coverage criteria are based on the assumption that higher levels of coverage mean higher quality, and a specific quality goal can be translated into a specific coverage goal. However, we must realize that although there is a general positive correlation between coverage and quality, the relationship between the two is not a simple one. Many other factors need to be considered before an accurate quality assessment can be made based on coverage. For example, different testing techniques and sub-phases may be effective in detecting and removing different types of defects, leading to multi-stage reliability growth and saturation patterns (Horgan and Mathur, 1995). Nevertheless, coverage information gives us an approximate quality estimate, and can be used as the exit criterion when actual reliability assessment is unavailable, such as in the early sub-phases of testing.

Usage-based statistical testing (UBST) and operational profiles (OPs)

At one extreme, actual customer usage of software products can be viewed as a form of usage-based testing. When problems are experienced by these customers, some information about the problems, can be reported to software vendors, and integrated fixes can be constructed and delivered to all the customers to prevent similar problems from occurring. However, these post-product-release defect fixing activities could be very expensive because of the massive numbers of software installations. Frequent fixes could also damage the software vendor's reputation and long-term business viability. The so-called beta test makes use of this usage-and-fix to the advantage of software vendors, through controlled software release so that these beta customers help software development organizations improve their software quality.

In general, if the actual usage, or anticipated usage for a new product, can be captured and used in testing, product reliability could be most directly assured. In usage-based statistical testing (UBST), the overall testing environment resembles the actual operational environment for the software product in the field, and the overall testing sequence, as represented by the orderly execution of specific test cases in a test suite, resembles the usage scenarios, sequences, and patterns of actual software usage by the target customers. Because the massive number of customers and diverse usage patterns cannot be captured in an exhaustive set of test cases, statistical sampling is needed, thus the term "statistical" in the descriptive title of this strategy. For the same reason, "random testing" and "usage-based random testing" are also used in literature. However, we prefer to use the term "usage-based statistical testing" in this book to avoid the confusion between random testing and "ad hoc" testing, where no systematic strategy is implied in "ad hoc" testing.

For practical implementation of such a testing strategy, actual usage information needs to be captured in various models, commonly referred to as "operational profiles" or OPs.

Different OPs are associated with different testing techniques for UBST. Two primary types of usage models or OPs are:

- Flat OPs, or Musa OPs (Musa, 1993; Musa, 1998), which present commonly used operations in a list, a histogram, or a tree-structure, together with the associated occurrence probabilities. The main advantage of the flat OP is its simplicity, both in model construction and usage. This testing technique is described in Chapter 8.

- Markov chain based usage models, or Markov OPs (Mills, 1972; Mills et al., 1987b; Whittaker and Thomason, 1994; Kallepalli and Tian, 2001; Tian et al., 2003), which present commonly used operational units in Markov chains, where the state transition probabilities are history independent (Karlin and Taylor, 1975). Complete operations can be constructed by linking various states together following the state transitions, and the probability for the whole path is the product of its individual transition probabilities. Markov models based on state transitions can generally capture navigation patterns better than flat OPs, but are more expensive to maintain and to use. This testing technique is described in Chapter 10.

Usage-based statistical testing (UBST) is generally applicable to the final stage of testing, typically referred to as acceptance testing right before product release, so that stopping testing is equivalent to releasing the product. Other late sub-phases of testing, such as integration and system testing, could also benefit from the knowledge of actual customer usage situations to drive effective reliability improvement before product release, as demonstrated in some case studies in Chapter 22. Naturally, the termination criterion used to stop such testing is achievement of reliability goals.

Coverage and coverage-based testing (CBT)

As mentioned above, most traditional testing techniques, either functional testing (BBT) or structural testing (WBT), use various forms of test coverage as the stopping criteria. The simplest such criterion is in the form of completing various checklists, such as a checklist of major functions based on product specifications when BBT is used, or a checklist of all the product components or all the statements when WBT is used. Testing can be performed until all the items on the respective checklist have been checked off or exhausted. For most of the systematic testing techniques, some formal models beyond simple checklists are used. Some specific examples of such models and related coverage include:

- Formally defined partitions can be used as the basis for various testing techniques in Chapter 8, which are similar to checklists but ensure:
  - mutual exclusion of checklist items to avoid unnecessary repetition,
  - complete coverage defined accordingly.

- A specialized type of partitions, input domain partitions into sub-domains, can also be used to test these sub-domains and related boundary conditions, as described in Chapter 11.

- Various programming or functional states can be defined and linked together to form finite-state machines (FSMs) to model the system as the basis for various testing techniques in Chapter 10 to ensure state coverage and coverage of related state transitions and execution sequences.

- The above FSMs can also be extended to analyze and cover execution paths and data dependencies through various testing techniques in Chapter 11.

The generic steps and major sub-activities for CBT model construction and test preparation are described below:

- *Defining the model*: These models are often represented by some graphs, with individual nodes representing the basic model elements and links representing the interconnections. Some additional information may be attached to the graph as link or node properties (commonly referred to as weights in graph theory).

- *Checking individual model elements* to make sure the individual elements, such as links, nodes, and related properties, have been tested individually, typically in isolation, prior to testing using the whole model. This step also represents the self-checking of the model, to make sure that the model captures what is to be tested.

- *Defining coverage criteria*: Besides covering the basic model elements above, some other coverage criteria are typically used to cover the overall execution and interactions. For example, with the partition-based testing, we might want to cover the boundaries in addition to individual partitions; and for FSM-based testing, we might want to cover state transition sequences and execution paths.

- *Derive test cases*: Once the coverage criteria are defined, we can design our test cases to achieve them. The test cases need to be sensitized, that is, with its input values selected to realize specific tests, anticipated results defined, and ways to check the outcomes planned ahead of time.

Model construction and test preparation are more closely linked to individual testing techniques, which are described when each testing technique is introduced in Chapters 8 through 11. The other major testing related activities, including test execution, measurement, analysis, and follow-up activities, are typically similar for all testing techniques. Therefore, they are covered together in Chapter 7. Coverage analysis plays an important role in guiding testing and coverage criterion is used to determine when to stop testing. Automated tool support by for this analysis and related data collection is also discussed in Chapter 7.

Comparing CBT with UBST

To summarize, the key questions that distinguish coverage-based testing (CBT) from usage-based statistical testing (UBST) are the "perspective" question and the related stopping criteria:

- *Perspective*: UBST views the objects of testing from a user's perspective and focuses on the usage scenarios, sequences, patterns, and associated frequencies or probabilities; while CBT views the objects from a developer's perspective and focuses covering functional or implementation units and related entities.

- *Stopping criteria*: UBST use product reliability goals as the exit criterion; and CBT using coverage goals — surrogates or approximations of reliability goals — as the exit criterion.

CBT and UBST can also be compared by the way in which they address the following questions:

- *Objects*: Although the objects tested may overlap, CBT is generally used to test and cover small objects, such as small software products, small units of large software products, or large systems at a high level of abstraction, such major functions or components; while UBST is generally more suitable for large software systems as a whole.

- *Verification vs. validation*: Although both CBT and UBST can be used for both verification test and validation test, UBST is more likely to be used for validation test because of their relationship to customers and users.

- *Timeline*: For large software systems, CBT is often used in early sub-phases of testing, such as unit and component testing, while UBST is often used in late sub-phases of testing, such as system and acceptance testing.

- *Defect detection*: In UBST, failures that are more likely to be experienced by users are also more likely to be observed in testing, leading to corresponding faults being detected and removed for reliability improvement. In CBT, failures are more closely related to things tested, which may lead to effective fault removal but may not be directly linked to improved reliability due to different exposure ratios for software faults.

- *Testing environment*: UBST uses testing environment similar to that for in-field operation at customer installations; while CBT uses environment specifically set up for testing.

- *Techniques*: Various techniques can be used to build models and generate test cases to perform systematic CBT. When these models are augmented with usage information, typically as the probabilities associated with checklist items, partitions, states, and state transitions, they can be used as models for UBST also. This is why we cover UBST models and techniques together with corresponding basic CBT models and techniques in Chapter 8 and Chapter 10.

- *Customer and user roles*: UBST models are constructed with extensive customer and user input; while CBT models are usually constructed without active customer or user input. UBST is also more compatible with the customer and user focus in today's competitive market.

- *Tester*: Dedicated professional testers typically perform UBST; while CBT can be performed by either professional testers or by developers themselves.

6.5 CONCLUDING REMARKS

In this chapter, we described basic concepts of testing and examined various questions and issues related to testing. In addition, we classified the major testing techniques by two important criteria:

- *Functional vs. structural* testing techniques, with the former focusing on external functional behavior, the latter on internal implementations. Alternatively, they can be characterized by the ignorance or knowledge of implementation details: Functional testing is also referred to as black-box testing (BBT) because it ignores all implementation details, while structural testing is also referred to as white-box testing (WBT) because the transparent system boundary allows implementation details to be visible and to be used in testing.

- *Usage-based vs. coverage-based* stopping criteria and corresponding testing techniques, with the former attempting to reach certain reliability goals by focusing on functions and feature frequently used by target customers, and the latter focusing on attaining certain coverage levels defined internally.

Based on this examination, we will focus on two major items related to testing in subsequent chapters in Part II of this book:

- *Test activities, organization, management*, and related issues. We will examine in detail the major activities related to testing, their management, and automation in Chapter 7. These issues are common to different testing techniques and therefore covered before we cover specific techniques.

- *Testing techniques* and related issues. We will examine in detail the major testing techniques in Chapters 8 through 11. The adaptation and integration of different testing techniques for different testing sub-phases or specialized tasks are covered in Chapter 12.

Problems

6.1 Perform a critical analysis of the current practice of testing in your organization. If you are a full-time student, you can perform this critical analysis for the company your worked for previously, or based on the testing practice you employed in your previous course projects. Pay special attention to the following questions:

    a) What is the testing process used in your organization? How is it different from that in Figure 6.1?

    b) What is your role in software development? Are your performing any testing? What kind? What about your department and your organization?

    c) Is testing mostly informal or mostly formalized in your organization? In particular, what formal testing models and techniques are used?

6.2 Define the following terms related to testing: black-box testing, white-box testing, functional testing, structural testing, coverage-based testing, usage-based testing, operational profiles, statistical testing.

6.3 Can you applied the above terms and related concepts to inspection or other QA alternatives? If yes, give some examples. If no, briefly justify yourself.

CHAPTER 7

TEST ACTIVITIES, MANAGEMENT, AND AUTOMATION

In the previous chapter, we introduced major test activities and the generic testing process as part of the overall quality assurance (QA) activities. We expand on these topics in this chapter to take a detailed look of all the major test activities individually, including test planning and preparation in Section 7.1, test execution and measurement in Section 7.2, and test results analysis and follow-up in Section 7.3. We also examine the roles and responsibilities of different people in carrying out these activities and the related management issues in Section 7.4. Test automation issues are covered in Section 7.5.

7.1 TEST PLANNING AND PREPARATION

As illustrated in Figure 6.1, test planning and preparation is the most important activity in the generic testing process for systematic testing based on formal models. Most of the key decisions about testing are made during this stage. In this section, we first examine what key questions need to be answered in the high-level test planning, and then examine individual low-level activities related to test preparation. Test planning and test preparation are sometimes treated as separate groups of activities (Black, 2004).

7.1.1 Test planning: Goals, strategies, and techniques

The high-level task for test planning is to set goals and to determine a general testing strategy. This high-level decision should be based on answers to several key questions we examined in Chapter 6, particularly the objectives or goals of testing under a specific environment.

The answers to these questions not only determine the general types of testing to perform, but also determine the test termination or exit criteria. Overall environment needs to be considered because the environmental constraints imposed on testing also affect the choice of testing strategies.

Most of the testing we cover in this book focuses on the correctness aspect of quality. If the software is complete or nearly complete, then the above correctness-centered quality goals can be directly translated into reliability goals, which, in turn, requires us to use usage-based statistical testing. Sometimes, these quality goals can be translated indirectly into coverage goals, which can be achieved by black-box testing for the whole system. However, if only individual units and pieces are available, we might choose to focus on the implementation details and perform coverage-based white-box testing.

Therefore, we set an overall testing strategy by making the following decisions:

- *Overall objectives and goals*, which can be refined into specific goals for specific testing. Some specific goals include *reliability* for usage-based statistical testing or *coverage* for various traditional testing techniques.

- *Objects to be tested and the specific focus*: Functional testing views the software product as a black-box and focuses on testing the external functional behavior; while structural testing views the software product or component as a (transparent) white-box and focuses on testing the internal implementation details.

Once the overall testing strategy has be selected, we can plan to allocate resources and staff to implement it. The available staff and resources also affect the specific models and techniques that can be used to implement the strategy. For example, simple models based on checklists and partitions generally require less resources and prior knowledge by the testing staff, while more complex formal models and related testing techniques may require more resources and expertise. Different models and techniques are also associated with different effectiveness levels or different applicability to different types of problems and situations. Consequently, appropriate testing models and related techniques can be selected to optimize some form of cost–benefit measure.

Sometimes, existing models or test suites can be used with some minor modifications or adaptations, which would require minimal additional effort in test planning and preparation. Nevertheless, the above high-level activities still need to be carried out to arrive at this decision, because indiscriminately using exiting testing strategies, techniques, models, and test suites may not fulfill the need for the new situation and end up merely wasting valuable time and resources. In what follows, we focus on the situation where new models, procedures, and test cases need to be considered in testing planning and preparation. The situation of minor adaptations is dealt with in Chapter 12 in connection with regression testing as a specialized type or testing.

7.1.2   Testing models and test cases

Different models are closely linked to different testing techniques, and the modeling details can only be described together with their corresponding techniques, as we will do in Chapters 8 through 11. However, some generic steps and activities are involved in test model construction, as follows:

1. *Information source identification and data collection*: The information and data are generally affected by both what is required by specific models and what is available in

the project environment. For example, in usage-based statistical testing, information about actual in-field or anticipated usage by target customers needs to be gathered to construct operational profiles as the basis of testing; while in white-box unit testing, the tested unit provides the information source which can be analyzed to construct our testing models.

2. *Analysis and initial model construction*: The information and data collected above are analyzed to construct testing models. Expertise and familiarity with the specific testing techniques and models are required for people who perform this task. This step is typically the hardest to automate because of the human intelligence and expertise required.

3. *Model validation and incremental improvement*: This is an important step, particularly for large objects or for functions or usages associated with external customers. Iterative procedure might be necessary to fix inaccuracies and other problems found in the initial model or early versions of the candidate models.

Once the testing models have been constructed and validated, they can be used to generate test cases, which can then be executed by following some planned test procedure. First, we need to define and distinguish the static test cases and the dynamic test runs, as follows:

- A *test case* is a collection of entities and related information that allows a test to be executed or a test run to be performed.

- A *test run*, is a dynamic unit of specific test activities in the overall testing sequence on a selected testing object.

Each time a static test case is invoked, we have an individual dynamic test run. Therefore, each test case can correspond to multiple test runs. In some literature and organizations, each test run is also called an *attempt*.

The information included for a test case must enable the related test run to start, continue, and finish. For most of the testing situations, the starting and finishing points correspond to the initiation and termination of the operations for the whole software system, such as the compilation of a program when the compiler is tested. But there are exceptions, such as in operating systems and telecommunication systems, where continuous operation without stopping is the expected norm. In these cases, because the specific test is an activity associated with finite time for practical purposes, the starting and finishing points need to be artificially inserted, resulting in a subsection of the system execution as a test run.

Essential among the test case information is the specific input to the software object in operation, which includes both the initial input at the start of the test run and the input to allow it to continue and to finish. In addition, the test case often includes information about the expected output throughout the test run, which, together with the specific input and timing information, defines the program behavior under this test run. Such input, output, and timing information can be captured by the set of input variables, the set of output variables, and their values over time.

With the above understanding, we can view the construction of a specific test case as assigning its input values over a planned test run, which is referred to as test *sensitization* in testing literature. This assignment is typically derived from testing models we constructed in the previous step of test planning and preparation. Different criteria and steps may be involved in test sensitization when different testing techniques are used, as we will illustrate when individual testing techniques are covered in Chapters 8 through 11.

In addition to obtaining test cases from the sensitization step based on formal testing models, test cases can sometimes be derived from other sources directly. For example, actual runs from in-field operations of software products can sometimes be used to perform test runs. In this case, a simple strategy of "record-and-replay" is used. For some systems, if the required information is easy to obtain, this strategy might be an effective one. However, for most large systems, too much information might need to be recorded, making this strategy impractical. In addition, systematic analysis of recorded information may provide valuable insight into the usage situations of the product. Systematic models constructed using such recorded information may provide more efficient or more effective ways to test the software products than simply playing back the recorded runs.

7.1.3   Test suite preparation and management

The collection of individual test cases that will be run in a test sequence until some stopping criteria are satisfied is called a *test suite*. Test suite preparation involves the construction and allocation of individual test cases in some systematic way based on the specific testing techniques used. For example, when usage-based statistical testing is planned, the test case allocation will be determined by the operational profiles (OPs) constructed as the testing models, in proportion to individual usage probabilities. Similarly, when coverage-based testing is planned, the specific coverage criteria would dictate the allocation of test cases. For example, in control flow testing not involving loops, the exact number of test cases is determined by the number of paths for all-path coverage.

Another way to obtain a test suite is through reuse of test cases for earlier versions of the same product. This kind of testing is commonly referred to as *regression testing*. It ensures that common functionalities are still supported satisfactorily in addition to satisfactory performance of new functionalities. Special types of formal models are typically used to make the selection from existing test cases, as we will discuss in Chapter 12 in connection to regression testing.

In general, all the test cases should form an integrated suite, regardless of their origins, how they are derived, and what models are used to derive them. Sometimes, the test suite may evolve over time and its formation may overlap with the actual testing. In fact, in some testing techniques, test cases can be constructed dynamically, or "on-the-fly", during test execution. But even for such testing, some planning of the test cases and test suite is still necessary, at least to determine the specific method for dynamic test case construction and the precise stopping criteria. For most of the testing techniques we cover in this book, a significant part of test preparation must be done before actual testing starts.

In general, test cases cost time, effort, and expertise to be obtained, and are too valuable to be thrown away. It is worthwhile to spend some addition effort and resource to save them, organize them, and manage them as a test suite for easy reuse in the future. Test suite management includes managing the collection of both the existing test cases and the newly constructed ones. At a minimum, some consistent database for the test suite needs to be kept and shared by people who are working on similar areas. Some personnel information can also be kept in the test suite, such as the testers who designed specific test cases, to better supported future use of this test suite. The information contained in the test suite constitutes an indexed database with important information about individual test cases in the test suite, as well as pointers to actual test cases. The actual test cases, in turn, contains more detailed information about the exact scenario, test input, expected output and behavior, etc.

There are many ways to organize the test suite or test suites. The most common way is to organize them by sub-phases, because of the different objects, objectives, concerns, perspectives, priorities, and the testing techniques used. Various attributes can be used to describe, classify, and organize individual test cases in the suite. One concrete example is the use of the following attributes for an IBM product in its system testing phase (Tian, 1998):

- *sc* – scenario class

- *sn* – scenario number

- *vn* – variation number with a particular scenario

The scenario class *sc* corresponds to high-level functional areas or groups of functions. Within each *sc*, the scenario number *sn*, and the variation number *vn* within each *sn*, form a three-layer hierarchical organization of test cases in the suite. In addition, *sn* and *vn* are generally ordered in rough correspondence to the expected execution order, ranging from 1 to 99, with consecutive numbers used up to a point and then skipping to 99 to indicate some ad hoc test cases — those do not fall into some systematic sequence. Therefore, less than 99 scenarios or variations within scenarios are allowed, which was more than adequate for the product tested.

7.1.4 Preparation of test procedure

In addition to preparation of individual test cases and the overall test suite, the test procedure also needs to be prepared for effective testing. The basic question is the sequencing of the individual test cases and the switch-over from one test run to another. Several concerns affect the specific test procedure to be used, including:

- *Dependencies* among individual test cases. Some test cases can only be run after others because one is used to set up another. This is particularly true for systems that operate continuously, where the later test run may need to start at a state set up by the earlier one.

- *Defect detection* related sequencing. Many problems can only be effectively detected after others have been discovered and fixed. For example, integration of several components and related testing typically focus on interface and interaction problems, which can be masked by problems in individual components. Therefore, these components need to be individually tested before integration testing starts.

- Sequences to avoid *accidents*. For some systems, possibly severe problems and damages may incur during testing if certain areas were not checked through related test runs prior to the current test run. For example, in embedded software for safety critical systems, one does not want to start testing safety features before testing other related functions first. This can be considered as a special case of the problem or defect related sequencing where there is a very strong economical incentive for preferring certain sequencing to others.

- *Problem diagnosis* related sequencing. Some execution problems observed during testing may involve complicated scenarios and many possible sources of problems. Under this situation, related test runs focused on a single aspect or limited areas can be used to help with the problem diagnosis. Better yet, if such complicated problems are expected, we should run related simpler test cases first to eliminate certain possibilities and narrow down the problem areas. Therefore, one natural sequence for test case execution commonly used in practical testing procedures is to progress from simple and easy ones to complicated and difficult ones. The same idea has been used in defining coverage hierarchies.

- *Natural grouping* of test cases, such as by functional and structural areas or by usage frequencies, can also be used for test sequencing and to manage parallel testing. However, among areas where no such order exists, or when the incentive for following a certain order is not strong, we can carry out testing for them in parallel to speed up the testing process. In fact, this is what people do all the time for large-scale software testing, where parallelism and interleaving are common.

The key to test run transition in the test procedure preparation is to make sure that the next test run can start right after the current one is finished for each software installment. This consideration may place some additional requirements on individual test cases, either requiring them to leave the system in the same initial condition or in some specified final condition. In fact, the initial and final states of specific test cases can also be used to group individual test cases in the test suite. This is similar to the grouping of test cases when system configuration and environmental setup are considered in defining the operational mode in usage-based testing using Musa's operational profiles (Musa, 1998).

When test cases are derived dynamically, test procedure would naturally involve much more dynamic elements. However, the above considerations for test procedure preparation should still be incorporated in the corresponding test procedure. In this case, not only the execution but also the generation of dynamic test cases is affected by the dependency, effectiveness and efficiency concerns.

A related topic to test procedure preparation is the assignment of people to perform certain tests. Their roles and responsibilities need to be clearly specified, such as in Section 7.4. In addition, allocation of time and other resources also needs to be planned ahead of time before test execution starts, in accordance with test case grouping and allocation within a test suite. One specific type of resources is the test automation tools examined in Section 7.5, which could significantly reduce the time, staffing, and other resources required for test execution.

7.2 TEST EXECUTION, RESULT CHECKING, AND MEASUREMENT

The key to the overall test execution is the smooth transition from one test run to another, which also requires us to allocate all the required resources to ensure that individual test runs can be started, executed, and finished, and related problems can be handled seamlessly. General steps in test execution include:

1. Allocating test time and resources;

2. Invoking and running tests, and collecting execution information and measurements;

3. Checking testing results and identifying system failures.

The step to invoke and run tests is fairly straightforward with well-prepared test cases or already sensitized test cases. We can simply provide the input variable values over the whole execution duration as required and as already precisely specified in these test cases. The sequence of test runs can follow the pre-planned sequence we described in test procedure preparation in Section 7.1. In the case where test cases are generated dynamically, such as in various usage-based statistical testing approaches described in Chapter 8 and Chapter 10, much of the work we described in terms of test sensitization needs to be done at this stage.

The key in handling failed test runs is to ensure that they will not block the execution of other test cases. In addition, there will be test runs related to the re-verification of fixed problems, which can be treated much the same way as other planned test cases except the newly added dependency and its impact on test sequencing: Before an integrated fix becomes available, the test case that triggered the failure observation in the first place and other closely related test cases should be suspended to avoid repeatedly observing the same failure, which adds little new information to what is already known. The same test case can be re-run after the fix is in, and closely related test cases can also continue at this point. By doing so, we avoided unnecessary repetitions/re-runs, thus improving the overall test efficiency.

Test time and resources allocation is most closely related to the test planning and preparation activities described in the previous section. Although the allocation could be planned or even carried out at the previous stage, the monitoring, adjustment, and management of these resources need to be carried out during test execution. Test time allocation and management are closely related to people's roles and responsibility in carrying out specific testing activities, thus they are described in Section 7.4. Managing other test resources primarily involves the environmental set up and related facility management. For pure software systems, this is fairly straightforward, with the environment setup to include the hardware configuration and software environment that the finished product will operate within. Sometimes, limited number of simulation programs or hardware simulators can be used for testing some product components, but the overall system testing would very much resemble the actual operational environment. Once the general system configuration is decided, the facility management is mainly the allocation and monitoring of testing time on these facilities.

For embedded software systems or for heterogeneous systems with important software components, the environment and facility management issues involve the so-called "super-system". Coordination between different branches is a major issue where people have different perspectives and concerns. In addition, various techniques, such as simulation and prototyping techniques described in Chapter 12, will be used to aid testing or sometimes to replace part of the testing. We will also see some specific techniques to deal with interface, interaction, and interoperability problems among different sub-systems as part of the safety assurance program in Chapter 16.

Result checking: The oracle problem

Result checking, or the *oracle problem*, and the related failure identification is a difficult task, because of both the theoretical difficulties and practical limitations. In this book, we use the term *test oracle* to indicate any means to check the testing result. Long standing theoretical results state that result checking for testing in general is an undecidable problem. In other words, there is no hope for algorithmic or fully automated solution to the general test oracle problem. On the practical side, the expected behavior can hardly be precisely described so that the observed behavior can be compared against. Combined with the fact that software can fail in innumerable variations, the unexpected behavior can happen in truly unexpected ways, thus making result checking difficult or nearly impossible.

However, there are cases where specific types of system failures, such as irresponsive behavior or system crash, are easy to identify. In other cases, various other means, such as heuristic guesses, possible cross-checking, sampling of product internal information and/or execution states, etc., can be used to help us find approximate solutions to the oracle problem, as described below:

- Sometimes heuristics guesses can be used based on product domain knowledge, for example, what other similar products would do under similar situations. Consequently, similar products, such as previous releases of the same product or competitors' products with similar functionality, can often be used as the test oracle, to check execution results and to identify system failures.

- Knowledge of implementation details can also be used to link specific behavior to specific program units. We can also examine various product internal information and dynamic execution state to help solve the oracle problem. For example, if an external function is supported by some internal components, and these internal components were not invoked when we test for this external function, we can be almost certain there is something wrong with this test run. In addition, product experts or developers themselves can also help testers to perform this difficult task when some important problem is suspected, making effective use of these people's product knowledge.

- Various types of consistency checking during execution, such as checking for the database consistency, can also help us determine the execution failures. Such consistency checking can usually be done through sampling of some dynamic states and related product internal information, which could be analyzed either on-line during the test execution, or off-line with the detailed dynamic execution information.

Test measurement

Observed failures need to be recorded and tracked until their resolution. This defect handling or defect tracking process is typically considered part of the testing process itself, and the reporting of the observed failures is consider part the test execution activity. However, the handling of defects discovered during testing is not fundamentally different from that of defects discovered during other QA activities, as we described in the general context of QA activities in Chapter 4.

Detailed information about failure observations and the related activities is needed for problem diagnosis and defect fixing. Some specific information for failures and faults also includes various generic information about defects we will describe in Chapter 20, covering defect type, severity, impact areas, possible cause, when-injected, etc. This information could be collected either when the failure were observed and recorded or when the faults were fixed, or even afterward. When failures are not observed, the measurement of related test runs can be used to demonstrate product reliability or correct handling of input and dynamic situations.

Various other measurements can be taken during test execution for further analysis and follow-up actions. Successful executions also need to be recorded for various purposes, including documentation of test activities, possible use as oracle to check future execution results, etc. This is particularly important for regression testing to be described in Chapter 12 and for legacy products that are expected to change and evolve over the whole product lifespan. The timing and other related information can be important, when it can be used as input in analysis and follow-up activities described in Section 7.3 and in reliability analysis described in Chapter 22. In addition to the "on-line" measurement of the dynamic test

Table 7.1 A template for test execution measurements

- *rid* – run identification, consisting of:

  - *sc* – scenario class,

  - *sn* – scenario number,

  - *vn* – variation number with a particular scenario,

  - *an* – attempt number for the specific scenario variation

- *timing* – start time *t0* and end time *t1*

- *tester* – the tester who attempted the test run

- *trans* – transactions handled by the test run

- *result* – result of the test run (1 indicates success and 0 for failure)

---

runs and related failure information, the corresponding static test cases can be measured "off-line" to avoid interference with normal test execution. Various other information could also be collected, such as testing personnel, environment, configuration, test object, etc.

Table 7.1 is an example template for test execution information collected for an IBM product during system testing (Tian, 1995). Notice that a test run here corresponds to a specific *attempt* in the hierarchically organized test suite we described in Section 7.1: Each attempt or test run, numbered *an*, is drawn from a specific variation, with variation number *vn*, of a scenario numbered as *sn* that belong to a specific scenario class *sc*. Other information about individual test runs, such as timing, tester, workload measured in transactions, and the run result, is also recorded.

7.3 ANALYSIS AND FOLLOW-UP

The third group of major test activities is analysis and follow-up after test execution. The measurement data collected during test execution, together with other data about the testing and the overall environment, form the data input to these analyses, which, in turn, provide valuable feedback to test execution and other testing and development activities. Direct follow-up includes defect fixing and making other management decisions, such as product release and transition from one development phase or sub-phase to another. We examine these issues in this section.

Analysis and follow-up based on individual testing runs

Analysis of individual test runs includes result checking and failure identification we covered in the previous section as part of the test execution activities. When failures are identified, additional analyses are normally performed by software developers or "code owners" to diagnose the problem and locate the faults that caused the failures for defect removal. This activity may involve the following steps:

- *Understanding* the problem by studying the execution record, particularly those involving failures.

- Being able to *recreate* the same problem scenario and observe the same problem. This is important to confirm the problem and rule out possibilities of transient problems due to environmental disturbances or user errors. It also provides input to diagnose the problem causes.

- *Problem diagnosis* to examine what kind of problem it is, where, when, and possible causes. This may involve analyzing the above records and using some diagnostic tools or addition test runs to zoom in on possible causes or to eliminate other possibilities.

- *Fault locating*, to identify the exact location(s) of fault(s) based on information from the previous steps and product knowledge.

- *Defect fixing*, to fix the located fault(s) by adding, removing, or correcting certain parts of the code. Sometimes, design and requirement changes could also be triggered or propagated from the above changes due to logical linkage among the different software components.

As mentioned in Section 7.2, once an integrated fix is available, the failed test cases were re-run to verify the fix. If successful, the normal test execution continues; otherwise, another round of defect fixing as described above is again initiated.

Analysis and follow-up for overall testing results

Various analyses can be performed on the overall testing results and related data to provide various assessments about testing, and to drive follow-up activities, including:

- *Reliability analysis* for usage-based testing, which can be used to assess current product reliability and as input to determine if the pre-set reliability goal has been achieved. If so, product release or test termination decisions can be made. If not, future reliability as well as time and resources needed to reach the reliability goal can be estimated. Sometimes, low reliability areas can be identified for focused testing and reliability improvement. This analysis and its many uses in follow-up activities are described in Chapter 22.

- *Coverage analysis* for coverage-based testing, which can be used as a surrogate for reliability and used as the stopping criterion or as input to various decisions related to testing management. Specifics about this are presented when specific testing techniques and coverage hierarchies are introduced in Chapters 8 through 11.

- *Overall defect analysis*, which can be used to examine defect distribution and to identify high-defect areas for focused remedial actions. In addition, some product-internal measurements, such as size and complexity of individual components, and other measurements can also be used together with defect data to identify high-defect areas for focused quality improvement. These topics are covered in Chapters 20 and 21.

These analyses about overall testing results and related follow-up activities are described in Part IV, in connection with the overall analysis and feedback for all QA alternatives. Possible test process and overall development process improvement based on these and other analyses and feedback is also described therein.

7.4   ACTIVITIES, PEOPLE, AND MANAGEMENT

In this section, we examine people's roles and responsibilities in specific test activities as well as the related management issues.

People's role in informal vs. formal testing

Informal software testing and some types of formal testing could involve minimal prior knowledge of the software products or systems. One simple way to test the software is to just run it and observe its behavior. Some obvious problems can be easily recognized by people with almost no prior knowledge of computer software and software products. Some formal forms of testing, such as usability testing, can be performed with little prior knowledge as well. For example, to test some user-friendly, "plug-and-play" software products, novice users are often asked to start using the products. Their behavior and their difficulties in using the products are observed and related information is recorded for usability assessment and improvement. In this scenario, the testing involves the actual novice users as testers, but it may also involve experienced testers who observe and record the testing information. With automated information recording, the role of the experienced tester in this situation can be eliminated.

Because of the above situations, many people have the wrong perception that testing is "easy", and any "warm body" can perform testing. This misconception also contributes to various problems related to software management, where the least experienced and skilled people are assigned to testing groups. This problem can be corrected by a good knowledge of the technical skills and experience involved in testing, such as conveyed in this book, and through some organizational initiatives, such as creating a well-established and well-respected career path for testers (Weyuker et al., 2000).

For the large and complex software systems used in society today, any hope of assured quality needs to be supported by testing beyond informal ad hoc testing. We need to model the software systems, their operational environment, their users and usage scenarios, sequences, and patterns, so that systematic testing can be performed to ensure that these systems satisfy their customers' quality expectations. Test cases can be derived from these models and used systematically to detect and fix defects and to ensure software quality and reliability. All these activities are performed by individual testers or testing teams.

Various other development personnel also need to be involved in testing activities. For example, as part of the follow-up activity to testing, problems detected during testing need to be resolved by the people who are responsible for the creation of the product design or code. Therefore, software developers, particularly those designers and programmers whose code is tested, also need to be involved in testing, although mostly indirectly to follow up on failure observations and defect fixing.

Sometimes, people can play the dual role of developers and testers, when they test their own code, such as in the unit or component testing sub-phases. However, for the overall system, professional testers are typically employed to testing the integration of different components and the overall operation of the system as a whole in the integration, system, and acceptance testing sub-phases.

Testing teams: Organization and management

The test activities need to be managed by people with a good understanding of the testing techniques and processes. The feedback derived from analyses of measurement data needs to be used to help with various management decisions, such as product release, and to help quality improvement. Test managers are involved in these activities.

Testers and testing teams can be organized into various different structures, but basically following either a horizontal or a vertical model:

- A *vertical model* would organize around a product, where dedicated people perform one or more testing tasks for the product. For example, one or more teams can perform all the different types of testing for the product, from unit testing up to acceptance testing.

- A *horizontal model* is used in some large organizations so that a testing team only performs one kind of testing for many different products within the organization. For example, different products may share the same system testing team.

Depending on the demand for testers by different projects, staffing level may vary over time. In the vertical model, as the product development shifts from one phase to another or as the development focus shifts from one area to another, project personnel could be re-assigned to perform different tasks. One common practice in industry is to use programmers to perform various testing tasks when testing phase peaks. This practice may create various problems related to staffing management: If not done carefully, it may also lead to project delays, as in Brooks' famous observation that adding people to a late project will make it later (Brooks, 1995). The mismatch between people's expertise and their assignments may also result in more defects passing through the testing phase to cause additional in-field problems. This fact is part of the reason for people to adopt the horizontal model where staffing level variations can generally be better managed due to the different schedules and demands by different projects.

In reality, a mixture of the two is often used in large software organizations (Tian, 1998), with low-level testing performed by dedicated testers or testing teams, system testing shared across similar products, and general project support provided by a centralized support unit for the entire organization. The general project support includes process, technology, and tool support necessary for formal development and testing. This centralized support unit resembles the so-called experience factory that also packages experience and lessons learned from development for more effective future use (Basili, 1995). The idea of experience factory is described further in Chapter 13 in connection to defect prevention based on process improvement.

External participants: Users and third-party testers

Besides the above internal participants, external participants or users may also be involved in testing. The concept of users can also be expanded to include non-human users of software as well, such as other software and hardware environments that the software product in question interacts with (Whittaker, 2001). This extended user concept is particularly relevant to embedded systems or heterogeneous systems with extensive software components.

In general, the users' views and perspectives, their usage scenarios, sequences, and patterns, and the overall operational environment need to be captured in some models and used in testing to ensure satisfactory performance and reliability for the software products. This is particularly true for usage-based statistical testing, where active user participant is essential in model construction. Sometimes, the users can even serve informally as testers, such as in the usability testing example earlier.

For certain types of software systems, such as those used in defense industry or government, independent verification and validation (IV&V) model is extensively used, where software systems are independently tested or verified and validated using various techniques by third-party participants. This model has gained popularity for various other types of high-assurance software systems, where high reliability, high integrity, or other properties are required, resulting in the so-called certification model or certification pipeline (Voas, 1999).

Another reason for IV&V's popularity is the increasing use and focus on software development using COTS (commercial-off-the shelf) components and CBSE (component based software engineering, or CBSD — component-based software development). In such paradigms, independent testing and certification of software components or reusable parts are key to the possible selection, use, and adoption of software components, parts, or subsystems.

7.5 TEST AUTOMATION

Test automation aims to automate some manual tasks with the use of some software tools. The demand for test automation is strong, because purely manual testing from start to finish can be tedious and error-prone. On the other hand, long standing theoretical results tell us that no fully automated testing is possible. Even most of the major sub-activities, such as result checking or the oracle problem we discussed in Section 7.2, are undecidable. However, some level of automation for individual activities is possible, and can be supported by various commercial tools or tools developed within large organizations. The key in the use of test automation to relieve people of tedious and repetitive tasks and to improve overall testing productivity is to first examine what is possible, feasible, and economical, and then to set the right expectations and goals. Various issues related to test automation include:

- specific needs and potential for automation;
- selection of existing testing tools, if available;
- possibility and cost of constructing specific test automation tools;
- availability of user training for these tools and time/effort needed;
- overall cost, including costs for tool acquisition, support, training, and usage;
- impact on resource, schedule, and project management.

We next examine test automation in connection with the major test activities and people's roles and responsibilities in them.

Automation for test execution

Among the three major test activities, preparation, execution, and follow-up, execution is a prime candidate for automation. In fact, this is the area in which the earliest test automation tools found some unequivocal successes. For example, various semi-automatic debugging tools or debuggers allow testers to set and reset variable values and execution states during execution and observe the dynamic execution behavior at different observation points. These tools are semi-automatic because testers are still involved in test execution intervention.

Many of the modern test automation tools can be considered as enhanced debuggers that work for larger products, automate more individual testing activities, and are generally more flexible and more tailorable than earlier debuggers. Various automated task sequencing tools for job transfer from one test run to another work in much the same way as job dispatcher/scheduler in various operating systems. In fact, most such test run sequencing tools are platform-specific, and are often constructed within testing organizations using some system utilities or APIs (application program interfaces).

An additional functionality for many of the test automation tools is to allow information recording and collection. For example, in the testing of some commercial software product in IBM (Tian et al., 1995; Tian, 1998), an internal test automation tool called T3 was used to generate workload, monitor the execution, and record various execution details for a subset of test scenario classes listed in Table 7.1. The specific measurement data that need to be collected are dictated by the specific analyses to be performed. Therefore, we cover test measurement tools in conjunction with analysis tools later.

Automation for test planning and preparation

In test planning and preparation, the potential for automation is different for different sub-activities. The overall planning part can only be carried out by experienced personal with expertise in planning and management as well as a good understanding of testing and development technologies. Not much automation can be achieved in these sub-activities, nor is there a high demand for automation here. Similarly, test procedure planning is primarily done by experts, although the planned procedure can be later enforced and automated during actual test execution with the help of various test execution automation tools we discussed above.

Test case preparation is the area where there is some realistic potential for automation. For example, in testing of legacy products, various automated analysis can be performed to compare the current version of the product with its previous versions, and to screen the existing test suites to select the ones for regression testing. For construction of new test cases, automation is also possible. For example, in the T3 tool we mentioned above for test execution support, a script can be provided to generate different workload for testing, which effectively generates test cases and related test runs dynamically from test script. However, the test scripts, which are high-level descriptions of what to test, need to be constructed in the first place by the experienced testers. These test scripts are usually much simpler and shorter, thus much less costly to generate than actual test cases. Consequently, a semi-automated test case generation is supported in this case.

In general, test scripts or test cases are based on some formal models. The model construction for different test techniques requires high levels of human intelligence and expertise, and is therefore not easily automated. However, some individual steps in model construction can be automated, such as some automated data gathering, graphical or other aids for modeling, etc. For small-scale programs, some tools can be used to generate certain models and test cases directly, much like using compilers to generate object code from source code. However, these tools cannot scale up to large software systems. In addition, in most of the models, various decisions need to be made and parameters need to be selected for specific model variations, which can only be carried out by people with proper expertise.

Once such a model is constructed, various tools can be used to generate test cases automatically. Sometimes, even if a tool is not directly available, the testing model is typically associated with some algorithms that can be at least partially implemented for automatic generation of at least some test cases. For example, once an underlying usage model in the form of a Markov chain is constructed, several algorithms can be used for usage-based statistical testing to cover frequently used usage patterns, frequently visited states, and call-pairs (Avritzer and Weyuker, 1995). If there is a commercial tool or an existing tool within the organization available, the key in its adoption for test case generation is to understand what kind of model is supported and how difficult it is to construct models of this type, in order to match it with our purpose of testing.

Automation for test measurement, analysis, and follow-up

In terms of analyses of test results and follow-up actions, the situation is similar to test planning and preparation. Most of the follow-up actions involve problem fixing and various other remedial and improvement initiatives, very little of which can be automated. However, specific analysis activities can be supported by various analysis and modeling tools. For example, many of the reliability analysis activities described in Tian (1998) were automated. This was achieved after many rounds of studies that converged on the appropriate models and data to use. Many popular tools were discarded because they were found to be unsuitable for the type of commercial products from IBM. This experience told us that automated analysis tools should not be indiscriminately applied, but rather based on intelligent choice based on one's own specific environment and experience. A general tool support strategy for QA and development process measurement, data analysis, and follow-up is described in Chapter 18.

Closely related to test result analyses are coverage analysis for coverage-based testing and reliability analysis for usage-based testing. For traditional reliability analysis, we typically need results for individual test runs and related timing information (Lyu, 1995a). Sometimes, some additional information, such as test input, environment, and personnel information can also be used to link input states to reliability or to identify problematic areas for focused reliability improvement (Tian, 1995). These data can usually be automatically collected using various test execution tools or dedicated data collection tools.

Coverage analysis usually involves the use of more detailed information and measurement data than that for reliability analysis. But, fortunately, various coverage analysis tools exist to collect coverage information during test execution. For example, several popular commercial test tools collect and analyze coverage information to provide feedback and quality assessments to the testing process or the overall development process, including:

- McCabe Test from McCabe and Associates provides control flow coverage related information and analysis.

- S-TCAT (System Test Coverage Analysis Tool) from SRI (Software Research, Inc.) provides function-level coverage and call-pair information. S-TCAT can also be integrated into a tool suite called TestWorks from SRI for various other testing purposes.

- ATAC (Automatic Test Analysis for C) from Telecodia is a data flow coverage analysis tool for white-box testing.

To use these tools for coverage analysis, the source code is usually instrumented to build an instrumented test driver. When this instrumented code is run in testing, information related to coverage in the form of raw data is collected. Later on, the raw data are analyzed for coverage. Figure 7.1 illustrates these steps with the use of S-TCAT for test coverage analysis. Each of these steps is usually automated by the tools themselves. One interesting

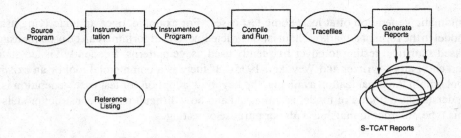

Figure 7.1 Test coverage analysis with S-TCAT

fact to notice is that, although these tools are designed for coverage-based testing, they can also be used sometimes to support usage-based testing, such as the use of S-TCAT to collect customer usage information for some IBM products (Lu and Tian, 1993b).

7.6 CONCLUDING REMARKS

To summarize, there are three major types of activities for testing, including:

1. *Test planning and preparation*: which include the following important sub-activities:

   - setting goals,
   - selecting overall strategies and techniques,
   - gathering information,
   - constructing testing models,
   - preparing individual test cases,
   - preparing the overall test suite ,
   - preparing the test procedure.

   Additional details about model construction and test case preparation will be included in Chapters 8 through 11, when specific testing techniques are introduced.

2. *Test execution and measurement*, which include three steps:

   - allocating and adjusting test time and resources,
   - invoking and running tests, and taking appropriate measurements,
   - checking testing results and identifying system failures.

   The important test oracle problem in connection to the last step above was discussed. We use the term *test oracle* to indicate any means to check the testing result.

3. *Test result analysis and follow-up* activities, including possible problem diagnosis and defect fixing as follow-up to individual test runs, and analyses of overall or cumulative test results for management decisions and quality improvement initiatives.

These activities for large-scale testing can generally be performed and managed with the involvement of many people who have different roles and responsibilities, including:

- dedicated professional testers and testing managers,

- developers who are responsible for fixing problems, who may also play the dual role of testers,

- customers and users, who may also serve as testers informally for usability or beta testing,

- independent professional testing organizations as trusted intermediary between software vendors and customers.

The important issue of test automation was also examined. We conclude this chapter with the following general observation: Although fully automated support are not possible, some automated support, combined with a good understanding of the specific test activities and related techniques by the testers and other people involved in testing, can help us carry out planned test activities to effectively detect many software problems and ensure product quality.

Problems

7.1   Is test planning an important activity in your organization? Why or why not?

7.2   Describe the major activities within test planning and examine how well they are performed in your organization.

7.3   What would be different when you perform test planning for different systems and application environments? Particularly, consider mass-market software products, commercial software products, internal-use-only software tools, software embedded in other systems.

7.4   Define the following important concepts related to test planning and preparation:
   a) dynamic test runs vs. static test cases,
   b) test suite and its organization,
   c) input and output variables, and how to use them to define program behavior,
   d) sensitization of test cases.

7.5   Test execution may be more sensitive to different environments that the other major testing activities. Describe testing execution for systems your are working on and compare it to the generic test execution issues we discussed in this chapter.

7.6   Besides dealing with defects, what kind of analysis and follow-up is usually needed?

7.7   What is a test oracle? What oracles are used in your testing currently?

7.8   What test automation tools are used in your organization? Can you classify them using the different areas of automation we described in this chapter?

7.9   Sort the test automation tools you are familiar with or the ones we mentioned in this chapter by their degree of automation.

7.10   One of the common problem associated with the use of test automation tools is unrealistic expectations: If I use so-and-so, all my testing problems will be solved. How would you explain to your managers or colleagues when they have unrealistic expectations?

7.11   When you have many test automation tools, do you still need to learn about the basic testing techniques?

CHAPTER 8

COVERAGE AND USAGE TESTING BASED ON CHECKLISTS AND PARTITIONS

In this chapter, we describe several formal test techniques whose models are based on simple structures such as lists and partitions. In particular, the following topics are covered:

- We start with informal and semi-formal testing with the use of various checklists in Section 8.1.

- These checklists are formalized into partitions in Section 8.2 to perform basic coverage-based testing.

- The basic usage-based testing for partitions using a similar testing model called Musa's operational profiles (OPs) is described in Section 8.3.

- We also cover the procedure for developing OPs in Section 8.4 and present a comprehensive case study in Section 8.5.

Additional testing techniques based on similar underlying models are covered in Chapter 9 for testing boundary conditions between partitioned input sub-domains.

8.1 CHECKLIST-BASED TESTING AND ITS LIMITATIONS

As already mentioned in Chapter 6, the simplest form of testing is to start running the software and make observations, in the hope that it is easy to distinguish between expected and unexpected behavior. Along the same line, software systems are sometimes tested in a similar way to see if some specific problems can be observed or if specific operational condition and input can be handled without resorting to some systematic method. We call these forms of simple and informal testing *ad hoc* testing.   Ad hoc testing is also called *random* testing in some literature.   However, we will avoid this use of the term random testing because of the possible confusion between it and usage-based statistical testing that is random testing based on specific operational profiles or distributions of likely operations or operational sequences.

When ad hoc testing is used repeatedly to test a software system, the testers then need to keep track of what has been done, in order to avoid wasting their time repeating the same tests.   In addition, an informal "to-do" list is commonly used to track what needs to be done.   Such to-do lists can be a physical list, an online list, or just a mental list.   The use of these informal lists forms the rudimentary and implicit *checklists*, where each item can be checked off when corresponding testing was performed, until every item on the lists is checked off.

Testing with checklists

The idea of checklists can be and has been generalized to perform systematic testing for many software systems (DeMillo et al., 1987; Kaner et al., 1999; Binder, 2000). For example, a specification checklist, or a checklist based on product specifications with each major specification item as a checklist item, can be used to perform black-box testing. Similarly, checklists of expected programming features that are supposed to be implemented in a software product, or coding standards that are supposed to be followed in implementation, are examples of white-box checklists, which can be used to support various types of white-box testing. In fact, the commonly used testing strategy of statement coverage in unit and component testing, or component coverage in integration and system testing, is also white-box checklist based testing, where each element in the checklists corresponds to a specific statement or a specific component, respectively. As we will also see in Section 8.3, usage-based statistical testing can also be supported by a special form of checklists called operational profiles (OPs), in which each item is associated with an operation to be performed together with its probability of usage.

In using these checklists, a specific testing based on a specific checklist can stop when every item on it has been tested (or "checked off"). By been "tested" or "checked off", we mean that the corresponding test case has been executed, and follow-up activities, such as fixing discovered problems, have been carried out and completed, which may also include rerunning the test case to verify that the problems have indeed been fixed. Some commonly used checklists for black-box or white-box coverage testing are listed below:

- Functional (black-box) checklists at different levels of abstraction and granularity, ranging from major high-level functions for the overall system to specific low-level functions of an individual unit or components.

- Checklists of system elements (white-box) at different levels of granularity, ranging from sub-systems and modules at the high level to individual statements or data items at the low level.

- Checklists of various structures or features that cut through different elements, such as list of call-pairs, consumers-and-producers for certain resources, modules sharing some common data, etc. These lists are concerned with implementation structures, therefore can be classified as white-box checklists as well.

Table 8.1   A high-level functional checklist for some relational database products

- abnormal termination
- backup and restore
- communication
- co-existence
- file I/O
- gateway
- index management
- installation
- logging and recovery
- locking
- migration
- stress

- Checklists about certain properties, such as coding standard, specific specification items, etc., which can be either black-box or white-box.

Other basic types of checklists are also possible. A common way to obtain usable checklists is to select items from several exhaustive checklists based on some criteria and to combine them. Many checklists can also be used together, to form some linked set of things to check during testing, as discussed below.

Table 8.1 gives a sample high-level checklist for some relational database products (Tian et al., 1995; Tian, 1998). In fact, each item corresponds to a specific high-level functional area or aspect important to the products as perceived by their users, which can be and was further refined into sub-areas using other checklists.

From basic checklists to hierarchical and combined checklists

The most commonly used form of multiple checklists is the hierarchical checklist, with each item in a higher-level checklist expandable to a full checklist at a lower level until we stop at a level of detail deemed enough by some criteria. In the checklist in Table 8.1, each high-level functional area represented by an individual item can be divided into sub-areas, and each sub-areas can be divided further. In fact, they form the hierarchical test suite we described in Chapter 7. Table 8.1 and its associated checklists form a set of hierarchical checklists that can be used as the basis for coverage based testing for these large software systems.

In addition to the use of individual checklists and hierarchical sets of checklists above, various checklists can also be combined in other forms. For example, a coding standard checklist can be combined with a component or unit checklist to make sure that each component follows all the recommended practice in the coding standards. This combination of two checklists forms a two dimensional checklist, or a table with each of its entries to be checked off, as illustrated in Table 8.2. Similarly, higher dimensional checklists can also be used. In addition, mixed checklists that mix the direct list combinations and hierarchies are also possible, but such mixed checklists should be used with care because of the possible confusion involved.

Table 8.2   A template for a two-dimensional checklist by combining a standards checklist and a component checklist

Component	Standards Items			
	s_1	s_2	$\cdots$	s_n
c_1				
c_2				
$\vdots$				
c_m				

Problems and limitations of general checklists

One of the important characteristics of these checklists is that they are typically not very specific, particularly those high-level ones. For example, a high-level functional checklist typically lists the major functions to be performed by a software product, but the list items are hardly detailed enough for testers to start a specific test run. The translation from this testing model to the test cases and then to test runs is not a simple matter. It usually involves experienced testers setting up the system and testing environment to execute specific test cases. In addition, repetition of the same test case in a later test run can only be guaranteed with this additional information about setup and environment, but not deduced from the checklist item itself. This would lead to difficulties when we try to rerun the failing execution to recreate the failure scenario for problem diagnosis, or when we need to re-verify the problem fixes. Therefore, additional information needs to be kept for these purposes.

With the increased demand for more automation, service, and functionality, modern software systems also become larger and more complex. Such systems consist of many components that are interconnected and interact with one another. There are also many different functions provided or supported by the systems for many different users. Both the structural complexity and functional complexity make it hard to effectively use checklists for testing and quality assurance, because of reasons below:

- It would be hard to come up with checklists that cover all the functional (black-box) or structural (white-box) components from different perspectives and at different levels of granularity, resulting in missed areas of coverage. These areas are the "holes" in coverage commonly referred to by practitioners.

- In an attempt to provide good coverage, a lot of overlaps between different items in the checklists may be introduced, resulting in redundant testing effort when such checklists are used.

- Some complex interactions of different system components or among major system functions are hard or impossible to describe using checklists.

To deal with the third problem, we will introduced finite-state machines (FSMs) and other related models as the basis for formal and systematic testing in Chapters 10 and 11. The first two problems can be resolved if we can derive a special type of checklists, called *partitions*, that can both achieve full coverage of some specifically defined entities or relationships and avoid overlaps. The formality and precision involved in defining these partitions would also help us obtain a more precisely defined set of test cases as compared to general checklist, thus making problem diagnosis, fix re-verification, and other tasks easier to perform.

8.2   TESTING FOR PARTITION COVERAGE

In the software testing context, partitions and partition-based testing are a special type of checklists and checklist-based testing. Partitions possess some desirable properties that set them apart from general checklists. Therefore, they can be used to better support testing and address some specific problems associated with general checklists in two areas: Better coverage because a partition is collectively exhaustive, and better efficiency because of the use of mutually exclusive partitions.

8.2.1   Some motivational examples

As described in the previous chapter, one essential step in testing is to sensitize test cases, or defining specific input variables and associated values to exercise certain parts of the program in the white-box view or to perform certain functions in the black-box view. If the input–output relation is a simple one, then test cases can be directly constructed by selecting corresponding input variable values through some systematic sampling. If the sample space is relatively small, exhaustive testing might be possible. Example of such cases include a decision based on a few input variables of the logical type, each can take a true (T) or false (F) value. Then the number of input combinations would be 2^n for n such input variables. Complete coverage of input combinations are possible as long as n remains small. However, even for simple input–output relations, such as a simple program calculating the root of quadratic equations in the form of:

$$ax^2 + bx + c = 0,$$

with the solution for the root r to be:

$$r = \frac{-b \pm \sqrt{b^2 - 4ac}}{2a}.$$

The number of input combinations between the three input variables a, b, and c could be huge. For example, if each of these three variables is represented by a 32 bit floating point number, the number of all possible input value combinations is then

$$2^{32} \times 2^{32} \times 2^{32} = 2^{96}.$$

Even for this fairly simple program, the number of test cases to cover all the input value combinations is beyond the testing resource for any organization.

However, the above example can also be used to illustrate the basic idea of partition-based testing. Notice that in our algebra classes, we all learned to distinguish the different cases for the root associated with different values for the part $d = b^2 - 4ac$. We know that the equation has two different roots if $d > 0$, two identical roots if $d = 0$, and no real root if $d < 0$. This relationship between d and r can be used in testing to see if the programs handles all three of these different situations correctly. In doing this, we effectively grouped the set of all possible input value combinations or test cases into three equivalent classes, or

Table 8.3 Sample test cases for the program solving the equation $ax^2 + bx + c = 0$

Test Case	Condition $d = b^2 - 4ac$	Input a	b	c
1	$d > 0$	1	2	-1
2	$d = 0$	1	2	1
3	$d < 0$	1	2	3

a partition into three subsets defined by the three conditions on d. Such partitioned subsets of input domains, or the set of possible input values, are called input sub-domains.

In this case, three test cases can be used, as illustrated in Table 8.3. Notice that the choice of specific test cases for each sub-domain that satisfy specific conditions is not unique. However, if simple sub-domain coverage is the goal, then it doesn't matter which one we choose, because every point in a given sub-domain receives the same kind of treatment, or belongs to the same equivalent class. In fact, this testing strategy directly corresponds to the checklist-based testing, with the domain partition as the checklist, and each sub-domain corresponding to a single element in the checklist.

This idea can be generalized to support partition-based testing for the general case: We can sample one test case from inside each subset in the partition, thus achieving complete coverage of all the subsets of corresponding equivalence classes. As illustrated in this example, the key to partition-based testing is to define the partitions first and then try to sensitize the test cases to achieve partition coverage.

8.2.2 Partition: Concepts and definitions

Partition is a basic mathematical concept, generally associated with set theory. Formally, a partition of a set S is a division of a set into a collection of subsets G_1, G_2, $\ldots$, G_n that satisfies the following properties:

- The subsets are *mutually exclusive*, that is, no two subsets share any common members, or formally,

$$\forall i, j, \ i \neq j \Rightarrow G_i \cap G_j = \emptyset.$$

That is, the intersection of any such two subsets must necessarily be empty.

- The subsets are *collectively exhaustive*, that is, they collectively *cover* or include all the elements in the original set, or formally,

$$\bigcup_{i=1}^{n} G_i = S.$$

That is, the union of all subsets (G_i's) is the set S.

Each of these subsets in a partition is called an *equivalent class* (or equivalence class), where each member is the same with respect to some specific property or relation used to define the subset. Formally, the specific relation for the members in an equivalent class is symmetric, transitive, and reflexive, where

- A *symmetric* relation is one that still holds if the order is changed. For a binary relation R defined on two elements a and b, R is symmetric if $R(a, b) \Rightarrow R(b, a)$. For example, "=" is symmetric; but ">" is not.

- A *transitive* relation is one that holds in a relation chain. A transitive binary relation R is one that $R(a, b) \land R(b, c) \Rightarrow R(a, c)$. For example, ">" is transitive; but "is-mother-of" is not.

- A *reflexive* relation is one that holds on every member by itself. A reflexive binary relation R is one that $R(a, a)$. For example, "=" is reflexive; but ">" is not.

Similarly, if a relation is not symmetric, not transitive, or not reflexive, we call it asymmetric, intransitive, or irreflexive, respectively.

With these formal definitions and descriptions of partition in mind, we next examine various uses of partitions and related ideas for software testing (White and Cohen, 1980; Clarke et al., 1982; Weyuker and Jeng, 1991; Beizer, 1990).

8.2.3 Testing decisions and predicates for partition coverage

Since partitions are a special subclass of checklists, the types of partitions can closely resemble the type of checklists we described in Section 8.1. However, we group them in a different way according to the specific decisions associated use in defining different types of partitions, as follows:

- Partitions of some product entities, such as external functions (black-box view), system components (white-box view), etc. The definition of such partitions are typically a simple "member" relation in sets, that is, $x \in S$ for x as a member of the set S. As a concrete example, whether a component belongs to a sub-system or not is easy to decide. The key is to ensure the partitioned subsets truly form a partition of the original set of all entities. That is, they are mutually exclusive and collectively exhaustive.

- Partitions based on certain properties, relations, and related logical conditions. These partitions can be further divided into two sub-groups:

    - Direct use of logical predicates, through logical variables (those take T/F or True/False values) and connected through logical operators AND ($\land$), OR ($\lor$), or NOT ($\neg$).

    - Comparison of numerical variables using some comparison operators, such as "$<$", "$=$", "$\leq$", "$\geq$", "$>$", and "$\neq$". For example, all possible values (a property) of a variable x can be partitions into two subsets S_1, and S_2 defined by $S_1 \equiv \{x : x < 0\}$ and $S_2 \equiv \{x : x \geq 0\}$.

- Combinations of the above basic types are also commonly used in decision making. For example, the sub-domain of non-negative integers less than 21 can be specified as $(x \in I) \land (x \geq 0) \land (x < 21)$, where I denotes the set of integers. The values range is also conveniently represented as $[0, 21)$, as we see in mathematical literature.

For the first type of partitions, the testing would be essentially the same as for checklist-based testing: we simply select one item for testing at a time from the subset as a representative of the corresponding equivalent class until we have exhausted all the subsets.

For the other types of partitions above, testing would involve some sensitization in determining the input variables and their values in consultation with the specific conditions or logical predicates used to define each partitioned subset. For example, to satisfy both conditions $(x \geq 0)$ and $(x < 21)$ for the subset $[0, 21)$ above, we might as well select $x = 10$. Notice that in each subset, there might be many elements. Partition-based testing selects one from each subset as the representative for the subset based on the equivalence relations defined.

In addition, the conditions for partitions, or the logical predicate values, are often closely related to either the product specifications (black-box view) or actual implementations (white-box view). For example, we might specify that a function works for certain data types, such as the distinction between integer arithmetic operations and floating point ones in most numerical computing systems. Similarly, many conditional statements in programs may be related to some partitioning conditions, such as those used to guard unexpected input. For example, most arithmetic software packages would not accept divide by 0 as legitimate input. In general, such domain partitions can be represented by simple decisions in product specification or multiple decisions in program code. When multiple decisions are involved, decision trees or decision tables can be used. Therefore, we can consider decision testing and related predicate testing as part of the general partition-based testing.

The above combinations of partition definitions can often be mapped to a series of decisions made along the way of program execution. These decisions in a sequence can be represented by a decision tree, starting from the initial decision, progressing through intermediate decisions, until we finish with a final decision and program termination. Sometimes, the decision can be organized into stages, with the same question asked at each stage regardless of the previous decisions. This would result in a uniform decision tree. Alternatively, some of the later decisions and questions asked may be dependent on the earlier ones, resulting in a non-uniform decision tree.

In either case, we can use the unique path property, from the initial decision node to the last decision outcome to enumerate all the series of decisions, and treat each unique path as a sub-domain and derive test cases to cover each sub-domain. In this way, a decision tree is equivalent to a hierarchical checklist, but with the items of each checklist at each decision point form a partition. For example, in the hierarchical checklist using test scenario classes, scenario numbers, and variation numbers in Section 8.1 can be interpreted as a three-level decision tree, and test cases can be selected to cover these individual variations from specific scenarios in different scenario classes.

The key to deriving coverage based testing for such decisions is to select values to make the test execution follow specific decision paths. For example, if we have decisions using logical variables P and Q in two stages, then we can realize the four combinations:

- $P \wedge Q$ or TT, that is, P = True and Q = True.

- $P \wedge \neg Q$ or TF, that is, P = True and Q = False.

- $\neg P \wedge Q$ or FT, that is, P = False and Q = True.

- $\neg P \wedge \neg Q$ or FF, that is, P = False and Q = False.

For a specific combination, if other numerical variables are involved, we need to select the numerical variable values to make them satisfy the conditions. For example, to select a test for $(x \geq 0) \wedge (x < 21)$, we can choose $x = 10$, that satisfies both $(x \geq 0)$ and $(x < 21)$. In more complicated situations, we might want to generate a list of candidate test cases based on one condition, and then use other conditions to eliminate certain elements from this initial candidate list. In this example, we might start with a list like $\{1, 10, 100, \ldots\}$, and the second condition would reduce it to $\{1, 10\}$, and we can finally select 10 or $x = 10$ as our test case to cover this specific decision combination.

8.3   USAGE-BASED STATISTICAL TESTING WITH MUSA'S OPERATIONAL PROFILES

One important testing technique, the usage-based statistical testing with Musa's operational profiles (OPs) (Musa, 1993; Musa, 1998), shares the basic model with partition testing techniques, and enhances it to include probabilistic usage information. We next describe Musa OPs and their usage in testing.

8.3.1   The cases for usage-based statistical testing

The many sub-domains for large software systems may include many different operations for each sub-domain. In such situations, the equivalence relation as represented by partition testing described earlier in this chapter represents a uniform sampling of one test point from each sub-domain. However, if operations associated with one particular sub-domain are used more often than others, each underlying defect related to this sub-domain is also more likely to cause more problems to users than problems associated with other sub-domains.

This likelihood for problems to customers, or related system failures defined accordingly, is captured in software product *reliability*. As already introduced in Chapter 2, reliability is defined to be the probability of failure-free operations for a specific time period or a specific input set (Musa et al., 1987; Lyu, 1995a; Tian, 1998). The best way to assess and ensure product reliability during testing is to test the software product as if it is used by customers through the following steps:

- The information related to usage scenarios, patterns, and related usage frequency by target customers and users needs to be collected.

- The information collected above needs to be analyzed and organized into some models — what we call operational profiles (OPs) — for use in testing.

- Testing needs to be performed in accordance with the OPs.

- Testing results can be analyzed to assess product reliability and provide feedback to the testing and the general software development process.

Most of the common testing related activities were described in Chapter 7, and reliability analysis is described in Chapter 22. Therefore, we concentrated on the information collection, OP construction, and it usage in testing in the rest of this chapter.

Like most test activities, the actual testing is typically performed late in the overall product development process, and the model construction could be and should be started much earlier. Usage-based statistical testing actually pushes both these activities to the extremes at both ends as compared with most other testing techniques. On the one hand, the operational profiles (OPs) need to be constructed with customer and user input. It makes more sense to start them right at the requirement analysis phase, or even earlier, in the product planning and market assessment phase. On the other hand, testing according to customer usage scenarios and frequencies captured in OPs cannot be performed until most of the product components have been implemented. Therefore, such OP-based testing

Table 8.4   Usage frequencies (hits) and probabilities (% of total) for different file types for SMU/SEAS

File type	Hits	% of total
.gif	438536	57.47%
.html	128869	16.89%
directory	87067	11.41%
.jpg	65876	8.63%
.pdf	10784	1.41%
.class	10055	1.32%
.ps	2737	0.36%
.ppt	2510	0.33%
.css	2008	0.26%
.txt	1597	0.21%
.doc	1567	0.21%
.c	1254	0.16%
.ico	849	0.11%
Cumulative	753709	98.78%
Total	763021	100%

could only be performed in the very late sub-phases of testing, such as in the integration, system, or acceptance testing sub-phases.

8.3.2 Musa OP: Basic ideas

According to Musa (Musa, 1993; Musa, 1998), an operational profile, or an OP for short, is a list of disjoint set of operations and their associated probabilities of occurrence. It is a quantitative characterization of the way a software system is or will be used. As a simple example, consider the usage of www.seas.smu.edu, the official web site for the School of Engineering (which used to be called School of Engineering and Applied Science, or SEAS) of Southern Methodist University (SMU/SEAS). Table 8.4 gives the OP for this site, or the number of requests for different types of files by web users over 26 days and the related probabilities.

The "operations" represented in the operational profiles are usually associated with multiple possible test cases or multiple runs. Therefore, we typically assume that each "operation" in an OP can be tested through multiple runs without repeating the exact execution under exactly the same environment. In a sense, each operation corresponds to an individual sub-domain in domain partitions, thus representing a whole equivalence class. In this example, each item in the table, or each operation, represents a type of file requested by a web user, instead of individual web pages. Of course, we could represent each web page as an operation, but it would be at a much finer granularity. When the granularity is too fine, the statistical testing ideas may not be as applicable, because repeated testing may end up repeating a lot of the same test runs, which adds little to test effectiveness. In addition, such fine-granularity OPs would be too large to be practical. For example, the number of individual web pages on an average web site would be more than tens of thousands, while the number of file types is usually limited to a hundred or so, including many variations

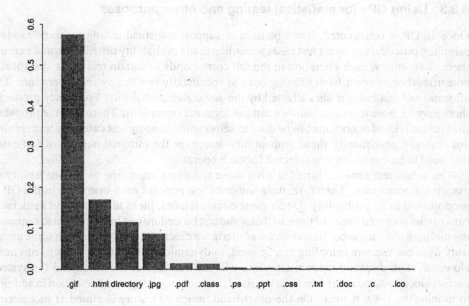

Figure 8.1   An operational profile (OP) of requested file types for the SMU/SEAS web site

of the same type, such as HTML files with extensions of ".HTML", ".html", ".htm", etc. There are more than 11,000 web pages but only about a hundred file types for SMU/SEAS.

There are also several other key points worth noting about such OPs, including:

- It is customary to sort the operations by descending probabilities of usage and present the results in that order.

- It is common to have quite uneven distribution of usage probabilities, with a few frequently used ones account for most of the usage frequencies. For example, the top 13 out of a hundred or so files types account for more than 98% of the web hits or individual requests for SMU/SEAS.

- Related to the uneven distribution of usage probabilities is the probability threshold for individual operations. The basis of statistical testing is to perform more testing for those operations that are used more by the customers. Therefore, if some operations have very low probability of usage, we could omit them in the OP. This probability threshold plays an important role in limiting the numbers of operations to represent in the OP, especially when there are a large number of possible operations.

- The representation in forms similar to Table 8.4 is called tabular representation in literature, which can often be represented visually as a histogram, such as in Figure 8.1. The use of such histograms has several advantages, primary in the direct and intuitive information about the relative value and magnitude of the different usage probabilities associated with different operations.

Consequently, an OP can be considered to be a checklist or a partition, but with frequency or probability of usage associated with each item in the list or with each sub-domain in the partition.

8.3.3 Using OPs for statistical testing and other purposes

Once an OP is constructed, it can be used to support statistical testing by some random sampling procedure to select test cases according to the probability distribution and execute them. Essentially, each operation in the OP corresponds to certain test cases specifically constructed or selected from existing ones to specifically test this system operation. The allocation of test cases is also affected by the associated probability. For legacy products, there may be more test cases than we can use for some operations. Therefore, the probabilities for individual operations can be used to select some existing test cases while screening out others. Consequently, these probabilities determine the minimal number of test cases that need to be constructed or selected for each operation.

The actual test runs are sampled from these test cases according to the probability of associated operations. Therefore, the number of test runs for each operation in the OP is proportional to its probability. Under most circumstances, these test cases and associated runs can be prepared ahead of time, so that some test procedure can be employed to sequence the multiple test runs according to various criteria we described in Chapter 7. In some cases, truly dynamic random sampling can be used, to dynamically select test cases to run next. However, such dynamic random sampling will slow down test execution and the system performance because of the overhead involved in managing the test case selection in addition to monitoring the test runs. On the other hand, much of testing is aimed at monitoring the system performance and possible problems under "normal" operational conditions, particularly for usage-based statistical testing of common usage scenarios carried out under the environment that resembles target customers'. We would like to reduce such overhead and get a truly representative setting of in-field operations. Therefore, unless absolutely necessary, we should prepare the test cases and test procedures ahead of time to reduce the impact of testing overhead on normal system operations.

In addition to or in place of proportional sampling, progressive testing is often used with the help of OPs. For example, at the beginning of testing, higher probability threshold can be used to select a few very important or highly used operations for testing. As testing progresses, the threshold can be lowered to allow testing of less frequently used operations so that a wide variety of different operations can be covered. In a sense, the use of OPs can help us prioritize and organize our testing effort so that important or highly used areas are tested first, and other areas are progressively tested to ensure good coverage.

The use of OPs for statistical testing enables us to make of quantitative reliability assessment and ensure product reliability that is meaningful to target customers. Failure and test execution data from OP-guided testing should resemble the data that would be expected by target customers. It is for this reason that data from such statistical testing can be analyzed using various reliability models to assess product reliability, to determine if the product is reliable enough for release. If the reliability goal has not been achieved yet, the analysis results can often help us predict time and resource to reach the reliability goal, and sometimes to identify problematic areas for focused improvement actions. These reliability models and their usage are described in Chapter 22.

Besides the above use of OPs to help us prioritize testing and assure product reliability, OPs can also be used in other situations for various purposes, including:

- *Productivity improvement and schedule gains* could be achieved because of the focus on high-leverage parts with the use of OPs. The use of OPs would reduce the over-testing of lesser-used product components or functions: The same effort could be applied to most-used parts, with reduced effort for lesser-used parts. According to data from AT&T (Musa, 1993), a reduction of 56% system testing cost or 11.5% overall cost could be achieved.

- *Introducing new products* by implementing highly used features quickly to capture market share and then gradually adding lesser-used features in subsequent releases or product updates. OP-guided testing would make this approach work. This use of OP is similar to and can be combined with spiral development process (Boehm, 1988), or the use of software prototypes to resolve important product design questions before proceeding with other implementation activities.

- *Better communications with customers and better customer relations*: The use of OPs can foster better communications with target customers and help establish and maintain better customer relations. There are several reasons for these, including:

  - The construction of operational profiles needs the direct or indirect involvement of customers. Customer's perspectives of quality, product features, relative importance, and possible usage scenarios and associated problems are adopted in testing when OPs are used. Therefore, it's more likely for the software development organization and the customers to appreciate each other's views and efforts in such a collaborative instead of an adversarial environment.

  - The use of OPs can help develop more precise product requirements and specifications, which are more likely to satisfy customers' needs.

  - Customer and user training can be better focused on those features that the customers use the most instead of esoteric ones more likely to be used by internal users.

- *High return on investment*: According to data from AT&T (Musa, 1993), the OP development cost for an "average" product is about one staff-month. The average product is one that contains 100 KLOC (thousand lines of code) and takes 10 developers 18 months to finish. There is also a sub-linear increase of OP development cost for larger products. The cost–benefit ratio is reported to be about 1:10.

Because of these tangible and intangible benefits, OPs should always be a prime candidate for testing in large software system with many users or with diverse usage environments.

8.4 CONSTRUCTING OPERATIONAL PROFILES

An important question before actual OPs are constructed is whether a single OP would be enough or multiple OPs have to be constructed. The decision should be based on the homogeneity or similarity of product usages by different customers: If there are no fundamental differences, one OP would be appropriate. However, if qualitative or substantial differences exist, then one OP for each individual group of customers would be appropriate. The basic assumption is that one OP would be sufficient to capture the usage scenarios and probabilities for all the customers within a group. Sometimes, a mixed strategy might be meaningful, to develop separate OPs for individual groups, and then the combined OP can be used to provide an overall picture of the product's use by all customers. We next examine the generic methods for OP construction and some proven procedures that have been successfully used in industry.

8.4.1 Generic methods and participants

There are three generic methods for information gathering and OP construction: actually *measurement* of usage at customer installations, *survey* of target customers, and usage estimation based on *expert opinions*. For existing software products, the most precise way to obtain customer usage scenarios and associated probabilities is through actual measurement of the in-field operations at the customer installations. Actual measurement provides ultimate accuracy but also faces various limitations, including:

- For new products or new applications, there won't be in-field customer installations. Therefore, actual measurement would not be possible. One way to bridge this gap is to use measurement from similar products or earlier versions of the product for different applications, and then make certain adjustment to the measurement results to obtain the OP for the new products or new applications. However, this adjustment would be difficult and would involve a substantial amount of subjective judgment. Therefore, other approaches to for OP construction might be preferable.

- Even if there are in-field customer installations for existing products or earlier versions of new product releases, the actual usage information and the environment may contain a substantial amount of business sensitive and proprietary data. Therefore, the customers would not be willing to share the data with the software development organizations. In fact, this situation covers most of the commercial products and the business relations between software development organizations and their customers. One way to overcome this is through some voluntary participation of selected customers, similar to beta testing that we will describe in Chapter 12. Alternatively, instead of measuring at the customers' sites, a few customers could be invited in, to run their applications on the new versions of software products before product release, such as in the ECI (early customer involvement) program by IBM, through which information was collected to build OPs (Lu and Tian, 1993a). However, both these types of remedial solutions suffer from their own limitations, primary in the late availability of such OPs and the doubtful representativeness of the information collected.

In addition to the above difficulties and limitations, actual measurements are also expensive to implement. Consequently, various other ways have been suggested, primarily customer surveys to obtain information from the customers directly and expert opinions to obtain customer usage information indirectly. Both of these ways of information gathering can be carried out much earlier in the software development process, typically in the requirement analysis stage. They are even applicable for brand new products, to get information about the "intended" customer usage by surveying potential customers or obtaining expert opinions. In addition, these techniques are typically much simpler and cheaper to implement than actual measurement.

Customer surveys can provide more objective and potentially more accurate information regarding a product's usage than expert opinions that are indirect information about product use by customers. For different products and market segments, such surveys may be implemented differently. For example, for products with a single customer or limited number of customers, such as many defense-related software products whose customers are typically the government(s) or government branches, the survey might be more manageable. However, for commercial products and other mass-market products, such as commercial database products or operating systems for PCs, the massive user population requires careful planning to reduce the survey cost while maintaining result accuracy. Another problem we have to deal with in using customer surveys is that the accuracy of the information obtained is largely affected by the product knowledge of the individuals who complete the survey.

The main advantages of using expert opinions to construct OPs are the ready availability of these mostly internal experts and the much lower cost. Therefore, many of the rough OPs can be obtained this way, which can be cross-validated later on when customer survey and measurement information is obtained. Other information sources include many of the existing product and system documentations, such as architectural and design documents, technical memos, and documents of understanding with customers and partners, as well as product specifications and relevant standards. From these information sources, high-level structures, major components, interconnections among these components, as well as rough usage frequency and importance information, can be easily obtained by some product experts or with consultation with such experts.

Musa suggested that the operational profile should be developed by a combination of system engineers, high-level designers, and test planners, with strong participation from product planning and marketing functions (Musa, 1993; Musa, 1998). The involvement of customers is implicitly assumed here as a primary source of information. If we consider the test planners as the coordinator of OP construction activities and the testing team as the main user of the OPs, we can then consider the other parties above as representing experts whose opinions are used in the process for OP construction. Each party bring unique expertise to OP construction, as follows:

- *Planning and marketing personnel* are the primary contact with customers, and their involvement would ensure that customers' concerns and their perspectives are reflected in the resulting OPs. Initially product requirements are also gathered by these people, which may as well contain various OP related information. Gathering of such information could also be a part of requirement gathering.

- *System engineers* are responsible for the overall product requirement and specification, including high-level functions and features to be implemented in the product. Therefore, their participation would ensure a comprehensive system view of the resulting OPs.

- *High-level designers* are responsible to produce high-level product designs based on product specifications. Their participation would help map the external functions or features expected by customers into internal product components, modules, or sub-systems that are tested.

On the other hand, the large software systems usually involve many customers who use the software products differently under different environments or settings. It would be highly unlikely that all the information about the operations can be obtained and organized in one step. Consequently, some procedural support is usually needed for such situations. In what follows, we will describe two such procedures developed by Musa: a top-down procedure with multiple profiles refined along the way labeled as Musa-1 (Musa, 1993) and a single profile procedure labeled as Musa-2 (Musa, 1998). Musa-1 is also used in our case study in Section 8.5.

8.4.2 OP development procedure: Musa-1

In Musa's top-down approach (Musa, 1993) or Musa-1 procedure, one OP is developed for each homogeneous group of users or operations by following five basic steps below:

Table 8.5 A sample customer profile

Customer Type	Weight
corporation	0.5
government	0.4
education	0.05
other	0.05

1. *Find the customer profile* by defining a complete set of customer categories weighted per a usage factor.

2. *Establish the user profile* by defining user types weighted in relation to the customer groups and relative usage rates.

3. *Define the system modes and related profile* by identifying the sets of operations commonly used together and obtaining their related weights.

4. *Determine the functional profile* by identifying individual (high-level) functions and obtaining their related weights based on analysis of the system modes and environmental variables.

5. *Determine the operational profile* by refining high-level functions into detailed operations and obtaining their usage probabilities.

Notice that in this top-down approach, each step results in a profile in progressively more detail, culminating in the final operational profile. The focus is on the external users and their usage of the software systems. And the general view is that these users are affiliated with large organizations or are authorized to use certain software products; while each customer represents an organization.

The main difference between a customer and a user is that the former is responsible for the acquisition of the software products, while the latter uses them. For example, a database product could be targeted toward corporate, governmental, educational, and other large organizations as potential customers. In this case, both the number of customers in each category, as well as their importance to the software vendors, can be captured in this customer profile. The resulting customer profile would be in the form of pairs of customer types and associated probabilities or weighting factors, such as in Table 8.5.

Within each customer group or type, there are different user groups, frequently with some similar user groups across different customers. For example, in the example above with database product for large organizations, there may be end users, database administrators (dba), application programmers, third party contractors. The usage probabilities by these user types or their weights within each customer type can be determined first, and then the weighted sums give us the overall user profile, as illustrated in Table 8.6. Notice that the customer types (ctype) are abbreviated in Table 8.6, with "com", "gov", "edu", and "etc" for corporate, governmental, educational, and other organizations respectively. Notice that some user types are absent from some customer types, such as third party contractors are represented in governmental and educational organizations but not in corporate and other organizations. When a user type is missing, it is indicated in Table 8.6 by a "–", and its weight is interpreted as 0. The customer profile (or weights by customer types) is used to determine the overall user profile. For example the weight for end users is calculated as:

Table 8.6 A sample user profile

User Type	User Profile by Customer Type					Overall User Profile
	ctype	com	gov	edu	etc	
	weight	0.5	0.4	0.05	0.05	
end user		0.8	0.9	0.9	0.7	0.84
dba		0.02	0.02	0.02	0.02	0.02
programmer		0.18	–	–	0.28	0.104
third party		–	0.08	0.08	–	0.036

$$0.8 \times 0.5 \text{ (com)} + 0.9 \times 0.4 \text{ (gov)} + 0.9 \times 0.05 \text{ (edu)} + 0.7 \times 0.05 \text{ (etc)} = 0.84 \ .$$

The computation for the next three steps, system mode definition and profile, functional profile, and operational profile, follows essentially the same procedure as that for user profile: Individual profiles are obtained first, and then the weights from the previous step are used to calculate the overall profile for this step as the weighted sums of the individual profiles. Therefore, we will omit numerical examples in describing the next three steps.

System modes are associated with different sets of functions or operations that are commonly used together within a mode. For example, the differences of normal operation mode and maintenance mode for many systems are significant, and each mode can be associated with its own functions and operations. In this case, various system maintenance functions, such as some backup and patching functions, are only applied under system maintenance mode but not under normal operations.

The last two steps, functional profile and operational profile, are essentially the same except granularity differences and sometimes implementation status differences. System *functions* are high-level tasks of the projected system in the requirement, which can be mapped to various lower-level *operations* in the implemented system. The function list can be created from various sources, such as system requirement, prototypes, previous release, user manual, etc., and then consolidated. The functional profile can then be derived, followed by the operational profile.

One of the decisions to be made for functional and operational profiles is to use explicit or implicit profiles. An explicit profile is similar to that in Table 8.4 and in examples we used so far: the alternatives are disjoint and the weights (or probabilities) for them add up to 1. These explicit profiles usually correspond to end-to-end operational sequences and their associated probabilities. However, for many systems, staged or repeated selections, independent of each other, of operational units may be more meaningful to the users. For example, if a system operation can be divided into two stages, A, and B, and the selections are independent of each other, we can then specify the implicit profile for A and B separately. That is, we specify the distribution for A with $p_i = prob(A = A_i)$ and for B with $p_j = prob(B = B_j)$. The profile for A-B selections can be calculated as the product of their probabilities, that is, $p_{ij} = prob(A = A_i, B = B_j) = p_i \times p_j$.

8.4.3 OP development procedure: Musa-2

The above development procedure for OPs is suitable for large software systems, where there are potentially many customers or users involved and their usage situations can be quite diverse. Consequently, successive profiles are used, with one for each of the 5 steps, culminating into the final OP. However, for smaller products or ones with more homogeneous user population, one profile would probably be enough. The primary areas of procedure support needed might be in the specific information source identification and data collection. Another OP construction procedure, also proposed by Musa (Musa, 1998) and labeled Musa-2 in this book, is suitable for such situations. One OP is constructed for each operational mode, similar to the system mode in Musa-1 above, because testing is typically performed under a specific operational mode instead of being in mixed modes. There are also 5 generic steps:

1. Identify *initiators* of operations: These initiators include human users as well as other software, hardware, network, etc. The human users will be the primary information sources themselves. However, for non-human users, people who are familiar with them, or sometimes existing documents and recorded data can be information sources.

2. Determine tabular or graphical *representation*: In fact, this representation used by Musa here goes beyond simple representation to determine the type of OP will be constructed, as we will elaborate later.

3. Operations *lists*: First, individual operations lists can be obtained from identified initiators of these operations. Then, these lists can be consolidated into a comprehensive list. For example, from the original lists $\{A, B, C\}$ and $\{B, D\}$, we can obtain a consolidate list $\{A, B, C, D\}$. Sometimes, some adjustments are also made to ensure proper granularity for the comprehensive list, particularly when the initial lists are based on different levels of granularity.

4. Determine the occurrence *rate* (per hour): Actual measurement is typically used to obtain data about the occurrence rate or frequency for individual operations in the above consolidated operations list and tabulated. This tabulation may be affected by the type of OPs used, as we will elaborate later.

5. Determine the occurrence *probability*: With the measurement and tabulation results from the previous step, this step is straightforward: When we normalized the occurrence rate or frequency, we get the occurrence probability, which satisfies the two conditions $0 \leq p_i \leq 1$ and $\sum_i p_i = 1$. When actual measurement is not available, surveys, expert opinions, or other estimates can be used. In the latter case, we typically directly estimate the occurrence probability while skipping the previous step.

The tabular representation is similar to the explicit OP in Musa-1, such as Table 8.4 above. Such OPs can also be represented graphically as histograms, such as in Figure 8.1, which is not what is referred to as graphical representation by Musa. The measurement and tabulation in step 4 are carried out for each item in the consolidated operations list, and these results are normalized by dividing them by the total occurrences in step 5.

The graphical representation used in Musa-2 actually correspond to a tree-structured OP that somewhat resembles (but it is not exactly the same) the implicit OP in Musa-1 above. In this type of OPs, the complete operational sequence can be divided into fixed number of stages, with fixed number of choices for each stage. When we combine these stages, it gives us a tree, much like a decision tree, but with occurrence rates and probabilities attached to each tree branch. Therefore, a complete end-to-end operation would be a path in the tree from the root node to one of the leaf nodes, and the path probability is the product of its individual branch probabilities. This is best illustrated through an example in Figure 8.2 for web usage by a group of users modeled as a two-stage process:

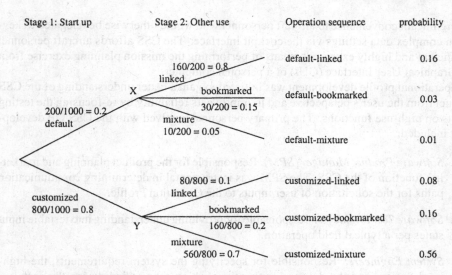

Figure 8.2 A tree-structured or graphical operational profile

- *Stage 1.* Starting the browser with two choices: either on the default starting page or a customized starting page.

- *Stage 2.* All subsequent usage is modeled as one stage, with three choices: following links in visited pages, following bookmarked pages, or a mixture of the two.

Occurrences of specific usage choices at each stage are also tabulated separately, thus resulting in different probability distributions at points X and Y in Figure 8.2. In other words, the probability distributions at later stages in such trees can be different, depending on different earlier choices. However, if implicit OPs in Musa-1 are used, the probability distributions at points X and Y would be the same. Consequently, the tree-structured graphical OPs in Musa-2 are more powerful in representing different usage situation than implicit OPs in Musa-1. Explicit OPs in Musa-1 and tabular OPs in Musa-2 are the same, and can both be treated as degenerated multi-stage OPs when there is only one stage.

8.5 CASE STUDY: OP FOR THE CARTRIDGE SUPPORT SOFTWARE

We next describe a case study constructing an operation profile for the Lockheed Martin Tactical Aircraft System's (LMTAS) Cartridge Support Software (CSS) (Chruscielski and Tian, 1997). The process is an adaptation of Musa's 5-step approach, Musa-1, described above. This operational profile allowed the LMTAS software engineering team to derive some clear insights about the usage rate of the CSS functions from the customer's perspective.

8.5.1 Background and participants

The Cartridge Support Software (CSS) developed by Lockheed Martin Tactical Aircraft Systems (LMTAS) is used by aircraft personnel to load mission planning data to a read/writable media. The read/writable media is used by pilots to upload data to the avionic computers residing on an aircraft. The ability to use a personal computer to load mission planning data is a significant convenience to aircraft personnel who would otherwise be relegated to key-ing in complex data settings via the cockpit interface. The CSS affords aircraft personnel an efficient and highly expedient means of performing the mission planning exercise from the Graphical User Interface (GUI) of a personal computer.

Operational profile development was initiated to gain a better understanding of the CSS product from the user's perspective and to improve its reliability by re-focusing the testing efforts on high-use functions. The primary personnel involved with the CSS OP develop-ment included:

1. *Software Product Manager (SPM):* Responsible for the product planning and market-ing function of the CSS. The SPM was instrumental in determining communication paths for the solicitation of user inputs to the Operation Profile.

2. *Software Test Engineers:* Responsible for providing understanding into testable input states per a typical field operation.

3. *System Engineers:* Responsible for specifying the system requirements, the high-level design, and the deliverable functions which are verified during the software testing phase.

Both authors of the reported case study (Chruscielski and Tian, 1997) were also involved in a graduate-level class "CSE 5314: Software Testing and Quality Assurance" at Southern Methodist University, with Chruscielski taking the class and performed the initial work described here as a course project, and Tian teaching the class.

8.5.2 OP development in five steps

The customers of the CSS are the air forces (US Air Force or Other Air Forces) that use the LMTAS tactical aircrafts. The CSS also has internal users labeled as "Avionic System Test and Flight Test." For the purposes of the CSS operational profile the investigation into the customer profile did not result in a "weighting" of the customers, as each customer had a similar use of the CSS. However, this exercise did serve as a means of establishing communication paths for the collection of user inputs.

The users of the CSS include the following types of flight personnel and engineering support:

1. *Air Force Pilots*, the primary users of the CSS. The pilots are directly involved with the mission planning exercise, however their use can be very infrequent.

2. *Flight Test Support:* These frequent users of the CSS interface directly with test pilots during the mission planning exercise.

3. *Avionic System Test:* These users are involved in integrating the entire suite of avionics residing in the aircraft.

4. *System Administrators:* This user group's functions are performed by Air Force Pilots. Therefore, it is combined into the Air Force Pilot group.

The user groups were weighted as shown in Table 8.7. In addition to the usage frequencies used in weight assignments, marketing concerns were also considered as an important weighting factor. For example, although the pilots were found to be very infrequent users,

Table 8.7 CSS user profile

User Group	Marketing Concerns	Frequency of Use	Total Weighting Factor
Air Force Pilot	0.85	0.05	0.45
Flight Test Support	0.10	0.80	0.45
Avionics System Test	0.05	0.15	0.1

they are the primary contractual customers of the CSS. Consequently, they were weighted accordingly due to both marketing concerns and usage frequencies.

The system modes for the CSS were determined to fall into the following categories:

1. *Preflight Mission Planning:* The Pilot or Flight Test Support personnel plan a mission.

2. *Avionic System Test:* The system test engineers use the CSS to stimulate avionics as part of the verification process during system integration.

3. *System Administration:* The administrator uses the CSS to maintain a database of preflight mission files.

An analysis of the system operational behavior revealed that there is not an appreciable difference accounted for between the system modes. Therefore a categorization and weighting of identified system modes was not performed. The derivation of the CSS user profile and the associated weighting factors remains the most significant component for determining the CSS operational profile.

For CSS, there is no significant distinction between high-level intended functions and low-level implemented operations. Therefore, the steps of functional profile and operational profile in Musa-1 was collapsed into one in this case study. Each function of the CSS is typically associated with it's own dialog or window. The user has the ability to enter one or more individual functions and then terminate the mission planning session. The user does not have a defined order in which the functions must be executed. Because of this, an implicit functional profile described in Musa-1 was used, listing only the occurrence probability for each individual function, rather than the end-to-end functional sequences that define an explicit functional profile. These functions were analyzed for the operational profile in Table 8.8.

An indication of how each user group uses the CSS was found to be beneficial to the System Engineers and Test Engineers. The user groups all have a significant contribution during the lifecycle of a tactical aircraft and each user and their requirements have to be satisfied. Therefore, an operational profile was created for each of the user groups. From these individual operational profiles, a comprehensive operational profile was created.

In the existing development and testing environment, a small minority of functions is considered to be of prime importance and receive a copious amount of emphasis in the development lifecycle. Those functions that are considered to be of very low importance are given a brief cursory test to determine their functionality. The formation of the CSS operational profile was intended to appraise this current approach that is used in software testing. Because of this specific usage concerns for operational profiles, the raw comprehensive operational profile were grouped into high, medium-high, medium-low, and low use categories in Table 8.8 as the final operational profile. These classifications correspond to the software management concern for the prioritization of defect resolution.

Table 8.8   CSS OP: CSS functions classified according to usage probabilities

High	Medium-high	Medium-low	Low
DTC Load	DTC Read	Wpn Prof	RetrCanned
Inventory	Delete	Hot Keys	Save Canned
Save	Retrieve Route	Comm	DTC Test
Route Planning		Retr/Save SCL	
Print		Help	
		Base Default	
		FCR	
		Mstr Mode	
High usage	Medium-high usage	Medium-low usage	Low usage
= 100% – 75%	= 74.9% – 50%	= 49.9% – 25%	= 24.9% – 0%

8.5.3 Metrics collection, result validation, and lessons learned

The generation of the CSS operational profile required the participation of the Software Product Manager (SPM) to outline the marketing aspects of the software product. Several short interviews with the SPM over the span of a few weeks identified key areas of the CSS and several communication paths to the users. Follow-up discussions with the SPM helped to define the requirements for the user profile and functional profile. Much of the existing system design of the CSS guided the generation of the functional list. Consultations with system engineers and test engineers, during a two week period, were instrumental in the development of the survey form that was sent out to the CSS users.

The numbers for the operational profile were derived from e-mail and fax copies of user surveys through the identified communication channels. The advantage of using electronic communications was that it allowed for a quick transmission of the surveys to remote locations. The desirable prospect of this approach was that one user would "forward' the survey to other users — thus creating a "chain letter" effect, and thereby increasing user participation in the survey. The disadvantage of this approach was that the status of the survey replies was a difficult factor to correctly determine. The projected response to the survey was 30–50 users. The actual response was 12 users. However, the participants who did engage in the survey were considered to be significantly reflective of their user groups.

The final results evaluation required each member of the software engineering team to interpret the operation profile. Individual interviews with each member of the software engineering team was beneficial in capturing unique perspectives on the operational profile. Initially, team members were not aware of how the data could be used in practical situations. Over the course of the interview each member began to suggest possible explanations for the results of the data. This led the review team to contrast current testing strategies with the identified needs of the customers. Individuals then offered action plans to accommodate customer needs and improve software reliability.

The LMTAS software engineering team, including the SPM, System Engineer, and Test engineers, reviewed and evaluated the operational profile results and the usage probability classifications shown in Table 8.8. The test engineers felt that the operational profile confirmed some of the expectations of their customers. In particular, validation the current software engineering efforts towards these "high" use functions provides confirmation that

LMTAS's efforts are on target. However, there were several unexpected results that lead to related actions:

- The medium use classification of the Hot Keys Function was found as a completely unexpected result. This function has been considered to be of low importance to the customer. The user's continued reliance on Hot Keys should require modifications of current testing strategies.

- The classification of the Help function as a "medium to low" use function was another unexpected result. The CSS developers had believed that most users are familiar with the overall operation of the software functions, and as such, would require a minimal amount of help.

Prior to the generation of the CSS operational profile there had never been a comprehensive review of the CSS product from the customer perspective. A higher appreciation for communicating with the customer and an increased opportunity for improving the CSS testing strategy were direct results of the operational profile. The increased emphasis on the customer perspective also affected the system and high-level design effort. As demonstrated by this case study, an operational profile can be developed for the LMTAS CSS with a reasonable amount of effort by following and adapting Musa-1 steps. Cross-validation through peer review was also found to be valuable not only in validating the results but also help derived specific follow-up actions based on these results. On the practical side, a simple classification of usage frequencies also adds value in highlighting the findings and helping initiate discussions and follow-up actions.

From the OP development procedure perspective, we can see that the 5 steps in Musa-1 may not necessarily lead to a complete profile each step along the way. In this case study, customer and system mode profiles were not generated because the homogeneous usage of CSS by customers under different systems modes. The similarity between high-level intended functions and low-level implemented operations for CSS also reduced functional and operational profiles into one step. However, even for such reduced steps, the specific activities carried out were beneficial, for example, in identifying customers and communication channels to them.

8.6 CONCLUDING REMARKS

Checklist-based testing has been around ever since the first programs were tested. It is still widely used today due to its simplicity. Various types of checklists covering internal components, external functions, environments, as well as other related properties, can be used for testing where each item in the lists needs to be tested and "checked off". However, due to the possible problems of overlapping and insufficient coverage, partitions were introduced as a special kind of checklists that ensure both coverage by the whole and mutual exclusion among different elements. Therefore, both coverage and efficiency can be assured.

Partition-based testing models are constructed based on the simple assumption that various things that we would like to test can be partitioned into subsets of equivalent classes. The use of equivalent classes can significantly reduce the number of possible tests required for a product, while still covering diverse situations. Like their checklist counterparts, partitions can be derived based on either external descriptions or internal components and implementation details. Various external and internal decisions related to product functions and information processing can be easily tested by such partition-based testing. As a special case of such partition-based testing, input domain partitioning and related boundary testing is described in Chapter 9.

Statistical testing with Musa's operational profiles (OPs) shares the same basic model for testing, but focuses on highly used system functions and operations with the help of usage information by target customers captured in the OPs as probabilities associated with list items or tree-branches. The development procedures, Musa-1 and Musa-2 (Musa, 1993; Musa, 1998), provide practical guidance in the actual development of OPs. These procedures can be adapted for different products under different environments, as demonstrated by the case study in Section 8.5.

The main advantage of these testing techniques based on such checklists or partitions is their simplicity, which makes them easy to perform under practical testing situations. These techniques can also be extended to cover some specific problems, such as boundary problems closely related to input-domain partitions in Chapter 9. However, for testing more complex program execution, interaction, and usage situations, alternative models, such as based on finite-state machines (FSMs) in Chapter 10 and Chapter 11, are called for.

Problems

8.1 What is the main difference between checklists and partitions?

8.2 Stepwise refinement is a commonly used strategy for software design and development. Can you use associated designs or documents as your checklists in testing?

8.3 Define the following terms and give some examples: relation, symmetric relation, transitive relation, reflexive relation, and equivalence class.

8.4 Perform decision analysis for a small program and outline the test cases using partition-based testing.

8.5 Repeat the previous exercise based on the manual or specifications of a small software product or a utility program.

8.6 Assess the general applicability of Musa's OPs for a software product that your are working on or one that you are familiar with. Pay attention to the following issues: customer identification, difference between users and customers, means for data collection, Musa-1 vs. Musa-2. If possible, try to construct an OP for this product.

8.7 Is OP appropriate for a unit, a component, or a sub-system?

8.8 What would be an OP for this book like?

8.9 What is the impact if a new customer type is introduced in Table 8.6? What about a new user type? Use some concrete examples to illustrate your points.

8.10 The graphical OP in Figure 8.2 is a specialized tree. What is the impact if a general tree structure can be used as an OP?

8.11 As a customer or an external user, would you like to see OP used in testing of some specific software products that you buy or use? Be specific with the products and related properties/attributes that you care about.

CHAPTER 9

INPUT DOMAIN PARTITIONING AND BOUNDARY TESTING

One of the most important areas where partition-based testing has made a strong impact is domain testing or input domain testing (White and Cohen, 1980; Clarke et al., 1982; Jeng and Weyuker, 1994; Beizer, 1990). In this chapter, the idea of partition-based testing is applied to partition the overall input domain into sub-domains and to test them accordingly. However, the simple strategies for sub-domain coverage are found to be inadequate for many situations. This inadequacy is particularly noted in dealing with problems specifying or implementing the sub-domains involving numeric input variables. Many problems are commonly observed at the boundaries, leading us to examine various boundary testing strategies in this chapter, in particular:

- We first examine possible input domain partitions and related partition coverage testing ideas in Section 9.1. A special type of common problems associated with partitions, the boundary problems, is also discussed therein.

- Several important boundary testing strategies are described, including extreme point combination (EPC) in Section 9.2, and weak $N \times 1$ and weak 1×1 in Section 9.3.

- We finally extend the above strategies and generalize boundary testing for testing based on other boundary-like situations in Section 9.4.

All these testing strategies and techniques are based on the same models described in Chapter 8, that is, input domain partitions, but we focus on the related boundary conditions that distinguish one sub-domain from another. As selective or non-uniform testing strategies, boundary testing shares some commonalities with usage-based testing using Musa's operational profiles (OPs): Sub-domains with more complex boundaries will be tested more in boundary testing, thus reducing the number of boundary problems that are the likely causes for many potential in-field failures; while frequently used functions and components will be tested more under OP-guide statistical testing, thus reducing the chance of failures when the software is used by target customers.

9.1   INPUT DOMAIN PARTITIONING AND TESTING

We next examine the partitioning of the overall input domain into sub-domains, the associated boundaries, and the general idea of input domain testing.

9.1.1   Basic concepts, definitions, and terminology

The basic idea of domain testing is to generate test cases by assigning specific values to input variables based on some analyses of the input domain. This analysis is called domain analysis, or input domain analysis. By doing so, we hope to avoid exhaustive coverage of all the possible input variable value combinations by sampling a small number of input values or test points to systematically cover different input situations. There are several important characteristics for this testing technique:

- It tests I/O (input/output) relations by providing input values associated with all the individual input variables.

- The output variable values are not explicitly specified. But, we assume that there are ways to check if the expected output is obtained for any given input.

- Although the technique is black-box in nature, by focusing on the I/O relations, the internal implementation details can be used to analyze the input variables and the input domain. Therefore, the technique can be classified either as white-box or black-box, depending on whether the implementation information is used in analysis and modeling.

Before we describe any specific domain testing techniques or strategies, several basic definitions are needed, as described below:

- Let $x_1, x_2, \ldots, x_n$ denote the input variables. Then these n variables form an n-dimensional space that we call *input space*. Each of these variables corresponds to a single data item in a program or an input to the program that can be assigned a value. They include both program variables as well as some constants. On the other hand, compound data structures, such as arrays, used as program input might need to be represented by multiple input variables.

- The input space can be represented by a vector X, we call *input vector*, where $X = [x_1, x_2, \ldots, x_n]$.

- When the input vector X takes a specific value, that is, each of its elements $x_1, x_2, \ldots, x_n$ is assigned a specific value, we call it a *test point* or a *test case*, which corresponds to a point in the n-dimensional input space.

- The *input domain* consists of all the points representing all the allowable input combinations specified for the program in the product specification.

- An input *sub-domain* is a subset of the input domain. In general, a sub-domain can be defined by a set of inequalities in the form of

$$f(x_1, x_2, \ldots, x_n) < K,$$

where "$<$" can also be replaced by other relational operators such as "$>$", "$=$", "$\neq$", "$\leq$", or "$\geq$".

- A *domain partition*, or input domain partition, is a partition of the input domain into a number of sub-domains. That is, these sub-domains are mutually exclusive, and collectively exhaustive.

- A *boundary* is where two sub-domains meet. When inequalities are used to define sub-domains as above, the following equation would give us a specific boundary:

$$f(x_1, x_2, \ldots, x_n) = K.$$

- A boundary is a *linear boundary* if it is defined by:

$$a_1 x_1 + a_2 x_2 + \ldots + a_n x_n = K.$$

Otherwise, it is called a *nonlinear boundary*. If a sub-domain whose boundaries are all linear ones, it is called a *linear sub-domain*. In describing all the input domain testing strategies, we will restrict ourselves to linear sub-domains first before dealing with the complicated nonlinear boundaries and sub-domains in Section 9.4.

- A point on a boundary is called a *boundary point*.

- A boundary is a *closed* one with respect to a specific sub-domain if all the boundary points belong to the sub-domain.

- A boundary is an *open* one with respect to a specific sub-domain if none of the boundary points belong to the sub-domain.

- A sub-domain with all open boundaries is called an *open sub-domain*; one with all closed boundaries is called a *closed sub-domain*; otherwise it is a mixed sub-domain.

- A point belonging to a sub-domain but not on the boundary is called an *interior point*. The opposite is an *exterior point*, that is, not belonging to a sub-domain and not on its boundary.

- A point where two or more boundaries intersect is called a *vertex point*.

Corresponding to these terms and definitions for the input, we can define output variable, space, vector, point, range (corresponding to input domain), etc. Since the output is only implicitly specified in most domain testing strategies, we omit the corresponding definitions.

9.1.2 Input domain testing for partition and boundary problems

With the above definitions, we can restate the general idea of domain testing as trying to achieve domain coverage, through the following steps:

1. Identifying the input variable, input vector, input space, and define the input domain based on specifications (black-box view) or implementation details (white-box view) for the program unit under testing.

2. Dividing or classifying the input domain into sub-domains to form a partition.

3. Performing domain analysis for each sub-domain to examine its limits in each dimension and its boundary properties, such as the specific boundary definitions and the related closure properties.

4. Selecting test points to cover these partitioned sub-domains based on domain analysis results from the previous step.

5. Testing with the above selected test points as input, checking the results (output values), dealing with observed problems, and carrying out analysis and follow-up activities.

Notice that there is not much variability in the first two steps, because the input and partitions are generally determined by the external specifications or internal implementation details for the program unit under testing. The last step is also a standard step similar to any other forms of testing. Therefore, the specific variations of domain testing depend on how this third step is carried out. That is, how specific test points are selected defines a specific domain testing strategy.

The simplest strategy is to sample one test point from inside each sub-domain in the partition, thus achieving complete coverage of all the sub-domains. This is exactly the same as partition coverage testing we described in the previous chapter. However, there is empirical evidence that problems with input domain partitions most commonly occur at sub-domain boundaries. Therefore, some specialized testing techniques are called for to deal with such problems, as we describe in the rest of this chapter. We next examine the common problems associated with input domain partitions to set the stage to develop appropriate testing techniques to deal with these problems.

General problems with input domain partitions

In general, the problems in the computation or information processing for a given input can generally fall into two categories:

- *Ambiguity or under-defined processing for some given input*: Some input values or test points in the input domain cannot be handled by the program unit under testing. In other words, these test points are *under-defined*, because we cannot find a solution for them. The most common situations for this kind of problems to occur are when computational procedures are defined for individual sub-domains, but these sub-domains do not cover the complete input domain, thus creating *ambiguity* for some input. The practitioners often refer to this as having "holes" in the input domain.

- *Contradiction or over-defined processing for some given input*: In contrast to the above, some input values or test points have contradictory computation associated with them, or are *over-defined*. Most of such cases indicate problems in the product specification or in the implementation, which result in different output for the same input or the system behaves incorrectly, such as fail to stop computation because it cannot resolve the conflicting results. The most common situations for this kind of problems to occur is when computational procedures are defined for individual sub-domains, but some of these sub-domains overlap with one another, thus causing contradictions.

It has been observed both by practitioners and researchers that the above problems are most likely to happen at boundaries as discussed below.

Boundary problems

Several specific manifestations of input domain partition problems on the boundaries between different sub-domains include the following:

- *Closure problem*, that is, the problem with whether the boundary points belong to this sub-domain under consideration. A closure problem would be an implementation that disagrees with the specification, or the specification that disagrees with the intention. For example, an intended open boundary is specified or implemented as a closed one.

- *Boundary shift*: This problem refers to the disagreement with where exactly a boundary is between the intended and the actual boundary. In the form of boundary specifications,

$$f(x_1, x_2, \ldots, x_n) = K,$$

a (small) change in K is associated with a boundary shift.

- Other boundary changes are possible too, if the boundary equation

$$f(x_1, x_2, \ldots, x_n) = K$$

is changed. One common such change is called *boundary tilt*, when some parameters in the equation are changed slightly.

- *Missing boundary*: If a boundary is missing, that means the two neighboring sub-domains will collapse into one sub-domain, or into one equivalent class. Therefore, all points in them would receive the same treatment or processing.

- *Extra boundary*: If there is an extra boundary within a sub-domain, the sub-domain has been further partitioned and different points would receive different treatments because they belong to different equivalent classes.

To deal with such problems, various specific domain testing strategies can be used to focus on testing related to the sub-domain boundaries, resulting in the so-called *boundary testing strategies*. Notice that we assume the existence of "intended" or correct partitions and/or boundaries in discussing both partition and boundary problems above. The actual specification (black-box view) or implementation (white-box view) of these intended partitions or boundaries may contain some mistakes. With the above assumption, the result checking for testing can be done by using the intended partitions or boundaries as oracles. In addition, the differences or discrepancies between the intended and actual partitions or boundaries represent problems that need to be detected and corrected.

The specification problems can usually be detected through input-domain and boundary analysis, and the implementation problems can be detected through input-domain and boundary testing. Because such testing typically involves analysis as the first step, we refer to both the analysis and testing simply as input domain and boundary testing in subsequent discussions.

9.2 SIMPLE DOMAIN ANALYSIS AND THE EXTREME POINT COMBINATION STRATEGY

Extreme-point combination (EPC) is one of the oldest domain testing strategies that are still used by people and supported by some testing tools. We first examine this strategy based on simple domain analysis in this section.

The idea of EPC is fairly simple and similar to the idea of capacity testing, stress testing, or robustness testing commonly performed for many systems (DeMillo et al., 1987; Myers, 1979). At extreme input values, system capacities or some other limits might be contested. Therefore, the logic goes that testing for such extreme values would help reveal system design and implementation problems. In addition, when we attempt such extreme values, we are pushing the envelope to exceed the limits and observing how the system behaves. This is also related to robust design principle commonly recommended for highly-dependable systems (Leveson, 1995), where system dependability or safety needs to be assured even if it is subjected to unexpected input or environments.

The systematic definition and usage of such extreme values when multiple variables are involved give us the so-called extreme-point (or extreme-value) combination (EPC) strategy. This strategy can be summarized in the following steps:

- A set of test points is associated with each sub-domain.

- For each sub-domain, a simple domain analysis is carried out to identify the domain limits in each dimension. That is, we need to find out, for each variable x_i the maximal, "max_i", and minimal, "min_i", values for this sub-domain. In addition, we would like to stretch these values to test the limits, in an attempt to test the boundaries. We define the values "$under_i$", to be slightly under "min_i", and "$over_i$", to be slightly over "max_i".

- Produce all the possible combinations of input with each of its variables x_i taking on one of the four values defined above, "$under_i$", "min_i", "max_i", and "$over_i$". Each of these combinations will be a test case or a test point in this n-dimensional space. Therefore the number of test cases would be $4^n + 1$, with 4^n defined here by the cross product of those four values for each dimension, plus 1 for sampling inside the sub-domain as in the simple domain coverage strategy above.

We next illustrate this strategy through some examples and evaluate its effectiveness.

EPC for 1-dimensional sub-domains

When the input only consists of a single variable, that is, in a 1-dimensional input space, we can directly use the four values, "under", "min", "max", and "over", and an interior point for testing. For example, for an input sub-domain, $0 \leq x < 21$, the test points according this EPC would be: $-1, 0, 10, 21$, and 22, if we are testing integers. The interior point is

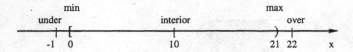

Figure 9.1 1-dimensional domain testing with EPC strategy

arbitrarily selected at $x = 10$, and the "under" and "over" points are 1 under or 1 over. If we go beyond integers, the choice of "under" and "over" will be somewhat problematic. We will deal with it later in connection with other testing strategies. This example can be illustrated graphically in Figure 9.1.

To evaluate this testing strategy, we can consider the handling of the common problems with sub-domains and boundaries we described in Section 9.1, as follows:

- *Closure problem*: In this example, the lower bound is a closed one and the upper bound is an open one, because $x = 0$ belongs to the sub-domain $\{0 \leq x < 21\}$, but not $x = 21$. In fact, we specify such 1-dimensional sub-domain as $[0, 21)$ in mathematics, using "[" and "]" for closed boundaries and "(" and ")" for open boundaries. If there is a closure problem with the lower bound, the test point "min", or $x = 0$, would catch it: If it was implemented as an open boundary, it would be treated differently than points within the sub-domain, leading to the detection of this closure problem. Similarly, the closure problem with the upper bound can be caught by the test point "max".

- *Boundary shift*: With the sub-domain $[0, 21)$, if we implemented $[1, 20)$, we have a right boundary shift for the lower bound, and a left boundary shift for the upper bound. In this case, the pair of test points "min" ($x = 0$) and "under" ($x = -1$) would detect the problem, because the right-shift of the lower bound would mean the $x = 0$ will now be treated as an exterior point. At the upper end, the boundary shift to the left would not be detected, because both before and after the shift, both "max" and "over" will be treated as exterior points. Therefore, we can see that some boundary shift problems can be detected by EPC, but not others.

- *Missing boundary*: In this example, if the lower boundary is missing in $[0, 21)$, then the point $x = -1$ (under) would be treated as an interior point, thus detecting the problem. Similarly, if the upper boundary is missing, then both $x = 21$ (max) and $x = 22$ (over) would be treated as interior points, thus detecting the problem.

- *Extra boundary*: In this example, depending on where the extra boundary is, we may or may not be able to detect it with EPC. For example, if the extra boundary is at $x = 5$, then the test points $x = 0$ (min) and $x = 10$ (interior) would receive different processing, and thus detecting the extra boundary problem. However, if the extra boundary is at $x = 15$, there is no way it can be detected by EPC, because all the 5 test points still receive the same treatment as if no extra boundary is there.

From this example, we can see that EPC can consistently detect closure and missing boundary problems for the single input situations; but cannot consistently detect boundary shift or extra boundary problems.

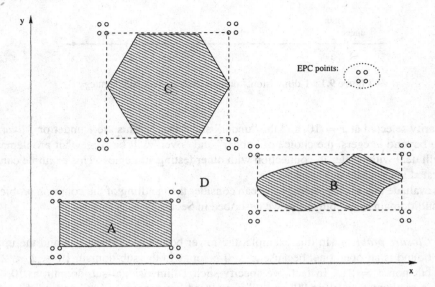

Figure 9.2 2-dimensional domain testing with EPC strategy

EPC for higher dimension sub-domains

For n-dimensional sub-domains, the combination of extreme points for individual dimensions will come into play when EPC strategy is used. We use 2-dimensional examples below to illustrate the effect of such combinations. Consider the three sub-domains in Figure 9.2:

- A, the shaded rectangular region;

- B, the shaded irregular region;

- C, the shaded hexagon, which is often used to depict the coverage area for a cell-phone transmission tower (Garg, 1999);

- D, the rest of the 2-d space not belonging to either A, B, or C.

The 16 EPC test points each for A, B, and C are also illustrated in Figure 9.2. However, we have difficulties with the 16 EPC points for D, because it goes from $-\infty$ to $+\infty$ in both its x and y dimensions. In fact, EPC would not be applicable to sub-domains like D. The interior points are omitted because their choices are obvious. The effectiveness of EPC for sub-domains A, B, and C can be evaluated as follows:

- The EPC test points for region A test around the vertex points, which may include more complex logic to combine the multiple boundaries. The effectiveness in detecting common domain boundary problems would be similar to that for the 1-dimensional example above but would involve more complex analysis because of the multiple boundaries involved at these vertex points.

- The EPC points for regions B and C are totally unrelated to any of the boundaries, and are all exterior points to B and C. Therefore, they are completely useless in detecting boundary problems.

In fact, this example, particularly regions B, C, and D, illustrates the shortcomings of EPC strategy. Alternative strategies, such as those we described next, are needed.

9.3   TESTING STRATEGIES BASED ON BOUNDARY ANALYSIS

The EPC strategy described above is simple but may miss the boundaries entirely. Alternatively, we can directly work with the boundaries and the related boundary conditions to derive our testing strategy, as described below.

9.3.1   Weak $N \times 1$ strategy

This strategy is called weak $N \times 1$ (Cohen, 1978; White and Cohen, 1980), because it uses n ON points and 1 OFF points to be defined below for each boundary. The term "weak" is used to indicate that one set of test points is associated with each boundary instead of a boundary segment as in "strong" domain testing strategies that we will describe later in Section 9.4.

Basic ideas to detect boundary shift problems

In an n-dimensional space, a boundary defined by an equation in the form of

$$f(x_1, x_2, \ldots, x_n) = K$$

would need n linearly independent points to define it. Therefore, we can select n such boundary points to precisely define the boundary. Any change in boundary would result in some or all of these points no longer on the boundary. We call these boundary points "ON" points, simply because they are on the boundary.

Once these ON points are defined, we need to compare them against a point that receives different processing — what we call an "OFF" point. In an open boundary, all the ON points receive exterior processing. Therefore, we would like to select an interior point as our OFF point close to the boundary that receives interior processing. The idea is to pick the OFF point so close to the boundary that any small amount of boundary shift inward would move past this point, thus making the movement detectable. Problem detection is achieved because this interior point will receive exterior processing after the move. If the boundary moves outward, the ON points would detect the movement because all of them would be receiving interior processing after the move. Therefore, this set of test points would detect boundary shift problems.

For a closed boundary, we would like to select an exterior point close to the boundary as our OFF to detect boundary shifts. It mirrors the above situation with open boundaries: Any movement inward would be caught by the ON points because now they will receive exterior processing instead of interior one as specified; and any movement outward would be caught by the OFF point because it will receive interior processing instead of exterior one as specified.

Weak $N \times 1$ strategy: Formal definitions

One practical problem that is key to this strategy is the selection of one OFF point for each boundary and its distance to the boundary. The general recommendation is that this distance, ϵ, should be small, so that any small movement would result in a change in distance that is larger than ϵ. In practical applications, this should be set to the numerical precision of the data type used. For example, for integers, $\epsilon = 1$; while for numbers with n binary digits after the decimal point, $\epsilon = \dfrac{1}{2^n}$. With the above choice of ON and OFF points and definition of ϵ distance, we can detect boundary shift problems in the weak $N \times 1$ input domain testing strategy (Cohen, 1978; White and Cohen, 1980) summarized below:

- For each sub-domain boundary in a n-dimensional input space, n linearly independent boundary points are selected as the ON points.

- The OFF point will be "on the open side of boundary" (White and Cohen, 1980), that is, it will always receive different processing than that for the ON points. Therefore, we have two situations:

  - If the boundary is a closed boundary with respect to the sub-domain under consideration, the OFF point will be outside the sub-domain or be an exterior point.

  - If the boundary is an open boundary with respect to the sub-domain under consideration, the OFF point will be inside the sub-domain or be an interior point.

In either of the above cases, the OFF point will be ϵ distance away from the boundary.

- In general, an interior point is also sampled as the representative of the equivalence class representing all the points in the sub-domain under consideration, resulting in $(n + 1) \times b + 1$ test points for each domain with b boundaries.

Weak $N \times 1$ strategy: Other detectable problems

In addition to the boundary shift problem, other problems can be detected as well, which we describe in general terms here. However, the readers might want to refer to concrete examples given later when examining general descriptions below:

- *Closure problems* can be easily detected because such problems will be manifested as ON and OFF points receiving the same processing instead of the expected different processing. For an open boundary, the ON points should receive exterior processing while the OFF point should receive interior processing. A closure problem would cause ON points to receive interior processing. For a closed boundary, the ON points should receive interior processing while the OFF point should receive exterior processing. A closure problem would cause ON points to receive exterior processing.

- *Boundary tilt* and other boundary changes can be easily detected by the ON and OFF points because any such change would result in some or all the ON points not on the boundary anymore. For each of these ON points falling off the boundary, the part of boundary associated with it is either pushed inward or outward, which can be detected the same way as the boundary shift problem we described above.

- *Missing boundary* would be detected by the same processing received by the ON and OFF points as opposed to the different processing expected.

- *Extra boundary* would likely be detected by the different processing associated with some of the ON or OFF points for different boundaries. For each boundary, there will be an OFF point or n ON points which receive interior processing. Let's call these ON or OFF points that receive interior processing "IN" points. All these IN points as well as the selected interior test point should received the same processing.

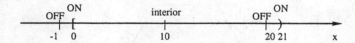

Figure 9.3 1-dimensional domain testing with weak $N \times 1$ strategy

An extra boundary would likely to cause some of these IN points to receive different processing if it separates them apart. However, there are cases in which this extra boundary will not separate any of these IN points apart, resulting in extra boundary not being detected in these situations. One example of such as an extra boundary is one near a vertex point that is far away from any of the ON, OFF, or the selected interior test points.

Therefore, we can see that weak $N \times 1$ strategy is a fairly effective strategy in dealing with most boundary problems.

Another practical consideration for the OFF point selection is that it should be "central" to all the ON points for easy comparison. For example, in the two-dimensional space, it should be chosen by:

1. Choosing the midpoint between the two ON points,

2. Then moving ϵ distance off the boundary, outward or inward for closed or open boundary, respectively.

This selection of ON and OFF points for 2-dimensional sub-domains is illustrated in Figure 9.4. For higher dimensions, this problem becomes more complicated, but the general idea is to still find some kind of center on the boundary among the ON points, and then we can move ϵ distance away to get the OFF point.

Weak $N \times 1$ strategy: Application examples

To contrast weak $N \times 1$ strategy with EPC strategy, we revisit the same examples. For the 1-dimensional example with sub-domain $[0, 21)$, the ON points would be $x = 0$ and $x = 21$, and the OFF points would be $x = -1$ and $x = 20$, and we can keep the interior point at $x = 10$. This set of testing points, -1, 0, 10, 20, and 21, is depicted in Figure 9.3. Notice that the only difference in testing point selection with EPC is the OFF point at $x = 20$ instead of the original "over" point at $x = 22$. The same upper boundary shift to $[1, 20)$ that cannot be detected by EPC can be detected by this OFF point at $x = 20$, because it now receives exterior processing in violation of the expectation. In fact, if we follow the description above about the weak $N \times 1$ detectable problems, we can conclude the all these problems can be detected.

The 2-dimensional example for the hexagon in Figure 9.2 is re-examined and illustrated in Figure 9.4. We only illustrated one set of two ON points and one OFF between regions C0 and C2. As mentioned before, such hexagons are often used to depict coverage areas for cell-phone transmission towers. When a mobile user passes from one region to another, a hand-off transaction is processed by the cell-phone communication networks to ensure continued communication for the user. Therefore, the region can be considered a closed sub-domain: A hand-off will not occur unless a user crosses the boundary. In this case, there is a huge superiority of weak $N \times 1$ testing over EPC testing.

We can also use this 2-dimensional example to illustrate the way weak $N \times 1$ detects boundary tilt problem. Figure 9.5 illustrate the original boundary (solid line) and the tilted

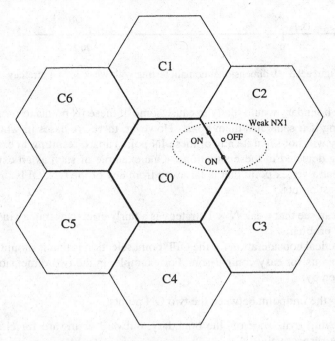

Figure 9.4 2-dimensional domain testing with weak $N \times 1$ strategy for the boundary between C0 and C2

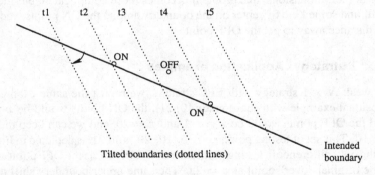

Figure 9.5 2-dimensional boundary tilt detection by the weak $N \times 1$ strategy

boundaries (dotted lines) that tilt clockwise at different points. Then we can consider all the possible tilting points, as below:

- Any tilt outside the segment between these two ON points would make them receive the same processing as the OFF point, as illustrated by tilted boundaries t1 and t5. Therefore, such problems can be detected.

- Any tilt inside the segment between these two ON points would result in the two ON points receiving different processing, as illustrated by the tilted boundary t3. Therefore, such problems can be detected also.

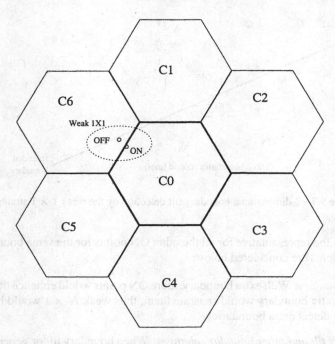

Figure 9.6 2-dimensional domain testing with weak 1×1 strategy for the boundary between C0 and C6

- Any tilt on one of the ON points would make the other ON point and the OFF point receiving the same processing, as illustrated by tilted boundaries t2 and t4. Therefore, such problems can be detected also.

Notice that ϵ distance plays a very important role in the above argument: Any tilting towards the OFF point, such as tilted boundaries t4 and t5 in Figure 9.5, would rotate past it.

9.3.2 Weak 1×1 strategy

One of the major drawbacks of weak $N \times 1$ strategy is the number of test points used, $(n + 1) \times b + 1$ for n input variables and b boundaries, although it is significantly less than that for EPC ($4^n + 1$) when n is large. Therefore, a reduced strategy, called weak 1×1 strategy, has been proposed and successfully used in place of weak $N \times 1$ (Jeng and Weyuker, 1994). Weak 1×1 strategy uses just one ON point for each boundary, thus reducing the total number of test points to $2b + 1$. The choice of the ON and OFF points in the 2-dimensional space was also illustrated in Figure 9.6. In fact, we no longer have the difficulties with the OFF point choice associated with weak $N \times 1$ strategy any more: After we choose the ON point, the OFF point is just ϵ distance from ON point and perpendicular to the boundary.

However, most of the problems that can be detected by the weak $N \times 1$ strategy can still be detected by the weak 1×1 strategy. This can be simply shown by observing that all the n ON points receive the same processing in the closure, shift, and missing boundary problems in the weak $N \times 1$ strategy. Therefore, in detection these problems, one ON

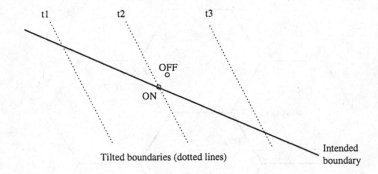

Figure 9.7   2-dimensional boundary tilt detection by the weak 1×1 strategy

point can act as the representative for all the other ON points for the same boundary. Other boundary problems are considered below:

- *Extra boundary*: With extra boundary, more ON points would enhance the possibility that the extra boundary would separate them, thus weak $N \times 1$ would have a better ability to detect extra boundaries.

- *Boundary tilt and other boundary changes*: When boundary tilt or general boundary change is concerned, weak $N \times 1$ can always detect the problem, because the n ON points exactly define the boundary. Weak 1×1 can detect the problem most of the times, but may occasionally miss some problems. Consider the boundary tilt in Figure 9.7 on the single ON point in weak 1×1: the processing received by the ON and OFF points after tilting would be exactly the same as before. Therefore, weak 1×1 would miss this boundary tilt. However, if we tilt on any other point, the ON-OFF pair would receive the same processing after the tilt, thus detecting the problem.

Consequently, by moving from weak $N \times 1$ strategy to weak 1×1, we significantly reduced the number of test points, without sacrificing much of the problem detection ability. Therefore, weak 1×1 should be used in practical applications, unless there is a compelling reason for the other choices.

9.4   OTHER BOUNDARY TEST STRATEGIES AND APPLICATIONS

Beside the weak $N \times 1$ and weak 1×1 strategies described above, various other boundary testing strategies may be used in different situations to deal with different problems. In addition, the basic idea of boundary testing can be extended beyond basic input sub-domain boundaries to other applications where a logical boundary exists between different information processing needs. We examine these testing strategies and their applications in this section.

9.4.1   Strong and approximate strategies

In contrast to the weak boundary testing strategies above, strong boundary testing strategies may be used for various situations, such as when there are boundary inconsistencies.

Common boundary inconsistencies include changing closures along the boundary, singular points, or some kind of "holes". Under such situations, each segment should be treated separately, much like a separate boundary itself. This treatment would require multiple sets of ON and OFF points, one for each segment, resulting in the so-called strong testing strategies, such as strong $N \times 1$ and strong 1×1 strategies.

For nonlinear boundaries, n points are not enough to define the boundary. For example, the boundary for region B in Figure 9.2 would require more than two points to define. Accordingly, we may select many more ON points, or approximate the boundary as a series of (linear) line segments, with one set of ON-OFF points for each segment. This latter strategy is in fact a strong testing strategy. Linear approximations can be used to test imprecise or rough boundaries that may occur in various applications.

Another general extension to boundary testing strategies is to perform vertex testing, because such points are also commonly associated with problems. However, vertex testing would involve more complicated logic and interactions. Therefore, they should generally be done after a regular boundary test.

9.4.2   Other types of boundaries and extensions

The primary application domain of boundary testing is the boundary problems related to input domain partitioning into sub-domains. However, various other situations involving boundaries can also benefit from the general idea of boundary testing, primarily because there are typically problems associated with such boundaries and related boundary conditions. Some such particular situations include:

- Limits or boundaries associated with various compound data structures and their implementations. For example, in array implementations and usage, problems associated with the lower and upper bounds are much more likely than problems associated with other "interior" array elements. Therefore, boundary testing ideas can be used to derive test cases around such data boundaries. We will see a specific example of such an adapted strategy applied to test queues at the end of this section.

- The ideas can be used for capacity testing, which is usually associated with stress testing for various systems. The upper bound in capacity is typically the focus of capacity testing, which can be planned and carried out with the help of boundary testing ideas, such as using test cases to test system operations slightly under or over this capacity limit. However, people typically don't pay much attention to lower bound in capacity, which can be included as part of the systematic boundary testing.

- There are also other dynamic situations where boundary testing ideas might be applicable. One such situation is the execution of loops, which may be totally bypassed, or going through a number of iterations until some conditions are met or until a predetermined number of iterations has been reached. We will deal with loop testing in Chapter 11 in connection to control flow testing, where boundary testing idea is also used.

- For some systems, output range partitions might be more meaningful than input domain partitions. For example, in safety critical systems, some output or system variables are monitored and controlled through some input or control variables, such as temperature (output) regulation in boilers or nuclear reactors. In this example, the output or system variable we care about is the temperature. The input or control variables are the heating/cooling system parameters, through the settings for these parameters we can control the heating or cooling processes to regulate the temperature. In such cases, we can apply the input domain partition and boundary testing ideas to output range partition and related boundary testing. But the test sensitization will be more difficult because we are no longer directly working with input variables and their values. These input values need to be derived through control system equations and related analyses. In fact, one of the most important analyses, called hazard analysis, deals with the output partition of system failures that may or may not lead to accidents. Fault-tree analysis and event-tree analysis are used to analyze the system accidents scenarios to derive the preconditions or system input so that the accident can be avoided. These specific analysis techniques for safety critical systems are covered in Chapter 16.

In addition to the above direct adaptations of boundary testing ideas in various other application domains, the general concepts of associating test points with boundaries instead of uniform domain coverage can be extended to usage-based statistical testing. In boundary testing, the number of test points is generally determined by the number of boundaries, the type of boundaries, and the specific testing strategies used. Therefore, sub-domains with more boundaries or with more complicated boundary situations are receiving more attention than those with fewer and simpler boundaries. The rationale behind this uneven distribution of test points and the associated test resources is that those with larger numbers of and more complex boundaries are more likely to have defects or problems. Along the same line, if a sub-domain is used more often, it is more likely to cause more problems to users even if it contains exactly the same number of defects as another sub-domain that is used less often. This latter rationale led us to build domain partitions and associated probability of usage as the basis for usage based statistical testing in Chapter 8.

9.4.3 Queuing testing as boundary testing

Queuing testing is primarily associated with the many dynamic situations where queues are involved, such as in store-and-forward strategies commonly used in computer networks and our global information infrastructure such as the Internet and the world wide web (WWW). The classical definition of queues is a special type of data structure where the processing or removal order follows precisely the arrival or inserting order. It has been generalized in many applications to indicate any buffering scheme employed, with some priority scheme to select the next element for processing, as follows:

- *Priority* or queuing discipline: Most of the selection or service decisions are based on prioritized queuing disciplines, including the classical queue. In the classical queues, earlier arrivals receive higher priorities in the priority scheme commonly referred to as FCFS (first come, first served) or FIFO (first in, first out). Other explicit priorities and mixed priorities are also commonly used. For example, with the use of a few priority classes, items from higher priority classes will take precedence to the ones from lower priority classes, but items within each class are processed in FIFO order. Strictly random or non-prioritized queuing discipline is rarely used.

- *Buffer capacity*: Because queuing implementation needs some buffer space or queuing space for items to be queued, most queues have either an adjustable or fixed upper bound. In some special cases, theoretically unbounded queues can be implemented by making all the system resources available. In either case, the queues are bounded from below, because we cannot have negative number of elements in the queue. Boundary testing ideas can be easily adapted to test these queue boundaries.

- In addition to the above important characteristics, some other parameters can be specified for queues, including:

  - *Pre-emptive or not*: Whether the queue is pre-emptive or not, that is, can an item currently receiving service or being served be pre-emptied to make room for another item of higher priority?

  - *Batching*: One common practice is to wait until a batch is full before all the items in the batch are processed.

  - *Synchronization*: A special case of batching is synchronization, where some items have to wait for other specific items before they can be processed together.

In what follows, we concentrate on testing prioritized queues without pre-emption or batching. Techniques for synchronization testing are described in Chapter 11 in connection to data flow testing. We can adapt boundary testing ideas to test the handling of the following important situations:

- We always test the lower bound with 0 (empty), 1, or 2 elements in the queue. In particular, the following sub-cases are tested:

  - When the queue is empty, the server could be busy or idle. Depending on the server status, the new arrival may be served immediately or entered into the queue.

  - The cases with 1 or 2 elements already in the queue test the insertion function (or enqueue) to make sure interactions between the new and existing items in the queue are handled correctly.

- If there is an upper bound B, we need to test the queue at capacity limit, that is, with B or $B \pm 1$ items in the queue, in particular:

  - The case with $B - 1$ tests the handling when a new arrival pushes the queue to capacity limit.

  - The case with B tests the handling of new arrival when the queue is already full. Different systems might have different specifications, with the most common ones being discarding the new arrivals, or blocking the arrival stream so that no new arrivals are allowed.

  - The case with $B + 1$ resembles OFF point with closed sub-domains, which may cause system problems, but needs to be guarded to make sure the system is robust in handling unexpected situations.

- In addition to the above cases around upper and lower bounds, a "typical" case is used to test the normal operation of the queue, much like the interior point used in domain testing strategies. This is particularly useful for unbounded queues, because we need some information about queue handling beyond a few items.

Notice that in queuing testing, various natural testing sequences can be used to make the testing run more smoothly. For example, it would make more sense to run the lower bound before running the typical and upper bound test cases. This sequence follows the natural progression from simple to complex test cases. The setup of these later test cases would most likely involve filling the queue that would start from empty. In addition to these concerns, the testing of queuing discipline does not usually need separate test cases. It could be incorporated into the above test cases by observing both the arrival of jobs/items and the departure or processing of them. Of course, this would imply that each job or item can be uniquely identified and various static and dynamic information can be kept for it throughout the testing process. The result checking or the oracle problem in this case is closely associated with observing and analyzing both the handling of individual arrivals as well as the overall arrival/departure sequences.

One significant different between queuing testing and input domain boundary testing is the dynamic and continuous nature of the former as compared with the simple one-decision processing model of the latter. In fact, in performance evaluation and analysis of systems and networks, queuing at a single server or in a queuing network is typically supported and tested with a traffic generator based on measurement and characterization of normal operational traffic so that realistic operational conditions can be tested (Trivedi, 2001). This idea is similar to the usage measurement and usage-based statistical testing using Musa's operational profiles to ensure product reliability we discussed in Chapter 8.

9.5 CONCLUDING REMARKS

One of the most important areas where partition-based testing has made a strong impact is input domain testing, where the overall input domain is partitioned into sub-domains, and the associated boundaries as well as the sub-domains themselves are tested. The basic testing models are constructed based on the simple assumption that the input domain can be partitioned into sub-domains of equivalent classes. The information processing model is assumed to be a simple classify–and–process one, with input classified into sub-domains and processed accordingly, much like a "case–switch" structure in various programming languages. The models are often constructed based on external descriptions, resulting in black-box coverage-based testing. However, implemented decisions can often be consulted in model construction, in testing, and in problem analysis. Therefore, the input domain testing strategies need not be purely black-box.

Unlike the strategies for basic partition coverage in the previous chapter, we focus on the boundary problems between neighboring sub-domains. The types of problems that can usually be detected by boundary testing strategies generally include the following:

- Closure problems;

- Bound changes, most commonly boundary shift and boundary tilt;

- Extra or missing boundaries.

Because of these reasons, input domain or boundary testing is mostly applicable to the situations of well-defined input data, such as numerical processing. Testing for I/O relations, such as used in system testing, is also a common place for domain testing to be applied.

The most widely used and effective strategies include weak $N \times 1$ and weak 1×1 strategies, particularly the latter for economical reasons as well. For an n-dimensional sub-domain with b boundaries, weak 1×1 uses $2b+1$ test points; weak $N \times 1$ uses $(n+1) \times b+1$ test points; and extreme point combination (EPC) uses $4^n + 1$ test points. Other strong testing strategies also use significantly more testing points than corresponding weak ones. We summarize these testing strategies below:

- Weak 1×1 uses few test points and can detect most of the boundary problems most of the time. Therefore, it should be a primary candidate for boundary testing.

- When high quality requirements need to be met or specific types of problems that weak 1×1 cannot address are suspected, weak $N \times 1$ or other testing strategies can be selectively used.

- If inconsistencies exist in some boundaries, strong testing strategies can be used to select one set of test points for each boundary segment.

- When non-linear boundaries are involved, some approximate testing strategies can be used, where one set of test points is used for each segment in the linear approximations of non-linear boundaries.

In addition to its original applications in testing input domain partitions, the basic idea of boundary testing can be applied to other situations where a logical boundary exist between different information processing needs. One such concrete example is the queuing testing we described in Section 9.4, where the upper and lower bounds of the queue buffer can be tested. Additional examples of this nature will be included in Chapter 11, when we apply boundary testing ideas to testing loops.

There are some practical problems with various boundary testing strategies, particularly in the choice of OFF points and related ϵ-limits. OFF point selection for closed domain might extend into undefined territory to cause system crash if the system is not robust enough to guard against unexpected input. In addition, coincidental correctness is common. For example, when different processing gives same results, much of the basis for our problem detection is taken away. These testing strategies are also limited by their simple processing models for more complex interactions. We examine alternative testing strategies based on more complicated models in subsequent chapters.

Problems

9.1   Define the terms: input, input space, input vector, test point, input domain, domain partition, sub-domain, boundary, boundary point, interior point, exterior point, vertex point, under-defined point, over-defined point.

9.2   Give some concrete examples in drawing for the boundary problems in a 2-dimensional space.

9.3   Of the different boundary problems, which ones are observed most often at your work?

9.4   If we have three sub-domains defined by $f(x_1, x_2, \ldots, x_n) < K$, $f(x_1, x_2, \ldots, x_n) = K$, and $f(x_1, x_2, \ldots, x_n) > K$ respectively. Define the boundaries, and discuss how boundary problems would be different in this case.

9.5   So far, we have assumed that each sub-domain is connected. A disconnected sub-domain consists of several disconnected parts or regions. What would be the effect of disconnected sub-domains on boundary problems, and how would you perform boundary testing for them?

9.6   For some of the programs/projects your are working on, find some domain/sub-domain or boundary problems, apply the different boundary testing strategies described in this chapter, and discuss the result.

9.7   What are the EPC, Weak 1×1, and Weak $N \times 1$ testing points for a round sub-domain. (I.e., $(x - x_0)^2 + (y - y_0)^2 \leq r^2$.)

9.8   In the above example, non-linear boundary is used. Discuss the impact on the ability of different testing strategies to detect boundary problems for such non-linear boundaries.

9.9   Can you think of other possible applications of boundary testing idea not mentioned in Section 9.4?

CHAPTER 10

COVERAGE AND USAGE TESTING
BASED ON FINITE-STATE MACHINES
AND MARKOV CHAINS

There are many limitations with the testing techniques based on simple models, such as checklists, partitions, and trees, described in the previous two chapters. Program execution details, interactions among different parts of programs, as well as detailed usage information cannot be adequately represented in such simple models for testing. In this chapter, we introduce finite-state machines (FSMs) as the basis for various testing techniques, in particular:

- The basic concepts of FSMs are introduced in Section 10.1.

- The direct use of FSMs in testing to cover the modeled states is described in Section 10.2.

- A comprehensive case study to model web testing and web crawling using FSMs is presented in Section 10.3.

- The enhancement of FSMs into Markov chains and Unified Markov Models (UMMs) as usage models is described in Section 10.4.

- The usage based testing using Markov chains and UMMs is described in Section 10.5

- A comprehensive case study of statistical web testing based on UMMs is presented in Section 10.6.

As extensions to FSM-based testing that focus on interactions along execution paths and data dependencies, control flow and data flow testing techniques are covered in Chapter 11.

10.1   FINITE-STATE MACHINES AND TESTING

The basic idea of FSMs is to use an intermediate formalism to model the program execution or behavior that strikes a balance between expressive power and simplicity (Chow, 1978). At one extreme, lists and partitions covered in the previous two chapters provide simple processing models that may not be expressive enough to represent complex program executions and behavior. On the other hand, the actual implementation, or the programs themselves, contains too much detail that needs to be abstracted into models so that specific aspects or features can be analyzed and tested. FSMs lie in between these two extremes, and possess some flexibility in the level of details that can be modeled by the number of states, the number of links among them, and related input/output.

10.1.1   Overcoming limitations of simple processing models

The processing model used in the previous two chapters is a single stage one in the form of "input–process–output". Both the input and the output are associated with this single stage of processing. We focused on the input in test model construction and test case sensitization, while implicitly assuming that the corresponding output can be obtained and checked through some oracle. As extensions to the single stage processing model, we also introduced multi-stage ones such as the use of hierarchical lists, multi-dimensional lists, and tree-structured decision models. Some of the basic assumptions in those extensions include:

- There is a finite number of stages or lists.

- Each stage or list is unique, that is, no stage or list is a repetition of another.

- The final choices made through multiple stages or lists are uniquely determined by the items in each list involved or by the choices made at every stage.

Consequently, although multiple lists or multiple decision stages are involved, the final choices or complete operations can still be represented by a global one-level list or decision by collapsing the lists or stages. In the case of tree-structured processing model that can represent both hierarchical lists and graphical operational profiles in Chapter 8, there is always a unique path from the root to each leaf node. The whole paths associated with these leaf nodes represent the series of decisions or stages of processing. Therefore all the information can be represented at the leaf node, as in Figure 8.2 in Chapter 8. In the case of multi-dimensional lists, each individual choice can be represented as a point in the multi-dimensional space, such as in Table 8.2 in Chapter 8. All these points can be enumerated as long as there are finite dimensions and finite choices for each dimension.

However, we know in information processing, repetition or looping is a common way to handle various tasks, and the program behavior also shows repetition. It would be desirable under such situations to relax the unique stage or decision assumption above so that such repeated processing or behavior can also be modeled. This relaxation actually leads us to finite-state machines, if we do the following:

- We simply replace the above decision points associated with individual lists or processing stages by states.

- The selection of an individual list item or the processing decision can be replaced by a stage or state transition.

- Looping back to some list or stage is allowed from any state.

Such models can be formalized and used to precisely specify the behavior and interactions for many systems and components and serve as the basis for testing. In addition, many of the sub-operations within end-to-end operations specified in checklists or associated with partitions may be in common. The construction of FSMs could highlight these commonly used core sub-operations. The use of FSMs could lead to more effective testing by focusing on these core sub-operations and their connections to the rest of the system operations. Similarly, more economical testing could also be achieved by avoiding exact repetition of some of these common sub-operations.

10.1.2 FSMs: Basic concepts and examples

Finite-state machines (FSMs) are standard models in the basic studies of computer science. There are four basic elements for FSMs, which can be grouped into two subsets:

- *Static elements*: The subset of static elements includes *states* and *state transitions*. The state transitions are often referred to as just transitions. The number of states is finite. By not allowing duplicate transitions from one state to another, that is, a direct transition from state A to state B can only follow a unique link labeled A-B, the number of state transitions is also finite.

- *Dynamic elements*: The subset of dynamic elements includes the *input* provided to the FSMs and the *output* generated from the FSMs in dynamic executions of the FSMs. In general, both the number of different input and the number of different output are also finite. In the case that such input and output may take a large number or an infinite number of values, we generally need to group them into partitions, much like what we did in checklist and partition based testing in Chapter 8. These finite groups or partitions will correspond to transitions from one state to another. Therefore, they form some special types of equivalence classes.

At any time, the system can be in one state or in transition from one state to another. If we ignore the transition time, the system is in exactly one state at any time — in what we call the "current" state. If the output and the next state are both uniquely determined by the current state and the input, we call it a "deterministic" FSM. We first deal with testing based on deterministic FSMs in this chapter, with non-deterministic or probabilistic FSMs used in Section 10.4 for usage-based testing.

The FSMs and their elements are typically represented graphically. The main graphical elements include:

- Each state is represented as a node in a graph.

- Each transition is represented as a directed link from one state to another.

- Input and output are associated with state transitions, and are represented as link weights or annotations by the transitions.

The above representation is called the Mealy model (Mealy, 1955). An alternative model is to represent each output as a state, resulting in the so-called Moore model (Moore, 1956). We use Mealy model in this book primarily for its simplicity in reducing the number of states.

So far, we have not directly dealt with the question: "What is represented by a state in FSMs?". The answer depends on what we want to model. Most commonly, a state corresponds to some program execution state, or a specific time period or instance between certain actions. For example, consider the following execution sequence:

- When a program starts, it is in the "initial" state.

- After performing a user-oriented function (black-box view), or executing a statement or an internal procedure (white-box view), the program execution is transitioned to another state.

- The above step can be repeated a number of times, with some of the states possibly repeated as well.

- The state where program execution terminates is called the "final" state.

- In each of the transitions, some input might be needed, and some output might be produced.

In the above example, the states represent some abstraction of execution status or states, and most of the operations are associated with the links or state transitions. A concrete example familiar to almost everyone in modern society is the use of the world wide web (WWW or simply the web): Each web page a user is viewing can be considered a state. When we start a web browser, the default starting page or our customized starting page will be loaded, which corresponds to the initial state. Each time we follow a link in a page or specifically request a page through the use of bookmark/favorite selections or by directly typing in a URL (universal resource locator, or the unique address for a specific web page), we start a transition to another web page. We can stop anytime by exiting the web browser, or implicitly by no longer requesting pages. This last page visited is then the final state. In this example of web usage, most of the operations such as requesting and loading a page, as well as the related error or other messages, are associated with the transitions. The FSM states are clearly visible to the users and represent the main purpose of using the web.

Alternatively, various individual operations, functions, or tasks can be represented by the states, and the transitions merely indicate their logical connections or precedence relations. For example, the flow-charts commonly used in product design, program implementation, and program analysis are examples of this type. We will see many examples of such FSMs when we discuss control flow testing in Chapter 11.

In many applications, a mixture of the above two types of FSMs can be used as long as there is no confusion. A concrete example of FSM of this type is Figure 10.1 that depicts the states and state transitions for call processing in a cellular communication system (TIA/EIA, 1994; Garg, 1999). Specific information includes:

- Specific states related to different operations or system status are identified, for example, "Power-up", "Mobile Station Initialization", "Mobile Station Idle", etc., and are identified by their labels A, B, C, D, E, respectively.

- Some transitions are not associated with any input (null input) or output (null output). They simply follow after the completion of the task associated with the current state. In such cases, there is usually only one possible transition, because otherwise specific input or conditions will be needed to specify which allowable transition to take. For example, after state A (Power-up), the next state to follow is always B (MS

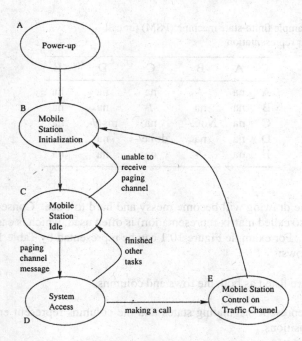

Figure 10.1   An example finite-state machine (FSM) for call processing

Initialization). Similarly, after state B the next state to follow is always C (MS Idle); and state E (Mobile Station Control on Traffic Channel) is always followed by state B. In general, such transitions are not associated with any processing but only a logical relation between the states, just like "is-followed-by" relation in control flow graphs in Chapter 11.

- Other transitions in Figure 10.1 are associated with specific messages or conditions as input and some possible output. For example, the states to follow C (MS Idle) could be D (System Access), associated with receiving a paging channel message requiring response, originating a call, or performing registration. State B (MS Initialization) could also follow C for the condition that MS is unable to receive paging channel. Similarly, State D can be followed by state E (Mobile Station Control on Traffic Channel) if a call is originated, or followed by state B if other System Access tasks are completed.

10.1.3 Representations of FSMs

The most intuitive and most straightforward way to represent FSMs is to use graphical means, such as in Figure 10.1. As we know from graph theory (Deo, 1974), such graphs can also be formally specified as a set of states, a set of allowable state transitions, and associated input/output. For example, the set of states corresponding to Figure 10.1 is {A, B, C, D, E}. The transition from C to B is represented as {C, B, "unable to receive paging channel", –}, with input as specified by the third element and null output (–). The set of state transitions and input/output includes this and other similar items as its elements.

Although the graphical representation is intuitive and easy to interpret by human subjects, it becomes impractical when the number of states becomes large. When we have more than

Table 10.1   An example finite-state machine (FSM) for call processing in tabular representation

	A	B	C	D	E
A	na	-/-	na	na	na
B	na	na	-/-	na	na
C	na	NoC/-	na	msg/-	na
D	na	na	done/-	na	call/-
E	na	-/-	na	na	na

20 or 30 states, the drawing will become messy and hard to trace. Consequently, tabular representation (also called matrix representation) is often used, which is easy for computer to process as well. For example Figure 10.1 can be represented by Table 10.1 that can be interpreted as follows:

- The states are listed as both the rows and columns.

- The rows represent originating states and the columns represent ending states for specific transitions.

- If a transition from state X (row X) to state Y (column Y) is allowed, then the corresponding cell (row X, column Y) is marked by its input and output. A null input or a null output is marked by "–". For the specific input conditions or messages in Table 10.1, we used shorthands msg, NoC, call, and done to represent "paging channel message", "unable to receive paging channel", "making a call", and "finished with other tasks", respectively.

- If a cell is marked with "na" or not marked (left empty), the corresponding transition is not allowed.

As we can see, the tabular representation is systematic, regular (an $N \times N$ table), and not too hard to interpret. Therefore, it is used quite commonly to represent FSMs. The regularity makes computation and analysis based on tabular FSMs easy to perform.

However, when there are many empty cells, we end up wasting a lot of memory space to store the $N \times N$ table. Consequently, a third commonly used representation, what we call the list representation, is directly based on the formal specification for the graphs in graph theory formalisms (Deo, 1974). Basically, the set of states is represented by a list; and the set of allowable state transitions is also represented by a list, with its elements in the form of {C, B, "unable to receive paging channel", –} that we mentioned above. The list representation is more compact but less regular. The comparison between the list and tabular representations is similar to the comparison between the list and 2-dimensional array data structures in computing and information processing: The trade off is between storage savings for lists and faster indexed access for arrays.

All three types of representations of FSMs, graphical, tabular, and list, are commonly used in testing literature. Therefore, the readers should become familiar with all three, possibly through some additional exercises interpreting and converting among them. In what follows, we primarily use graphical representation to make it easy to present and illustrate the basic ideas and techniques.

10.2   FSM TESTING: STATE AND TRANSITION COVERAGE

We next examine the basic FSM-based testing that attempts to achieve basic coverage of states and transitions as the basic elements of FSMs, and using related input and output for test sensitization and result checking.

10.2.1   Some typical problems with systems modeled by FSMs

As mentioned above, FSMs can be used to model either external system behavior (black-box view) or detailed execution of specific implementations (white-box view). In either view, we can consider the four basic elements, namely, states, transitions, input, and output, to examine possible and likely problems of systems modeled by FSMs, as follows:

- *State problems*: missing, extra, or incorrect states:

  - An incorrect state is one with ill-defined behavior.

  - A missing state corresponds to one that has a valid current state and input but the next state is missing. A special case of the missing state is that the system with unspecified initial state.

  - Extra state may be related to unreachable state or dead state, where there is no path from any initial state to it through a number of state transitions. Multiple next states for the same input may also be linked to some extra states. In this case, the current state is also an incorrect state because its behavior is ill-defined.

- *Transition problems*: missing, extra, or incorrect transitions;

  - A missing transition is one that corresponds to a valid current state and input but the next state is missing or not specified.

  - An extra transition is associated with multiple transitions for the same current state and input.

  - An incorrect transition is a transition to an unexpected state or one that produces unexpected output.

- *Input problems*: In FSM-based testing, we typically treat input problems as part of state or transition problems, assuming that all input needs to be handled correctly through some state transitions by the FSM. As a general extension, even invalid input is expected to be handled correctly without causing system crash or other problems, such as through the following means:

  - ignoring invalid input, such as staying in the same state for invalid input.

  - direct handling of invalid input, such as outputting some error message and going through some exception handling and related state transitions.

- *Output problems*: We do not typically deal with output problems directly, but rather as part of the test oracle problem in state transitions. For example, if a state transition produces unexpected output, such as missing, extra, or incorrect output, we identify the transition as an incorrect transition.

Therefore, in FSM-based testing, we focus on state and transition problems. Input is primarily used for test sensitization, and output is primarily used for result checking.

10.2.2 Model construction and checking for missing or extra states or transitions

During model construction, all the basic elements of the FSMs need to be identified, including states, transitions, input, and output. Following the generic steps for test model construction in the test preparation activities we outlined in Chapter 7, some self-checking or model validation is usually needed to make sure the model reflects reality. Therefore, checking for missing or extra states or transitions is usually carried out as part of the model construction process, in particular, as part of model validation step in this process.

Instantiating and expanding the generic steps for model construction we described in Chapter 7, we can construct FSMs and validate them in the following steps:

- *Step 1. Information source identification and data collection*: Depending on whether external functional behavior is modeled (black-box view) or internal program execution states are modeled (white-box view) in FSMs, we can identify different sources of information. In the former case, the information sources include external product specification or expected usage scenarios. They represent functional and logical relations between different subsets of operations and interfaces. In the latter case, internal product information, such as structure and connections of the implemented components in product design documents and the program code can be used for model construction. For many existing products, existing test cases and checklists can also be used as an important source of information. The sub-operations need to be extracted from such existing sources and linked together to form FSMs.

- *Step 2. Construction of initial FSMs* based on the information sources identified in Step 1 above: We next consider the four basic elements, namely, states, transitions, input, and output, to construct the initial FSMs. Some of the elements are considered together for convenience in the following steps:

  - *Step 2.1. State identification and enumeration*: We need to keep the number of states to a manageable level, ranging from a handful to a few dozens, but not thousands. In cases where the real system needs to be represented by a large number of states, we can use nested or hierarchical FSMs, as we will describe in further detail in model refinement below.

  - *Step 2.2. Transition identification with the help of input values*: For each state, we can consider all the possible transitions in connection with all the possible input values. As mentioned in Section 10.1, when the number of possible input values is large or infinite, we can use input partitions to help identify specific transitions. These partitions represent equivalence classes defined with respect to the state transitions to be taken. Another side effect of this step is to identify some missing states from Step 2.1 above, where some transitions lead to states other than those already identified above.

  - *Step 2.3. Identifying input-output relations* related to individual transitions. This output will be used as part of the test oracle to check the testing results.

- *Step 3. Model refinement and validation*: This step includes two interconnected activities. In the process of validating the initial FSM, new states and/or new transitions might be identified, resulting in the refinement of the FSM. However, as we mentioned above, this process cannot be carried to excess, to include too many states and transitions in the FSM. Consequently, when large numbers of states and transitions need to be represented in a model, we typically use nested or hierarchical FSMs, with some of the specific states in the higher-level FSMs expandable to lower-level FSMs. This issue is examined further at the end of this section. We can also check the information sources to identify missing or extra states or transitions as part of the model validation exercise. This issue is elaborated below.

The basic idea for identifying missing states or transitions is similar to checklist- and partition-based testing. For example, a checklist based on product functional specifications can be used to directly check the missing states or transitions. However, such functional specifications usually correspond to high-level states and state transitions, which need to be refined to the same level of the states and transitions captured by the FSMs. For lower-level FSMs, product design information and documents, or program code, can usually be used to help identify missing states or transitions.

Checking for extra states and transitions can follow essentially the same procedure by cross-validating them with the information sources. However, this checking is typically more difficult than identifying missing ones, similar to the situation that requires product requirement traceability: If every state and every transition can be traced back to the corresponding information sources for their creation, this checking can be done easily. However, one should not expect complete documentation associated with every state or transition to be included in the FSMs. This fact makes it hard to identify extra states and transitions if we don't know what led to their creation in the first place. As an alternative to this procedure of checking for extra states or transitions, we can perform reachability analysis to identify individual unreachable states or clusters of unreachable states. Usually, these unreachable states or clusters represent extra states or some other problems. The reachability analysis algorithms from graph theory (Deo, 1974; Knuth, 1973) and related tools can be used to perform such analyses.

In addition to the above methods of checking the missing or extra states and transitions, sometimes, they can also be checked together with incorrect ones. To actually test the states and transitions, we need to start from an initial state or from an intermediate current state saved in some means, and then follow a series of transitions to test the correct state that we try to reach and the correct transitions we try to follow.

10.2.3 Testing for correct states and transitions

The general testing based on FSMs and the particular checking of correct states and correct transitions can be treated as two separate problems:

- *State or node coverage*: We need to make sure that each state can be reached and visited by some test cases. This is essentially a state or node traversal problem in graph theory (Deo, 1974; Knuth, 1973). Consequently, various graph node traversal algorithms can be used to help us with the development of test cases.

- *Transition or link coverage*: We need to make sure that each link or state transition is covered by some test cases. Although this problem can also be treated as link traversal in graph theory, the above state coverage testing already helped us reach each reachable states. It would be more economical to combine the visit to these states with the possible input values to cover all the links or transitions originated from this current state.

In trying to reach a specific state, each test case is essentially a series of input values that enables us to make the transitions from an initial state to some target state, possibly through multiple hops by way of some intermediate states. It is possible that one test case could potentially enable us to visit all the states thus achieving complete state coverage. However, we need multiple test cases under most circumstances because there might be multiple initial states, multiple final states, and multiple sequences of transitions leading from an initial state to a specific state. In most systems modeled by FSMs, the initial states are the ones without incoming links and the final states are the ones without outgoing links. Under such circumstances, whenever multiple initial or final states exist, we would need at least as many test cases, and most likely much more.

From the current state, the next state to visit is determined by the input. Therefore, this one-step state transition can be viewed as first classifying the input into equivalence classes and then follow a specific transition according to the classification. With our knowledge for checklist- and partition-based testing in Chapter 8 and its special cases of input domain boundary testing in Chapter 9, we can easily perform link coverage starting from each state that we can reach. The one-step "classify-and-process" model from the current state to the next state fits perfectly with the processing model we used for those testing techniques. All the input variables and associated values, as well as input domain partitioning in correspondence to the specific transitions to take, can be examined to derive our test cases as described in those chapters.

Test case sensitization for FSM-based testing is fairly easy and straightforward. For each test case of state coverage, we have a specific initial state and a series of state transitions to lead to a target state. Since each transition is associated with specific input values, we can simply select such input values to sensitize the test case. The key in this sensitization is to remember that in FSM-modeled systems, input and output are associated with individual transitions instead of as an indistinguishable lump of initial input for many other systems. Consequently, the input sequencing is as important as correct values for the specific input.

For link coverage, the testing we described above is essentially the same as partition-based input domain testing. We can follow the corresponding techniques to achieve partition coverage, or if necessary, to test the boundary conditions related to these partitions. The test sensitization issues are also the same as in those testing techniques described in Chapters 8 and 9.

One useful capability for test execution is the ability to save some "current state" that can be restored when we start testing. This would significantly shorten the series of state transitions needed to reach a target state, which may be important because in some systems these transitions may take a long time. This capability is especially useful for link coverage testing starting from a specific state: If we can start from this saved state, we can go directly into link coverage testing without waiting for the state transitions to reach this state from a specific initial state.

The result checking is similarly easy and straightforward, since the output for each transition is also specified in FSMs in addition to the next state. The key to this result checking is to make sure that both the next state and the output are checked.

10.2.4 Applications and limitations

The most common application domain for FSM-based testing is the menu-driven software, where each menu demands some input and produces some output that is often accompanied by a new menu. This situation with interactive input is also different from various more autonomous systems where mostly an initial set of input is required but little or no interaction with the user is needed. A special case of menu-driven software is the use of the web that we will examine in more detail in Section 10.3.

FSM-based testing is generally suitable for systems with clearly identifiable states and state transitions. The situation covers various real-time systems, control systems, and systems that operate continuously. In many of these systems, it is more common to relate various system properties, such as status, controllability, safety, etc., to the current system states than to the beginning or end of systems operations. Related protocols for such systems can also be easily specified as FSMs and tested accordingly. Our example of call processing given in Figure 10.1 is an example of such systems.

Another area where FSM-based testing has received significant attention is the testing of object-oriented software and systems (OOS). Object-state testing typically resembles FSM testing, with some specific customization (Binder, 2000; Kung et al., 1998). There are various other application domains, such as device drivers, software for installation, backup and recovery, and software that replaces certain hardware (Beizer, 1995).

The primary limitation of FSM-based testing is its inability to handle large number of states. Although nested or hierarchical FSMs can help alleviate the problems, they have their own limitations in assuming clear-cut hierarchies: In lower-level models, we general assume a common source and common sink as its interface with higher-level models. However, the interactions may well be cutting through hierarchy boundaries in real systems. For large software products, the complete coverage of all these hierarchical FSMs would still be impractical because of the size as well as the generally uneven distribution of problems and usage frequencies in different areas and product components. Selective testing focused on highly used operations or product components can be supported by extending FSMs with usage information to form Markov chains and using them for statistical usage-based testing, as we describe in Section 10.4.

10.3 CASE STUDY: FSM-BASED TESTING OF WEB-BASED APPLICATIONS

Web-based applications provide cross-platform universal access to web resources for the massive user population. With the prevalence of the world wide web (WWW), testing and quality assurance for the web is becoming increasingly important. We next examine the characteristics of the web and discuss the use of FSM-models for web testing.

10.3.1 Characteristics of web-based applications

Web applications possess various unique characteristics that affect the choices of appropriate techniques for web testing. One of the fundamental differences is the *document and information focus* for the web as compared to the computational focus for most traditional software. Although some computational capability has evolved in newer web applications, document and information search and retrieval still remain the dominant usage for most web users. In addition, navigational facility is a central part of web-based applications, with the most commonly used HTML (hyper-text markup language) documents play a central role in providing both information and navigational links. In this respect, web-based applications resemble many menu-driven software products. However, there are also some significant differences, as follows:

- Traditional menu-driven software still focuses on some computation; while web-based applications focus on information and documents.

| Client – Web Browsers |
| Web Server |
| Middleware |
| Database – Backend |

Figure 10.2   Multi-layered web applications

- Traditional menu-driven software usually separates its navigation from its computation; while the two are tightly mingled for web-based applications.

- In traditional menu-driven software, there is usually a single top menu that serves as the entry point; while for web-based applications, potentially any web page or web content can be the starting point. These entry or starting points typically correspond to initial states in an FSM. Similar differences exist for the end points or final states, with traditional menu-driven software having limited exits while web-based applications typically can end at any point when the user chooses to exit the web browser or stop web browsing activities.

- Another significant difference is the qualitative difference in the huge number of navigational pages of web-based applications even for moderately sized web sites and the limited number of menus for all traditional menu-driven applications.

- Web-based applications typically involve much more diverse support facilities than traditional menu-driven software. Web functionalities are typically distributed across multiple layers and subsystems as illustrated in Figure 10.2. We need to make sure all these functionalities and related components work well together, to eliminate failure sources or to reduce failure chances.

Similar to general testing, testing for web applications focuses on the prevention of web failures or the reduction of chances for such failures. Therefore, we need to examine the common problems and associated concepts such as web failures, faults, and errors, before we can proceed with the selection of appropriate testing techniques to identify and remove these problems and problems sources.

10.3.2   What to test: Characteristics of web problems

We define web failures as inability to correctly deliver information or documents required by web users. This definition also conforms to the standard definition of failures as the behavioral deviations from user expectations (correct delivery expected by web users) we outlined in Chapter 2. Based on this definition, we can consider the following failure sources:

- *Host or network failures:* Hardware or systems failures at the destination host or home host, as well as network failures, may lead to web failures. These failures are mostly linked to middleware and web server layers in Figure 10.2. However, such failures are no different from the regular system or network failures, and can be analyzed by existing techniques.

- *Browser failures:* Browser failures are linked to problems at the highest layer in Figure 10.2 on the client side. These failures can be treated the same way as software product failures, thus existing techniques for software testing can be used.

- *Source or content failures:* Web failures can also be caused by the information source itself at the server side, associated with the lowest layer in Figure 10.2.

In addition, user errors may also cause problems, which can be addressed through user education, better usability design, etc. The host, network, and browser failures mentioned above can be addressed by the "global" web community using existing techniques. However, web source or content failures are typically directly related to the services or functions that web-based applications are trying to provide. In addition, although usability is one of the primary concerns for novice web users, reliability is increasingly become a primary concern for sophisticated web users (Vatanasombut et al., 2004). Therefore, we will focus on web source failures and trying to ensure *reliability* of such web-based applications from a user's perspective in this case study. Related web components (Miller, 2000) include the following:

- *HTML document*, still the most common form for documents on the web.

- *Java, JavaScript, and ActiveX* commonly used to support platform independent executions.

- *Cgi-Bin Scripts* used to pass data or perform some other activities.

- *Database*, a major part of the backend.

- *Multi-media components* used to present and process multi-media information.

We need to ensure the functionality, performance, reliability, usability, etc. of these web components and their applications. To do this, various types of existing web testing can be performed (Bowers, 1996; Bachiochi et al., 1997; Fromme, 1998; Miller, 2000), including: functionality testing, load and stress testing, browser rendering, and usability testing. However, such testing typically focus on a small area or a specific aspect of the web quality problems. We next describe the use of FSMs in web testing to ensure the overall satisfactory performance from the user's perspective for the operational usage scenarios and sequences.

10.3.3 FSMs for web testing

From the web user's point of view, each web-based application or function consists of various components, stages, or steps, visible to the web users, and typically initiated by them. Consequently, state transition based FSMs models are appropriate for this kind of applications. We next consider the four basic elements of FSMs and map them to web-based applications:

- Each web page corresponds to a state in an FSM. Potentially any page can be the initial state and any page can be the final state.

- State transitions correspond to web navigations following hypertext links embedded in HTML documents and other web contents. One special case is that a user may choose to follow a previous saved link (bookmarked favorites) or to directly type a

URL (universal resource locator, the address of a specific page). The use of these latter navigation tools makes state transitions more unpredictable. However, there are also two factors worth noting in modeling web navigations as state transitions in FSMs:

- From the point of view of Internet- and web-based service providers, it is more important to ensure that the "official" contents on the providers web site are correct than to ensure that the user's bookmarks or typed URLs are up-to-date or correct.

- There is empirical evidence to show that the vast majority of web navigations are following embedded hypertext links instead of using bookmarked or typed URLs. For example, for the www.seas.smu.edu web site studied in (Ma and Tian, 2003), 75.84% of the navigations are originated from embedded links within the same web site, only 12.42% are user originated, and the rest from external and other links.

Consequently, we choose to focus on the embedded navigation links and capture them in FSMs for web testing.

- The input and output associated with such navigations are fairly simple and straightforward: The input is the clicking of the embedded link shown as highlighted content; and the corresponding output is the loading of the requested page or content with accompanying messages indicating the HTML status, error or other messages, etc.

Existing techniques that attempt to "cover" certain aspects can still be used, but at a lower level than the FSM-based testing. For example, syntax and form testing can still be performed on individual pages and Java testing can be performed for Java components. Link checking can be considered as part of this FSM-based testing for transition coverage, but not based on formal models. The overall FSMs can guide the overall testing of the web navigations. In fact, web robots used by various Internet search engines or index services commonly "crawl" the web by systematically following the embedded hypertext links to create indexes or databases of the overall web contents. This crawling is very much like the state traversal for FSMs, with appropriate graph node traversal algorithm typically used.

There is one obvious drawback to web testing using such FSMs: the number of web pages for even a moderate-sized web site can be thousands or much more. Consequently, there would be significant numbers of states in these FSMs, which makes any detailed testing beyond simple indexing impractical, even with some automated support. In fact, even such simple indexing by the most powerful robot for major web search engines or index sites only cover a small percentage of the entire web. On the other hand, as a general rule, usage and problem distribution among different software components is highly uneven, which is also demonstrated to be true among different web contents (Li and Tian, 2003). Consequently, some kind of selective testing is needed to focus on highly-used and problematic areas to ensure maximal web site reliability improvement, such as through usage-based statistical testing we discuss next.

10.4 MARKOV CHAINS AND UNIFIED MARKOV MODELS FOR TESTING

Parallel to the situation with the use of flat or Musa's operational profiles (OPs) for usage-based statistical testing using partitions, we can also augment FSMs with probabilistic usage information so that usage scenarios and navigation sequences commonly used by target customers can be tested more thoroughly than the less frequently used ones. The use of this approach would help us ensure and maximize product reliability from a customer's perspective. Such augmented FSMs are our OPs, which typically form Markov chains, to be described in this section.

10.4.1 Markov chains and operational profiles

For large systems, the state explosion problem (massive number of states in FSMs) calls for selective testing instead complete coverage. As a basic assumption for usage-based testing, if some functions or components are used more often, the likelihood that an underlying fault is going to be triggered through such usage is also higher. Therefore, we need to focus on those highly used parts in the FSMs. Both the need for selective testing to deal with the size problem and the need for focused testing of highly used FSM parts can be supported by augmented FSMs in the form of Markov chains. The use of Markov chains in usage-based statistical testing also allows us to obtain realistic and meaningful evaluation of system reliability under an environment that resembles the actual usage environment by the target customers. The additional information for the FSMs is the probabilities associated with different state transitions that satisfy the following property:

- From the current state $X_n = i$ at time n or stage n, the probability of state transition to state $X_{n+1} = j$ for the next time period or stage $n + 1$ is denoted as p_{ij}, which is independent of the history, that is,

$$P\{X_{n+1} = j | X_n = i, X_{n-1} = s_{n-1}, \ldots, X_0 = s_0\}$$
$$= P\{X_{n+1} = j | X_n = i, \}$$
$$= p_{ij}.$$

In other words, the probability that the system will be in state j only depends on the current state i and the history-independent transition probability p_{ij}. Equivalently, the complete history is summarized in the current state, thus removing the need to look back into the past history to determine the next transition to take. This property is call the memoryless, Markov, or Markovian property in stochastic processes (Karlin and Taylor, 1975).

- Since p_{ij}'s are probabilities, they also obey the following equations:

$$0 \leq p_{ij} \leq 1, \quad \text{and} \quad \sum_j p_{ij} = 1.$$

- If the above conditions hold for every state in an FSM, the FSM forms a Markov chain. Although there are also other types of Markov chains, such as continuous time and infinite-state ones (Karlin and Taylor, 1975), we restrict our attentions to the ones based on our FSMs: Current state is associated with a stage of the FSM but not necessarily associated with fixed amount of time within the state, and state transition may take unspecified time to complete. In the context that we use it for usage-based statistical testing, this Markov chain is also called a Markov OP, because it constitutes the specific operational profile (OP) for the system.

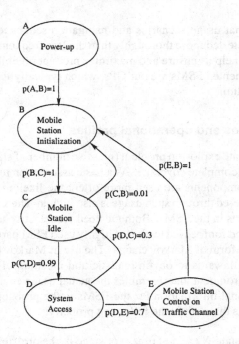

Figure 10.3   Example Markov chain for call processing FSM in Figure 10.1

Figure 10.3 is a sample Markov chain enhanced from the FSM in Figure 10.1. The transitions here are probabilistic instead of deterministic. Specific messages or conditions in the corresponding FSM are augmented with the associated probability. For example, after state B the next state to follow is always C, as represented by the transition probability of $p(B, C) = 1$. While the states to follow C could be D, with probability $p(C, D) = 0.99$ for the normal case, or B, with probability $p(C, B) = 0.01$ for the rare occasion that MS is unable to receive paging channel. Notice that we omitted the input/output information in such Markov OPs to keep the illustration simple, with the understanding that the input/output information is available for us to sensitize testing.

10.4.2 From individual Markov chains to unified Markov models

Statistical testing using Markov chains started with (Mills, 1972), which was integrated with formal verification to create Cleanroom technology (Mills et al., 1987b), and formalized later (Whittaker and Poore, 1993; Whittaker and Thomason, 1994). Recently, hierarchical Markov chains in a framework called unified Markov models (UMMs) to support statistical testing, performance evaluation, and reliability improvement were developed (Tian and Lin, 1998; Tian and Nguyen, 1999; Kallepalli and Tian, 2001; Tian et al., 2003; Tian et al., 2004). In what follows, we focus on the use of UMMs to support effective and flexible statistical usage-based testing.

The usage information is represented in UMMs as a set of hierarchical Markov chains. For example, the top-level Markov chain in UMMs for call processing in a cellular communication network is represented in Figure 10.3. However, various sub-operations may be associated with each individual state in the top-level Markov chain, and could be modeled by more detailed Markov chains, such as the Markov chain in Figure 10.4 for expanded

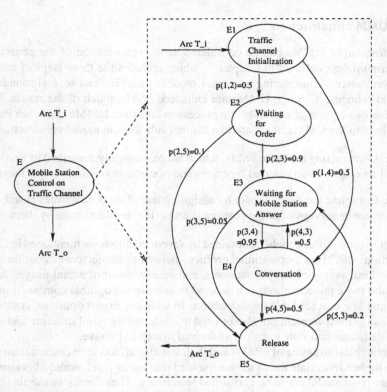

Figure 10.4 Example UMM (unified Markov model): Expanding state E of the top-level UMM in Figure 10.3 into a lower-level UMM

state E. Notice that in some of these Markov chains, the sum of probabilities for transitions out from a given state may be less than 1, because the external destinations (and sources) are omitted to keep the models simple. The implicit understanding in UMMs is that the missing probabilities go to external destinations.

Such UMMs make it easy to model individual operational units and link them together to form the global operations. The higher-level operations can be expanded into lower-level models for more thorough testing. Therefore, they are more suitable for large systems with complex operational scenarios and sequences than Musa's OPs we described in Chapter 8 or deterministic FSMs described earlier in this chapter. This hierarchical structure and the associated flexibility that can be tailored to multi-purpose applications set this approach apart from earlier approaches to statistical testing using Markov chains.

Each state or transition represents an individual operation, workload, or execution stage. They form the building blocks for the end-to-end operations by following the probabilistic state transitions. We will focus on the use of UMMs in testing in Section 10.5, with some discussion on reliability analysis and improvement covered in Chapter 22. For practical implementations, predefined procedures and automated tools can be used to support information gathering, model construction, measurement collection, and result analysis, which we discuss next.

10.4.3   UMM construction

The construction of UMMs can be considered as the instantiation of the general model construction process outlined in Chapter 7, which includes the three steps of identifying information sources, constructing the initial model or models, and several rounds of validation and refinement. Since UMMs are enhanced FSMs, much of the results for FSM construction can be reused as part of the process to construct UMMs. For each individual Markov chain in the UMMs, there are two distinct sub-steps in model construction:

Step M1: Constructing the basic FSMs, which we have already described in Section 10.2, with an emphasis on external functions and operations visible to target users.

Step M2: Complete the usage model by assigning transition probabilities based on measurement or surveys of target customers and actual product usage by them.

   Transition probabilities could be obtained by several methods we mentioned in Chapter 8 in connection with Musa's operational profiles, including: Subjective evaluation based on *expert opinions*, *survey* of target customers, and *measurement* of actual usage. A combination of the these three methods can be used to achieve the optimal combination of high accuracy and low cost for UMM construction. In addition, expert opinions, customer surveys, and usage measurement can also be used to confirm the overall structure and elements of the FSMs (states and state transitions) derived in step M1 above.

   The hierarchical structure of UMMs and their use also affects their construction process: Not every higher-level state needs to be expanded into lower-level models, because testing using lower-level model are to be performed selectively. Therefore, a threshold should be set up so that only the ones above it need to be expanded with their corresponding lower-level UMMs constructed. In the case that the usage is expected to fluctuate, we might need to use a lower threshold so that more candidate models of lower-level can be constructed to handle different usage situations. However, there should be a balance between the number of UMMs and the flexibility depending on the specific application environment.

10.5   USING UMMS FOR USAGE-BASED STATISTICAL TESTING

We next describe the use of UMMs in usage-based statistical testing and illustrate them with some concrete examples.

10.5.1   Testing based on usage frequencies in UMMs

Test cases can be generated by following the states and state transitions in UMMs to select individual operational units (states) and link them together (transitions) to form overall end-to-end operations. Possible test cases with probabilities above or at specific thresholds can be generated to cover frequently used operations. In practical applications, thresholds can be adjusted to control the numbers of test cases to be generated and executed. For example, we can start with a high threshold to test only the most frequently used operations, and gradually lower the threshold to cover more distinct situations and ensure satisfactory performance and reliability for a wider variety of operations. Several thresholds have been initially proposed (Avritzer and Weyuker, 1995) and used in developing UMMs (Tian and Lin, 1998; Kallepalli and Tian, 2001). In this book, we use three kind of thresholds for usage-based statistical testing, including:

- *Overall probability threshold* for complete end-to-end operations to ensure that commonly used complete operation sequences by target customers are covered and adequately tested.

- *Stationary probability threshold* to ensure that frequently visited states are covered and adequately tested.

- *Transition probability threshold* to ensure commonly used operation pairs, their interconnections and interfaces are covered and adequately tested.

To use the overall probability threshold, the probability for possible test cases (or complete operations) need be calculated can compared to this threshold. For example, the probability of the sequence ABCDEBCDC in Figure 10.3 can be calculated as the products of its transitions, that is,

$$1 \times 1 \times 0.99 \times 0.7 \times 1 \times 1 \times 0.99 \times 0.3 = 0.205821.$$

If this is above the overall end-to-end probability threshold, this test case will be selected and executed.

If the Markov chain is stationary, it can reach an equilibrium or become "stationary" (Karlin and Taylor, 1975). In such a state, the stationary probability π_i for being in state i remains the same before and after state transitions over time. The set $\{\pi_i\}$ can be obtained by solving the following set of equations:

$$\pi_j = \sum_i \pi_i p_{ij}, \quad \pi_i \geq 0, \quad \text{and} \quad \sum_i \pi_i = 1,$$

where p_{ij} is the transition probability from state i to state j. The stationary probability π_i indicates the relative frequency of visits to a specific state i after the Markov chain reaches this equilibrium. Therefore, testing states above a given threshold is to focus on frequently used individual operations or system states. For the many Markov chains that are not stationary (Karlin and Taylor, 1975), the same idea of focused testing can still be used by approximating stationary probabilities with the recorded relative frequencies of visit.

A mirror case to test states with stationary probabilities above a given threshold is to test links with transition probabilities above a given threshold. In this case, the testing is actually much easier to perform, because all the p_{ij}'s are specified in the UMMs. A larger value of p_{ij} indicates a commonly used operations (if we associate individual operations with transitions) or operational pairs (if we associate individual operations with states) in the sense that whenever i is reached, j is likely to follow.

Some combinations of these thresholds could also be used if they make sense for some specialized situations. For example, if state i is visited very infrequently (low π_i), then even larger values of p_{ij} may not be that meaningful if state j is not tightly connected as the destination of other links (that is, low p_{kj}, $k \neq i$). In this example, we would combine stationary probability threshold with link probability threshold to select our test cases.

10.5.2 Testing based on other criteria and UMM hierarchies

Coverage, importance and other information or criteria may also be used to generate test cases. In a sense, we need to generate test cases to reduce the risks involved in different usage scenarios and product components, and sometimes to identify such risks as well (Frankl and Weyuker, 2000). The direct risks involved in selective testing including missing important areas or not covering them adequately. These "important" areas can be characterized by various external or internal information, as discussed below.

As a basic principle, all implemented functions or sub-functions should at least be covered once and found to be satisfactory before product release. This coverage requirement can be handled similarly by adjusting the probabilities to ensure that all things we would like to cover stays above a certain threshold, or by adjusting our test case selection procedures.

In addition to the coverage requirement, some critical functions of low usage frequencies also must be thoroughly tested because of the severe consequences if faults exist in them. For example, some recovery procedures may have little chance of being invoked in customer settings, but they still need to be adequately tested because of the critical role they play in emergency situations. Similar adjustments as above can be used to ensure such test cases are generated, selected, and executed.

In general, importance information can be used in conjunction to usage frequencies to establish various probabilities or weights, as we have already seen in the case study of usage-based testing in Chapter 8. The same idea can be carried over to UMMs, weighing link probabilities accordingly. The importance information can be obtained by consulting product experts. In addition, the complexity of the implemented components may also influence the choice of functions or sub-functions to test. Test case allocation can be adjusted accordingly to compensate for increased complexity.

As mentioned before, models of different granularity can be constructed and then be used with the above methods for test case generation. Test efficiency concerns may require that we cover different functions with a minimal of test cases. The hierarchical structure of UMMs also gives us the flexibility to improve test efficiency by avoiding redundant executions once a subpart has been visited already. This is particularly true when there are numerous common sub-operations within or among different end-to-end operations.

When revisiting certain states, exact repetition of the execution states that have been visited before is less likely to reveal new problems. The revisited part can be dynamically expanded to allow for different lower-level paths or states to be covered. For example, when state E is revisited in the high-level Markov chain in Figure 10.3, it can be expanded by using the more detailed Markov chain in Figure 10.4, and possibly execute different sub-paths there. In general, to avoid exact repetition, we could expand revisited states with operations of finer granularity, and more thoroughly test those frequently used parts.

10.5.3 Implementation, application, and other issues

The test sensitization and outcome prediction are relatively simple and straightforward, as we discussed above for testing based on general FSMs in Section 10.2. Because UMMs are based on FSMs with augmented probabilistic transitions, once a series of state transitions is selected using the criteria above, the sensitization simply follows the required sequence of input and the result checking simply compares the actual output and next states to what are specified in the corresponding FSMs. In effect, we can prepare all the input and specify the anticipated output and transitions ahead of time. However, under some dynamic situations, it would be hard to anticipate the input as well as the next state. One may also argue that such prepared tests are not truly random in the statistical sense. Under such situations, dynamic test cases may be generated in the following way: From a current state, the transition or branching probabilities can be used directly to dynamically select the next state to visit, and sensitized on the spot. As discussed in Chapter 7, such dynamic test cases also have their own drawbacks, primarily in the reduced system performance due to the overhead to dynamically prepare and sensitize these test cases.

The usage-based testing based on UMMs also yield data that can be used directly to evaluate the reliability of the implemented system, to provide an objective assessment of product reliability based on observation of testing failures and other related information. Such use of statistical testing data in reliability analysis is described in Chapter 22. Unique to the usage of UMMs is that the failures can be associated with specific states or transitions. We can use such information to evaluate individual state reliability as well as overall system reliability, to extrapolate system reliability to different environments, and to identify high-risk (low-reliability) areas for focused reliability improvement.

The general applicability of UMMs is similar to that for FSMs, such as menu-driven, interactive, and real-time systems, especially to large software systems of these types. In addition, the hierarchical UMMs fit well with incremental, iterative, and spiral development processes, where new software increments or sub-systems can be treated as a new top-level node in UMMs to be added, expanded, and tested, while the rest of the models can remain essentially the same. Reuse of software components or use of COTS (commercial off-the-shelf) components can be supported, modeled, and tested similarly.

10.6   CASE STUDY CONTINUED: TESTING BASED ON WEB USAGES

Continuing our case study in Section 10.3 about web testing, we can use statistical testing based on UMMs to overcome some of the difficulties of using pure FSM-based testing due to the size and other factors. The key to this usage-based statistical testing strategy based on a series of studies is the automatic extraction of web usage information from existing web logs to build UMMs as web usage models (Tian and Nguyen, 1999; Kallepalli and Tian, 2001; Ma and Tian, 2003; Tian et al., 2004).

10.6.1   Usage-based web testing: Motivations and basic approach

We characterized web-based applications in Section 10.3 by their information/document focus, integration between information and navigation, and multi-layered support infrastructure to derive FSMs for web-based applications. In addition, we also noticed the inadequacies of using pure FSMs in testing such web-based application due to the size and other factors, as follows:

- *Massive user population*: Virtually anyone from anywhere with an Internet access can be a user of a given web-site. Although some traditional software systems, such as operating systems, also serve a massive user population, the systems are usually accessed locally, thus scattering the user population into sub-groups of limited size.

- *Diverse usage environments*: Web users employ different hardware equipments, network connections, operating systems, middleware and web server support, and web browsers, as compared to pre-specified platforms for most traditional software.

The combination of these characteristics and other characteristics noticed in Section 10.3 above also make traditional coverage-based testing such as basic state and link coverage based on FSMs inadequate for web-based applications. Instead, statistical testing techniques described above can be used to selectively test those components or usage patterns frequently used by the massive number of users under diverse usage environments. These techniques can help us prioritize testing effort based on usage scenarios and frequencies for individual web resources and navigation patterns to ensure the reliability of web-based applications.

```
129.119.4.17 - - [16/Aug/1999:00:00:11 -0500] "GET
/img/XredSeal.gif HTTP/1.1" 301 328 "http://www.seas.smu.edu/"
"Mozilla/4.0 (compatible; MSIE 4.01; Windows NT)"
129.119.4.17 - - [16/Aug/1999:00:00:11 -0500] "GET /img/ecom.gif
HTTP/1.1" 304 - "http://www.seas.smu.edu/" "Mozilla/4.0
(compatible; MSIE 4.01; Windows NT)".
```

Figure 10.5 Sample entries in an access log

Once we have decided on the use of usage-based statistical web testing, the immediate question is the choice of which types of usage models or operational profiles (OPs), or more specifically, the choice between Musa's flat OP covered in Chapter 8 and the UMMs covered earlier in this chapter. Web applications consist of various components, stages, or steps, visible to the web users, and typically initiated by them. Consequently, state transition based Markov models such as UMMs are generally more appropriate for this kind of applications than flat OP.

As mentioned in Section 10.4, the construction of UMMs includes two steps: Constructing the basic model elements and the structure first (or the underlying FSMs), and then assigning transition probabilities. In our case study in Section 10.3, we have already constructed the FSMs. Therefore, we can concentrate on obtaining the probabilistic transition information. As pointed out in Chapter 8 in connection to flat (Musa) OPs, such information can be obtained by expert opinions, customer surveys, or actual measurement, with the last one the most accurate but also typically the most difficult and costly to obtain. Fortunately, various log files are routinely kept at web servers for normal support of various web-based applications. This availability offers us the opportunities of automatic collection of usage information for OP construction. We next describe this approach and also illustrate it with examples for www.seas.smu.edu, the official web site of the School of Engineering and Applied Science at Southern Methodist University (SMU/SEAS). Access log data covering 26 consecutive days were used in these examples.

10.6.2 Constructing UMMs for statistical web testing

A "hit" is registered in the access log if a file corresponding to an HTML page, a document, or other web content is explicitly requested, or if some embedded content is implicitly requested or activated. Most web servers record relevant information about individual accesses in their access logs.

Every hit is logged as a separate entry in the server's *access log* file. Some sample entries from the access log for the www.seas.smu.edu web site using Apache Web Server (Behlandorf, 1996) is given in Figure 10.5. Specific information in this access log includes:

- The reverse-DNS hostname of the machine making the request. If the machine has no reverse-DNS hostname mapped to the IP number, or if the reverse-DNS lookup is disabled, this will just be the IP number.

- The user name used in any authentication information supplied with the request.

- If "identd" checking is turned on, the user name as returned by the remote host.

- Date and time that the transfer took place, including offset from GMT (Greenwich Mean Time).

- The complete first line of the HTTP request, in quotes.

- The HTTP response code.

- Total number of bytes transferred.

If the value for any of these data fields is not available, a "−" will be put in its place. Although different web servers record different information, the following is almost always present: the requesting computer, the date and time of the request, the file that the client requested, the size of the requested file, and an HTTP status code.

UMMs can be constructed based on analyzing the access logs using a combination of existing tools and internally implemented utility programs. However, as with most model construction activities, fully automated supported is neither practical nor necessary. Human involvement is essential in making various modeling decisions, such as to extract UMM hierarchies and to group pages or links, as follows:

- For traditional organizations, there is usually a natural hierarchy, such as university-school-department-individual for universities, which is also reflected in their official web sites. There are generally closer interconnections as represented by more frequent referrals within a unit than across units. This natural hierarchy is used as the starting point for the hierarchies in these UMMs for web testing, which are later adjusted based on other referral frequencies.

- For links associated with very small link probability values because they are followed infrequently, grouping them together to form a single link would significantly simplify the resulting model, and highlight the frequently used navigation patterns. A simple lower-level model for this group can be obtained by linking this single grouped node to all those it represents to form a one-level tree. Web pages related by contents or location in the overall site structure can also be grouped together to simplify UMMs.

This approach to UMM construction based on web logs is similar to the use of data mining techniques on web logs for web site evaluation (Spiliopoulou, 2000), but the focus here is to construct integrated models instead of a loose collection of results and patterns.

10.6.3 Statistical web testing: Details and examples

Although any web page can be a potential entry point or initial state in an FSM or its corresponding Markov chain, one basic idea in statistical testing is to narrow this down to one or a few entry points based on their actual usage as entry point to a web site. The destinations of incoming links to a web site from external sources are the entry points for UMMs. These links include URL accesses from dialog boxes, user bookmarks, search engine results, explicit links from external pages, or other external sources. All these accesses were recorded in the access log, and the analysis result is summarized in the entry page report in Table 10.2. For this web site, the root page "/index.html" outnumber other pages as the entry page by a large margin. In addition, these top entry pages are not tightly connected. These facts lead to the decision of building a single set of UMMs with this root page as the main entry node to the top-level Markov chain presented in Figure 10.6.

Table 10.2 Top entry pages to SMU/SEAS

Entry Page	Occurrences
/index.html	18646
/ce/index.html	2778
/co/cams/index.html	2568
/ce/smu/index.html	2327
/netech/index.html	2139
/disted/phd/index.html	1036
/co/cams/clemscam.html	963
/disted/index.html	878
/cse/index.html	813

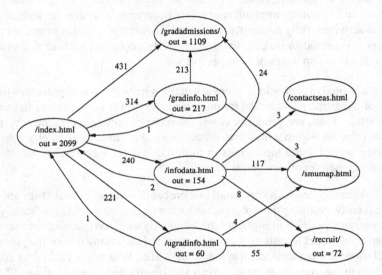

Figure 10.6 Top-level UMM for SMU/SEAS

The issue with exit points is more complicated. Potentially any page can be the exit point, if the user decides to end accessing the web site. That is probably why no such exit page report is produced by any existing analyzer. This problem can be handled implicitly by specific usage sequences associated with specific test cases: The end of a usage sequence is the exit point from the UMM. This decision implies that frequently visited pages are also more likely to be the exit node than infrequently visited pages, which makes logical sense.

Figure 10.6 shows the top-level Markov chain of the UMM for the SMU/SEAS web site. The following information is captured and presented:

- Each node is labeled by its associated web file or directory name, and the total outgoing direct hits calculated. For example, out = 2099 for the root node "/index.html", indicates that the total direct hits from this node to its children pages is 2099.

- Each link is labeled with its direct hit count, instead of branching probability, to make it easier to add missing branching information should such information become available later. Only when such content is requested and loaded, a hit is recorded in the access log, but not when a user accesses a specific content using browser navigation buttons ("Back", "Forward", etc.), because the local cache is used for the latter type of accesses. Therefore, branching information represented by the use of these browser navigation buttons can only be extracted from other information sources, such as a collection of user-side records, which would be much harder to obtain than server access logs. However, relative frequencies and conditional branching probabilities for links originating from a given node can be deduced easily. For example, the direct hit count from the page "/index.html" to the page "gradinfo.html" is 314; and the conditional branching probability for this link is 314/2099 = 20.5%.

- Infrequent direct hits to other pages are omitted from the model to simplify the model and highlight frequently followed sequences. However, the omitted direct hits can be calculated by subtracting out direct hits represented in the diagram from the total "out" hits of the originating node. For example, there are direct hits to nine other pages from the root page "/index.html". The combined direct hits are: $2099 - 431 - 314 - 240 - 221 = 893$.

- Lower-level models (not shown) are also produced for the nodes "/gradadmission/" and "/recruit/" in the top-level model. These models can be used to support our hierarchical strategy for statistical usage-based testing.

- For nodes needing no further analysis, such as "/smumap.html" and "/contactseas.html", neither lower-level models nor "out" hits are produced. Such pages either do not contain outlinks, or are visited with very low frequency, that further analysis is impossible or unnecessary.

10.7 CONCLUDING REMARKS

Finite-state machines (FSMs) are often suitable models for many software systems where system functions or operations cannot be adequately modeled by a one-step or fixed step information processing models such as those based on checklists, partitions, or decision trees. FSMs use states and transitions to model the individual units of system operations or current status, and link them together to form the overall usage scenarios and sequences, with possible repetitions or loops handled easily. Testing based on FSMs can be performed on these systems for basic coverage of states and transitions by directly using the FSMs, or for focused testing of highly used or important parts by using Markov operational profiles (OPs) as extended FSMs with usage probabilities associated with transitions.

In gaining the power of being able to model and test more realistic steps and transitions with possible repetitions, we lost the simplicity of simple processing and testing models covered in Chapter 8. In addition, the intrinsic complexity associated with the number of states and transitions limits our ability to model large systems in detail where large numbers of states and transitions are required. Hierarchical FSMs can be used to alleviate the problem by limiting transactions across boundaries of different FSMs in the hierarchy. Selective testing based on Markov OPs can also alleviate the problem to some degree by focusing on highly used states and transitions while omitting infrequently used ones or grouping them together. The combination of these hierarchical FSMs and Markov OPs led us to unified Markov models (UMMs) described in this chapter. UMMs can help us prioritize testing effort, perform usage-based statistical testing, improve test efficiency, and support reliability analysis and improvement activities.

These testing techniques can be effectively applied to various systems, such as menu-driven, object-oriented, and real-time systems, and systems that operate continuously. We illustrated the use of these testing techniques through a comprehensive case study of testing web-based applications using both the basic FSMs and the extended FSMs in the form of UMMs. Not only can the usage of individual web pages and possible links be captured by FSMs, but also the related usage frequencies and navigation patterns by web users can be captured automatically in UMMs by extracting information from web access logs routinely kept by web server for normal web operations. Therefore, FSM- and UMM-based testing techniques are viable, practical, and effective techniques for web-based applications.

However, complex interactions along execution paths and detailed dependencies among different data items cannot be adequately modeled and tested by using the testing techniques described in this chapter. On the other hand, the FSMs can be the starting point for us to perform various analyses and build additional models as extensions to the basic FSMs to test more complex interactions, as we will describe in the next chapter.

Problems

10.1   What are the similarities and differences between FSMs and flow charts? You might want to include some sample flow charts.

10.2   Can the checklists, partitions, and decision trees described in the previous two chapters considered FSMs?

10.3   Convert the FSM in Figure 10.1 or in Table 10.1 to its list representation. Which conversion is easier, from graphical to list representation or from tabular to list representation? What about converting them back?

10.4   As described in this chapter, we can use the three different representations of FSMs. What about Markov chains? Can you convert the Markov chains in Figure 10.3 and Figure 10.4 into tabular or list representations? What about the graph in Figure 10.6?

10.5   As we mentioned in Section 10.1, there might be many common sub-operations in complete end-to-end operations. How would problems related to such sub-operations or complete operations manifest into problems in FSMs? In particular, can they be mapped to state problems, transition problems, input problems, or output problems?

10.6   Build an FSM for some menu-driven software you are familiar with.

10.7   What is the main problem of modeling individual web pages as individual FSM states?

10.8   Many realistic usage situations of software products may be influenced by both the individual characteristics of the user, the past usage history, as well as the current dynamic environment. Can you incorporate such information into Markov chains? If yes, how? If no, why not?

10.9   Can you still use Markov chains to model your software systems if the memoryless property is not strictly satisfied?

10.10   Compare the probability thresholds in Section 10.5 to the use of Musa OPs we studied in Chapter 8.

10.11   In your opinion, is it easier to incorporated information other than usage frequencies into UMMs or into Musa OPs?

10.12   There are still many open questions about statistical usage-based web testing, particularly with the missing information or information not recorded in server access logs. Can you suggest some alternative ways to obtain such missing information or to deal with other open questions?

CHAPTER 11

CONTROL FLOW, DATA DEPENDENCY, AND INTERACTION TESTING

From the structural or implementation view, a software system is made up of interacting components, modules, or sub-systems. As it appears to target customers, the overall system consists of linked functions or operations. Finite-state machines (FSMs) and related usage models we described in the previous chapter can be used to model and test these interconnected system functions, implementations, and related usage. We focused on covering the states, transitions, and related usage without paying too much attention to interactions beyond simple links. In this chapter, we describe testing techniques to deal with complex interactions beyond one-step links in FSMs. Two primary types of such complex interactions are:

- Interactions along an execution path, where later executions are affected by all that went on before them.

- More specific interactions among data items in execution, with some of the later ones depending on the definitions and values of earlier ones for their definitions and values.

The testing of the above interactions is through what are commonly called control flow testing (CFT) and data flow testing (DFT), respectively. These techniques are traditionally white-box techniques due to the level of detail captured in their models (Myers, 1979; Beizer, 1990), but they have also found some applications as black-box testing techniques applicable to testing system-level functional flow, data dependencies, and related interactions (Howden, 1980; Beizer, 1995). In fact, these techniques and related studies represent some of the earliest formal studies of software testing (Allen and Cocke, 1972; Goodenough and Gerhart, 1975; Clarke, 1976; Howden, 1976; Miller and Howden, 1981).

11.1 BASIC CONTROL FLOW TESTING

Control flow testing (CFT) is a direct and natural extension to coverage-based FSM testing with a specialized type of FSMs called control flow graphs (CFGs) and with a focus on complete execution *paths* instead of on state or link coverage.

11.1.1 General concepts

When we introduced finite-state machines (FSMs) in Chapter 10, we distinguished the type whose information processing is associated with transitions from the type whose information processing is associated with states. Control flow graphs (CFGs) can be considered as special cases of the latter type, with their elements and characteristics specified as follows:

- *Nodes*: Each node in a CFG represents a unit of information processing (white-box view) or workload to be handled by the software (black-box view). The nodes in CFGs correspond to the states in FSMs.

- *Links*: Each link in a CFG simply represents the relation "is followed by": If we have a directed link from node A to node B, it is interpreted as A is followed by B, or B follows A. The links in CFGs correspond to the state transitions in FSMs, but no processing or workload is associated with links in CFGs. Duplicate links are not needed in CFGs because there is no need to specify the simple relation "is followed by" more than once.

- *Initial/entry* and *final/exit nodes*: The nodes where program execution starts are called the initial or entry nodes and the ones where program execution ends are called the final or exit nodes. In CFT, we mostly deal with proper programs or functions where there is only a single entry node and a single exit node.

- *Outlinks*: A link that originates from a node is called an outlink with respect to that node. When there are multiple outlinks from a node, each of them will be labeled with its specific condition. The actual execution will only follow one of these outlinks.

- *Inlinks*: A link that ends up in a node is called an inlink with respect to that node. When there are multiple inlinks to a node, the actual execution will only follow one of these inlinks because the above condition on outlinks guarantees that program execution will only follow one link at a time.

- *Decision, junction,* and *processing nodes*: A node associated with multiple outlinks is called a decision node because a decision is made at this node to select an outlink to follow in an actual execution. It is also called a branching node for obvious reasons. Similarly, a node associated with multiple inlinks is called a junction node. A node that is neither a decision node nor a junction node is called a processing node because it usually corresponds to some internal or external processing. Two special cases are the entry nodes, where there may not be any inlink, and exit nodes, where there may not be any outlink. However, they are still grouped as processing nodes, because they are generally associated with some initial or final processing. For clarity, we generally separate out the three types of nodes, with information processing associated with only processing nodes and with one junction node corresponding to each branching node.

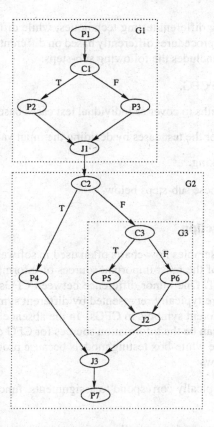

Figure 11.1 A sample control flow graph (CFG)

- *Path*: A complete path, or simply a path, is one that starts from an entry node, follows a number of links and visits a number of intermediate nodes, and ends up in an exit node. Since no duplicate link is allowed, we can simply identify the path by the sequence of nodes visited.

- *Segment*: A path segment, or simply a segment, is a subpart of a complete path where the first node may not be an entry node and the last node may not be an exit node.

- *Loop*: A path or a segment contains a loop if some nodes in the path or segment are revisited. In what follows, we will deal with CFGs without loops first. Section 11.2 is dedicated to loop testing.

Figure 11.1 is a sample CFG with processing nodes P1, P2, P3, P4, P5, P6, and P7; decision nodes C1, C2, and C3; and junction node J1, J2, and J3. The CFG is also divided into three different parts G1, G2, and G3, with each part shown inside a dotted rectangle. In another variation of CFGs often used by practitioners and in literature, some of the nodes could be merged if we allow processing in all the nodes. In that variation, we would merge J1 and C2 into one node, and J2, J3 and P7 into another.

The basic idea for control flow testing (CFT) is to select paths as test cases and sensitize them by assigning corresponding input values. As described in Chapter 7, among the three major activities of test preparation, execution, and follow-up, the last two share much of the same sub-activities among different testing techniques; while different testing techniques prepare test cases and test procedures differently based on different underlying models. For CFT, the test preparation includes the following sub-steps:

- Build and verify the CFG.

- Define and select paths to cover as individual test cases based on the CFG.

- Sensitize the paths or the test cases by deciding the input values.

- Plan for result checking.

We elaborate on each of these sub-steps below.

11.1.2 Model construction

Notice that Figure 11.1 resembles flow charts often used in software development. In fact, such flow charts are one of the most important sources of information for us to construct CFGs and to perform CFT. One minor difference between CFGs and flow charts is that different types of nodes are typically represented by different symbols in flow charts, but we do not usually use different symbols in CFGs. In the absence of flow charts, program code or program designs can be the information sources for CFG construction. The CFGs constructed in this way are white-box testing models because product implementation information is used, as follows:

- Processing nodes typically correspond to assignments, function calls, or procedure calls.

- Decision or branching nodes typically correspond to branching statements such as binary branching in the form of "if-then-else" or "if-then" (empty "else"), or multi-way branching such as "switch-case". Each outgoing branch will be marked by its specific condition. For example, for binary branching, it is typically marked by the truth value (T/F, or True/False) of the associated condition. For multi-way branching, more specific conditions will be marked.

- Loop statements correspond to a special type of branching nodes that we will deal with in Section 11.2.

- The entry and exit nodes are usually easy to identify, corresponding to the first and last statement or processing unit in the program code or some corresponding flow-chart.

One of the problems with the above procedure for CFG construction is that a lot of nodes will be used and represented in the CFG. However, since CFG is used for path testing, we can group some nodes together, such as a number of sequential processing nodes, to form super-nodes if such grouping will not affect the execution paths.

Notice that the use of "goto" was not covered in the above procedure for CFG construction. The free use of goto's will create truly horrible programs and corresponding CFGs that are hard to test — one of the main reasons that goto is considered harmful (Dijkstra, 1968). Fortunately, with structured programming and its successor, object-oriented programming, commonly employed for today's software product development, we do not encounter too many goto's. The commonly used structures are sequential concatenation, such as between the parts G1 and G2 in Figure 11.1, and nesting, such as G3

L1:   input(a, b, c);
L2:   d ← b * b - 4 * a * c;
L3:   if (d > 0) then
L4:   r ← 2
L5:   else_if (d = 0) then
L6:   r ← 1
L7:   else_if (d < 0) then
L8:   r ← 0;
L9:   output(r);

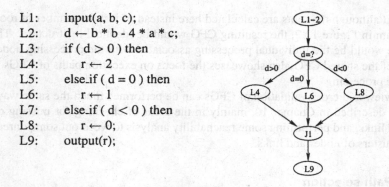

Figure 11.2   A sample program and its control flow graph (CFG)

nested inside G2 in Figure 11.1. Of course, multiple concatenations or multiple levels of nesting can be used in programs and reflected in their CFGs. We will deal with them in our path selection and sensitization later.

Figure 11.2 gives a program in pseudo-code form that determines the number of roots for the equation $ax^2 + bx + c = 0$. Each line is individually numbered. We used a three-way branching implemented by "if-else_if-else_if" (called cascading if's). The corresponding CFG is given to the right of the program. We merged lines L3, L5, and L7 together because they basically specify a 3-way branching, with the branching node in Figure 11.2 marked by condition $d =?$. Lines L1 and L2 were also merged because such sequential statements do not affect the control flow. In addition, a junction node J1 was introduced to clearly mark the junction.

CFGs can also be derived from external functional specification or descriptions of customer usage scenarios, thus could also be considered as black-box testing models. We can directly adapt and modify flow-charts for these product specifications or usage scenario descriptions into our CFGs. If the flow-charts are not available, we need to extract information from these specifications and descriptions by examining the structure and relations in them, as follows:

- Processing nodes typically correspond to some described actions, typically associated with phrases such as "do/enter/calculate" something.

- Branching nodes are typically associated with decisions or conditions.

- Entry and exit nodes typically correspond to the first and last items respectively in the specifications or descriptions, although they are also often explicitly specified.

For example, the CFG in Figure 11.2 can be conceivably derived from the following product description:

- To solve the equation $ax^2 + bx + c = 0$, the user needs to enter the parameters.

- If $b^2 - 4ac < 0$, there is no real root, and the user should be informed.

- If $b^2 - 4ac = 0$, the root $r = -b/(2a)$ will be calculated.

- If $b^2 - 4ac > 0$, two roots will be calculated as:

$$r = \frac{-b \pm \sqrt{b^2 - 4ac}}{2a}.$$

Notice that although the roots are calculated here instead of just the number of roots as in the program in Figure 11.2, the resulting CFG would be identical in structure. The only difference would be the individual processing associated with the processing node. This example of the shared CFG also showcases the focus on execution paths of CFGs instead of specific processing.

The review and cross-validation of CFGs can be performed much the same way as for FSMs we described in Chapter 10, mainly in the areas of checking for missing or extra nodes and links, and performing some reachability analysis to weed out some unreachable or dead clusters of nodes and links.

11.1.3 Path selection

We next describe a strategy to systematically select paths for structured CFGs (no explicit goto's). This strategy consists of two basic steps:

1. CFG decomposition.

2. Bottom-up path definition.

In doing this, we make use of some important properties about structured CFGs from graph theory and programming language theory (Maddux, 1985; Pratt and Zelkowitz, 2001). A structured CFG is one where only sequential concatenation and nesting are allowed, and where there is a unique entry and a unique exit node. Such structured CFGs can be decomposed into their sub-graphs (or sub-CFGs), with each one a proper structured CFG in its own right. The sub-CFGs are connected through sequential concatenation or nesting. If a sub-CFG cannot be decomposed further, it is called a prime CFG. The hierarchical CFGs yielded from this process are called a decomposition of the original CFG. For example, the CFG in Figure 11.1 can be decomposed into: G = G1 ∘ G2 (-, G3). with G3 nested inside G2, and G1 concatenated with G2. G2(-, G3) is used to indicate that G3 is nested in the F branch of G2, with use of "-" to indicate no more levels of nesting at the T branch. G2(G3) is used to indicate that G3 is nested in G2 but we do not know or do not care about which branch it is nested in. The boundaries for G1, G2, and G3 were also shown in Figure 11.1 by the dotted rectangles.

With the above CFG decomposition, we can perform bottom-up path definition. When two CFGs, G1 with M paths and G2 with N paths, are combined in a higher-level CFG, we can determine the paths as follows:

- For sequential concatenation, G = G1 ∘ G2, there will be $M \times N$ paths in G. That is, each of the M paths in G1 can be paired with one of the N paths in G2. Notice that these paths in G1 and in G2 form path segments in G. For example, the concatenation of two binary prime CFGs (each has two paths corresponding to the logical value T or F for its condition) would yield four paths: TT, TF, FT, FF.

- For nesting, G = G1 (G2), there will be $M + N - 1$ paths in G. That is, one of the M paths in G1 will be replaced by N paths in G2. For example, in the nesting of two binary prime CFGs with the one nested in the F path of another, the original T, F paths will become T, FT, and FF, or $2 + 2 - 1 = 3$ paths.

This process can be carried out for each level, by starting with the prime CFGs and continuing with higher-level combinations, until we have defined the complete path for the whole CFG. In the above example of Figure 11.1, we can follow the above procedure to select the paths. The CFG has already been decomposed, with G = G1 ∘ G2 (-, G3). We can then focus on the second step, the bottom-up use of concatenation and nesting to select paths, as follows:

- We first define the two paths in G3, corresponding to C3=T and C3=F.

- We next nest G3 paths into G2 to form three paths, corresponding to C2=T, C2=F and C3=T, and C2=F, C3=F. We can denote these paths as T-, FT, FF, with the letters in the sequence corresponding to C2 and C3 values respectively. A "-" indicates that a specific decision is irrelevant. In this case, when C2=T, we do not need to make a decision involving C3.

- We finally concatenate G2(G3) with G1 to form 6 paths: TT-, TFT, TFF, FT-, FFT, FFF.

11.1.4 Path sensitization and other activities

The key to path sensitization is the decision or branching nodes and the associated conditions. If all these conditions are independent of each other, then all the paths defined above can be sensitized by selecting variable values to satisfy the specific conditions for each path. For example, if logical variables are used for the CFG in Figure 11.1, then the six paths TT-, TFT, TFF, FT-, FFT, FFF are directly sensitized already. Similarly, if $C1 \equiv (x > 0)$, $C2 \equiv (y < 100), C3 \equiv (z = 10)$, then we can select values for x, y, and z to sensitize the corresponding conditions. For example, for the path TFT, we may sensitize it using $x = 1$, $y = 1024$, and $z = 10$. Notice that when numerical variables are involved, the sensitization is typically not unique. Essentially, we choose one test point from each equivalence class, as we described in Chapter 8.

If some of the conditions in a path are correlated through some shared logical or numerical variables, then further analysis is needed to eliminate certain paths that cannot be sensitized. For example, for a concatenation of two binary sub-graphs with exactly the opposite conditions, C1 = ¬ C2, we can eliminate two from the four paths TT, TF, FT, and FF to leave us with TF and FT paths, because TT and FF cannot be sensitized.

As another example, consider the concatenation of two binary sub-graphs with $C1 \equiv (x > 0)$ and $C2 \equiv (x < 100)$. The two conditions are linked through the shared variable x. In this case, the overall path FF can be eliminated because of the contradiction shown below:

$$(C1 = F) \wedge (C2 = F)$$
$$\equiv \neg(x > 0) \wedge \neg(x < 100)$$
$$\equiv (x \leq 0) \wedge (x \geq 100)$$
$$\equiv \emptyset.$$

That is, the set of x's that satisfies these conditions is empty ($\emptyset$).

A third situation is that the conditions might be related through some computation and assignment in between that link one variable in one condition to another one in a later condition. The analysis of such correlated conditions is essentially an analysis of data dependencies, which we address in Section 11.3 in connection to data flow testing.

Similar to the concatenation situations we considered above, nesting situations may also involve correlated conditions and need to be handled similarly. From these examples we can conclude that test sensitization for CFT could be difficult. Proper analysis and sensitization tools can help us to some degree. But the ultimate responsibility is with us, the testers. We need to have a good understanding of the sensitization issues and to check for possible conflicts or contradictions, instead of blindly trying all the different input combinations in the attempt to sensitize all the selected paths when some of them may be un-realizable due to contradictions.

Other activities involved in execution and follow-up for CFT are essentially the same as those for any other techniques. Some specifics relevant to CFT include:

- For test oracles, we can take advantage of the internal or intermediate steps in CFT to sample intermediate states for some consistency conditions.

- Execution can be helped by debugger and other testing tools, particularly for white-box CFT because it focuses on statement-oriented path definitions and executions.

- Some specific follow-up activities include verification of the intended paths against coverage target and confirmation that the intended paths were indeed followed to guard against coincidental correctness. Some program instrumentation is typically needed to collect coverage information and to confirm dynamic execution paths.

11.2 LOOP TESTING, CFT USAGE, AND OTHER ISSUES

So far, we have avoided loops in CFG and CFT. The primary reason for doing so is the intrinsic difficulties dealing with loop testing. For example, with just a few loops of moderate numbers of iterations, the complete coverage becomes impractical because the combinatorial explosion when we concatenate or nest them together. On the other hand, loops are common and important to almost all the program implementations, and are used as a primary means of flow control. Consequently, we must deal with loops in CFT, as we attempt to do next, by modifying the CFT techniques to address some practical difficulties. After discussing loop testing, we also deal with CFT application and other related issues at the end of this section.

11.2.1 Different types of loops and corresponding CFGs

Loops are associated with repetitive or iterative procedures of information processing, either corresponding to the actual implementations (white-box view) or user-oriented functions (black-box view). As mentioned above, if a path through a CFG contains one or more nodes visited more than once, a loop is formed. For example, if we have a path ABCDBE, then the middle sub-path BCDB forms a loop. Loops may also form implicitly through some programming language features, such as recursion and explicit goto's. A loop can be specified as follows:

- There must be a loop body that accomplishes something, and which may be repeated a number of times. It is usually represented by a node or some other CFG nested inside the loop.

- There must be some loop control to make the looping decision, or to determine whether to execute the loop body or exit the loop. This loop control may be used repeatedly for each iteration of the loop to make the decision under the current dynamic

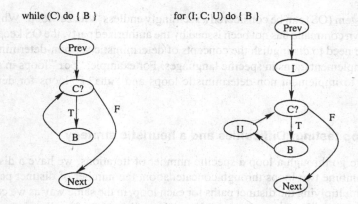

Figure 11.3 Control flow graphs (CFGs) for "for" and "while" loops

environment. It is usually represented by a node with associated predicate defined by some control variables whose dynamic values are used to make the looping decisions.

- There must be some loop entry and exit nodes. The ones we commonly deal with in structured programming typically have a single entry and a single exit point, such as the "while"and "for" loops.   In addition, in many of these loops the entry, exit, and loop control nodes are the same. The exceptions include "repeat-until" loops and unstructured loops using conditional or unconditional goto's.

- Two or more loops can be combined through nesting (one inside another) and con-catenation (one after another). Although non-structured combination using goto's are also allowed in many programming languages, their usage is discouraged and usually limited to rare situations.

Two of the most common loop instructions in various programming languages are the "while" and "for" loops:

- "while (C) do { B }", where C is the loop condition and B the loop body. The entry point is also the exit point.

- "for (I; C; U) do { B }", where I is the loop initialization before entering the loop, U the loop update after each iteration, C the loop condition, and B the loop body. The entry point is still also the exit point.

Figure 11.3 gives the CFGs for them.

One of the fundamental questions important to testing is whether we can determine the number of iterations for a loop ahead of time before actual test execution. If so, it is called a deterministic loop; otherwise a non-deterministic one. Deterministic loops are commonly used to process some known data or other entities, such as performing some processing for every element of an array of fixed size. One direct implementation is the "do" loop, in the form of "do (n) {B} , that repeats the loop-body B n times. In various languages, this "do" loop is implemented as a more commonly used "for" loop, which usually specifies the number of iterations through related entities in the loop control.

The most common form of the nondeterministic loop is the "while" loop, with the loop body repeated while some condition remains true. For example, the overall operation of an operating system (OS) can be considered a seemingly endless "while" loop: While the system shut-down command has not been issued by the authorized party, the OS keeps running. However, we need to distinguish the concepts of deterministic vs. non-deterministic loops from their implementations in specific languages. For example, "for" loops in a language can be used to implement non-deterministic loops and "while" loops for deterministic loops.

11.2.2 Loop testing: Difficulties and a heuristic strategy

Each time we go through a loop a specific number of iterations, we have a distinct path. When we combine two loops through concatenation, the number of distinct paths can be obtained by multiplying the distinct paths for each loop, in the same way as we concatenate two loop-free CFGs. However, the possible number of iterations for a loop is usually large. Therefore, the combination produces a larger number of overall paths.

The nesting of two loops is different from the nesting of loop-free CFGs: The resulting paths is no longer $M + N - 1$, but a much larger number due to repetition. For example, corresponding to each distinct path for the outer loop, say going through i iterations, each of the outer iterations may involve going through N distinct number of inner loop iterations (from 0 to $N-1$). If we unwind the outer loop while treating the inner loop as one indivisible unit, the nested loop would be equivalent to having the inner loop unit concatenated i times. Applying the concatenation rule for path combinations, we obtain N^i combined paths — a huge number even for moderate N and i values. The total number of possible control flow paths can be calculated as:

$$\sum_{i=0}^{M-1} N^i = \frac{N^M - 1}{N - 1},$$

which would be beyond complete coverage for almost all cases except very small M and N values. Consequently, we have to abandon any realistic hope for complete path coverage when nested loops are involved, and choose instead selective coverage strategies.

One of the common basis for selective coverage strategies is the empirical evidence or observation of likely problems, much like what we did for boundary testing related to input domain partitions in Chapter 9. For loops, it was observed by practitioners and researchers that we typically have more problems with loop boundaries. For example, for many computational tasks associated with arrays where loops are often used, we often have problems with the lower end, such as initialization problems and special handling of empty, and single item cases. At the upper end, we often have array limit problems commonly manifested as the N $\pm$ 1 problems. We can derive our test cases accordingly.

On the other hand, if the upper bound for a loop is N, say N = 1000, and if we have tested for the loop with N/2 iterations without discovering a problem, it is also reasonable to expect that we will not likely to discover a problem when we test with N/2 +1 iterations. In a sense, this is similar to the equivalence class testing related to different input sub-domains: We typically only need to sample one interior point, while focusing on boundary conditions and related problems. The same idea can be carried to loop testing, as we describe below.

Based on the above discussion, the following execution paths related to lower bound for loops should be used:

- *Bypass* the loop: This test case can often reveal loop initialization problems. Many operations, such as those associated with the loop body in this case, need proper set-up or initialization, and need some restoration or clean-up to allow for further operations. For example, if the initialization is done before the loop and restoration is done inside the loop, there would be a problem if we bypass the loop, and this test case would reveal the problem.

- Going through the loop *once*: This test case can often reveal loop initialization or set up problems, such as not initializing certain variable or data items for use in the loop body.

- Going through the loop *twice*: This test case can often reveal problems that prevent loop repetition.

In some specialized loops, there might be minimum number of iterations. In such cases, the above test cases can be adapted to min and min $\pm$ 1 iterations. One other fact worth noting is that every loop has a lower bound but not every one has an upper bound. Therefore, lower bound testing is more universally applied in loop testing than upper bound testing. When an upper bound N exist for a loop, it should also be tested using the test cases of N, $N \pm 1$ iterations. This set of test cases can typically reveal capacity problems.

In addition to the above boundary test cases, we should also use some typical cases to make sure that normal executions can be handled properly.

When we test concatenation of loops, we can combine the above test cases that define separate path segments to form overall paths. For example, for each typical loop we have seven path segments (bypass, once, twice, typical, max $-$ 1, max, max $+$ 1). The concatenation of two such loops would result in 49 test paths, a large number but still manageable. However, if we have more than a few loops concatenated together, we need to reduce this further.

A more dire situation is with loop nesting. Even with such reduced test cases, when we test for the upper bound of N iterations for the outer loop, we have 7^N combination paths because we have seven cases for the inner loop corresponding to each outer iteration. This would be a truly astronomical number even for moderately large N. Therefore, we need to reduce the test cases further. For example, after testing the inner loop independently, we can fix the inner loop with a single test case when we test the outer loop, thus resulting in only seven test cases for the outer loop. In this case, we used a hierarchical testing strategy, where we tested the inner loop first, and then effectively reduced it to a single node for outer loop testing. If such a strategy sounds too restrictive, we may combine it with a randomly selected inner loop test case whenever the inner loop is invoked to bring more variety to testing without increasing the number of test cases. This idea is similar to the use of hierarchical FSMs or hierarchical Markov chains we described in Chapter 10. In either of these cases, we loose some interactions between the outer and inner loops, but significantly reduce the number of test cases. This may be a worthwhile tradeoff for many situations.

The same combinatorial or hierarchical testing ideas can be used to combine loop testing with general CFT. For example, we can combine the heuristic loop test cases with complete coverage test cases for loop-free CFG for concatenation situations. However, when nesting is involved, particularly when something is nested in some loops, we are probably forced to use hierarchical testing ideas as above: First testing the inner CFG or loop in isolation, and then treating it as a node when testing the outer loop.

The other testing related activities, such as path sensitization, execution, result checking, follow-up actions, etc., are not fundamentally different from those for regular loop-free CFT we described in Section 11.1. The only difference is quantitative, with a larger number of conditions to consider, a longer execution time, etc., which would require more meticulous effort by the testers.

11.2.3 CFT Usage and Other Issues

As compared to testing based on FSMs, CFT based on CFGs focuses on the complete paths and the decisions as well as interactions along these execution paths. Because of this emphasis on paths, the number of test cases also increases substantially over FSM-based testing based on the similar underlying structures (states and links), particularly when loops are involved. Consequently, the increased power in covering dynamic decisions and interaction problems is accompanied by the additional cost related to the substantially more test cases. The gain needs to be balanced against the cost to arrive at an optimal solution for specific application environments. For most computation intensive applications, which cover most of the traditional software systems, mere state and link coverage would not be enough because of the interconnected dynamic decisions along execution paths. Therefore, CFT is generally a necessary step in the repertoire of different testing techniques for such systems. More often than not, we need to go beyond just CFT to examine detailed interactions that are captured in data dependency analysis and related data flow testing (DFT).

Because of the complexity with large number of paths when multiple control structures are used, particularly when nested loops are used, CFT is typically applicable as a white-box testing technique to small programs, or to small program units during unit testing. If we want to use it for larger software systems, we have to use a coarse granularity to reduce the number of paths to a manageable level, such as using coarse-grain system-level CFGs, with each node representing a major function (black-box view) or a major component (white-box view) instead of individual program instructions.

CFT can also be enhanced to support usage-based statistical testing. If the branching probabilities are history independent, the corresponding Markov OPs we covered in Chapter 10 can be used. If the probabilities associated with some usage sequences are context and history sensitive (memoryless property for Markov chains not satisfied), we can enumerate individual complete paths and associate usage probabilities with them, similar to the use of Musa's explicit OPs for complete end-to-end operations we covered in Chapter 8. These OPs can then be used to guide our usage-based statistical testing.

11.3 DATA DEPENDENCY AND DATA FLOW TESTING

In the sensitization of CFT test cases, we have encountered some difficulties when shared variables instead of constants are involved in the decision points, and analyses of these variable values were performed to eliminate un-realizable paths. In fact, the correlated decisions need not necessarily involve the shared variable. If some computation and assignments link variables used in later decisions to those used earlier ones, the decisions are correlated. The analysis of this and other data relations is the subject of data dependency analysis (DDA) and the verification of correct handling of such data relations during program execution is the subject of data flow testing (DFT).

11.3.1   Basic concepts: Operations on data and data dependencies

The use of variables or data items in CFG decisions is called *P-use* in data dependency analysis to indicate their use in predicates or conditions. The other kind of use is called *C-use*, or computational use. One common understanding of these usage situations is that these variables or data must be defined earlier, so that we can determine their types and obtain their values, and use them for various purposes. Formally, we can define these data operations as follows:

- Data *definition* through data creation, initialization, assignment, all explicitly, or sometimes through side effects such as through shared memory locations, mailboxes, read/write parameters, etc. It is commonly abbreviated as D-operation, or just D. The key characteristic of the D-operation is that it is destructive, that is, whatever was stored in the data item is destroyed after this operation and cannot be recovered unless some specialized recovery mechanism is used.

- Data *use* in general computation or in predicate, commonly referred to as C-use or P-use. Both these types of uses are collectively called U-operation, or just U. The key characteristic of the U-operation is that it is non-destructive, that is, the value of the data item remains the same after this operation. However, P-use of a data item in a predicate might affect the execution path to be selected and followed. C-use of data items usually occurs in the form of variables and constants in a computational expression or as parameters in a program function or procedure. Such C-use typically affects some computational results, with some result variables being defined.

With the definitions of these two types of data operations, we can next consider the pair-wise ordinal relations on the same data objects:

- D-U relation: This is the normal usage case. When a data item is used, we need to obtain (or "fetch") its value defined previously. Most of the data dependency analysis (DDA) and data flow testing (DFT) focus on this type of usage.

- D-D relation: This represents the overloading or masking situation, where the later D-operation destroys the previous contents. One special case is when D-D relation exists without a U-operation in between, that is, a data item is redefined without its previous definition ever being used. This situation might represent some error in the software, or at least some inefficiencies, because the previous definition was totally wasted. Another special situation is the racing condition, where multiple execution streams or parallel processes/devices are all trying to "write" to a shared data item. Again, the unused D-D relation represents problems with control protocol or inefficiencies. However, under the normal circumstances with one or more U-operations in between, we could focus on the corresponding D-U relations after each D-operation in DDA and DFT while leaving the D-D analysis as specialized tasks for other activities.

- U-U relation: There is no effect or data dependency due to the nature of non-destructive U-operation. Therefore, these relations are ignored in DDA and DFT. As we mentioned before, such correlation might affect the realizability of different execution path. However, as we will see later, we can focus on the corresponding D-U relation for each usage situation to realize different paths in CFT or different slices in DFT, which implicitly takes care of correlated conditions.

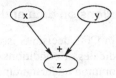

Figure 11.4   Data dependency graph (DDG) element: An example of data definition through assignment

- U-D relation: This is called anti-usage. The only interesting situation with it is that a data item is used without ever been defined previously (no D-operation precedes the first U-operation), which usually indicate a problem in the software.

Therefore, with this basic identification and analysis of data operation pairs, some possible problems can be identified immediately. For overall data dependency analysis (DDA) used in data flow testing (DFT), we focus on the D-U relation and related issues.

11.3.2 Basics of DFT and DDG

The basic idea of data flow testing (DFT) is to test the correct handling of data dependencies during program execution. Since program execution typically follows a sequential execution model, we can view the data dependencies as embedded in the data flow, where the data flow is the mechanism that data are carried along during program execution. The test cases are derived from data dependency analysis (DDA), with a focus on D-U relations, and the related model we call data dependency graph (DDG).

In DDGs, each node represents the definition of a data item, such as a variable, a constant, and a compound data structure. The links in DDGs represent the D-U relation, or "is used by". That is, if we have a link from A to B, we interpret it as that the data defined in A is used to define the data in B. For example, the assignment statement "$z \leftarrow x + y$" can be represented in Figure 11.4, with the definitions for x and y used (C-use) in defining z. This analysis of chains of D-U relations used in defining later data items can be carried out to identify the definitions of those earlier items, until we resolve all the definitions. This backward chaining process, starting from the computational result back to all its input and constants represents the model construction process, which we will elaborate later.

In DFT, we directly focus on the data dependencies captured in DDGs instead of the computational sequences or control flow in CFT. One may argue that DFT is closer to testing the essence of computation because such data dependencies directly affect the computational results, while sequencing or control flow is used mainly due to the limitations of our sequential machines and programming languages used (otherwise, much of the computation can be carried out in parallel). For example, the dependency relations in Figure 11.4 must be obeyed to ensure computational result in z. One the other hand, sequencing in program implementations might be altered without affecting the results. For example, the order of the two statements in a sequence

$$z \leftarrow x + y;$$
$$i \leftarrow i + 1;$$

can be switched without changing the computational results. Therefore, in performing DDA and DFT, we separate out essential data dependencies from program execution sequencing to focus on the correct handling of data items and their dependencies, and ultimately the correct computational results.

Similar to any other systematic testing techniques, we focus on the test preparation part for our DFT, with the test execution and follow-up activities essentially the same as that for other testing techniques described in Chapter 7. For DFT, test preparation includes the following steps:

- Build and verify the DDGs.

- Define and select data slices to cover as individual test cases based on the DDGs. A data slice consists of a data item, usually an output variable, with its definition in terms of other data items, possibly selected from among multiple definitions (Weiser, 1984).

- Sensitize the data slices or the test cases by deciding the input values.

- Plan for result checking.

We elaborate on each of these sub-steps below, with a focus on building the DDGs. Once such a DDG is constructed, slice definition and selection is fairly straightforward, and test case sensitization also directly follows. Outcome prediction is also easy with DFT because the selected and sensitized slice directly defines the computational results. Another reason that we focus on DDG construction is that its form and structure are quite different from the program structure and flow-chart that most software developers are familiar with.

We next describe the ways to construct DDGs by first examining the specific characteristics of them, identifying the information sources, outlining a generic DDG construction procedure, and finally an indirect but easy-to-follow procedure for people who are familiar with traditional sequential programming and flow-charts.

11.3.3   DDG elements and characteristics

In DFT, we are focusing on testing the correct handling of different data items involved in producing the final computational output through data dependency analysis (DDA) using DDGs. Therefore, we can view a DDG as a logical graph where computational results are expressed in terms of input variables and constants through the possible use of some intermediate data items as nodes and related D-U relations as links. Based on this view, we can characterize the different graph elements in DDGs as follows:

- Each node represents the definition of a data item x, denoted as $D(x)$ and represented as x inside an oval in a DDG. The nodes can be classified into three categories:

  - Output or result nodes that represent computational results for the program under testing. These nodes will be analyzed and expressed in terms of other nodes, except in the rare situation that the program does nothing with respect to some data items (that is, some input direct passed down as output).

  - Input or constant nodes that represent user-provided input or pre-defined constants. These nodes represent the "terminal" nodes that do not need to be analyzed any further.

  - Intermediate or storage nodes are those who are neither input nor output nodes. In most computations, these nodes are introduced to facilitate computational procedures to make it easy to obtain the results from input.

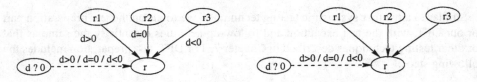

Figure 11.5 DDG element: An example of data selector node

- The relations modeled in DDGs are always D-U relations, or "is-used-by" relation. as in the normal usage situations such as "$z \leftarrow x + y$" depicted in Figure 11.4.

A special case to the above DDG elements is the selective or conditional definitions of certain data items using the so-called data selector nodes. For example, in determining the number of real roots r for the equation $ax^2 + bx + c = 0$, the result r depend on the value $d = b^2 - 4ac$ in such a way:

$$(d > 0) \Rightarrow r \leftarrow 2;$$
$$(d = 0) \Rightarrow r \leftarrow 1;$$
$$(d < 0) \Rightarrow r \leftarrow 0;$$

The three possible values for the result r can be marked as $r1$, $r2$, and $r3$. The final result r will be selected among these three values based on the condition on d. Therefore, we can place r in a data selector node, connect $r1$, $r2$, and $r3$ to r as data inlink, and the condition node "$d?0$" to r as the control inlink. We distinguish control inlink from data inlink by using a dotted instead of a solid link. Only one value will be selected for r from candidate values, $r1$, $r2$, and $r3$, by matching their specific conditions to the control inlink evaluation result. The resulting DDG for this data selector is shown in Figure 11.5 (left figure). Although the specific conditions can be shown explicitly in DDGs, we omit some specific labels for conditions where there is no danger for confusion. By doing so, we simplify the DDG by implicitly matching conditions to positions, such as in the right figure in Figure 11.5.

Notice that in this example, both P-use and C-use are present: C-use is associated with computation for the variables $r1$, $r2$, and $r3$ within each DDG branches, where the constants 0, 1, and 2 are used. P-use is associated with the variable d and constant 0 for the predicate in the control inlink.

In general, such conditional definitions can be expressed as some parallel conditional assignments, in the form of a collection of conditional pairs:

$$(C = C_i) \Rightarrow y \leftarrow f(x_1, x_2, \ldots, x_n).$$

Each of these possible definitions of y is labeled y_i. We can use a data selector node for y to select from y_i's by matching their condition C_i's to the condition node C evaluation result represented in the control inlink. For example, $C = C_2$, then the condition for the y_2 data inlink to y would match the control inlink result, leading to y_2 value been carried over to y.

Unlike the situation with other data definitions where all the data connected to the current data item being defined are used, data selectors only need the condition node and *one* data inlink to uniquely define the current data item. This fact plays a critical role in our data slice definition and related testing to be discussed in Section 11.4.

In most traditional programming languages that support only sequential execution, the above conditional assignments can be implemented using a sequence of assignments controlled by "`if`", "`switch-case`", or similar statements. We will deal with such implementations and DDGs derived from them later in this section, where the mental mapping between parallel conditional assignments and actual program implementations plays an important role in DDG construction.

With the above details about DDGs, we can consider a DDG as consisting of input nodes, output nodes, intermediate nodes, data selector nodes, and associated links and properties. Again, the focus is on the output or results, and their resolution through DDGs in terms of input variables and constants. Because of this procedure for data resolution through backward chaining using D-U relations, the DDGs typically show the following characteristics:

- There is usually one output data item or variable, or at most a few of them.

- There are typically more input variables and constants.

- Multiple inlinks are common.

- Since the DDG is typically shown as flowing from top to bottom, we have the "fan" shaped DDGs as the most common type. This shape is also often described as tree-shaped (like a real tree on the ground, not the upside-down ones in computing literature), or shaped like a river with its tributaries.

11.3.4 Information sources and generic procedure for DDG construction

Because of its focus on details, DFT and its DDGs are usually derived from detailed data information about small components such as represented in the program code or detailed design (white-box view) or detailed functional specifications (black-box view). Traditionally, DFT is more often white-box than black-box, because detailed functional specifications for individual components are not commonly used: Instead of such detailed specifications, the refinement of high-level product specifications is usually accompanied by implementation choices for the components directly. However, for object-oriented methodology, detailed functional specifications might be more meaningful for individual objects, thus making black-box DFT more likely to be used.

When actual code (or detailed design) is available, our natural tendency is to trace it from beginning to end in order to construct our DDGs. In doing so, we could identify input variables and constants first, then follow the code to identify other intermediate variables, link them, and finally conclude with the output variables. This is more akin to following the programmer's train of thought in the (optimistic) hope that everything will fall into its place when we finish.

In its focus on computational results, DFT construction is more naturally aligned to stepwise data resolution backward from output to input. In addition, a model and view independent of the programmer's train of thoughts are also beneficial in detecting problems and ensure product quality. Therefore, the following DDG construction procedure based on backward data resolution is generally preferred:

- Identify output variables.

- Backward chaining to resolve these variables using other variables and constants by consulting the specific computation involved.

- If there are unresolved variables, the above step is repeated for each one of them, until we have no unresolved variables left.

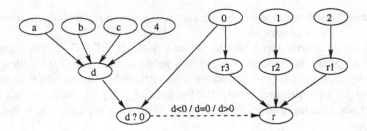

Figure 11.6 A sample data flow graph (DDG)

An unresolved variable is one that is neither an input variable nor a pre-defined constant. Therefore, the above procedure ensures that at the end of DDG construction, all leaf nodes are either input variables or constants. For example, we can follow the above procedure to finish the DDG for Figure 11.5 by resolving the variables d, $r1$, $r2$, and $r3$. The resulting DDG is shown in Figure 11.6, where all the leaf nodes are either input variables (a, b, and c) or constants (0, 1, 2, 4). Notice that we also switched the positions of r3 and r1 and the corresponding conditions in the control inlink so that the sharing of the same constant 0 can be more easily depicted.

One immediate use of such constructed DDGs is the identification of variables in specifications or implementations that are not connected to the DDGs, thus not contributing to the computational results. Such disconnected nodes or sub-graphs are called dead nodes or dead sub-graphs, which usually represent some data problems either in the software or in the model, or at least some wasted system resources in computing something that is not used or returned as results. Such problems can also be detected using DDGs constructed from forward tracing of code by identifying nodes that do not end up in some linked path to output nodes. In this case, effort has already been wasted constructing part of the forward DDGs that lead to nowhere.

11.3.5 Building DDG indirectly

In following the backward chaining procedure for DDG construction, various specific situations specified by conditional parallel assignments in specifications or in implementation can be easily handled. However, in most system implementations using traditional programming languages, they are achieved by sequential assignments and use of conditional statements such as "if" and "switch-case". In addition, most software developers and testers are generally more familiar with such sequential conditional statements. We can customize the above backward chaining procedure to construct DDGs based on information represented in such code and related flow-charts or CFGs. If these CFGs are not available, it is usually much less difficult for people with the traditional training of computer science or software engineering to construct them first and then construct DDGs indirectly. We still follow the same general procedure specified above by starting with the output variables and try to resolve them in terms of other variables and constants until all non-terminal data items are resolved. However, whenever we are dealing with a specific non-terminal node, we can use the corresponding code or CFG in the following steps:

1. Identify all the variables and constants, $x_1, x_2, \ldots, x_n$, used in defining the current node y as in the $D(y)$ operation: $y \leftarrow f(x_1, x_2, \ldots, x_n)$.

2. For each of these data items x_i used, we can trace back to its latest definition by identifying the D-U pair for x_i. If $D(y)$ is not in a branch, we can directly link node x_i to node y.

3. If $D(y)$ is in a binary control flow branch, there are two possible definitions for y after the branching statement is done (after the junction point). The actual definition of y can be handled in the following way:

   (a) We can denote the situation as: "blockI; if C then A else B", where "blockI" is the initial block before the branching statement; C is the branching condition, and A and B are the "then" and "else" parts where $D(y)$ occurs.

   (b) Build sequential subgraph for each branch independently by treating them as:

   - blockI; A
   - blockI; B

   We know how to do such sequential situations from step 2 above. This step gives us two y definitions, labeled as $y1$ and $y2$.

   (c) Build data selector condition subgraph for: "blockI; C". This step gives the definition of C.

   (d) A data selector node will be used for y to select from data definitions $y1$ and $y2$ as follows:

   - The definitions, $y1$ and $y2$, can be directly linked to the data selector node y.
   - The control inlink to y is from C above in the selector condition subgraph.

The above step can be repeated for every data definition, until all unresolved variables are resolved. Multi-way branches can be treated similarly as binary branches, but with a multi-way selector instead of a binary selector above.

Following the procedure above, we should be able to obtain the DDG in Figure 11.6 from the pseudo-code or the CFG in Figure 11.2. Also worth noting is the conventions we adopted in such pseudo-code, with explicitly identified input and output variables. In actual programs, they are often implicit, such as through parameter passing or user-prompt for input, and implicitly returned variables (writable parameters or parameters by reference) or explicit returned variable or values using "exit" or "return" statements.

In the above derivation, one common case where mistakes are often made is with the case of empty "else" part. We need to remember that there are still two choices, corresponding to two execution paths, for the variables involved after this "if-then" statement with empty "else": one updated value and another unchanged. For example, consider the following pseudo-code:

```
input(x);
y ← x;
if ( x < 0 ) then y ← −x;
output(y);
```

In this case, the output variable y still has two possible values, $-x$ and x, depending on whether the condition $x < 0$ is true, which can be represented by a data selector on y values in the DDG.

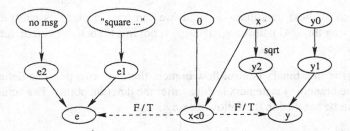

Figure 11.7 Data selectors for multiple variables in branches

Another complication with branching is the situation with multiple variables being used. In this case, we can treat each variable separately, just like in the examples above. However, since the conditions will be the same, they can be shared through control inlinks from the same node. For example, consider the following pseudo-code:

```
input(x);
if ( x < 0 ) then
        exit("square root undefined for negative numbers");
else y ← sqrt(x)
return(y);
```

There are two output variables, one explicitly returned y and another implicitly returned error message e. The DDG can be derived and is shown in Figure 11.7. If the "then" branch is executed (or corresponding data slice realized), we have an error message and the variable y will keep its original value $y0$. Otherwise, y is assigned $sqrt(x)$ and no error message is produced.

11.3.6 Dealing with loops

The use of loops would significantly complicate the DDGs because of the many possible data dependencies involved. The data used within each iteration would be dependent on all the previous iterations, similar to an n-level sequential concatenation. With the difficulties noted above for selector combinations for sequential concatenations, full data dependency analysis for even a loop with moderate number of iterations would be impractical. The situation is much worse than in CFT, where only execution path is analyzed but not the detailed computations and related data definitions within each iteration captured in DDG.

However, many of the loops in actual implementations may not correspond to loops in conceptual models or functional specifications. One concrete example is the summation of an array: conceptually, it can be defined as:

$$S = \sum_{i=1}^{n} A[i],$$

which can be implemented in whichever way supported by a computational model. However, due to the limitations of most sequential programming languages, this is often implemented as a loop.

When we test such non-essential loops, we can choose to focus on the conceptual data dependency between S and A, instead of the individual elements $A[i]$'s. We could adopt a two-phase strategy, testing the loop by CFT, and then collapsing the loop into one processing

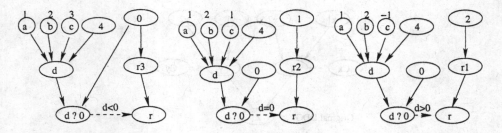

Figure 11.8   Three data slices for the DDG in Figure 11.6 and their sensitization

node, for example, in the form of "S ← arraysum(A);", in performing our data flow testing.

For essential loops that could not be processed without loops even in conceptual models we can attempt to unwind the loops once or twice, treating them as nested if's. In this way, "while C do B" is unwound into: "if C then {B; if C then B}". That is, we have empty else's for both the inner and the outer if's. From what we have described above, we know how to handle such if's. Therefore, by unwinding the loops once or twice, we can test basic data relations but avoid complications with multiple iterations that would be too complex to handle.

11.4   DFT: COVERAGE AND APPLICATIONS

With the data dependency graphs (DDGs) constructed above, data flow testing can be carried out easily by selecting data slices and other entities to cover and sensitize them.   Both these selection and sensitization steps are relatively easy and straightforward, as described below.

11.4.1   Achieving slice and other coverage

As with testing based on complex models, we can always start with testing the basic model elements and then complex interactions and dependencies in DFT. For DFT based on DDGs, we can start with the nodes that represent data items.   The simplest testing would be to provide input and check the output, while ignoring all that is going on inside. We can then repeat the same type of testing for other variables involved, for the links, etc. All these could be done similar to the way we did for simple testing based on checklists in Chapter 8. One special case in the above elementary coverage based on DDGs is the testing with different predicate values, which would be similar to CFT where decision and related paths are tested.

What really makes DFT different from CFT is the use of DDGs in slice testing, where a slice is a specific realization of an output variable value through a specific set of input variable and constant values (Weiser, 1984). When there is a single output variable and no selector nodes, then all the used input variables and constants will be covered in one slice. However, when there are selectors, each selector will choose one specific data inlink from multiple data inlinks with the control inlink takes a corresponding value.   Therefore, we have as many data slices associated with each data selector as the number of corresponding data inlinks. For example, the DDG in Figure 11.6 has three slices, corresponding to the three candidates $r1$, $r2$ and $r3$ data definitions for the variable r, as shown in Figure 11.8.

In general, there will be multiple slices for each output variable, and the number of slices depends on the number of specific selectors and their combinations. The combination of

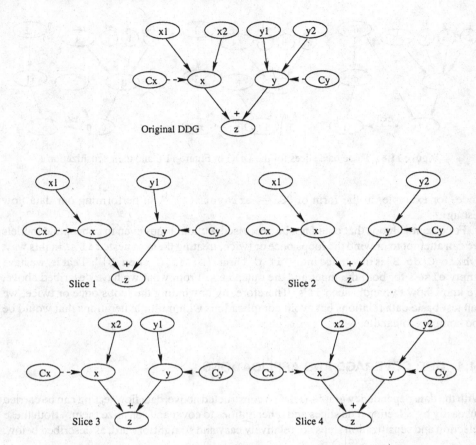

Figure 11.9 Combination of independent data selectors and related slices

two selectors is similar to the path combination involving nesting (when one selector is in the slice of another) or sequential concatenation (when neither is inside the other's slice, thus called *independent* selectors). For example, in computing $z \leftarrow x + y$, if x uses a binary selector and so does y, then the candidate values $x1$, $x2$, $y1$, $y2$ and related conditions can be combined to produce four slices representing the following pairs of values taken by x and y under corresponding conditions: $\{(x1, y1), (x1, y2), (x2, y1), (x2, y2)\}$. Figure 11.9 illustrates this DFG (top figure) and its four slices.

Similarly, if we have a selector for x above (but not for y) between $x1$ and $x2$, and if $x2$ involves another binary selection between $x21$ and $x22$, then there will be three slices corresponding to $\{x1, x21, x22\}$. Notice here $x2$ is going to takes the values of $x21$ or $x22$. Figure 11.10 illustrates this DFG (top left figure) and its three slices.

The above steps for combining two selectors can be repeatedly applied to combine multiple selectors. This process would yield multiple slices from DDGs, and each slice can be selected for testing. The sensitization is fairly easy and straightforward for a selected slice, as follows:

• Every input variable and constant involved in the slice needs to be initialized with specific values, as follows.

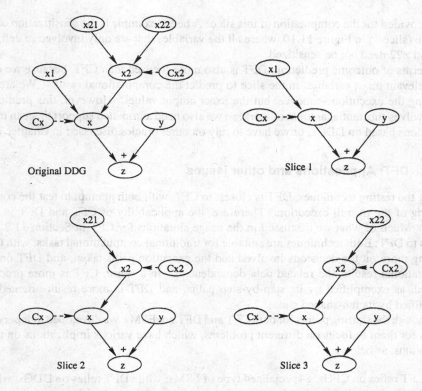

Figure 11.10   Combination of nested data selectors and related slices

- If it is involved in a predicate, the values selected must ensure the realization of the desired predicate value. To do so, we can work backwards with the desired predicate value, and select its input value, possibly through several steps and using several intermediate variables.

- If it is involved as a data input, potentially any value is allowable.

Again, worth noting is that these input values are not uniquely determined by the data slice selected. We can always use ideas from partition-based, usage-based, or boundary testing covered in Chapters 8 and 9 as well as other practical considerations to make such selections.

• For variables and constants not involved in the slice, they would not have any effect on the computational results of the slice according to the definition of slice (Weiser, 1984). However, we still need to assign values to them under most circumstances because data input is usually handled as an indivisible group of actions in the execution of sequential programs. Default or random values, sometimes labeled as "don't care" values, can be used.

The above separation of variables and constants that matter from those that don't in computational results is one significant difference between DFT and CFT. For example, to sensitize the left slice in Figure 11.8, we need to have $d < 0$, which can be carried back to values such as $a = 1$, $b = 2$, $c = 3$, also shown for this slice. Notice here that the constants 1 and 2 involved in $r2$ and $r1$ branches in the other two slices are not used, thus need not to be provided for the computation of this slice. A better example is the sensitization of the $x1$ slice (slice 1) in Figure 11.10, where all the variables that are only involved in defining $x21$ and $x22$ need not be sensitized.

In terms of outcome prediction, DFT is also more focused than CFT, because we only need relevant input variables in the slice to predict the computational results. We are not verifying the execution sequence, but the exact output values. However, this prediction also involves substantial amount of work, so we also need automated support that can make predictions based on DDGs, or we have to rely on other oracles discussed in Chapter 7.

11.4.2   DFT: Applications and other issues

Among the testing techniques, DFT is closest to CFT, with both attempt to test the correct handling of the overall execution. Therefore, the applicability of CFT and DFT is also similar. Much of what we discussed in the usage situations for CFT in Section 11.2 also applies to DFT: Both techniques are suitable for traditional computational tasks, with CFT focusing more on the decisions involved and the execution paths taken, and DFT on the computational results and related data dependencies. In a sense, CFT is more process-oriented, as exemplified by its step-by-step paths, and DFT is more result-oriented, as exemplified by its fan-shaped slices.

Although the starting points for both CFT and DFT are FSMs, we developed independent models for them to focus on different problems, which have various implications on their applications, as below:

- CFT relies on CFGs, a specialized type of FSMs; while DFT relies on DDGs, which deviates greatly from FSMs.

- CFGs closely resemble the program code or overall execution flow commonly associated with sequential computation models. DDGs capture more details about interactions and essential dependencies while omitting the non-essential sequencing information captured in CFGs. This difference manifests in testing in the fan-shaped slices in DFT as contrast to step-by-step paths in CFT.

- DDGs are generally more complex than CFGs.

- The ability for loop handling is much more limited in DFT than in CFT.

Because of the above, our assessment of the limits on applications due to product size and granularity for CFT above is even more true for DFT due to the increasing details in DDGs used in DFT: Both CFT and DFT are generally applicable to small programs, small units of large software systems, or overall system operations for large systems at coarse granularity levels. Automated tool support, such as those discussed in Chapter 7, would help make DFT scale-up to some degree. On the other hand, some of the difficulties with one testing technique can often be compensated for by using the other one. For example, we can use CFT for loops within DFT to form a hierarchical testing strategy. For many systems, CFT and DFT can be used together to ensure product quality, usually with CFT performed before DFT due to its relative simplicity and closer ties to program code.

Similar to CFT, DFT contains much detail in its models and uses it in testing. Typically such detailed information can only be obtained based on program code and detailed design, making them more likely to be used as white-box testing techniques. However, DFT is closer to specification than CFT in its focus on the result instead of the process or path taken to obtain the result. In this respect, DFT is more likely to be used as a black-box testing technique for various situations, including object-level testing for object-oriented systems.

DFT can also be enhanced to support usage-based statistical testing. For example, when we used hierarchical models to perform DFT for large systems, the important data slices or those associated with higher usage probabilities can be expanded into lower-level DDGs, much like we did in our unified Markov models (UMMs) in Chapter 10. Such information can also be used to determine what we want to do with loops. For example, if the loops are associated with frequently used slices, we should probably unwind it (once or twice) to test the basic data relations through the loops. Otherwise, we could just perform CFT for the loops and treat them as a functional node in performing DFT.

In addition to its application to computational and result-oriented system functions and implementation, DFT can be applied in various other application situations due to the information captured in its DDGs. The most important among its other applications is the many uses of data dependency analyses in parallel and distributed systems. If we generalize DDGs to capture the essential dependency among different system tasks instead of data items, we can use such DDGs to help maximize overall system performances: Whenever no dependency is represented in DDGs among different computations tasks, they can be executed in parallel. The parallel execution results can then be synchronized to produce the overall results. In fact, synchronization is a built-in mechanism in DFT, if we interpret the input to a node in a DDG as tasks. We next explore this application of DFT for task synchronization and related testing.

11.4.3   DFT application in synchronization testing

As we described in Section 11.3, for situations like $y \leftarrow f(x_1, x_2, \ldots, x_n)$, that is, when data items x_1, x_2, $\ldots$, x_n are used and processed to define the value for y, we can draw links from them to y. When we interpret these x_i's as parallel tasks carried out before our next task y, these links represent the synchronization situation: All the x_i tasks must finish before y can be completed. That is, if some of the x_i's finish early, we still have to wait for the other to finish before we can finish y. Because of the dynamic nature of such individual tasks executed in parallel, the testing of the correct handling of such synchronizations involves two elements:

- Correct (computational) result (y value) is obtained or appropriate processing (y processing) is applied for given input x_i's. One special case for this is that no result should be produced or no processing should be applied if we do not have all the x_i's available.

- Synchronization of arrivals among x_i's in all possible orders, including time ordered arrivals as well as the possibility of one or more x_i's arriving at exactly the same time.

In synchronization testing, we would combine the above two conditions to test the arrivals of x_i's in all different arriving orders, and to check for the correct outcome. For example, with two way synchronization of input A and B to produce C, we can run the following synchronization testing cases:

- Nothing arrives ⇒ no output.

- One arrives (2 cases: A alone or B alone) ⇒ no output.

- Both arrive (3 cases: A then B, B then A, or A and B together)
  $\Rightarrow$ verify that correct C is obtained.

As we can see, even for such a simple situation, we have 6 synchronization test cases. When the number of x_i's goes up, we need significantly more synchronization test cases due to the combinatorial explosion of possible arriving orders. One way to simplify such testing is through hierarchical models to form groups among the x_i and then synchronize the grouped results. For example, for a 4-way synchronization, if we can group them into two groups of 2-way synchronizations, we can then use 6 test cases for each group and then 6 additional test cases to synchronize the two groups by treating each group as a single input in the higher-level model, resulting in 18 total synchronization test cases. The raw 4-way synchronization would involve substantially more test cases.

11.5 CONCLUDING REMARKS

Generally speaking, there are two basic elements in any computation or information processing task: the data element and the control element, which are organized together through some implemented algorithms. In this chapter, we extended the basic analysis based on FSMs further to analyze and test the overall control flow paths and the overall interactions among different data items through control flow testing (CFT) and data flow testing (DFT). The basis for CFT is the construction of control flow graphs (CFGs) as a special type of FSMs and the related path analysis. The basis for DFT is the data dependency analysis (DDA) using data dependency graphs (DDGs). CFT tests for basic decision or control flow problems and, to a limited degree, interactions along execution paths. More thorough testing of the interactions can be achieved through DFT. Both CFT and DFT models can be either white-box ones based on implementation details or black-box ones based on external functions and usage scenarios. However, due to the details involved and the close resemblance to program code, their white-box variations are more likely to be produced and used.

In addition to CFT and DFT used individually, they can also be combined into the so called transaction flow testing (Beizer, 1995), where the basic structure resembles control flow while the dynamic tokens and the token relations resemble data flow and parallelism common in many systems. Another specialized analysis technique and related testing is the use of Petri-net models (Ghezzi et al., 2003), which can be considered as a special kind of FSMs with two distinct types of nodes called places and transitions (Peterson, 1981). In fact, Petri net shares many of the important characteristics of transaction flow models, such as marking and token relations. These analysis and testing techniques are generally more suitable for overall workload handling in complex systems where parallel execution and process coordination play a central role.

One of the common characteristics that runs through all these testing techniques is their focus on details and the use of such detailed information in performing actual testing. Therefore, these techniques are generally appropriate for small-scale testing, unit testing of large software systems, and high-level control, data, and transaction integration for large systems. In general, for large software systems, people are more like to use a combination of different testing techniques for different purposes and under different environments to maximize the effectiveness of different testing techniques while keeping the overall cost at a reasonable level. These are the subjects that we will examine in the next chapter, to integrate different testing techniques for more effective and efficient testing.

Problems

11.1 Construct a CFG for a small program.

11.2 Construct a CFG from a specification or description of a product or a module.

11.3 Select one of the CFGs you constructed above, sensitize all the paths in your CFG. If it contains loops, treat it as a binary decision (that is, going through the loop or not going through the loop).

11.4 Consider the sensitization of a CFG that consists of sequential concatenation of two subgraphs G1 and G2 (that is, $G = G1 \circ G2$). G1 and G2 each contains a binary branching with conditions C1 and C2 respectively. Discuss the possible sensitization issues for the following cases:

a) C1 and C2 unrelated (or independent of each other).
b) $C1 = C2$.
c) $C1 = \neg C2$.
d) $C1 \Rightarrow C2$. (C1 implies C2, for example, $(x > 100) \Rightarrow (x \geq 0)$)
e) $C2 \Rightarrow C1$.
f) C1 and C2 overlaps, for example, $C1 \equiv (0 \leq x \leq 100)$ and $C2 \equiv (50 \leq x \leq 200)$.
g) C1 and C2 are disjoint, for example, $C1 \equiv (0 \leq x \leq 10)$ and $C2 \equiv (50 \leq x \leq 200)$.

11.5 Repeat the question above for the situation where G2 is nested in G1.

11.6 Is combinatorial explosion a big problem for CFGs without loops? What about when numerous multiple branching statements are used?

11.7 Consider the "`repeat-until`" and the "`do`" loops, where "`repeat {B} until (C)`" keeps on executing the loop-body B until C becomes True, and "`do (n) {B}`" repeats the loop-body B n times.

a) Draw the CFGs for these loops or for related sample programs, and design your test cases to test these CFGs.
b) Are they deterministic or non-deterministic loops?
c) Can you use "`while`" or "`for`" loops to implement them or vice versa? If yes, show your implementation. If no, state why not.

11.8 Enumerate a few different paths systematically for nested loops to get a feel for the enormous number of paths.

11.9 Construct a DDG for a small program.

11.10 Construct a DDG from a specification or description of a product or a module.

11.11 One simple way to check your DDGs is to examine its shape: If it looks like a single-entry/single-exit graph, you have most likely made some mistakes. Why is this the case?

11.12 Define slices for one of the DDGs above, and sensitize them.

11.13 Similar to correlated branches in CFGs, we also have correlated data selectors in DDGs. How can you detect such correlations in DDGs, and how do you deal with them?

Discuss the relative difficulties in identifying and dealing with such correlations in CFGs and DDGs.

11.14 Discuss the relative importance of P-use and C-use in slice sensitization.

11.15 Construct the test cases for a 3-way synchronization.

11.16 Construct the test cases for a 4-way synchronization and compare your test cases to the 2-staged 2-way synchronization described in Section 11.4.

CHAPTER 12

TESTING TECHNIQUES: ADAPTATION, SPECIALIZATION, AND INTEGRATION

For large-scale testing for today's large and complexity software systems, many tasks are carried out to fulfill multiple goals and objectives. Different testing techniques might be used and integrated, and many resources are also involved. In this chapter, we examine these issues in detail, including,

- Individual testing sub-phases and appropriate techniques for them are discussed in Section 12.1.

- Other specialized tasks and specialized testing techniques are described in Section 12.2.

- Integration of different testing techniques covered in the previous chapters to fulfill some specific purposes in practical applications are described in Section 12.3, and illustrated through a strategy for web testing that integrates both usage-based and coverage-based testing at different levels in Section 12.4.

12.1 TESTING SUB-PHASES AND APPLICABLE TESTING TECHNIQUES

For large-scale testing, typically multiple testing techniques are used to test multiple objects. The test activities spread out over time, lasting over months or more than a year. The overall testing is commonly divided further into various *sub-phases* to allow testing to be carried out in a smaller, more manageable scale. In this section, we examine the problems and focuses of these sub-phases and suitable testing techniques for them.

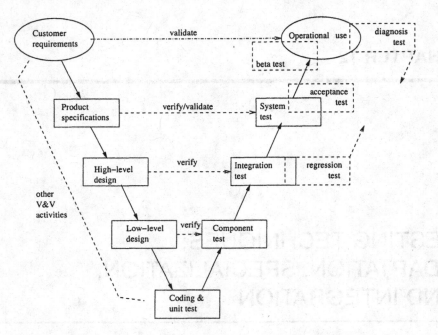

Figure 12.1 Testing sub-phases associated with the V-Model

Testing sub-phases

Figure 12.1 illustrates the testing sub-phases through the use of V-model, a variation of the commonly used waterfall process with an emphasis on verification and validation activities. It shows an annotated V-model with additional information about the specific testing sub-phases. All the sub-phases not included in the original V-model are shown in dashed boxes, with their relationship to the other sub-phases also illustrated. Specific information about these sub-phases is described below:

- When problems are reported by customers during operational use, *diagnosis testing* can be used to recreate and diagnose the problems. Diagnosis testing can also be used for other sub-phases of testing for the same purpose as well, as illustrated by the downward arrow in Figure 12.1.

- Controlled product release and operational use by limited customers lead to *beta testing*. Beta testing can be considered as an additional testing sub-phase closely linked to operational use. It often directly precedes operational use or is carried out at the very beginning of it, as depicted accordingly in Figure 12.1.

- A special testing sub-phases, *acceptance testing*, is attached to the end of system testing, because it is typically performed right after system testing to determine if the product should be released. Sometimes, the late part of system testing is used as acceptance test instead of a dedicated acceptance testing sub-phases. Therefore, we also show possible overlap between the two in Figure 12.1.

- As a direct division of the testing phase in the waterfall process, several specific sub-phases of testing, such as *system testing, integration testing,* and *component testing* have already been represented in the V-model originally. Therefore, no modification or annotation is necessary to represent these sub-phases in Figure 12.1.

- Similarly, *unit testing* is depicted as is, both as a sub-phase of overall testing and as a part of the coding-and-unit-testing phase.

- A special case is *regression testing*, which typically spreads over the overall test activities for new product releases based on previous ones or other similar products. However, since a significant part of the existing product is used, the focus of regression testing is typically on the integration testing sub-phase and thereafter, where old and new product components are integrated. On the other hand, the unit and component testing for the new components are similar to those for traditional new products. The existing components can typically forgo full-fledged unit and component testing, while only subjected to testing focused on interface and interaction problems with the new components, typically in the integration testing sub-phase and after. Therefore, we depict regression testing in Figure 12.1 as linked to integration testing, with an additional arrow pointing to later testing sub-phases.

Unit testing for implementation details

Unit testing tests a small software unit at a time, which is typically performed by the individual programmer who implemented the unit. Depending on the different programming languages used, this unit may correspond to a function, a procedure, or a subroutine for traditional structured programming languages such as C, PASCAL, or FORTRAN, or correspond to a method in object-oriented languages such as C++, Java, and Smalltalk.

Unit testing typically focuses on the implementation details and uses white-box testing techniques, with various coverage criteria as the exit criteria. It typically focuses on the executable statements and related control and data elements. The commonly used testing techniques for unit testing include:

- Ad hoc testing or informal debugging are often used to execute the unit in isolation, typically with the help of some debugging tools to relate specific execution state to the execution of specific statements. Complete statement coverage is a common goal for such testing. For units where interaction with other units is essential, a specific testing environment or testbed may need to be used to simulate this interaction without actually involving other units.

- Input domain partitions based on input variables for the unit are often used to perform input domain partition testing and related boundary testing, as described in Chapter 8.

- Various traditional structural testing techniques, such as control flow testing (CFT) and data flow testing (DFT) described in Chapter 11, are often used, with the models built based on analyzing the code through control flow analysis and data dependency analysis.

Black-box testing could also be performed on the unit, while focusing on the input–output relations. However, it is used much less frequently than white-box coverage testing because of the implementation knowledge possessed by the programmers who test their own code.

Component testing for implementation details and specific functions

Component testing tests a software component at a time, typically by a small group of developers. A component generally includes a collection of smaller units that together accomplish something or form an object. For traditional software products, such as those developed using structured programming and high-level structured programming languages such as C, PASCAL, and FORTRAN, there isn't a clear-cut distinction between units and components, except that components are general larger and each of them typically includes a few units. Consequently, component testing is almost identical to unit testing, except at a slightly larger scale.

For some new programming models and software development paradigms, component testing and unit testing are more likely to be different. For example, for object-oriented (OO) systems, a components is typically an object or a class, which include both the internally defined data objects as well as the pre-defined operations (or methods) on them. Although the same white-box approach for unit testing can still be used for testing such components, it runs contrary to information hiding principle, one of the fundamental ideas in object-orientation. Black-box view is more in line with such objects as components. Corresponding black-box testing techniques or usage-based testing techniques can be used, similar to those we describe with system testing below. In addition, some recent work has been focused on adapting traditional testing techniques to work for object-oriented systems (Binder, 2000; Kung et al., 1998), which attempts to adapt use cases and design pattern ideas in testing as well as in product development.

The increasing use of software development based on COTS (commercial-off-the shelf) components and CBSE (component based software engineering, or CBSD — component-based software development) has also altered people's perception of component testing. In such paradigms, components play a much more important role, which also increases the need for us to ensure and demonstrate the quality and reliability of individual components. Independent testing and certification of software components or reusable parts is key to the possible selection, use, and adoption of certain software components. Therefore, independent verification and validation (IV&V) by third-party participants described in Chapter 7 are often performed for such situations. As for the testing techniques used, the situation is similar to system testing we describe later in this section, where black-box and usage-based techniques dominate, but at a smaller scale.

Integration testing for interface and interactions

Integration testing deals with the integration of different product components to work together, with the focus on interface and interaction problems among these components. Therefore, in integration testing, each component is treated as an atomic unit or as a black-box, while the interconnections among them are examined and modeled to test component interfaces and interactions. Most of the integration testing uses white-box testing techniques. However, the individual units are no longer individual statements or programming unit, but individual components instead. Again, coverage is typically used as the exit criterion for such testing. From integration testing onward, testing is typically performed by dedicated professional testers.

The execution control in such integration situations typically passes from one component to another and back-and-forth, which can be modeled by a finite-state machine (FSM). Therefore, FSM-based testing described in Chapter 10. is often used to cover the different states and transitions to ensure correct handling of interfaces, interactions, and execution control.

Sometimes, we may choose to adopt a completely black-box view for integration testing, and treat the whole collection of the components to be integrated as a black-box and test it accordingly. This view is similar to the system testing view below, and the testing techniques also correspond to those used in system testing. In fact, in many organizations, integration testing is considered as part of system testing instead of a separate testing sub-phase. We make the distinction in this book, using integration testing to indicate the part of testing that focuses on the interface and interactions among different product components, and using system testing to indicate the part of testing that focuses on the overall system operations.

System testing for overall system operations

System testing tests the overall system operations as a whole, typically from a customer's perspective. The primary concern is how the software system works as a whole under the operational environment of actual customers. Therefore, in system testing, the whole system is treated as a black-box, where external functions are tested. In addition, because of the customer's perspective adopted for this testing sub-phase, usage-based statistical testing techniques are often used.

Because of this concern and perspective, the entities to be tested stay at fairly high levels of abstraction. For example, high-level functions or components may be tested, typically those directly visible to the customers, but not implementation details or those elements far removed from customers. As for the team who performs the testing, knowledge about overall product functions, application domain and market segment, and customer expectations and their usage of the system is more important than product implementation details. The commonly used techniques include:

- High-level functional checklists are often used to ensure that all the major functions expected by the customers are present and perform satisfactorily. We can either try to achieve complete coverage of all major functions, therefore resulting in coverage-based testing, or to achieve reliability goals by emphasizing functions important to and frequently used by customers, resulting in usage-based statistical testing. With the latter technique variation, Musa's operational profile (OP) can be used. Both these coverage-based and usage-based system testing techniques were covered in Chapter 8.

- Finite-state machines (FSMs) for the above system functions may be constructed for more systematic testing than merely using the checklists above. Each state here represents a major function expected by and visible to target customers. These testing models and techniques are black-box ones, because they are based on external functions instead of internal implementations. Various coverage criteria can be used as stopping criteria.

- Similar to the way Musa OP enhances checklist to perform usage-based testing for direct reliability assurance. Markov OPs enhanced from FSMs can be used for usage-based statistical testing, as described in Chapter 10. ·

For embedded software systems or for heterogeneous systems with important software components, such as software controlled medical equipment and modern telecommunication networks, the term "system" typically means the complete system with the software part as a component or a sub-system. In such systems, system testing takes on additional meaning as well, which we refer to as super-system testing. Both integration testing and system testing described above can be applied to such super-system testing, to check for interface, interaction, and interoperability problems among different sub-systems, as well as to check for the overall super-system operations as a whole.

Acceptance testing and product release

In most organized development in mature software organizations, some form of acceptance testing is usually performed as the final sub-phase of testing to determine if the product should be released. Related questions also include:

- What is the expectations of product reliability in customer settings if the product is released now?

- What is the appropriate level of post-release product support?

Sometimes, acceptance testing can be a part of system testing, typically the last part that answers the product release questions. However, we distinguish it from regular system testing by the different focuses as well as the differences in defect fixing possibilities: In regular system testing, all major problems observed will be fixed before product release; while in acceptance testing, we assume that the problems will not be fixed because of imminent product release. The discovered problems in acceptance testing will be dealt with during post-release product support. In practical applications, critical problems observed in acceptance testing could cause costly delays to pre-planned and often pre-announced product release. The cost of delay needs to be weighed against the cost of delivering a product with major flaws, in order to arrive at a product release decision.

In terms of testing techniques, the ones usable for system testing are all potentially usable for acceptance testing. But with the focus on product release decisions and expected post-release product support, usage-based statistical testing techniques are typically favored over traditional black-box testing because of their direct linkage to reliability. Repeated random sampling without defect fixing (in statistical terms, without replacement) supported by either Musa or Markov OPs mentioned above is often used for acceptance testing.

Beta testing and testing based on operational problems

Although usage-based statistical testing can be used to ensure product reliability from the user's perspective, there are various limitation to the accuracy and practicality of these techniques. For example, the collection of information about actual usage scenarios, sequences, and patterns is often hindered or completely blocked by proprietary nature of such information, because much of it may be business sensitive. In addition, the diversity of customers and related population pool also present major obstacles in constructing OPs that are accurate for everyone involved.

An alternative to bring information "in" for usage-based testing is to ship the software product "out" in controlled release so that likely problems to be experienced by the general user population can be exposed and corrected before general product release. This model is commonly referred to as beta testing. The benefit is obvious and significant, especially for product with wide release and large user pool, and when usage-based statistical testing is inadequate. However, the cost of running such a testing program is also significant, including:

Table 12.1 Comparison of key characteristics and applicable testing techniques for different testing sub-phases

Sub-phase	Perspective	Stopping	Who	Techniques
unit	white-box	coverage	programmer	db, s-list, BT, CFT, DFT
component-I	white-box	coverage	programmer	s-list, BT, CFT, DFT
component-II	black-box	both	tester/3p	BT, CFT, DFT
integration	white-box	coverage	tester	FSM, CFT, DFT
system	black-box	both	tester	f-list, FSM, Musa, Markov
acceptance	black-box	usage	tester/3p	Musa, Markov
beta	black-box	usage	customer	normal usage

- Direct cost and limitations of running beta tests: A large enough and representative set of customers and users have to be identified; and the relationship with them often needs to be nurtured over a long period of time to gain their trust and cooperation. Sometimes, other criteria instead of representativeness can be used for selection of beta test customers, such as selecting customers who reported most field defects to effectively reduce such chances for similar problems after product release.

- Indirect cost in product delays could be significant, because beta test not only takes time to run, it also takes time and effort to prepare. In addition, enough time should be allowed for customers and users to get familiar with the product and start to use its full set of functionalities.

Therefore, whether to run a beta test, and what kind of beta test to run, its scope and length, etc., all need to be decided with all the factors considered. The general trend for increasing numbers of software products is to run some beta tests. In fact, direct involvement of the massive numbers of users who use the products and report problems, much similar to beta testing, but at a larger scale, has been credited as an important reason for high quality of various open source and Internet-based products (Raymond, 1999; Vixie, 1999).

Summary and comparison of testing sub-phases

Table 12.1 summarizes the different testing sub-phases in roughly the chronological order with respect to several important characteristics:

- *Perspective*: black-box (functional) vs. white-box (structural).

- *Stopping* criteria: coverage-based vs. usage based.

- *Who* is performing the test, including programmers, tester, customers, and independent third party (labeled "3p" in Table 12.1).

- Major types of specific testing *techniques* used, including, informal debugging (db), functional and structural checklists (f-list and s-list), boundary test (BT), finite-state machine based testing (FSM), control flow testing (CFT), data flow testing (DFT), Musa operation profiles (Musa), and Markov operational profiles (Markov).

Notice that main objectives are not directly stated but implied in the above characterization: Black-box testing focuses on external functions provided, while white-box testing focuses on internal implementations of different levels of detail; and coverage-based testing focuses on detecting problems for fixing, while usage-based testing focuses on reliability from a user's perspective.

Component testing is divided into two types, with type I (component-I) as loosely grouped components, and type II (component-II) as tightly packed components which form the basis of objects and reusable and resalable components in object-oriented (OO), component-based software engineering (CBSE), and commercial-off-the-shelf (COTS) component market.

12.2   SPECIALIZED TEST TASKS AND TECHNIQUES

In the above description of testing sub-phases, the tasks can be ordered in roughly chrono-logical order. However, some specialized tasks related to testing would cut through many of these sub-phases, such as defect diagnosis testing and regression testing mentioned above. There are also other specialized testing techniques that can be applied to different objects beyond programs, designed to fulfill different goals, or other techniques that can be used as substitute to testing. We next cover these specialized testing and analysis tasks and related techniques.

Defect diagnosis testing

When problems are reported by customers during normal operations or during beta testing, diagnosis testing is often used to help with the problem diagnosis by recreating the problem, observing program behavior associated with these problems, collecting relevant informa-tion, narrowing down the possibilities, and finally diagnosing the problems by analyzing all the information collected. Diagnosis testing can often help us find the exact location of the underlying faults in the program so that they can be fixed. In performing diagnosis testing, a series of test runs may be executed in succession to progressively narrow down the possible areas of problems. Therefore, highly correlated test runs based on similar scenarios are carried out, which is different from the normal testing or usage situations where a wider variety of usage scenarios are used.

Diagnosis testing can also be used to diagnose problems discovered during testing, as illustrated by the downward arrow in Figure 12.1. However, they may be used less extensively than the diagnosis testing for in-field problems reported by the customers. The key difference between the two situations is information availability: For in-house testing, all the test cases and the related test run details can be provided by the testers for code owners to diagnose the problems. However, actual customers are typically less willing to share detailed usage scenarios and detailed information when problems were encountered. Therefore, the code owners rely more on diagnosis testing to obtain more information for analyzing the in-field problems. The use of diagnosis testing in third-party testing in the IV&V (independent verification and validation) environment resembles in-field problem diagnosis.

In general, the more information that we can collect from specific testing or operational usage, the less our reliance on diagnosis testing. In addition, diagnosis testing can also be used to deal with other problems found through other means as well, such as through inspection and other QA activities. Therefore, diagnosis testing is an important specialized testing activity that cut through many related testing, usage, and QA activities.

Defect-based testing

Besides testing based on specification, implementation, and usage of the programs and other artifacts, testing can be based on the discovered defects or potential defects. The simplest form of such defect-based testing is the ad hoc testing based on guesses where potential faults might be located (not yet discovered, unlike in defect diagnosis testing) based on subjective feelings or some objective evidence, so that related functions or components can be tested accordingly. Systematic application of defect-based testing results in several strategies, including the following:

- *Defect risk based testing*: If the guesswork on where defects are likely can be replaced by estimates supported by quantifiable evidence, the above ad hoc defect based testing can then be more effectively used to focus on the identified high-risk areas, or those areas more likely to contain more defects.

- *Defect injection and testing*: This technique is also call fault seeding and testing (Mills, 1972). The idea is to inject known faults into the software system, and then use testing to catch both injected/seeded faults and original faults to ensure that certain types of defects are detected and removed, much like what immunization do to keep people healthy.

- *Mutation testing*: The basic idea of mutation testing is similar to fault injection/seeding above, but somewhat more systematic in creating slightly changed programs from the original ones. Such slightly changed programs, or mutants, are then subjected to testing by running a test suite to see if the mutants can be detected and "killed". This technique could be used effectively to detect various syntactic variations and related faults, as well as used to evaluate the "strength" or "kill rate" of existing test suites.

Due to the size limit of this book, we will omit detailed discussions of these more specialized testing techniques (Mills, 1972; Hamlet, 1977; Howden, 1982; Voas, 1998). Risk-based testing is covered in connection with the general topic of risk identification and risk-based QA activities in Chapter 21.

Software maintenance, product updates, and regression testing

For software maintenance and post-release product support, problems reported by customers need to be analyzed to fix the underlying defects. In doing so, diagnosis testing is typically used to recreate the problem scenario and to diagnose the problem.

Besides the above corrective software maintenance activities, software maintenance often includes adaptive and perfective activities to adapt the product to different operational environment, or to improve the product in various ways, as a pro-active move. Various product updates through new releases can be considered as an extension to such maintenance activities. The products with a long history and numerous previous releases are commonly referred to as *legacy* products. For these maintenance activities and for legacy products, a special form of testing called *regression testing* is typically used to make sure that previously supported software functions are not negatively affected by the updates.

Unlike problem diagnosis testing and defect-based testing, regression testing is more closely associated with specific testing phases for legacy products and for major software maintenance activities. For major new product releases, we usually go through a full cycle of testing, with the focus of regression testing typically on the integration testing sub-phases where old and new product components are integrated. For smaller product updates and software maintenance activities, regression testing may constitute the main part of the testing. The testing techniques for regression testing are typically more specialized (Rothermel and Harrold, 1996; Rosenblum and Weyuker, 1997), including the following components:

- An analysis of differences between the previous version of the product and the current version based on some formal or informal models to select from existing test cases, and to determine what new test cases are needed.

- The new test cases focus on two areas:
  - the newly developed or updated part, which is fundamentally the same as testing of new systems but on a smaller scale,
  - the interactions involving both old and new parts, which is similar to integration testing, but with a focus on specific kind of interfaces and interactions.

Testing beyond programs

The primary object of testing is program code produced in the software development process. However, this process also produces various other artifacts, such as product specifications, high-level (architectural), module-level, and detailed design documents, user manual, etc. If some of these artifacts can be implemented through some mockups or software proto-types, then the basic testing ideas and related techniques can be applied to test the general feasibility and performance of these prototypes, and testing results can be used to improve the prototypes for inclusion in the final products or for the construction of their successors.

As execution-based techniques for QA, testing can also be applied to various software-intensive systems instead of pure software systems we dealt with so far. Such software-intensive systems include embedded software used to monitor or control physical or hard-ware systems, equipments, or processes, as well as other general heterogeneous systems. Examples of embedded systems include software controlled medical equipments and pas-sive restraint systems in automobiles. Examples of general heterogeneous systems include telecommunication networks and distributed computing facilities over wide geographical areas, where software, hardware, and networks interact with one another. For such systems, it is sometimes hard to distinguish when software testing ends and overall system testing starts. Functional testing and usage-based statistical testing are typically more suitable for testing these system interactions than structural testing and coverage-based testing.

The Internet and the world wide web (WWW or simply the web) are some specific example of general heterogeneous systems. With the prevalence of them and people's reliance on them for their informal needs in daily life and work, testing and QA for these systems are also gaining importance. Various techniques for software testing can be adapted to test web-based applications, as we described in Chapter 10. The integration of different testing techniques for web testing is described in Section 12.4.

Testing to achieve other goals/objectives

As described in Chapter 2, the primary focus of this book is the correctness aspect of quality, which can be characterized by various reliability measures or defect-related entities.

Therefore, all the testing related topics we discussed so far had this focus in the background, that is, to achieve high-reliability or low-defect goals. However, as we have also noticed in Chapter 2, there are various other aspects of quality and related attributes and sub-attributes, which can be addressed by other types of testing, including:

- *Performance testing*, which focuses on the performance of the software system in realistic operational environments. Many such systems are real-time systems, where timely completion of computational tasks and overall workload handling are of critical importance.

- *Stress testing*, which is a special form of performance testing, where software system performance under stress is tested. This type of testing is also closely related to capacity testing, where the maximal system capacity is assessed.

- *Usability testing*, which assesses the overall usability of software systems, particularly for those systems where user interfaces play an important role, such as web browsers, GUI (graphical user interface) products, etc. For such software products and systems, usability may be more important than reliability.

In addition, there are other types of testing, although less formalized than the above to test the other quality aspects, such as testing the installation, maintainability, different environmental configurations, portability, interoperability, security, fault tolerance, recoverability, adaptability, etc. Again, we will omit detailed discussions about these specialized testing due to our book size limit.

Dynamic analyses and other related techniques for QA

Various analyses for problem diagnosis, fault locating, and other purposes associated with testing is the most commonly used dynamic analyses for defect detection and removal (Wallace et al., 1996). In addition, other dynamic, execution-based techniques, including simulation and prototyping, can help us detect and remove various defects early in the software development process, before large-scale testing becomes a viable alternative. On the other hand, in-field measurement and related analyses, such as timing and performance monitoring and analysis for real-time systems, and accident reconstruction using software event trees for safety-critical systems, can also help us locate and remove related defects. The basic ideas of these dynamic analyses and related techniques for QA are summarized below:

- *Simulation* is an important techniques early in the development process before fully operational systems become available, which can push the verification of some high-level design ideas or system architectural features to much earlier stages before expensive implementation and rework are involved. The expected behavior of part or even the whole system can be simulated through some simulation programs or hardware simulators, which capture the essential input/out and timing information. This could be a viable alternative when actual testing becomes exceedingly expensive. The most famous example is probably the extensive and exclusive use of computer simulation instead of wind-tunnel testing for Boeing 777, a product with extensive software components, throughout its entire design and development process.

- *Prototyping* is similar to simulation in basic ideas, where software prototypes, or simplified systems with some key features implemented, are built to test some high-level ideas in architecture, design, or operation environment. These prototypes could be thrown away later (throw-away prototypes) or revised to be included as part of the delivered system.

- *Timing and sequencing analyses* of operational systems can be similar to the analyses performed during problem diagnosis after failures are observed in testing. However, these analyses may be more limited by the amount of information available and different operational environments the system is subjected to. Therefore, various heuristics are used to approximate the causal relations and environmental impacts.

- *Event-tree analysis* is extensively used in accident reconstruction for safety critical systems, which is covered in Chapter 16 in connection to failure containment strategies commonly used for such systems.

12.3 TEST INTEGRATION

Many testing techniques and activities can be applied to test large software systems and to ensure their reliability and quality in general. On the other hand, each technique and related activities are only more effective than others for specific purposes under specific environment or product development phases. A collection of techniques and activities instead of a single one is called for because of the many different aspects of software systems that need to be tested for and many different problems we need to guard against for such large systems. The main advantages of such integrations include:

- *Benefit enhancement*: By taking advantage of the different techniques, the integrated strategies can be used to perform not only the original tasks the individual techniques were designed for, but also provide an "all-around" QA that may go above and beyond customer expectations to delight customers. The combination may yield some unforeseen insights into problem areas or quality aspects so that the combined total benefit may well be more that the sum of its individual elements.

- *Increased flexibility*: Such integrated strategies also offers more flexibility in overall QA and in deriving results that can be extrapolated to different situations and for different types of products and market segments. For example, if we are shifting from new product development to product support and update, much of the suite of testing techniques can still be used but with more of a focus on integrating updated parts with the existing parts.

- *Cost reduction*: By consolidating the models and techniques, substantial savings could be realized because such integrated strategies eliminate much of the redundant work associated with different techniques and activities. For example, many of the information sources can be shared, some models can be reused, even testing results by different techniques can serve as oracles to cross-check each other, etc.

12.4 CASE STUDY: HIERARCHICAL WEB TESTING

The realization of many of the advantages of test integration can be best illustrated in the following integrated strategy for web testing. Continuing our case study of web testing described in Chapter 10, we next examine the different testing techniques that are applicable to web testing and the possible integration of them to effectively assure quality from the perspective of web users.

Techniques applicable to web testing

Most existing work on web testing focus on *functionality testing* to test web components to ensure that the web site performs its intended functions as expected. This type of testing usually involves analyzing given web components, and checking their conformance to relevant standards and external specifications (Bowers, 1996). Specific types of functionality testing include:

- *HTML syntax checking*:   HTML validators, such as Weblint (`www.weblint.org`) and W3C Validator (`validator.w3.org`), can parse HTML files and check their conformance to relevant language specifications and document standards. Most of such validators and similar tools can also perform spelling checking on these files. This testing technique corresponds to automated testing based on checklists we discussed in Chapter 8 or automated syntax testing (Beizer, 1990).

- *Link checking* can be performed to check the entire site for broken links, with the help of tools like Net Mechanic (`www.netmechanic.com`). This is similar to link coverage testing we discussed above for FSM-based testing, but without formally constructing a FSM.

- *Form testing* checks input types and variable names in various forms, with the help of tools such as Doctor HTML (`www2.imagiware.com/RxHTML`). This can be considered as rudimentary input domain testing covered in Chapter 8.

- *Verification of end-to-end transactions*, which is similar to testing complete execution paths in control flow testing covered in Chapter 11.

- *Java component testing*:   Java applets, which work on the clients side, or other Java applications, which work on the server side, need to be tested, similar to traditional software testing we covered in the previous chapters.

Besides these forms of functionality testing, various other forms of testing and related testing techniques have been used for web testing and evaluation:

- *Load testing* is a subset of stress (or performance) testing. It verifies that a web site can handle a large number of concurrent users while maintaining acceptable response time.

- *Usability testing* focuses on the ease-of-use issues of different web designs, overall layout, and navigations. A lot of work has been done on web usability testing. However, such work relies heavily on subjective preferences of selected users. The focus is not on the reliability (the correct delivery of required information or documents), but rather on the appearance and usability. Therefore, it is not included as a part of this case study.

- *Browser rendering* problems may affects the delivery as well as presentation of web contents. For example, HTML files that look good on one browser may look bad on another. We need to make sure that the web site functions appropriately with all these different browser versions. However, the browser checking is done manually to assess the "look & feel" of the GUI etc., similar to usability testing discussed above. Other basic tests to detect browser rendering problems can be done to test for functionality and download time using different browsers.

Besides the above coverage-based testing for individual web components and some other limited aspect, other techniques have been used to test the overall usage scenarios and navigation patterns and evaluate web reliability (Tian and Lin, 1998; Tian and Nguyen, 1999; Kallepalli and Tian, 2001; Tian et al., 2004). In particular, selective functional testing based-on FSM and unified Markov models (UMMs) was performed for frequently used web contents and navigation patterns was supported automated information extraction from existing web logs. This approach was described in our case studies of web testing in Chapter 10.

On the other hand, loosely related collections of web pages can be more appropriately represented and tested by using some simpler usage models based on a flat list of operations and associated probabilities, such as Musa's operational profiles (OPs) we described in Chapter 8. The introduction of statistical testing strategies based on such OPs or UMMs is not to replace traditional testing techniques, but to use them selectively on important or frequently used functions or components, as in the following integrated strategy.

An integrated hierarchical strategy for web testing

We next describe an integrated strategy that integrates existing testing techniques and reliability analyses in a hierarchical framework (Tian et al., 2003). This strategy combines various usage models for statistical testing to perform high-level testing and to guide selective testing of critical and frequently used subparts or components using traditional coverage-based structural testing. There are three-tiers to this strategy, as follows:

1. Development of the high-level operational profile (OP), which enumerates major functions to be supported by web-based applications and their usage frequencies by target customers. This list-like flat OP will be augmented with additional information and supported by lower-level models based on unified Markov models (UMMs). The additional information includes grouping of related functions and mapping of major external functions to primary web sources or components.

2. For each of the high-level function groups, a UMM can be constructed to thoroughly test related operations and components. UMMs capture desired behavior, usage, and criticality information for web-based applications, and can be used to generate test cases to exhaustively cover high-level operations and selectively cover important low-level implementations. The testing results can be analyzed to identify system bottlenecks for focused remedial actions, and to assess and improve system performance and reliability.

3. Critical parts identified by UMMs can be thoroughly tested using lower-level models based on traditional testing techniques. Other QA alternatives, such as inspection, static and dynamic analyses, formal verification, preventive actions, etc., can also be used to satisfy user needs and expectations for these particular areas.

Reliability analysis and risk identification form an integral part of this strategy to help assure and improve the overall reliability for web-based applications. The use of this integrated testing strategy also yield data for use to perform various reliability analyses for several purposes, including: 1) providing an objective assessment of current web reliability from the user's perspective, 2) predicting future reliability (reliability growth) if we continue with testing using our integrated strategy 3) identifying problematic areas or software components for focused reliability improvement. Some examples of such reliability analysis and improvement activities can be found in Chapter 22.

Implementation of the integrated strategy

The following reports can be easily produced from analyzing the web access logs kept at the web servers:

- *Top access report* (TAR) that lists frequently accessed (individual) services or web pages together with their access counts.

- *Call pair report* (CPR) which lists call pairs (transition from one individual service to another) and the associated frequency.

TAR is important because many of the individual services can be viewed as stand-alone ones in web-based applications, and a complete session can often be broken down into these individual pieces. This report, when normalized by the total access count or session count, resembles the flat OP (Musa, 1998) we covered in Chapter 8. Each service unit in a TAR may correspond to multiple pages grouped together instead of a single page. Such results provide useful information to give us an overall picture of the usage frequencies for individual web service units, but not navigation patterns and associated occurrence frequencies.

CPR connects individual services and provides the basic state transitions and transition probabilities for our UMMs. We can traverse through CPR for strong connections among TAR entries, which may also include additional connected individual services not represented in TAR because of their lower access frequencies or because they represent lower-level service units. A UMM can be constructed for each of these connected groups. In this way, we can construct our UMMs from TAR and CPR.

Notice that multiple OPs, particularly multiple UMMs in addition to TAR, our top-level OP, usually result for a single set of web-based applications using the above approach. This implementation of our integrated strategy in a hierarchical form is discussed below:

- At the top level, TAR can be used directly as our flat OP for statistical usage-based testing.

- Entries in TAR can be grouped according to their connections via CPR, and a UMM can be constructed for each of these groups, forming our middle-level usage models, or our individual UMMs.

- The hierarchical nature of our UMMs will allow us to have lower-level UMMs as well as other lower-level testing models to thoroughly test selected functional areas or web components.

This hierarchical implementation of our integrated strategy is graphically depicted in Figure 12.2. We focus on testing frequently used individual functions or services at the top level, testing common navigation patterns and usage sequences at the middle level, and covering selected areas at the bottom level. Specific low-level UMMs or other coverage-based testing models can be built to thoroughly test the related features or critical components in the higher-level flat OPs or UMMs. Coverage, criticality, and other information can also be easily used to generate test cases using lower-level models under our OPs.

12.5 CONCLUDING REMARKS

When testing can be divided and performed in several sub-phases, each one can focus on some specific aspects and try to achieve some specific objectives. Various testing techniques

Top Level:	Top Access Report (TAR) a flat list of frequently accessed services in ranking order (may be grouped by interconnection in customer usage scenarios)
Middle Level:	Unified Markov Models (UMMs) for groups of TAR entries linked by CPR (call-pair report) (may be expanded into lower-level UMMs or other models)
Bottom Level:	Detailed UMMs or other Models associated with frequently visited or critical nodes of UMMs (may correspond to testing models other than UMMs)

Figure 12.2   Hierarchical implementation of an integrated web testing strategy

covered in the previous four chapters can be adapted and used in these testing sub-phases. The major testing sub-phases covered in this chapter and applicable testing techniques are summarized in Table 12.1.

In addition to these sub-phases, various specialized tasks and related testing techniques were also described in this chapter, including:

- problem diagnosis testing,

- defect-based testing, such as defect injection and mutation testing,

- regression testing for product maintenance, updates, and for legacy products,

- testing to achieve other objectives, such specialized testing for usability, stress, performance, etc.

- other execution and dynamic alternatives to testing, such as simulation, prototyping, and dynamic analysis techniques.

Another important issue addressed in this chapter is the possible integration of multiple testing techniques and related activities in a concerted effort to test large software systems and ensure their quality from different perspectives or to guard against different problems. Substantial amount of savings can also be achieved through such integrated strategies due to sharing of many common information sources, models, and other artifacts and results. We demonstrated such testing integration ideas in a case study of hierarchical testing of web-based applications:

- The user focus of web-based applications are supported in this integrated strategy by testing functions, usage scenarios, and navigation patterns important to and frequently used by end users under our top-tier usage model based on the list-like Musa's operational profiles described in Chapter 8 as well as our middle-tier usage models based on Unified Markov Models (UMMs) described in Chapter 10.

- On the other hand, internal components and structures for web-based applications can also be thoroughly exercised by using our bottom-tier models based on traditional coverage-based testing, under the guidance of the upper-level usage models.

In general, a collection of appropriate testing techniques can be selected and adapted to help us perform testing for different purposes and under different project environments.

The integration of them would also enable us to achieve our testing goals more effectively and efficiently.

Problems

12.1 What testing related phases and sub-phases are used in your projects? Can you map them to the standard sub-phases in Figure 12.1?

12.2 What would be the impact on different sub-phase organization and individual sub-phases if the following processes are used: spiral, incremental, iterative, and XP (extreme programming)?

12.3 Repeat the above question by examining the impact of the following technologies: OO, Cleanroom, and CBSE?

12.4 Defect injection testing and mutation testing are not used as widely as many other testing techniques we covered in this book. Why?

12.5 Usability testing is typically tightly integrated with design-for-usability or user-centered-design activities. Can you find some such integration between testing and design for other types of testing we described in this book?

12.6 If you are working on a large software product or a large system with extensive software components, list the types of testing performed, examine the current status of test integration in your project, and give some improvement suggestions.

PART III

QUALITY ASSURANCE
BEYOND TESTING

Although software testing plays a central role in software quality assurance (QA) and is the most commonly performed QA activity, it is neither the only viable nor the most effective QA technique under all circumstances. There are many other QA activities beyond testing. Among the chapters in Part III, Chapter 13 is devoted to defect prevention and related techniques and activities, and Chapters 14, 15, and 16 are devoted to inspection, formal verification, and defect containment, respectively. We compare all these QA alternatives to testing as well as among themselves in Chapter 17.

PART VIII

QUALITY ASSURANCE
BEYOND TESTING

CHAPTER 13

DEFECT PREVENTION
AND PROCESS IMPROVEMENT

Unlike most other commonly used QA techniques, defect prevention deals directly with errors instead of with faults or failures, In this chapter, we first examine the basic concepts and overall approaches to defect prevention, and then describe specific defect prevention techniques.

13.1 BASIC CONCEPTS AND GENERIC APPROACHES

Broadly speaking, testing and most QA activities deal with defects or faults already injected into the software system by a two-step process:

1. Detecting the presence or effect of defects through some observation, examination, or monitoring activities;

2. Applying certain actions to locate and remove the detected defects for most situations, or tolerate their presence if such defect removal activities are impossible or impractical for some special situations.

These activities consume a substantial share of total software development and maintenance cost, ranging from about one quarter to more than half. In addition, the longer a defect lies dormant in a software system, the more likely it is to cause other related problems. Therefore, problems or defects related to product requirement, specification, and high-level design are particularly damaging and costly because of the subsequent chain-effect due to these problems (Boehm, 1991). Unfortunately, most of the testing techniques are much less effective in dealing with such early defects because of the lack of executable program implementations at these early stages. Other QA techniques that can be applied to deal with some such early problems, such as inspection and formal verification, also have their individual limitations.

To summarize, there are two major problems with the existing QA approaches we have covered so far and in the rest of Part III:

- The significant cost for dealing with defects already injected into software systems;

- The ineffectiveness or limitations of existing QA techniques in dealing with early problems or defects.

Because of these, one natural question to ask is:

"Is it possible to prevent the injection of defects, or at least a subset of certain defects, in the first place?"

As defined in Chapter 2, "errors" are missing or incorrect human actions that result in certain fault(s) being injected into a software system. Therefore, if we can automatically provide some of the missing actions or correct some of the incorrect ones, we can prevent the injection of certain faults. We call such direct interventions *error blocking*, because they block the injection of some faults. This can be achieved through strict adherence to selected software process steps or relevant standards, or by using certain software tools that support the implementation languages and development methodologies.

On the other hand, we can analyze the reasons or causes behind the missing or incorrect human actions, and deal with the root causes, or the error sources, instead. This generic approach is called *error source removal*. The focus of these activities is typically on the people and their conceptual mistakes, which may lead to the selection and use of inappropriate development methodologies, languages, algorithms, QA strategies, etc. Such inappropriate selections or wrong uses then may lead to numerous fault injections.

Through error blocking or error source removal, some fault injections can be prevented in either of the above cases. Therefore, these techniques are commonly referred to as defect prevention techniques. They can be used for most software systems to reduce the chance of defect injections and the subsequent cost of dealing with these injected defects. However, the effective usage of defect prevention techniques depends on the specific product development environment and the common problems associated with it. Therefore, appropriate defect prevention actions need to be selected for specific applications.

13.2 ROOT CAUSE ANALYSIS FOR DEFECT PREVENTION

Root cause analyses can be performed on the product under development to identify the common defects and their causes, so that appropriate defect prevention activities can be selected and applied. However, because we aim for defect prevention right at the beginning of the product development, when there is typically a lack of actual product defect data, these root cause analyses are more often based on the predecessors of the current product, or based on similar products from the same company or even from other companies. In general, if there is a closer match between the product under development and the products the root cause analyses are based upon, the more likely that the analysis results can be used more effectively to drive defect prevention actions. Root cause analyses can usually taken two forms:

- *Logical analysis* examines the logical link between the faults (effects) and the corresponding errors (causes), and establishes general causal relations. This analysis is human intensive, and should be performed by experts with thorough knowledge about the product, the development process, the application domain, and the general environment.

- *Statistical analysis* is based on empirical evidence collected either locally or from other similar projects. These empirical data can be fed to various models to establish probable predictive relations between causes and effects.

Once such causal relations are established, either logically or statistically, appropriate defect prevention activities can then be selected and applied for error blocking or error source removal.

Particularly relevant to defect prevention is the root cause analysis that identifies specific error sources or missing/incorrect actions that result in fault injections. Typical causes, appropriate actions, and focus areas include:

- If human misconceptions or wrong conceptual models are the error sources, education and training should be part of the solution. The two main problem areas are: product domain knowledge and development methodology or technology knowledge. In this case, we focus on project personnel in our defect prevention activities, as described in Section 13.3.

- If imprecise designs and implementations that deviate from product specifications or design intentions are the causes for faults, formal methods should be part of the solution. In this case, we focus on the selection and use of a specific development methodology in our defect prevention activities, as described in detail in Chapter 15.

- As a generalization of the above case, if there is empirical or logical evidence that certain standards, tools, or technologies can reduce fault injections under similar environments, they should be adopted and followed. The key is the match between the project environment for the product under development and the effective application domain of the tools and technologies. We address these defect prevention activities focused on the product or project in Section 13.4.

- If non-conformance to selected processes is the problem that leads to fault injections, then process conformance should be part of the solution. Similarly, if various development activities are not precisely defined, measured, and managed, people may not have a process to follow for effective QA. We address these defect prevention activities focused on process in Section 13.5.

Therefore, root cause analyses are needed to establish these predictive relations and related pre-conditions, so that appropriate defect prevention activities can be applied for error blocking or error source removal. Information about how to perform these analyses as well as other related analyses is presented in Chapter 20. Specific types of defect prevention activities are described below in subsequent sections.

13.3 EDUCATION AND TRAINING FOR DEFECT PREVENTION

It has long been observed by software practitioners that the people factor is the most important factor that determines the quality and, ultimately, the success or failure of most software projects. For example, in a recent empirical study of software projects implemented in seven different programming languages (Prechelt, 2000), it was found that the performance variability that derives from differences among programmers of the same language is on average as large or larger than the variability found among the different languages. Software project management and process maturity work, to be described in Section 13.5, has also been extended recently to include process-related education and training for individual programmers, such as through the personal software process (PSP) (Humphrey, 1995).

Education and training of software professionals can help them control, manage, and improve the way they work, thus preventing the injection of certain defects based on their good software engineering practice. The injection of defects similar to those already discovered in the current or previous products can also be prevented if they can learn from these problems and their collective experience. Therefore, this learning effect takes place both *a priori* and *a posteriori* to the actual software development experience. Such activities can also help ensure that they have few misconceptions related to the product in particular and the product development in general. The elimination of these human misconceptions will help prevent certain types of faults from being injected into software products.

Based on the above discussion, the education and training effort for defect prevention should focus on two major areas: generic software development knowledge and specific product domain knowledge. In terms of timeline, both pre-project education and on-the-job training are important in effective defect prevention. We describe these topics below.

Generic knowledge about software development

Software development knowledge plays an important role in developing high-quality software products. As a discipline and profession, software engineering is still immature as compared to other engineering branches, such as mechanical, chemical, civil, and electrical engineering. Consequently, it is still common to have people who lack basic education in computer science and software engineering involved in software development and maintenance activities. For example, a lack of fundamental knowledge and familiarity about the programming language(s) used in product implementation could lead to improper use of language features. Wrong data structures or algorithms could be selected to implement certain product functions, if the programmers lack relevant knowledge. On the positive side, the use of the information hiding principle (Parnas, 1972) can help reduce the complexity of program interfaces and interactions among different components, thus reducing the possibility of interface or interaction problems.

The above problems can be addressed by basic computer science education, to ensure that programmers have a solid knowledge of programming, data structure, algorithms, and other basic topics in computer science. However, many computer science graduates who have a basic knowledge of the above but lack basic knowledge about development processes and activities for large software systems are commonly entrusted with system design and implementation tasks. This situation could lead to misunderstanding of customer requirements, and the lack of expertise with requirement analysis and product specification usually leads to many problems and rework in subsequent design, coding, and testing activities. Similarly, poor overall design could result due to the designers' inability to deal with the complexity associated with large software systems. These problems, in turn, can lead to the injection of numerous defects into the product, and represent more serious problems than the implementation problems noted above. Therefore, acquiring necessary knowledge about software engineering is a pre-requisite to successful and high-quality software products.

Table 13.1 Distribution of modules of different maturity for an IBM product

Module Type	Metric Value(s)	Modules	%
unchanged	SMI = 1	685	52.82
moderately changed	0 < SMI < 1	482	37.22
all new	SMI = 0	129	9.96
all	0 ≤ SMI ≤ 1	1295	100

A related issue is the required expertise with relevant software processes, standards, technologies, and tools. For example, in an implementation of Cleanroom technology (Mills et al., 1987b), if the developers are not familiar with the key components of formal verification or statistical testing, there is little chance for them to produce high-quality products. Similarly, if the project personnel do not have a good understanding of the development process used, there is little chance that the process can be implemented correctly. We deal with these issues in Section 13.4 in connection to technologies and tools for defect prevention, and in Section 13.5 in connection to process-based defect prevention, process maturity and quality improvement.

Product and domain specific knowledge

If the people involved are not familiar with the product type or application domain, there is a good chance that wrong solutions will be implemented. For example, if some programmers only experienced with numerical computation were asked to design and implement telecommunication software systems, they may not recognize the importance of making the software work within the existing infrastructure, thus creating incompatible software. On the other hand, people generally realize the important of familiarity with the product under development as a whole, instead of just limiting themselves to the modules or components they are responsible for, because of the interface and interaction among different product components.

Similarly, if project personnel are not familiar with the product specific history and other characteristics, fault injections are also likely. For example, very few large software projects are developed from scratch these days. For successive releases of software products, typically only a small proportion is newly implemented, while the vast majority of system components are adapted or changed slightly from previous releases. For example, for the IBM product LS (Troster and Tian, 1995), CSI, or changed source instructions, and SMI, or software maturity index, were used to characterize the extent of change for individual modules. SMI is defined by:

$$SMI = 1 - \frac{CSI}{LOC},$$

where LOC is the total lines of code for the module. SMI measures relative change, with untouched modules having SMI = 1 (or CSI = 0) and completely new module having SMI = 0 (or CSI = LOC, all lines are new lines) at the two extremes. For this product, the distribution of modules over different SMI values is given in Table 13.1.

For software products like LS, it is critical for project personal, particularly product designers and programmers, to have a thorough knowledge of not only the modules they are responsible for, but also both old and new modules they interact with, to ensure overall interoperability and the correct and smooth operation for the whole system. This familiarity would also help prevent injection of related faults.

Education vs. on-the-job training

Notice that most of the education and training activities discussed above need to be completed before the project is started, with most of the background information in software development knowledge through formal education, and product domain knowledge through education and training within the company. On the other hand, various other on-the-job training activities can be carried out to help project personnel to prevent the injection of defects similar to those already discovered in the current or previous products. This on-the-job training can take several forms:

- Formal training sponsored by the software development organizations, third-party technical training organizations who address industry-specific training needs, or other parties closely related to the product's domain. This form of training is particularly appropriate for gaining the general product domain knowledge.

- Formal and informal training within the company for product history and product-specific characteristics. Some formal classes as well as informal mentoring can be used for this kind of training.

- On-the-job learning by individual project participants under the guidance of some project expert. This form of learning and training is particularly suitable for preventing future defects similar to those already injected into the software system. An implicit assumption of these learning and training activities is the collection and analysis of existing defect data, which is covered in detail in Chapter 20.

13.4   OTHER TECHNIQUES FOR DEFECT PREVENTION

Appropriate software technologies and tools can also help prevent defect injection. The key in selecting and using such strategies for defect prevention is a good understanding of these technologies and tools on one hand, and a good understanding of the overall project environment on the other hand, so that a match can be made to use appropriate strategies for the product under development.

13.4.1   Analysis and modeling for defect prevention

As noted in Section 13.1, the pre-requisite for defect prevention is some root cause analysis to identify common defects and their causes, and to select effective ways to deal with such defect causes. Similar to the use of root cause analysis, research findings, analysis results, and models related to defects, defect distribution, and relations, can also provide opportunities for defect prevention, such as those covered in Part IV of this book. For example, if we have identified that certain types or classes of defects are concentrated in some product areas or injected during a specific development phase based on historical data, we could selectively apply certain defect prevention techniques to reduce or eliminate the injection of similar defects in the current product release. These analyses and related defect classification scheme are described in Chapter 20.

Most of the defect prevention actions based on analysis results are concentrated on high-risk or potentially high-defect areas, instead of being applied uniformly. For example, if we have established predictive relations between defects and module complexity or architectural features, then we can identify certain critical or high-risk modules or product components that are associated with high defects historically, using selected risk identification techniques described in Chapter 21. This identification of high-risk modules can help us take some pro-active actions, such as assigning the best designers to similar modules to prevent the possible injection of large numbers of faults. In fact, this effect has been observed by many practitioners, where the modules with the highest complexity are not typically the ones with the most observed defects, due to such pro-active actions as well as focused reactive or remedial actions and follow-ups. This effect has also been statistically validated through formal hypothesis testing for some large software products from IBM and Nortel Networks (Koru and Tian, 2003).

Various other analyses of software artifacts related to QA can also be used to help defect prevention (Wallace et al., 1996), including static analysis techniques described in Chapter 14 in connection with inspection techniques and dynamic analysis techniques described in Chapter 6 in connection with general testing techniques. The usage of these analysis results is similar to the above: first identify problem areas and major causes, and then apply selected defect prevention actions that specifically deal with these problems or problem areas.

13.4.2 Technologies, standards, and methodologies for defect prevention

The idea of formal methods, which was introduced in Chapter 3 and will be described in detail in Chapter 15, is a good example of a methodology that can prevent injection of certain defects into the software system. Formal specification produces an unambiguous set of product specifications so that customer requirements, as well as environmental constraints and design intentions, are correctly reflected, thus eliminating certain error sources and reducing the chance of accidental fault injections. Formal verification checks the conformance of software design or code to these formal specifications, thus ensuring that the software is fault-free with respect to its formal specifications. Therefore, formal specification can be considered as a defect prevention strategy. Formal verification is similar to other software verification techniques, such as inspection and testing, but with a focus on the verification of defect absence instead of the detection of defect presence. As a side effect, defect presence can sometimes be detected by formal verification.

Appropriate use of other software technologies and suitable implementation languages can also help reduce the chance of fault injections. For example, Cleanroom technology (Mills et al., 1987b) combines formal verification in the early part of software development with statistical testing in the late part of development to produce high-quality products. As demonstrated in a set of empirical studies (Selby et al., 1987), the use of Cleanroom has lead to fewer defect injections and higher product quality, although various obstacles also exist to its widespread adoption. Similarly, component-based software engineering (CBSE), where assembly of reusable COTS (commercial off-the-shelf) components play a central role in software development, has been promoted as a way to reduce defect injection and to improve overall product quality. However, one must be cautious in adopting CBSE, because different usage profiles may lead to vastly different quality levels (Weyuker, 1998), and there are a lot of open issues with certification of COTS components (Voas, 1999; Voas, 2000). Similar situations exist for the adoption of other software technologies: Careful planning and evaluation need to be carried out before they can be adopted for effective product development and QA.

Similarly, enforcement of appropriately selected product or development standards or guidelines also reduces fault injections. Such standards offer a common understanding for all the people involved, thus reducing the chances for misunderstanding and miscommunication and eliminating a major source for defect injections. For example, the system designed following Coad-Yourdon's object-oriented design principles as a quality guideline was significantly easier to maintain, as demonstrated by a controlled experiment (Briand et al., 2001). These standards may take different forms: The scope may range from product-specific standards, to company-internal ones, to industrial-wide ones, all the way to universal standards. The areas covered may include implementation languages and supporting environments, development activities and processes, interface with other products, documentation, etc.

Various software development methodologies, which package individual techniques into systematic frameworks, can also be used to help with defect preventions. The most famous example is the structured development ushered in by the elimination or strictly limited use of GOTO statement (Dijkstra, 1968), which led to significantly higher levels of product quality and became widely adopted as the standard development methodology. The significant reduction in observed failures and detected faults can largely be attributed to the reduced defect injection, because structured development methodology eliminated a large class of control flow defects. More recently, object-oriented methodology and related programming languages and technologies have been widely used and adopted, but still haven't quite gained universal acceptance, probably due to some counter evidence (Hatton, 1998; Wiener, 1998) despite the general observations of improved product quality.

13.4.3   Software tools to block defect injection

Specific software tools, when used properly, can also help reduce the chance of fault injections. Development support tools are commonly used for this purpose, which typically support specific development activities and different aspects or phases of development. The focus of these tool support strategies is on blocking the fault injections by directly screening out or automatically correcting certain human actions associated with defect injection. Some examples of such tools for defect prevention include:

- *Tool support for programming language and programming environment*: For example, a syntax-directed editor that automatically balances out each open parenthesis, "{", with a close parenthesis, "}", can help reduce syntactical problems in programs written in the C language. Certain coding standards can be easily supported and automatically checked to allow only those meeting the standards to pass through.

- *Tool support for source code and version control*: These support tools can help maintain consistency of product design and code, particularly important for parallel or distributed development commonly used for large software systems or for open source software projects coordinated over the Internet. Specific examples include CMVC, an IBM product for configuration management and version control, and CVS, or Concurrent Versions System (see www.cvshome.org), the open-source network-transparent version control system. The use of these tools eliminates certain inconsistency or interface problems among different software versions or components. Worthy of noting is the fact that these tools, or extensions of them, are often used for defect tracking and quality management as well.

- *Tool support for individual development activities*: These tools can help us automate various repetitive tasks in which humans are more likely to make mistakes, and free us to perform tasks that only we can do better. For example:

  - Various test automation tools can help testers generate and maintain test case suite and select appropriate ones for execution, thus eliminating certain human errors in repeating many similar tasks.

  - Requirement solicitation tools can help us capture user requirements more accurately.

  - Design automation tools can help us with various design tasks.

- An extension to the above tools is the tool support for certain technologies described earlier in this section, as well as support for process implementation and enforcement. Typically, such support is provide by a tool suite or a collection of related tools. The most famous example is Rational Rose, a suite of tools for object-oriented development methodologies, with support for different platforms and implementation languages.

Additional work is needed to guide the selection of appropriate tools or to tailor them to fit the specific application environment. Effective monitoring and enforcement systems are also needed to ensure that the selected tools are used properly to reduce the chance of fault injection.

13.5 FOCUSING ON SOFTWARE PROCESSES

As described so far in this chapter, defect prevention may involve many individual pieces of tasks and many individual activities. Most of these individual pieces can be integrated in some overall framework of software processes. A better managed process or a more suitable process can also eliminate many systematic problems. Effective monitoring and enforcement systems are also needed to ensure that the selected process or standard is followed to reduce the chance of fault injection.

Work on software processes serves many purposes, primarily in software project management during product development and maintenance. However, from the QA perspective, the primary contribution to quality management by the process work is in the area of defect prevention during product development. These software development processes, when properly selected, enforced, and managed, help prevent the injection of certain software defects by integrating many individual defect prevention activities. They also provide an overall guideline that software developers can follow to produce high-quality products. We next focus on several important process issues related to defect prevention, including process selection, definition, conformance, maturity, and improvement.

13.5.1 Process selection, definition, and conformance

There are several commonly used processes for software development, including the traditional waterfall process, iterative and incremental processes and their more recent counterparts such as agile development and extreme programming, and spiral process. Different processes might be suitable for different product domains and different project environments. For example, waterfall process is generally suitable for large software systems with stable requirements, while other processes may be more suitable for newer products with less stable requirements. Consequently, matching the existing processes with the project environment is the key in process selection.

Once a general process is selected, it generally needs to be adapted and precisely defined for product development, in consideration with the specific project environment. Typically, some company-specific process definitions can be used. For example, a variation of water-fall process is defined in the so-called Programming Process Architecture (IBM, 1991) for IBM projects, which precisely defines the different development phases and individual activities associated with them. A well-defined process can be monitored and its conformance can be checked and assured.

The overall software processes, which are typically defined and applied to large software projects, can be tailored to work on smaller-scale projects and for individual programmers, such as through the personal software process (PSP) (Humphrey, 1995). These precisely defined and adapted processes can also be used to facilitate the education and training of software professionals for defect prevention. Therefore, ensuring appropriate process selection, definition, and conformance helps eliminate some such error sources.

In the other direction, work has been done over the last ten years or so to create international standards for software processes, noticeably in the effort culminating in the ISO 9000 series of standards for quality management by the International Organization for Standardization (see www.iso.ch). As it applies to software, the focus is on three areas:

1. Define the process, or "say what you do".

2. Follow the defined process, or "do what you say".

3. Demonstrate evidence, or "show me".

In other words, it requires the process definition and conformance verification covered in this section.

13.5.2 Process maturity

Much of the work in process maturity was pioneered and led by SEI (Software Engineering Institute) at CMU (Carnegie-Mellon University). As stated in its official website at www.sei.cmu.edu, SEI's core purpose is to help others make measured improvements in their software engineering capabilities. The cornerstone of this effort is the software capability maturity model (SEI/CMM) (Paulk et al., 1995). According the SEI vision statement:

> "The right software, delivered defect free, on time and on cost, every time."

> " 'Right software' implies software that satisfies requirements for functionality, performance, and cost throughout its lifetime."

It deals mostly with software fit-for-use or the validation aspect of quality we discussed in Chapter 4, and other management issues such as performance and cost. Furthermore, in the same vision statement, SEI stated:

> " 'Defect-free' software is achieved either through exhaustive testing after coding or by developing the code right the first time. The SEI's body of work in technical and management practices is focused on developing it right the first time, which results not only in higher quality, but also in predictable and improved schedule and cost."

There is a clear focus on defect prevention in SEI's work, through education and process maturity. Since we have covered education issues in Section 13.3 and in connection with process definition above, we focus on the process maturity issue here.

Table 13.2 Process maturity levels in CMM

Level	Description	Focus
1	initial (ad-hoc)	competent people (and heroics)
2	repeatable	project management processes
3	defined	engineering process and organizational support
4	managed	product and process quality
5	optimized	continual process improvement

There are five process maturity levels in CMM, with higher numbers associated with higher process maturity, as summarized in Table 13.2. Associated with each level, there are key practice areas (KPAs) (Paulk et al., 1993) which characterize and define specific practices that an organization needs to follow to reach that level. More recently, SEI has focus more on expanding CMM and the integration of it into the software process in CMMI (CMM Integration), and its use for people (P-CMM) and for software acquisition (SA-CMM). Various empirical studies have also been conducted to confirm the link between higher CMM levels and higher product quality, in selected publications available from the SEI web site. For example, a recent empirical study of 45 projects demonstrated that both consistent application of CMM and higher personal capability contribute to reduced product defects (Krishnan and Kellner, 1999).

CMM has exerted a strong influence in the US, especially in the defense software industry. Parallel international effort on process maturity, assessment, and improvement include ISO-9000 series of standards mentioned above, and two related approaches called SPICE and BOOTSTRAP, as follows:

- SPICE stands for Software Process Improvement and Capability dEtermination. According to the official website www.sqi.gu.edu.au, SPICE is a major international initiative to support the development of an International Standard for Software Process Assessment. The project has three principal goals:

  - to develop a working draft for a standard for software process assessment;
  - to conduct industry trials of the emerging standard;
  - to promote the technology transfer of software process assessment into the software industry worldwide.

- BOOTSTRAP was funded by the European Commission within the ESPRIT programme, with the objective to develop a methodology for software process assessment, quantitative measurement, and improvement, and validate the methodology by applying it to a number of companies (Kuvaja et al., 1994).

13.5.3 Process and quality improvement

Notice that in the above approaches for software process assessment, maturity and improvement, such as SEI/CMM, SPICE, and BOOTSTRAP, one of the ultimate goals is product quality improvement. Alternatively, one can focus directly on quality improvement through measurement, analysis, feedback, and organizational support, as in the TAME project and related work (Basili and Rombach, 1988; Oivo and Basili, 1992; Basili, 1995; Basili et al.,

1995; Seaman and Basili, 1997; van Solingen and Berghout, 1999). The key elements to this approach include: QIP or quality improvement paradigm, GQM or goal-question-metric paradigm, and EF or experience factory. We briefly describe the basic ideas below, with some examples of quality measurement, analysis, and feedback presented in Part IV.

QIP includes three interconnected steps, understanding, assessing, and packaging, which form a feedback and improvement loop. The first step is to *understand* the baseline so that improvement opportunities can be identified and clear, measurable goals can be set. All future process changes are measured against this baseline. The second step is to introduce process changes through experiments, pilot projects, *assess* their impact, and fine-tune these process changes. The last step is to *package* baseline data, experiment results, local experience, and updated process as the way to infuse the findings of the improvement program into the development organization.

In the QIP approach, various measurements need to be taken for the assessment step above. GQM paradigm identifies the measurement goals (conceptual level) first. For example, some specific process improvement goals in QIP, or quality improvement goals can be identified, under the environmental constraint of the software project. Then a set of questions (operational level) related to a specifically identified goal is used to characterize the assessment or achievement of it. Finally, a set of metrics is derived and associated with every question in order to answer it in a measurable way. GQM can be used to guide measurement-based process improvement as well as various other purposes, such as for general software measurement, analysis, and feedback we cover in Part IV.

EF, or experience factory, provides organizational support for process and quality improvement in the above approach. The key idea is the separation of concerns, with the project organization primarily concerned with product development and maintenance, and the experience factory concerned with process, quality, and development support. EF supports reuse of experience and collective learning from the project organization by developing, updating, and delivering experience packages back to the project organization. The most famous example of experience factory is the Software Engineering Laboratory (SEL) at NASA/GSFC (Basili et al., 1995). The most up-to-date information about this EF can be found at the official website sel.gsfc.nasa.gov.

13.6 CONCLUDING REMARKS

Defect prevention techniques can be a very effective and efficient way to deal with quality problems by preventing the injections of faults into the software systems. The primary advantage of these techniques is in the effective savings resulted from not having to deal with numerous software faults that would otherwise be injected without applying these defect prevention techniques. There are two general strategies for defect prevention:

- *Error blocking*: Identifying common errors, which are defined to be missing or incorrect human actions, and blocking them to prevent fault injections. Various techniques, such as following well-defined processes, standards, and methodologies, or using appropriate tools, can help block identified common errors.

- *Error source removal*: Identifying common error sources and removing them, thus preventing fault injections. Various activities focused on people and their product and process knowledge can be carried out to removal these identified error sources, such as through education and training, process maturity and improvement initiatives, and other techniques specifically based on causal analysis of injected or potential faults.

Consequently, the pre-requisite for these defect prevention techniques to work is the effective identification of these common errors and error sources, so that appropriate techniques can be applied to block or to remove them. For mature product lines or mature software development organizations, the rich historical data of past defects and related information can be used to identify common errors and error sources. Therefore, defect prevention should be a primary choice of QA techniques for such products and organizations.

However, for new products to be developed in a new environment for an emerging market, it would be hard to collect existing defect data and analyze them to formulate an overall defect prevention strategy. Anticipated defects, based on past experience or general knowledge, can be used for this purpose. However, the effectiveness of the selected defect prevention techniques would be somewhat questionable, and should be closely monitored and adjusted whenever necessary.

In either of the above situations with mature products or new ones, there are still some defects whose related errors or error sources we couldn't identify practically. This observation is particularly true for large software systems, where it would be infeasible to analyze all the actual and potential defects to find their corresponding causes in errors and in error sources. In addition, we cannot expect the selected defect prevention techniques to be 100% effective in blocking all the identified errors or removing all the identified error sources. These facts indicate that there would still be some defects that evade the defect prevention activities and get injected into large software systems. These defects then need to be dealt with by other software QA alternatives we cover in this book.

Problems

13.1   What are the commonly used defect prevention strategies and initiatives? Are they focusing on error source removal or error blocking? What more can be done in you view?

13.2   One of the difficulties with empirically validating better-quality claims for various defect prevention initiatives is in the part of hypothetical if's, such as in the claim: "If abc is not used, #xyz defects would be introduced." How would you validate such claims?

13.3   Do you think zero defect is a realistic or practical goal? What about the zero-defect mentality?

13.4   How much of your formal education and on-the-job training is related to defect prevention and how much related to other ways of dealing with defects? What changes would you suggest?

13.5   Is root cause analysis commonly performed in your organization? If so, what is the purpose? Does it have a strong impact on your software quality?

13.6   What relevant standards to your industry are consistently followed in your company for defect prevention?

13.7   What are the commonly used development methodologies in your organization? Was quality or defect prevention used as part of the justification for the introduction and adoption of these methodologies in the first place?

13.8   What tools are commonly used in your software development or maintenance? In your view, is any of them contributing to defect prevention?

13.9 Define process maturity levels and discuss their relationship to the quality. (You might want to browse the SEI web site at www.sei.cmu.edu and related publications for references.)

13.10 What is the focus of your organization's process work, conformance or improvement? Is your organization ISO certified or CMM assessed? If so, what's the impact on your product quality?

13.11 Do you have an experience factory within your organization or something similar, such as an experience warehouse or database? How are your past project data and experience kept?

CHAPTER 14

SOFTWARE INSPECTION

Software inspection is the most commonly performed software quality assurance (QA) activity besides testing. Unlike testing, inspection directly detects and corrects software problems without resorting to execution, therefore it can be applied to many types of software artifacts. Depending on various factors, such as the techniques used, software artifacts inspected, the formality of inspection, number of people involved, etc., inspection activities can be classified and examined individually, and then compared to one another. We next discussed these issues, with a focus on the technical aspects of inspection. As a general extension, we also consider static analyses of programs and other software artifacts that can be performed similar to the ways that software inspections are performed.

14.1 BASIC CONCEPTS AND GENERIC PROCESS

Software inspection deals with software defects already injected into the software system by detecting their presence through critical examination by human inspectors. As a result of this direct examination, the detected software defects are typically precisely located, and therefore can be fixed easily in the follow-up activities.

The case for inspection

The main difference between the object types of inspection and testing, namely executable programs for testing and all kinds of software artifacts for inspection, is also the primary reason for the existence of inspection: One does not have to wait for the availability of

237

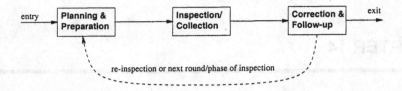

Figure 14.1 Generic inspection process

executable programs before one can start performing inspection. Consequently, the urgent need for QA and defect removal in the early phases of software development can be supported by inspection, but not by testing. In addition, various software artifacts available late in the development can be inspected but not tested, including product release and support plans, user manuals, project schedule and other management decisions, and other project documents. Basically, anything tangible can be inspected.

Because of this wide variety of objects for inspection, inspection techniques also vary considerably. For example, code inspection can use the program implementation details as well as product specifications and design documents to help with the inspection. Inspection of test plans may benefit from expected usage scenarios of the software product by its target customers. Inspection of product support plans must take into account the system configuration of the product in operation and its interaction with other products and the overall operational environment. Consequently, different inspection techniques need to be selected to perform effective inspection on specific objects.

Similarly, there are different degrees of formality, ranging from informal reviews and checks to very formal inspection techniques associated with precisely defined individual activities and exact steps to follow. Even at the informal end, some general process or guidelines need to be followed so that some minimal level of consistency can be assured, and adequate coverage of important areas can be guaranteed. In addition, some organizational and tool support for inspection is also needed.

Generic inspection process

Similar to the generic QA process we described in Chapter 3, all three basic elements of planning, execution, and follow-up are represented in the generic inspection process in Figure 14.1. The major elements are explained below:

- *Planning and preparation:* Inspection planning needs to answer the general questions about the inspection, including:

  - What are the objectives or goals of the inspection?
  - What are the software artifacts to be inspected or the objects of the inspection?
  - Who are performing the inspection?
  - Who else need to be involved, in what roles, and with what specific responsibilities?
  - What are the overall process, techniques, and follow-up activities of the inspection?

In the inspection literature, the term "inspection" is often used to denote the inspection meeting itself. Preparation for such meetings, as well as all the related activities leading up to these meeting, is often grouped with inspection planning, as the "planning and preparation" step.

- *Inspection or collection:* This step roughly corresponds to the execution of QA activities in our generic quality engineering process. However, as noted above, this step typically refers to the inspection meeting alone in literature, while all the activities leading up to this meeting are grouped in the previous step. This step is also referred to as collection or collection meeting. The focus of this step is to detect faults in the software artifacts inspected, and record the inspection results so that these faults can be resolved in the next step.

- *Correction and follow-up:* The discovered faults need to be corrected by people who are responsible for the specific software artifacts inspected. For example, in design or code inspection, the responsible designer or programmer, often labeled as design or code "owners" in industry, need to fix the design or code. There should be some follow-up activities to verify the fix. Sometimes, new inspection rounds can be planned and carried out, as illustrated by the dotted line leading back from the "correction & feedback" step to the "planning & preparation" step in Figure 14.1.

Therefore, faults are detected directly in inspection, in the preparation or the inspection steps, and removed in the follow-up step.

Within the generic inspection process above, there are numerous possible variations, primarily associated with the answers to the questions posed in the inspection planning step. There is generally a close integration between inspection techniques with inspection processes. Therefore, we introduce commonly used inspection techniques in connection with the corresponding inspection processes and examine their individual characteristics together in subsequent sections.

14.2 FAGAN INSPECTION

The earliest and most influential work in software inspection is Fagan inspection (Fagan, 1976), which is almost synonymous with the term "inspection" itself. Ever since its initial conception, Fagan inspection has been used widely across different industrial boundaries and on many different software artifacts, although most often on program code. Almost all the other inspection processes and techniques can be considered as derivatives of Fagan inspection, by enhancing, simplifying, or modifying it in various ways to fit specific application environment or to make it more effective or efficient with respect to certain criteria.

Process and participants

The original Fagan inspection process (Fagan, 1976) included five steps for actual inspection preceded by inspection planning. However, because of the tight connection between the planning and execution of inspections, they are generally considered together in the following six steps:

1. *Planning*: Deciding what to inspect, who should be involved, in what role, and if inspection is ready to start.

2. *Overview* meeting: The author meets with and gives an overview of the inspection object to the inspectors. Assignment of individual pieces among the inspectors is also done.

3. *Preparation*: Individual inspection is performed by each inspector, with attention focused on possible defects and question areas.

4. *Inspection* meeting to collect and consolidate individual inspection results. Fault identification in this meeting is carried out as a consensus building process.

5. *Rework*: The author fixes the identified problems or provides other responses.

6. *Follow-up*: Closing the inspection process by final validation.

Notice that in the Fagan inspection process, the term "inspection" is used to refer to the inspection meeting, while individual examination of the software artifacts under inspection, often referred to as individual inspection in later literature, is referred to as "preparation". We should keep this distinction in mind when examining inspection literature in order to avoid unnecessary confusion. In addition, Fagan inspection is typically carried out as an one-pass inspection. Although re-inspection for final validation is allowed, it is not interpreted as another complete round of inspection.

We can adapt the generic inspection program diagram in Figure 14.1 to depict Fagan inspection in the following:

- The "planning and preparation" block in Figure 14.1 can be expanded into three sequential steps, "planning", "overview", and "preparation" in Fagan inspection.

- The "inspection/collection" is directly mapped to the "inspection" step.

- The "correction and follow-up" block can be expanded into two sequential steps, "correction", and "follow-up".

- The dotted link for the next round of inspection is eliminated.

Fagan inspection typically involves about four people in the inspection team, large enough to allow group interaction to help with the defect detection, but small enough to allow individual voices to be heard. In general, the potential inspectors are identified in the planning stage (Step 1) from those designers, developers, testers, or other software professionals or managers, who are reasonably familiar with the software artifacts to be inspected, but not necessarily those who directly work on it. An ideal mix would include people with different roles, background, experience, and different personal or professional characteristics, to bring diverse views and perspectives to the inspection.

The assignment of individual pieces for inspection among the inspectors needs to take two issues into consideration: overall coverage and areas of focus. On the one hand, different inspectors will be assigned different pieces so as not to unnecessarily duplicate inspection effort. On the other hand, some important or critical pieces may need the focused attention of more than one inspector. A related inspection technique that uses extensive duplicate inspection on critical areas is described in Chapter 16, because they share the same basic idea of duplication for fault tolerance.

The inspection meeting should be an organized event, with one inspector identified as the leader or moderator, who oversees the meeting and ensures that it fulfills its main purpose of defect identification and consolidation. The meeting typically lasts two hours or less to avoid the ineffectiveness due to fatigue. The focus is on defect detection and consolidation only, but not on defect resolution, which may easily sidetrack the meeting. The assumption is that a group of people working together would find and confirm problems that individuals may not. However, each individual must be fully prepared and bring forward candidate problems for the team to examine together. In this group process, false alarms will be eliminated, and consolidated defects will be confirmed, recorded, and handed over for authors to fix.

General observations and findings

Ever since Fagan inspection was introduced in the 1970s, it has been widely adopted, adapted, and used in many companies covering diverse industries. Some important findings are summarized below:

- *The importance of preparation*: Many studies pointed out the great influence on inspection effectiveness by well-prepared inspectors and their individual inspections. In fact, the majority of defects discovered during inspection were initially noted by individual inspectors during their preparation, while the meetings are mainly used to consolidate the individual results to eliminate false alarms and confirm true defects (Porter and Johnson, 1997). This general observation has lead to several variations of Fagan inspection, as described in the next section.

- *Variations with team size, moderator role, and session coordination*: Depending on the size and complexity of the artifacts to be inspected, different team sizes may be appropriate. This has led to reduced team size for some situations, such as for small pieces of code or small increments in non-traditional (non-waterfall) development processes. In the other direction, larger sized teams or multiple sessions may be used for large or complex inspection objects. When multiple sessions are involved, the coordination issues also need to be addressed. No matter what the variations, the moderator plays a very important role not only in coordination but also directly affects the inspection effectiveness (Holmes, 2003).

- *Defect detection techniques used in inspection*: Various defect detection techniques have been proposed and used in inspection. The general idea is that systematic techniques are more likely to uncover defects during inspection than ad hoc checking (Porter et al., 1996). We will address this issue in Section 14.4.

- *Additional use of inspection feedback*: In addition to correction and direct follow-up actions based on feedback from inspection, the inspection process itself or the overall software development process and product quality can be improved. If root cause analysis is carried out to identify some of the common sources of the defects found during inspection, preventive actions can be carried out to prevent the injection of similar defects in future projects. The performance of these additional analyses or the use of such feedback forms an integral part of some modified inspection processes, such as Gilb Inspection (Gilb and Graham, 1993) to be described in the next section. These causal analysis results can also be used to guide defect prevention activities by removing identified error sources or correcting identified missing/incorrect human actions, as described in Chapter 13.

14.3 OTHER INSPECTIONS AND RELATED ACTIVITIES

Variations to Fagan inspection have been proposed and used to effectively conduct inspection under different environments. Some of them are direct responses to some of the general findings of Fagan inspection described above. We organize these inspection techniques and processes along two dimensions:

- size and scope of the inspection,

- formality of the inspection.

Since most of them were initially conceived and introduced as alternatives to Fagan inspection, the original descriptions are typically accompanied by comparison to Fagan inspection or empirical studies of the effectiveness of the newly proposed alternatives. We summarize some important inspection techniques and processes below.

14.3.1 Inspections of reduced scope or team size

As described above, Fagan inspection teams typically consist of four members to allow for the potential benefit of group process to discover defects that would otherwise escape the individuals. However, some software artifacts are small enough to be inspected by one or two inspectors. Similarly, such reduced-size inspection teams can be used to inspect software artifacts of limited size, scope, or complexity. Consequently, the so-called two-person inspection (Bisant and Lyle, 1989) was proposed to simplify the Fagan inspection, with an author-inspector pair, but following essentially the same process for Fagan inspection. This technique is cheaper and more suitable for smaller-scale programs, small increments of design and/or code in the incremental or iterative development, or other software artifacts of similarly smaller size.

A typical implementation of two-person inspection is the reversible or symmetric author-inspector pair, that is, the individuals in the pair complement their roles by inspecting each other's software artifacts. Consequently, on the organization level, this technique is also easier to manage because of the mutual benefit to both individuals instead of the asymmetric relation in Fagan inspection, where the author is the main beneficiary while the inspectors are performing "service" to others or to the company. The idea of two-person inspection has also found renewed interest in the new development paradigm called agile development and extreme programming (Beck, 1999), where the so-called paired programming resembles the author-inspector pair.

On the other hand, there has been empirical evidence pointing to the fact that most of the discovered defects are indeed discovered by individual inspectors during the "preparation" step of Fagan inspection, with the gains of defect detection by the meeting ranging approximately from 5% to 30% (Humphrey, 1989; Porter et al., 1996). Therefore, there is a possibility of eliminating inspection meetings entirely, thus significantly reducing the overall inspection cost without sacrificing many of the benefits from inspection. This results in the so-called meetingless inspection or the use of nominal inspection teams, where individual inspectors do not communicate with each other as a part of inspection (Biffl and Halling, 2003). One issue to deal with in this kind of inspection is the significantly higher false alarm rate (Porter and Johnson, 1997). Various ways of communication can be used to pass the individual inspection results to the author, for example, through direct communication with the author, or through some data or defect repository.

14.3.2 Inspections of enlarged scope or team size

One direct extension to Fagan inspection is based on the common observation about inspection meetings in Fagan inspection, where people tend to linger on discovered defects and try to both find the causes for them and suggest fixes. These additional activities in the meeting would interfere with the main task of defect detection and confirmation in Fagan inspection and tend to prolong the meeting, leading to diminishing returns as the meeting drags on. On the other hand, these activities do add valuable information to the feedback that can be used to improve the overall inspection process and product quality.

A solution to this problem is proposed in the Gilb inspection (Gilb and Graham, 1993), where an additional step, called "process brainstorming", is added right after the inspection meeting in Fagan inspection. The focus of this step is root cause analysis aimed at preventive actions and process improvement in the form of reduced defect injections for future development activities. There are several other special features to Gilb inspection, as characterized below:

- The input to the overall inspection process is the product document, rules, checklists, source documents, and kin documents. The emphasis is that any technical documentation, even diagrams, can be inspected.

- The output from the overall inspection process is the inspected (and corrected) input documents, change requests, and suggested process improvements.

- The inspection process forms a feedback loop, with the forward part resembling Fagan inspection but with the added step for process brainstorming, and the feedback part consisting of inspection statistics and adjustment to inspection strategies. Multiple inspection sessions are likely through this feedback loop, by making the dotted line in the generic inspection process in Figure 14.1 into a solid line. In a sense, this overall process resembles our quality engineering process in Figure 5.1 more closely, where analysis and feedback play an important role.

- The inner inspection steps (forward part of the overall feedback loop) are labeled somewhat differently than in the Fagan inspection, as follows (with Fagan inspection equivalent given inside parenthesis):

  1. planning (same),
  2. kickoff (overview),
  3. individual checking (preparation),
  4. logging meeting (inspection),
  5a. edit (rework),
  5b. process brainstorming (),
  6. edit audit (follow-up).

  Notice that 5a and 5b are carried out in parallel in Gilb inspection.

- The team size is typically about four to six.

- Checklists are extensively used, particularly for step 3, individual checking.

Another variation to the above is the phased inspection (Knight and Myers, 1992), where the overall inspection is divided into multiple phases with each focusing on a specific area or a specific class of problems. These problems not only include the defects (correctness problems), but also issues with portability, maintainability, etc. This inspection is typically supported by some form of checklist and related software tools. The dynamic team make-up reflects the different focus and skill requirements for individual phases.

14.3.3 Informal desk checks, reviews, and walkthroughs

As mentioned at the beginning of this chapter, inspection is most commonly applied to code, but it could also be applied to requirement specifications, designs, test plans and test cases, user manuals, and other documents or software artifacts. However, these other software artifacts are typically less formal or less precise than the program code itself, which partially explains the need for less formal forms of inspection.

Desk check typically refers to informal check or inspection of technical documents produced by oneself, which is not too different from proofreading one's own writings to catch and correct obvious mistakes. However, with the advance and widespread use of various software tools, many of which come packaged with the compilers or programming support software, we should not be focusing on such things as mis-spelling, format, syntactical errors, and other problems that can be easily detected and/or corrected by these tools. Instead, desk checks should focus on logical and conceptual problems, to make effective use of the valuable time of software professionals.

Similar to desk check, *review* typically refers to informal check or inspection of technical documents, but in this case, produced by someone else, either organized as individual effort, or as group effort in meetings, conference calls, etc. The focus of these reviews should be similar to desk checks, that is, on logical and conceptual problems. The differences in views, experience, and skill set are the primary reasons to use some reviews to complement desk checks. In most companies, the completion of a development phase or sub-phase and important project events or milestones are typically accompanied by a review, such as requirement review, design review, code review, test case review, etc.

A special form of review is called *walkthrough*, a more organized review typically applied to software design and code. Meetings are usually used for these walkthroughs. The designer or the code owner usually leads the meeting, explaining the intentions and rationales for the design or the code, and the other reviewers (meeting participants) examine these design/code for overall logical and environmental soundness and offer their feedback and suggestions. Defect detection is not the focus. Typically, these meetings require less time and preparation by the participants except for the owners.

In practical applications, these informal checks, reviews, and walkthroughs can be used in combination with formal inspections. For example, desk checks should precede any other reviews or inspections because we do not want to waste other people's time and effort on trivial and obvious mistakes we have made in product development. Information from reviews and walkthroughs can be used to plan for inspections and to determine which part to inspect, inspection techniques or processes to use, whom to invite as inspectors, etc. In addition, follow-up on inspection results and defect fixing can often be an informal review instead of another round of formal inspection.

14.3.4 Code reading

In addition to informal reviews and walkthroughs, various formal review techniques have also been proposed and used on various software artifacts. The most commonly used such formal reviews are various code reading techniques, typically applied by readers to

```
1    input(x);              1    y ← x;
2    if(x > 0) then         2    if(x > 0) then
3        y ← x;             3    else
4    else                   4    output(y);
5        y ← −x;            5    y ← −x;
6    output(y);             6    input(x);
```

Figure 14.2 A program segment (left) and its permutation (right)

individually examine program code to detect defects. The inspectors or readers focus on reading source code and looking for defects, with feedback to the author either through meetings or other means of communication.

An effective code reading technique for structured programs is top-down hierarchical decomposition combined with bottom-up abstraction. This technique, particularly its bottom-up abstraction, is called code reading with stepwise abstraction (Basili and Mills, 1982). The decomposition allows readers or inspectors to focus on one subpart of a program at a time; and the abstraction builds up a conceptual understanding of the pieces and connects them together in a structural hierarchy to form an overall picture. This divide-and-conquer strategy, which is intrinsically in agreement with structured programming philosophy, applies well to structured programs. In a recent study (Dunsmore et al., 2003b), this reading technique was found to perform well for object-oriented software, although with high cost. It can also be complemented by alternative defect-detection techniques, such as use case driven ones.

The basic idea of coding reading by stepwise abstraction shares many things in common with the mental models programmers use to design and implement programs and readers use to comprehend them. In the program design and implementation process, the overall tasks are decomposed into smaller and smaller ones recursively, until we reach the level that the individual tasks are small enough for implementation as an individual unit (for example, a function, a procedure, or a subroutine). This is the essential idea of structured programming or structured development.

Program comprehension works in the opposite direction: The readers start with individual lines or statements and abstract out individual blocks or units, and then use the abstract representation of them in comprehending higher-level units. This mental model has been empirically validated by some early experiments (Shneiderman, 1977; Shneiderman, 1980). Some of the findings can be best illustrated through the example in Figure 14.2: The left figure resembles a real program segment in pseudo-code, while the right one is the left one reshuffled (or a permutation or mutation of the left). The experienced programmers are much more effective in recalling and reconstructing programs like the left one in experiments than the scrabbled programs like the right one. The explanation is that they can abstract out the "meaning" of such meaningful programs, but for texts like the right one in Figure 14.2, the only way to recall or to reconstruct them is strictly through memorization.

We can also use Figure 14.2, particularly the left figure, to illustrate the ideas of code reading by stepwise abstraction. This program can be divided into three parts: input–processing–output. The middle processing part can be abstracted by an experience reader or programmer to $y = |x|$. Consequently, when this segment is used inside a larger segment or unit, this mental abstraction $y = |x|$ can be used to connect it to the rest of the unit. Therefore, we can build up higher and higher levels of program comprehension for larger and larger units by following such steps. Problems can also be detected along the way.

In this way, the readers or inspectors are focusing on the semantics or the "meaning" of the program, instead of the syntactical problems that can be easily detected by various programming or debugging tools.

One fact worth noting in the above abstraction is the formalism used, for example, $y = |x|$. In keeping track of larger and larger units and their functions or "meanings", we might need to describe them or specify them in formal ways. This is similar to the formalism used in formal program specifications that we discuss in Chapter 15 in connection with formal verification of program correctness.

14.3.5 Other formal reviews and static analyses

In addition to formal reviews of program code using various reading techniques above, various formal reviews can also be applied to other software artifacts. For example, in the active design reviews (ADR) (Parnas and Weiss, 1985), to ensure inspectors' active participation, the author prepares questionnaires to focus on specific scenarios or areas. ADR usually involves many participants, ranging from managers, designers, and programmers. The questions are designed in such a way that they can only be answered by careful study and analysis of the design document. This emphasis on the importance of preparation would likely lead to active participation. The typical ADR meetings are broken down into smaller ones or multiple sessions, with each participated by two to four people to allow for better interaction between reviewers and the author.

Formal reviews and inspections can also be supported, or substituted in some cases, by other analysis techniques for technical documents for software. Inspection belongs to the category of static analysis techniques that directly analyzes the form and structure of a product without executing the product (Wallace et al., 1996). Other static and/or formal analysis techniques can also be used, including various formal model based analyses such as algorithm analysis, decision table analysis, boundary value analysis, finite-state machine analysis, control flow and data dependency analyses, software fault trees, etc. Most of these analyses can be used in testing or other QA activities, and are covered accordingly in connection with corresponding techniques and activities, as described below:

- Decision table and decision tree analyses are related to partitions of choices and partition-based testing. Therefore, they are covered in Chapter 8.

- Boundary value analysis is related to testing for boundary coverage. Therefore, it is covered in Chapter 9.

- Finite-state machine analysis is most closely related to state-based testing, and covered in Chapter 10.

- Control flow and data dependency analyses, and to some degree, algorithm analysis, are most closely related to control flow testing and data dependency testing. Therefore, they are covered in Chapter 11.

- Various analyses related to symbolic executions and program state descriptions or formal specifications, such as in the form of logical pre-/post-conditions and mathematical functions computed by a program, are closely related to formal verifications. Therefore, they are covered in Chapter 15.

- Software fault trees are mostly used in analyzing accidents for safety-critical systems. Therefore, they are covered in Chapter 16 in connection to failure containment strategies commonly used for such systems.

14.4   DEFECT DETECTION TECHNIQUES, TOOL/PROCESS SUPPORT, AND EFFECTIVENESS

As an integral part of any software inspection technique and process, defect detection can be carried out and supported by various specific techniques and tools. The overall inspection processes and techniques as well as other factors affect the inspection effectiveness. We discuss these issues below.

Defect detection techniques

In the above descriptions of individual inspection techniques and related processes, we have already mentioned the use of checklist, scenarios, stepwise abstraction, etc. for defect detection. We next examine these and other defect detection techniques in more detail.

When no systematic defect detection technique is recommended or used in a specific inspection process, we call it *ad hoc* defect detection. The inspection team could choose to use some systematic defect detection technique to improve inspection effectiveness. For example, although no specific defect detection technique is specified in Fagan inspection, one may choose to leave it as is, thus using ad hoc defect detection, or use other defect detection methods, such as checklist- or scenario-based defect detection. The rationale that motivates people to seek out other defect detection techniques is that systematic defect detection techniques are less likely to miss major areas that we try to cover, thus leading to more defect discoveries and better quality. We will keep this point in mind when we examine various empirical studies about inspection effectiveness at the end of this section.

Checklist-based defect detection techniques use various forms of checklists to ensure coverage of important areas for inspection:

- Artifact-based checklist: Examples include checklists for major functions or features in requirement and specification inspections, components in design inspections, program functions/routines, data structures and other data definitions, etc., in code inspections. Notice that most of these checklists can also be followed in informal reviews or walkthroughs.

- Property-based checklist: Examples include checklists for coding style and standards, conformance to development methodologies, dependencies or coupling between different components, modules, or program parts, etc. This kind of checklists can be constructed based on analysis of common defects in previous releases of the product or similar products from industry, so that these problematic areas can be the focus of effective inspections. Such checklists are more likely to be used in formal inspections instead of informal reviews or walkthroughs.

Notice that these checklists look remarkably similar to the checklists used in our checklist-based testing in Chapter 8. In fact, many of these checklists can be shared between inspection and related testing to reduce the overall QA cost.

Scenario-based inspection is closer to usage-based testing we described in Part II of this book than coverage-based testing that checklist-based inspection is akin to. In scenario-based inspection, usage scenarios are used to guide the areas of focus, and typically tie together multiple product components that are involved in the scenario. For example, for an implemented product, customer usage scenarios can be used to inspect the code of the components involved to see if the usage scenarios can be handled properly by the product. An important variation of scenario-based inspection is the use case based inspection for object-oriented systems, which has gained popularity in QA for such systems, because of the importance that use cases play in object-oriented methodology.

Abstraction-based inspection, similar to the technique of code reading with stepwise abstraction described in Section 14.3, is a special defect detection technique particularly suited for code reading and code inspection for structured programs.

Tool support and process integration

Inspection process is human intensive, with the involvement of inspectors spending their valuable time to perform various inspection activities. It is virtually impossible to automate most of these activities. However, proper software tool support can reduce the routine effort and free the inspectors to focus on what they can do best. For example, inspection for syntax errors is a waste of inspectors' valuable time, because they can usually be more effectively detected by some programming tools. Therefore, the inspectors can focus on logical or conceptual problems.

Communication support, data repository, and groupware can also facilitate the inspection processes better. For example, proper groupware support can help lessen the burdens of inspection meetings, where interactions among the inspectors can be facilitated and recorded, and inspection reports can be easily produced. Communication via asynchronous means and data repositories can help with the communication between inspectors and the author in meetingless inspections as well as in other inspection tasks, such as supporting the use of background information for preparation in Fagan inspection.

To enhance the likelihood for success, inspection needs to be integrated into the overall quality engineering process and software development process. Adequate resources need to be allocated for inspection, and inspection results, as well as possible process improvement suggestions, need to be handled accordingly. As inspections can consume a substantial amount of resources, particularly software professionals' valuable time, upper management support for these activities is a critical success factor for inspections.

As follow-ups to the completed inspections, we need to go beyond just fixing the discovered defects. Various analyses can be and need to be performed, either within the inspection process, such as in Gilb inspection, or after the inspection process, to extract valuable information and lessons learned from the inspection activities just completed. These analyses and follow-up activities are described in Part IV of this book. A specific analysis technique called orthogonal defect classification (or ODC) (Chillarege et al., 1992) is described in Chapter 20, which can be used to analyze defects discovered during inspection to provide specifically tailored feedback to improve the inspection process and its effectiveness.

Inspection effectiveness and related studies

Inspection effectiveness can be assessed from several different perspectives. For example, inspection productivity can be assessed as the number, size, or amount of technical documents inspected per unit time or per session. Inspection intervals, effort, process changes, product modifications and defect fixed, etc., can also be used to assess inspection effectiveness. With the correctness-centered quality perspective in this book, defect-related measures can be directly used to measure inspection effectiveness.

Ideally, the defect measure should be about the latent defects and downstream failures and problems caused by these latent defects or faults that escaped the inspection. However, there are many other factors affecting these latent defects. The usage environment also affects the likelihood for failures. Therefore, most of the inspection effectiveness studies use the number of defects detected, either directly or normalized by size or some other measurement of the inspection objects, to measure the inspection effectiveness.

Among the reported inspection effectiveness studies in literature, most agree that defect detection method used has a strong influence on the inspection effective, while the impact assessments of different inspection processes and techniques were less than unanimous. Most also agree that inspector expertise or skills also have a strong impact on inspection effectiveness, but it is hard to quantify. In a series of studies summarized in Porter and Votta (1997), it was noted that better defect detection techniques, not better process structures, are the key to improving inspection effectiveness. In addition, they found that scenario-based inspection is better than ad hoc or checklist based inspections, and the latter two are about the same in effectiveness.

Other studies also point out similar effects, but the details are different. For example, it was observed that both abstraction-driven and use case driven inspections for object-oriented systems are superior to checklist-based inspection, with the abstraction-driven inspection obtaining high payoff but also incurring high cost, while use cases are easy to use and cost little to implement (Dunsmore et al., 2003b; Dunsmore et al., 2003a). On the topic of reading techniques related to abstraction-driven inspections, it was found that use of multiple reading techniques are superior than using the single best reading technique alone for individual inspections (Biffl and Halling, 2003). Other factors, such as organizational structure, working relationship among participants, and physical proximity, were also found to affect the contents and durations of inspection meeting and inspection effectiveness (Seaman and Basili, 1998).

Therefore, these empirical studies and follow-up studies in the same direction would help us choose appropriate inspection techniques and processes to maximize their effectiveness. In particular, the selection of defect detection techniques can be guided by these studies. On the other hand, the selection of inspection processes and participant is largely determined by the type of technical document to be inspected, the scope of the inspection, and the availability of experts for inspections.

14.5 CONCLUDING REMARKS

To summarize, inspection can be a very effective and efficient way to deal with quality problems caused by faults that have already been injected into software systems. Inspection works by directly examining the software artifacts, identifying problems or faults, and removing them. Sometimes, it is the only way, before execution becomes possible during early development phases, or for informal artifacts where formal analyses cannot be performed. This early and wide applicability is the main advantage of inspection over its close competitor, testing, although both detect the presence of faults, either directly in inspection or indirectly by observing execution failures in testing, and remove them.

As a human-intensive QA alternative, inspection also suffers from its own limitations, including:

- Difficulties in dealing with dynamic and complex interactions often present among many different components or functions in large software systems;

- Difficulties with task automation because of the human expertise involved. Communication and analysis tools can only help inspection to a limited degree, but are not able to replace human inspectors whose ability to detect conceptual problems cannot be matched by any software tool.

Consequently, inspection forms an important component in an overall suite of techniques and activities to ensure product quality. Detailed comparison of inspection with other common QA alternatives and techniques is presented in Chapter 17.

Problems

14.1 Assess the use of inspection in your organization and describe the forms of inspection used, scope and pervasiveness, formality and process, data collection and data keeping, and integration with other QA activities.

14.2 Find a piece of code or some technical document and perform a Fagan inspection on it. Document and discuss your experience and findings based on this exercise.

14.3 Repeat the inspection above, but use a different inspection technique.

14.4 Document your experience with various review meetings, and discuss the similarities and differences between them and inspection.

14.5 What is the technique, if any, that you use when you read your own programs or those of someone else's? Compare your mental process in understanding and checking the code when it is written in a language that your are familiar with that for programs in an unfamiliar language.

14.6 Despite many empirical studies that compare inspection favorably to testing, it is still not as widely used as testing. What is your assessment of the reason behind this fact?

14.7 Conduct some small-scale experiments about code reading and understanding similar to that described in Section 14.3 and Figure 14.2 and see how people build up conceptual understanding of programs. For example, you may ask some of your co-workers or classmates to make some changes to a program or rewrite it in a different language, and observe/measure the way they approach this task and the result produced.

CHAPTER 15

FORMAL VERIFICATION

As mentioned in the previous chapter, formal reviews and inspections can be supported or substituted in some cases by other analysis techniques for some software artifacts. Some of these analysis techniques attempt to formally verify program correctness through logical or other formal inferences, or to check certain properties. We next describe these formal analyses based on formal models of programs and their expected behavior, as an alternative way for software quality assurance (QA).

15.1 BASIC CONCEPTS: FORMAL VERIFICATION AND FORMAL SPECIFICATION

As Dijkstra pointed out: Testing shows the presence of defects, not their absence. (See E.W. Dijkstra Archive at www.cs.utexas.edu/users/EWD, particularly manuscripts numbered EWD268, EWD273, EWD303, and EWD1036.) In response to this and other similar observations, formal verification techniques attempt to show the absence of defects or faults in the implemented software systems.

Formal methods and their components

The basic idea of formal verification is to verify the correctness, or absence of faults, of some given program code or design against its formal specifications. Therefore, the existence of formal specifications is a prerequisite for formal verifications. Both formal specification techniques and formal verification techniques are referred to as *formal methods*

251

collectively in literature. When formal methods are used for software development, formal specifications are used upstream for requirement analysis and product specifications, and formal verifications or analyses are used downstream to verify the design and code before additional verification and validation (V&V) activities are carried out. Therefore, the use of formal methods can be summarized in the following two-step process:

1. *Constructing formal specifications*: The expected behavior and other properties of the software artifacts are represented in formal models. These models of program code, design, and expected behavior are typically product-dependent, which can be specifically constructed for formal verification and analysis purposes. However, to reduce cost as well as to benefit from formal development methods, these models can be the same as the formal specifications or adapted by formalizing informal specifications for the product.

2. *Performing formal verifications*: Formal analysis techniques are applied on the product components, typically product code or formal designs, to verify their correctness with respect to their formal specifications, or to check for certain properties. These techniques are typically organized as a product-independent framework of rules that serve as the basis of formal inferences or analyses. The most common type is a set of *axioms* used in correctness verification, which we describe in Section 15.2. Other frameworks used for formal verification and analysis are also described in this chapter.

Therefore, the analysis and verification activities are similar to formal reviews and inspections against requirement documents, product specifications, standards, etc. However, they focus on verifying the correctness or fault absence, or checking for other properties, instead of detecting defect in inspections and reviews. The formal specifications here serve similar purposes as the checklists for inspections in Chapter 14.

Formal specifications

Formal specification is concerned with producing an unambiguous set of product specifications so that customer requirements, as well as environmental constraints and design intentions, are correctly reflected, thus reducing the chances of accidental fault injections. It is similar in idea to various other defect prevention strategies based on development methodologies described in Chapter 13.

Formal specifications typically focus on the functional aspect or the correctness of expected program behavior, instead of non-functional aspects such as development schedule, personnel, cost, process, etc. With formal specifications, the desirable properties for software specifications, the so-called 3Cs (completeness, clarity, consistency) can be more easily and sometimes formally analyzed and assured through various formal analysis and verification techniques. Formal specifications can be produced in several different forms, falling into two general categories, descriptive specifications and operational specifications (Ghezzi et al., 2003), as follows:

- *Descriptive specifications* focus on the properties or conditions associated with software products and their components. For example:

  - Entity-relationship diagrams are commonly used to describe product components and connections.

- Logical (or logic) specifications focus on the formal properties associated with different product components or the product as a whole.

- Algebraic specifications focus on functional computation carried out by a program or program-segment and related properties.

- *Operational specifications* focus on the dynamic behavior of the software systems. For example:

    - Data flow diagrams specify information flow among the major functional units.

    - UML diagrams specify individual behavior for major objects or product components.

    - Finite-state machines (FSMs) describe control flow in state transitions.

Notice that most of the operational specifications can be tested by using various testing techniques we described in Part II, and analyzed by various formal analysis techniques briefly summarized in Chapter 14. Therefore, we focus on formally verifying descriptive specifications, particularly the logic subtype. In what follows, we will only introduce the basic ideas associated with individual specification techniques in connection to the specific formal verification techniques.

Formal verification and analysis

Formal verification checks the conformance of software design or code to its formal specifications described above, thus ensuring that the software is fault-free with respect to its formal specifications. To do this, some formal frameworks of models and rules are needed to support the arguments or inferences based on logical reasoning, algebraic relations, etc. The most influential and widely used ones include axiomatic correctness (Hoare, 1969; Zelkowitz, 1993), weakest pre-conditions (Dijkstra, 1975; Gries, 1987), and functional correctness (Mills et al., 1987a). The basic ideas are summarized below:

- The *axiomatic* approach works with the logical specifications of programs or formal designs by associating with each type of program or design elements with an *axiom* to prescribe the logical transformation of program state before and after the execution of this element type. When connected together through a formal set of inference rules, this approach can produce a correctness proof for a program, a program-segment, or a formal design, with respect to its formal specifications.

- The *weakest pre-condition* approach works in much of the same way as the axiomatic approach above, but with the focus on the goal or the computational result that is captured by the final state of the execution sequence. A series of backward chaining operations through the use of the so-called *weakest pre-conditions* transform this final state and its properties into an initial state and its properties, which verifies the correctness of the verification object if the initial state properties can be satisfied.

- The *functional correctness* or *program calculus* approach is similar to the axiomatic approach in the sense that some basic axioms or *meanings* of program elements are prescribed. Symbolic executions are used to connect these elements in a program. The program correctness, or the mathematical function specified and computed by the program, is verified through this process.

We single out the axiomatic approach in Section 15.2 to give readers a glimpse of a typical formal verification techniques and their applications. Related observations, such as the substantial amount of verification effort required, make subsequent discussions about different issues with formal verification and analysis techniques rooted in solid ground.

Each of the above approaches produces a full proof of program correctness. However, sometimes, we can accept partial proof or verification of certain properties instead of the full proof to reduce the verification cost while still verifying features or properties important to the specific product or its application environment. Model checking and other formal and semi-formal analyses of programs and formal designs offer such opportunities, as described in Section 15.3.

15.2 FORMAL VERIFICATION: AXIOMATIC APPROACH

The axiomatic approach is among the earliest work in the direction of formally verifying the correctness of programs (Hoare, 1969), and as such, influenced almost all the later work in this areas (Zelkowitz, 1993). We next outline this approach and give some concrete examples.

15.2.1 Formal logic specifications

The specifications to be used with axiomatic verification fall into the category of descriptive specifications introduced earlier. They are logical statements or conditions associated with the states, or program states, of programs or program segments. In what follows, we use programs and program segments interchangeably, because they are treated essentially the same way in this approach. The basic elements of these logical specifications include:

- Let S denote a program segment.

- The program state *before* executing S can be described by its *pre-condition* P and denoted as $\{P\}$ when it is shown with programs or in the proof or verification process. For example, if a program accepts non-negative input for its input variable x, the pre-condition can then be described by the logical predicate $P, \{x \geq 0\}$, or $\{P \equiv x \geq 0\}$.

- The program state *after* executing S can be described by its *post-condition* Q and denoted as $\{Q\}$. For example, if the above program accepting non-negative input for its input variable x computes its output y as the square root of x, the post-condition can be described by $Q, \{y = \sqrt{x}\}$, or $\{Q \equiv y = \sqrt{x}\}$.

- This pair of logical predicates around program segment S, denoted as $\{P\}S\{Q\}$, which is also referred to as a schema, constitutes the formal specifications for S, indicating that "if P is true before executing S and S terminates normally, then Q will be true".

The above notations are generally associated with program code. However, they can also be extended to deal with program designs, through various specification languages, notations, and methods, such as Z, VDM (Vienna Definition Method), etc. (Ghezzi et al., 2003; Zelkowitz, 1993). We next describe the verification techniques to verify $\{P\}S\{Q\}$, for S against its formal specifications.

15.2.2 Axioms

The logical inference rules usually take the form:

$$\frac{\text{conditions or schemas}}{\text{conclusion}}.$$

This kind of rules is interpreted as, "if we know that the expressions above the line are true, then we can infer that the expression below the line follows". The basic logical operations include logical AND ($\land$), OR ($\lor$), NOT (negation, or $\neg$), and IMPLIES ($\Rightarrow$).

We start with the so-called consequence axioms for logical implications and deductions that link different predicates. One variation sets up logical inferences for more restrictive pre-conditions, as follows:

$$\text{Axiom A1}: \quad \frac{\{P\} \Rightarrow \{R\},\ \{R\}S\{Q\}}{\{P\}S\{Q\}}.$$

Axiom A1 states that if a program works for a given pre-condition, it also works for a more restrictive (or stronger) pre-condition. For example, if we have already proven that our program S works for all non-negative inputs, or $\{R\}S\{Q\}$, with $R \equiv \{x \geq 0\}$, then by applying axiom A1, we can concluded that it also works for a positive input of bounded value, that is, $\{P\}S\{Q\}$, with $P \equiv \{0 < x \leq 1000\}$, because $P \Rightarrow R$ in this case.

Another variation of the consequence axiom sets up logical inferences for more relaxed post-conditions, as follows:

$$\text{Axiom A2}: \quad \frac{\{P\}S\{R\},\ \{R\} \Rightarrow \{Q\}}{\{P\}S\{Q\}}.$$

Axiom A2 states that if a program works for a given post-condition it also works for a less restrictive (or relaxed) post-condition. For example, if we have already proven that our program S calculates our results r within ϵ of the true results γ, that is, $|\gamma - r| \leq \epsilon$, then we can relax the precision requirement to 2ϵ, and still calculate an acceptable result, because $|\gamma - r| \leq \epsilon \Rightarrow |\gamma - r| \leq 2\epsilon$.

For each type of basic program elements, an axiom can be derived as the basis for correctness verification. Here we restrict ourselves to only the following basic statement types:

- Assignment in the form: $y \leftarrow expr(x_1, x_2, ..., x_n)$, where the right hand side (rhs) is an expression involving variables $x_1, x_2, ..., x_n$,

- Sequential concatenation in the form: $S_1; S_2$

- Conditional or "`if`" statement, either as an "`if-then`" statement in the form of:

  if B then S

  or an "`if-then-else`" statement in the form of:

  if B then S_1 else S_2

- Loop or "`while`" statement in the form of:

  while B do S

In addition, any number of sequential statements, or a *block*, can be grouped as:

$$\text{begin } S_1; \ S_2; \ ...; \ S_n \text{ end}$$

In general, other statements can be reduced to or converted to one or more of the above statements, while more complex language constructs, such as arrays, procedures, functions, etc., are covered elsewhere (Zelkowitz, 1993).

We need axioms or inference rules for each of the above statements, The first type of such axioms is simply in the form of $\{P\}S\{Q\}$. For example, the axiom for the assignment statement is given by:

$$\text{Axiom A3}: \qquad \{P_x^y\} \ y \leftarrow x \ \{P\}.$$

where $\{P_x^y\}$ is derived from expression P with all free occurrences of y (y is not bound to other conditions) replaced by x. As a practical example, consider a program that balances a banking account: If no negative balance is allowed after each transaction, that is, $\{b \geq 0\}$ is the post-condition P, the pre-condition P_x^y, before the withdrawal of money as represented by the assignment statement, $b \leftarrow b - w$, is then represented by $\{b - w \geq 0\}$, or $\{b \geq w\}$, by the above axiom. That is, the pre-condition for maintaining non-negative balance is that sufficient fund exists before each withdrawal transaction.

Another type of axioms for language elements defines the inference rules for multi-part statements. The so-called composition axiom for sequential concatenations states:

$$\text{Axiom A4}: \qquad \frac{\{P\}S_1\{Q\}, \ \{Q\}S_2\{R\}}{\{P\} \ S_1 \ ; \ S_2 \ \{R\}}.$$

As we will see in examples later, such sequential concatenations and the use of Axiom A4 help us build up our correctness proofs by linking individual elements to form bigger blocks, in essentially a bottom-up approach.

There are two variations of the conditional axiom. The following axiom gives the "meaning" for the "if-then-else" statement:

$$\text{Axiom A5}: \qquad \frac{\{P \wedge B\}S_1\{Q\}, \ \{P \wedge \neg B\}S_2\{Q\}}{\{P\} \ \text{if } B \text{ then } S_1 \text{ else } S_2 \ \{Q\}}.$$

As a practical example, consider the following statement:

$$\text{if } x \geq 0 \text{ then } y \leftarrow x \text{ else } y \leftarrow -x$$

with post-condition $Q \equiv \{y = |x|\}$, pre-condition $P \equiv \text{TRUE}$, and $B \equiv \{x \geq 0\}$. To verify this statement, we need to verify: $\{P \wedge B\}S_1\{Q\}$ and $\{P \wedge \neg B\}S_2\{Q\}$. The first branch ($B$) to verify is:

$$\{x \geq 0\} \ y \leftarrow x \ \{y = |x|\}.$$

Applying axiom A3 above, we have:

$$\{x = |x|\} \ y \leftarrow x \ \{y = |x|\}.$$

Combined with the logical relation $\{x \geq 0\} \Rightarrow \{x = |x|\}$, by applying axiom A1, this branch is verified. The second branch ($\neg B$), can be verified similarly. Therefore, through these verification steps, we have verified the above conditional statement.

The second variation of the conditional axiom is the following axiom for the *if-then* statement:

$$\text{Axiom A6}: \quad \frac{\{P \wedge B\}S\{Q\}, \ \{P \wedge \neg B\} \Rightarrow \{Q\}}{\{P\} \ \texttt{if } B \texttt{ then } S \ \{Q\}}.$$

This axiom can be considered as a special case of Axiom A5.

For the loop statement, we have the axiom:

$$\text{Axiom A7}: \quad \frac{\{P \wedge B\}S\{P\}}{\{P\} \ \texttt{while } B \texttt{ do } S \ \{P \wedge \neg B\}}.$$

This P (often labeled I) is called the loop invariant, which is the key to loop verification. Another property that we need to verify for loops is program termination (that is, it is not an infinite loop), through some property P_i for the ith iteration of a loop. This can be done by showing that

- P_i is positive within a loop, or $\forall i, P_i > 0$, and

- $P_i > P_{i+1}$.

We will see some examples of loop verification after we introduce the general procedure for axiomatic proofs.

15.2.3 Axiomatic proofs and a comprehensive example

The verification process, often referred to as the *proof of correctness*, is a bottom-up process much like the above verification example for the conditional statement: We start from individual statements and associated intermediate conditions we annotated before and after them, verify intermediate conditions through axioms or inference rules, and finally verify the pre- and post-conditions for the complete program. Although this is a bottom-up process, the main goal is to verify the result (post-condition) for the input (pre-condition), therefore, the annotations or intermediate conditions are guided by these pre- and post-conditions. Because of the post-condition is typically more specific and contains more information, we typically start with it and work backward, in the backward-chaining process to derive and verify intermediate conditions until we verify the whole program.

The hardest part is usually the verification of loops, and the hardest part in it is to find appropriate loop invariant that helps the verification. Consequently, a lot of the verification process often focuses on loop verifications, which also covers program termination verification.

As a comprehensive example, consider the program segment that calculates the factorial of a positive integer in Figure 15.1. The formal specification in the form of pre- and post-conditions is given, and the lines are individually numbered. The program segment has a "while" loop at the end, therefore, we need to verify that the loop terminates, and it terminated in the desired state.

Loop termination is easy to verify in this case: We notice that $i > 0$ throughout this loop, and i is decremented by 1 through each iteration of the loop. By apply the loop termination criterion, we have verified that this program terminates.

As for the correct results, we notice that the program segment ends with a "while" statement, and the post-condition for it is $I \wedge \neg B$. We also notice that y holds the current running factorial, or $n!/i!$ as the partial result. We denote it as:

$$I_1 \equiv \left(y = \frac{n!}{i!} \right).$$

$$\{n \geq 1\}$$

```
1        y ← 1;
2        i ← n;
3        while i > 1 do
4        begin
5            y ← y × i;
6            i ← i − 1;
7        end
```

$$\{y = n!\}$$

Figure 15.1 A program segment with its formal specification

In addition, when we finished loop, we should have $i = 1$. Therefore, we select our loop invariant to be $I_1 \wedge (i \geq 1)$, or :

$$I \equiv \left(y = \frac{n!}{i!}\right) \wedge (i \geq 1).$$

The loop condition is: $B \equiv i > 1$, and $\neg B \equiv i \leq 1$. Therefore, at loop termination, we have the post-conditions as: $I \wedge \neg B$, with:

$$
\begin{aligned}
& I \wedge \neg B \\
& \equiv I_1 \wedge (i \geq 1) \wedge (i \leq 1) \\
& \equiv I_1 \wedge (i = 1) \\
& \equiv (y = \tfrac{n!}{i!}) \wedge (i = 1) \\
& \equiv (y = n!).
\end{aligned}
$$

which is exactly our post condition for the entire program segment.

Now we need to show that I is indeed the invariant for the loop. First, by applying Axiom A3 to line 6, we get:

$$
\begin{aligned}
& \{(y = \tfrac{n!}{(i-1)!}) \wedge (i - 1 \geq 1)\} \\
& i \leftarrow i - 1; \\
& \{(y = \tfrac{n!}{i!}) \wedge (i \geq 1)\}.
\end{aligned}
$$

And, again applying Axiom A3 to line 5, we get:

$$
\begin{aligned}
& \{\left(y \times i = \tfrac{n!}{(i-1)!}\right) \wedge (i - 1 \geq 1)\} \\
& y \leftarrow y \times i; \\
& \{\left(y = \tfrac{n!}{(i-1)!}\right) \wedge (i - 1 \geq 1)\}.
\end{aligned}
$$

However, because:

$$\left(y \times i = \frac{n!}{(i-1)!}\right) \wedge (i - 1 \geq 1) \equiv \left(y = \frac{n!}{i!}\right) \wedge (i \geq 0)$$

and $i \geq 1 \Rightarrow i \geq 0$, by applying Axiom A1, we verify for line 5:

$$\frac{\{(y = \tfrac{n!}{i!}) \wedge (i \geq 0)\}\, y \leftarrow y \times i;\, \{(y = \tfrac{n!}{(i-1)!}) \wedge (i - 1 \geq 1)\},\ i \geq 1 \Rightarrow i \geq 0}{\{(y = \tfrac{n!}{i!}) \wedge (i \geq 1)\}\, y \leftarrow y \times i;\, \{(y = \tfrac{n!}{(i-1)!}) \wedge (i - 1 \geq 1)\},}.$$

Notice that the verified pre-condition to line 5 is I itself.

Now, combining the above for line 5 and line 6 using Axiom A4, and letting $P_i \equiv (y = \frac{n!}{(i-1)!}) \wedge (i - 1 \geq 1)$, we get:

$$\frac{\{I\} y \leftarrow y \times i; \{P_i\}, \ \{P_i\} i \leftarrow i - 1; \{I\}}{\{I\} \ y \leftarrow y \times i; \ i \leftarrow i - 1; \ \{I\}}.$$

Also, because $I \wedge B \Rightarrow I$, by applying Axiom A1, we have:

$$\frac{\{I\} \ y \leftarrow y \times i; \ i \leftarrow i - 1; \ \{I\}, \ (I \wedge B \Rightarrow I)}{\{I \wedge B\} \ y \leftarrow y \times i; \ i \leftarrow i - 1; \ \{I\}}.$$

Now, when we apply Axiom A7, we get:

$$\frac{\{I \wedge B\} \ y \leftarrow y \times i; \ i \leftarrow i - 1; \ \{I\}}{\{I\} \ \texttt{while } B \ \texttt{do begin } y \leftarrow y \times i; \ i \leftarrow i - 1; \ \texttt{end} \ \{I \wedge \neg B\}}.$$

The last couple of steps for the statements before the "while" loop can then be verified. For line 2, using Axiom A3 with post-condition I, we get:

$$\left\{ \left(y = \frac{n!}{n!} \right) \wedge (n \geq 1) \right\} \ i \leftarrow n; \ \left\{ \left(y = \frac{n!}{i!} \right) \wedge (i \geq 1) \right\}.$$

The pre-condition to line 2 can be reduced to $(y = 1) \wedge (n \geq 1)$. Again, applying Axiom A3 to line 1 yields:

$$\{(1 = 1) \wedge (n \geq 1)\} \ y \leftarrow 1; \ \{(y = 1) \wedge (n \geq 1)\}.$$

The pre-condition to line 1 is exactly the same to the pre-condition of our program segment, $n \geq 1$. Now, combining line 1 and line 2 using Axiom A3, we get:

$$\frac{\{n \geq 1\} \ y \leftarrow 1; \ \{(y = 1) \wedge (n \geq 1)\}, \ \{(y = 1) \wedge (n \geq 1)\} \ i \leftarrow 1; \ \{I\}}{\{n \geq 1\} \ \text{line } 1 - 2 \ \{I\}}.$$

Finally, combine lines 1–2 with the "while" loop, again using Axiom A3, we get:

$$\frac{\{(n \geq 1)\} \ \text{line } 1 - 2 \ \{I\}, \ \{I\} \ \texttt{while} - \texttt{loop} \ \{y = n!\}}{\{(n \geq 1)\} \ \text{whole program} - \text{segment in Figure 15.1} \ \{y = n!\}}.$$

This finishes our verification process or the correctness proof for the program-segment in Figure 15.1.

15.3 OTHER APPROACHES

Besides the axiomatic approach described above, two other widely used formal verification approaches are the weakest pre-condition approach and the functional approach. We next introduce the basic ideas of these approaches, then discuss some limitations of all these three approaches, and introduce the idea of model checking and other formal or semi-formal approaches that attempt to provide only a partial verification of certain properties.

15.3.1 Weakest pre-conditions and backward chaining

The weakest pre-condition approach was introduced by Dijkstra (1975), and extended to cover all kinds of situations by Gries (1987). The basic idea is essentially the same as the axiomatic approach above, but with a focus on backward chaining for program verification through the use of the wp operator, or the weakest pre-condition operator. The wp operator incorporate axioms for basic program elements, and the inference rules can be stated in terms of wp's.

Formally, the weakest pre-condition to a given statement S and post-condition Q, denoted as $wp(S, Q)$, is the largest initial set of states for which S terminates and Q is true after the execution of S. With this definition, we can see that the formal specification in the form of $\{P\}S\{Q\}$ can be interpreted as $P \Rightarrow wp(S, Q)$. Therefore, if we can derive $wp(S, Q)$ for a program S, and show that $P \Rightarrow wp(S, Q)$, we then have effectively provided a proof for $\{P\}S\{Q\}$, or the correctness of program S, with respect to its formal specification pair P and Q.

Based on this definition, as well as the program semantics, similar basic wp definitions for different types of statements, similar to the corresponding axioms in Section 15.2, can be derived. Various inference rules, referred to as *theorems* in this approach, can also be derived. For example:

- $wp(S, F) = F$. Since no state satisfy the condition F, we do not have any state in $wp(S, F)$ for any program S.

- $wp(S, Q) \land wp(S, R) = wp(S, Q \land R)$.

- if $P \Rightarrow Q$ then $wp(S, P) \Rightarrow wp(S, Q)$.

Therefore, program development as well as its verification is treated as a goal-oriented activities, and backward chaining plays a central role in this verification approach. Closely related to this verification approach is the so-called guarded command for non-deterministic execution (Dijkstra, 1975; Gries, 1987).

15.3.2 Functional approach and symbolic execution

Unlike in the above two formal verification approaches, where logical predicates are used to annotate states before and after the execution of some program segments, functional approach views these program elements as mathematical functions, in the sense that they provide a functional mapping from their input values to their output values. Full details about this approach, also called program calculus, can be found in Mills et al. (1987a). However, many basic ideas are similar to the axiomatic or the wp approaches described earlier, such as:

- The (mathematical) function calculated by each type of program elements can be captured by its "meaning", similar to the axioms for program elements in the axiomatic approach. In particular, conditional assignments are used extensively to break down the traces for "if" statements, and the "meaning" of "while" statement is defined recursively using that for "if" and "while" statements.

- The combination of sequential statements can be treat as functional nesting. For example, if S_i computes f_i, then the function computed by S_1; S_2; ..., S_n, with original input I_0, is $f_n(...(f_2(f_1(I_0)))...)$.

Table 15.1 Example symbolic execution traces

Part	Condition	x	y	Part	Condition	x	y
if $x > 0$	$x > 0$			if $x > 0$	$x \leq 0$		
$y \leftarrow x$			x	$y \leftarrow -x$			$-x$

Symbolic execution plays an important role in this approach. For example, the different traces of "if" statement through symbolic execution are used to determine parallel conditional assignments. Similarly, "while" involves "if" in recursive definition, therefore also involves corresponding symbolic execution. The functional nesting can be traced through symbolic execution as well. For the above example of calculating the absolute values with

$$\text{if } x \geq 0 \text{ then } y \leftarrow x \text{ else } y \leftarrow -x$$

we have the two traces in the symbolic execution in Table 15.1.

Full details about symbolic execution and its used in this verification approach can be found in Mills et al. (1987a). In essence, symbolic execution is a forward flow techniques, contrasting with the backward chaining technique for the axiomatic and wp approaches.

15.3.3 Seeking alternatives: Model checking and other approaches

Although we didn't go through detailed examples for the functional and wp approaches, and the proof procedures are somewhat different, several observations are true for all three formal verification approaches, including:

- The difficulty of producing correctness proofs, particularly for loops, where the selection of proper loop invariant plays an important role, but there isn't a uniform formula for doing the selection. Some heuristics based on people's understanding, prior knowledge, or insight, are typically used to select such invariants. Sometimes, a trial-and-error strategy is necessary to consider multiple candidates before a workable solution can be found.

- In general, many steps are involved in the correctness proofs, and the proof can be fairly long and complicated even for relatively small-sized programs. As a rule of thumb, the length of the proof is typically one order of magnitude longer than the program itself.

- The proof process can generally benefit from some hierarchical structures and related abstractions as guide for different parts, in much of the same way as stepwise abstraction used as a code reading techniques described in Chapter 14. These abstractions can also help us in dealing with some of the difficulties noted above, such as deriving loop invariant based on abstraction of the loop body.

The first two of the above observations make it difficult to apply formal verification techniques on large-scale software products. In addition, we also need to deal with various other aspects and complications for larger programs, including: arrays and functions, procedures, modules, and other program components, and sometimes complications from things such as physical limitations, side effects, and aliases. Because of these, various "partial" and/or semi-formal verification techniques have been suggested, as described below.

One way to deal with the difficult and human-intensive formal verification activities is through automation and software tool support. However, the long standing theoretical results state that the correctness and other properties for general programs are undecidable problems, that is, there is no hope for algorithmic or fully automated solutions. Nevertheless, for some restricted subset of problems and properties, some automated solutions are possible. Model checking is such an approach that automatically or algorithmically checks certain properties for some software systems. A good introduction to this topic can be found in Ghezzi et al. (2003), and the following briefly summarize the key ideas:

- A software system is modeled as a finite-state machine (FSM), with some property of interest expressed as a suitable formula, or a *proposition*, defined with respect to the FSM. Ideally, this FSM and the propositions are both developed during the software specification process, much like the use of formal specifications in various formal methods.

- The *model checker* is a software that runs an algorithm to check the validity of the proposition. If it is checked to be true, a *proof* is said to be produced. Otherwise, a *counterexample* is given, much like a failed test case that can be analyzed further for defect fixing.

An alternative to the above is formal methods for specific subset of properties related to the overall correctness of software. For example, algebraic specification and verification can help us specify and verify correctness of data structures and related data properties (Guttag et al., 1978). This example may look very limited at first glance. However, if we consider the increasing popularity of object-oriented systems, algebraic specification and verification can be a powerful tool, due to its close link to verifying the implementation of abstract data types, which form part of the cornerstone of object-oriented technology.

Other formal model based analyses can also be used to check for certain properties, either by analysts alone or with the help of some software tools, but rarely with fully automated support, due to the same reason as noted above. For example, various algorithm analysis techniques and analytical modeling techniques can be applied to verified the key algorithms employed in product implementations (Wallace et al., 1996). Petri-net, a special type of FSM, and the rich set of theoretical results for it, can be used to model and analyze various properties for various software, particularly those related to parallel, distributed, and/or asynchronous systems (Peterson, 1981). Various other static and formal analysis techniques we covered in Chapter 14 in connection with formal software inspection and reviews also fall into the same category.

All the formal analysis techniques mentioned above are extensions to formal verification techniques we described earlier. By restricting to a smaller subset of problems, systems, or properties, these techniques may lead to additional opportunities for automation, thus making them easier to perform than formal verifications. Such automated approaches can be considered as combining the ideas and advantages of formal verification with testing. However, there are still serious obstacles to the wide application of these extensions in larger software systems due to the intrinsic complexity involved in these verification and analysis techniques. For example, state explosion for FSM for large software systems would make model checking impractical unless we focus on the high-level components or functions only. In general, these formal verification and analysis techniques cost more, and in many cases significantly so, than testing and inspection, thus limiting their application domains. We next discuss this and other related issues.

15.4 APPLICATIONS, EFFECTIVENESS, AND INTEGRATION ISSUES

So far, the biggest obstacle to formal methods is the high cost associated with the difficult task of performing these human intensive activities correctly without adequate automated support. Although model checking and some other formal analysis techniques have alleviated the problem to some degree, formal methods in general still remain a costly alternative for ensuring software quality. This and other factors affect the applicability and effectiveness of formal verification analysis techniques in the quality engineering process, which we examine below.

Applicability and implementation

The question of applicability can be answered in two steps:

1. The type of products or application domains that would benefit from using formal verification and analysis techniques.

2. The type of software artifacts in the above products that can be verified or analyzed by these techniques.

Any product can potentially benefit from the use of these formal techniques. However, due to the required expertise for the personnel involved in the verification and analysis activities and the related cost, these techniques are mostly used in small software, or in a small subset of larger software systems that require ultra-high quality or where the damage of failures is substantial. Such large software systems include software for safety critical systems, or critical components or functions for large software systems. Examples of the latter include operating system kernels, routing functions in communication network switching software, etc.

Even for safety critical systems, formal verification and analysis techniques are usually used selectively instead of uniformly on all system components. For example, when applied in software safety engineering, focused verification activities are carried out over development phases based on results obtained from hazard analysis. Ideas similar to model checking can also be used in such systems, such as through some assertion or prescription monitor. These techniques will be described in Chapter 16.

The most commonly verified or analyzed objects are the program code. However, other formal technical documents can be verified or analyzed as well. For example, one of the biggest advantage of producing a set of formal product specifications is that formal development method, such as stepwise refinement in lock-step with verification, can be applied. In this example, each level of product design and implementation detail added can be formally specified and verified, both with respect to this new detailed specification for correctness, and with respect to the previous specification for equivalence between the current and earlier specification sets. Basically, any technical document can potentially be formally verified or analyzed, as long as formal specifications can be constructed for them.

Similar ideas and techniques have also been used successfully in verifying and analyzing distributed programs, hardware systems and their functions, communication networks and protocols, etc. The basic reason behind this is the shared formalism and formal language that can be used to describe, model, and analyze different type of systems, not just limited to the software systems. However, due to our software quality focus in this book, we will omit detailed discussions about this topic.

Technology and process integration

In terms of the software artifacts from different development phases being verified and analyzed, these techniques are closely related to and depend upon the availability of formal system specifications, either as formal descriptions, such as through logical and algebraic statements, or operational definitions, such as using finite-state machines. The integration between these specification techniques and the verification and analysis covered in this chapter resulted in various formal methods, such as stepwise development and verification based on logical specifications and axiomatic correctness proofs noted above. In most of these formal methods, software development and verification work side-by-side in developing high-quality software products or components.

There are some intrinsic limitations of formal systems, primarily related to simplification of the physical realities in the abstraction process and difficulties in dealing with language and hardware limitations. Therefore, formal methods cannot guarantee perfection for software, but only assure it with respect to the formal specifications verified or the properties checked. Even this assurance is subject to the error-free construction of correctness proofs or performance of formal analyses, which cannot be absolutely guaranteed. Consequently, formal methods cannot be replacements to all other QA activities. Instead, they can be used together in software development and maintenance processes, or integrated into some software methodologies and/or technologies.

One concrete example of this integration is the cleanroom technology and the related process (Mills et al., 1987b), which include two important components:

- Formal verification based on functional correctness approach is used during product design and implementation.

- Statistical testing based on customer operational profile is used in the later part of product development. This topic was covered in Chapter 10 in relation to Markov chain operational profiles.

However, in some cleanroom implementations, formal verification is replaced by formal inspection and some related analyses.

In general, formal methods are suitable to stable product development and market environments, where product requirements can be captured into formal specifications and remain fairly stable thereafter to allow for later refinements and verifications. Fortunately, most software sub-systems used in safety critical systems fall into this category, so that they can benefit from such formal methods. For products in volatile market environments, frequently requirement changes and solution updates make the use of formal methods more difficult. However, if some risk analysis techniques is used to identify main risk areas and deal with them first, such as in the spiral process, adapted formal methods can be applied to core functions to assure their quality, much like the identification of safety critical features for focused safety assurance in Chapter 16.

Relation to and integration with other QA activities

Formal verification and analysis is most closely related to formal inspection, review, and static analysis covered in Chapter 14. In fact, they are often grouped together as non-execution based QA activities in existing software engineering literature. Some variations of formal verification and analysis techniques are also closely related to testing. For example, symbolic execution in functional correctness verification is similar to testing in the way execution flow is traced and analyzed, but with symbolic instead of actual variable values to produce more generalizable results in the form of correctness proof instead of checking the success or failure of a single test run. Model checking combines algorithmic checking of propositions through execution with formal assertions stated as the propositions with respect to software systems modeled as finite-state machines.

In our framework of treating QA strategies as different ways to deal with defects in Chapter 3, formal methods belong to the defect prevention category, with formal specifications eliminating certain error sources due to poor understanding of product requirements and formal verification confirming the absence of certain defects. By extension, when a correctness proof cannot be constructed, it might be an indication of defect presence, thus triggering additional activities for defect locating and removal. Therefore, this usage can also be categorized as defect detection and removal, similar to inspection and testing. However, this is an ineffective way to detect and remove defects due to its different focus. Model checking and other formal analyses are closer to inspection and testing, in the sense that they may produce *counterexamples* during model checking or identify problems directly during analyses. Such information can then be used to locate and fix related defects.

As a defect prevention strategy, formal verification and analysis is human intensive, and requires mathematical and logical rigor in performing the verifications or analyses. As illustrated in the examples in this chapter, correctness proofs are difficult to produce and lengthy, even for short programs. The infeasibility to fully automate these proofs means that the manual process involved for any reasonably-sized programs will be error-prone. Attempts to scale up formal correctness proofs through model checking and other formal analysis have produced some successes but still suffer from their own limitations in both the model and analyze capabilities and the types of analyses that can be performed.

Consequently, education and training are key to success of these techniques. However, this effort should not be limited only to people who perform the verification and analysis activities, but also software managers, clients, and other parties involved so that the results can be interpreted properly, appropriate strategies can be selected ahead of time, resources can be allocated, and parallel QA activities and follow-up actions can be carried out to complement the use of these techniques. Some practitioners and researchers have also observed that formal methods place substantially higher responsibilities and stress on the software developers (Selby et al., 1987), while prior formal education and on-the-job training can help reduce such stress and make the application of formal methods more likely to succeed.

15.5 CONCLUDING REMARKS

Formal verification and analysis techniques, especially when they are packaged into formal methods and related development technologies, have many advantages. Various success stories as well as effectiveness studies have also been reported in literature (Selby et al., 1987; Gerhart et al., 1994; Pfleeger and Hatton, 1997; King et al., 2000), indicating that formal methods are not only effective for ensuring higher quality for many applications, but also more cost effective than other QA alternatives under some circumstances.

However, as a QA alternative, formal verification and analysis techniques have not gained the wide usage and popularity anywhere close to that for inspection or testing. Besides their own limitations related to cost, process, and other issues, one key reason is the general lack of the required expertise, which can be partially solved or alleviated by our education system. In fact, one reason for formal verification techniques to be included in this book is to promote the awareness of formal verification as a viable alternative for consideration by software professionals to use in ensuring the quality and reliability of their software systems.

Although over-selling formal methods is not a good way to promote their use, which may even induce certain backlashes, people need to be aware of the many advantages of formal methods in general, and formal verification techniques in particular. We need to conclude this topic with a balanced view on formal methods as a potentially effective element in the overall suite of QA techniques that can be combined in an overall strategy to achieve quality goals under project constraints, particularly for those requiring high levels of quality.

Problems

15.1   Some of the best arguments for formal verification or mathematical/logical proof of correctness are by the late E.W. Dijkstra. You can read many relevant articles/manuscripts on this topic and on the *wp* approach at the E.W. Dijkstra Archive:

www.cs.utexas.edu/users/EWD

Enjoy.

15.2   If you have never been exposed to formal specifications, you can use Ghezzi et al. (2003) in our bibliography as the starting point to study this important topic, particularly if this chapter convinced you to try some formal verification at your own work.

15.3   Complete the formal verification for the following program segment we studied in Section 15.2:

$$\text{if } x \geq 0 \text{ then } y \leftarrow x \text{ else } y \leftarrow -x$$

15.4   Apply the axiomatic approach to some program code that you are working on or some (pseudo-)code examples in earlier chapters of this book. You really need to do it to get a feel for it.

15.5   Can you find some manufacturing process examples to illustrate some of the axioms? For example, it might be useful to consider the precision and tolerance of the machines and mechanical parts when we talk about more restrictive or more relaxed pre-/post-conditions.

15.6   How would you formally verify multi-way branches such as "switch-case" statements without inventing some new axioms?

15.7   How would you formally verify "for"-loops without inventing some new axioms? (*Hint*: Look at the loops in Figure 11.3, Chapter 11.)

15.8   The mechanism for the *wp* approach looks similar to data dependency analysis we studied in Chapter 11. What are the similarities and differences?

15.9   Have you used symbolic executions before? If not, it's an interesting thing to try out on some simple programs.

15.10   Model checking is a "hot" topic in software engineering research today. Try find some articles on it to get a feel for some latest research on this topic.

15.11   Some people have cited culture influence on the relative popularity of formal methods in Europe as compared to that in the United States. What is your opinion on that?

15.12   How would you approach the task to make formal methods more widely used and practiced in software and IT industries?

CHAPTER 16

FAULT TOLERANCE
AND FAILURE CONTAINMENT

We next explore additional quality assurance (QA) alternatives that can be used to keep systems operational even under software problems, thus tolerating local faults to avoid global failures, or to contain the damage due to software problems or failures. These two generic strategies are referred to as fault tolerance and failure containment, respectively. We call them collectively defect containment strategies, because both of them contain defects by limiting them either to local failures or global failures with much reduced damage. Notice that the term "defect containment" we used in this context is different from some uses of the same term to mean defect detection and removal within the same development phase. This latter use is related to our defect dynamics models that characterize defect injection and removal by development phases described in Chapter 20.

16.1 BASIC IDEAS AND CONCEPTS

Despite the use of QA techniques we have described so far, we can only keep the number of faults to a fairly low level for the large and complex software systems in use today, but not completely eliminate them. For software systems where failure impact is substantial, such as software that runs the global telecommunication infrastructure, financial and critical databases for large companies, and many real-time control software sub-systems used in medical, nuclear, transportation, and other embedded systems, this low defect level and failure risk may still not be adequate. One common-sense solution to such problems is duplication and backup to reduce the chances for software failures or damages due to them.

We first examine similar ideas applied to other systems and the potential adoption and/or adaptation of them to deal with software problems.

Ideas from other highly dependable systems

Traditional physical systems that require higher levels of reliability, availability, or dependability have used duplications and backups all the time. In such systems, spare parts and backup units are commonly used to keep the systems in operational conditions, maybe at a reduced capability, at the presence of unit, part, equipment, or sub-system failures. The use of multiple engines on aircrafts and the availability of co-pilot to backup the pilot for passenger jets are examples of such duplications and backups. In cases where failures are unavoidable, it would be desirable that the accidents could be avoided if at all possible, where an *accident* is a failure with severe consequences. For example, when power failure for an elevator occurs, backup power might be switched on (a fault tolerance feature). When the backup power also fails, the system should be kept in a fail-safe state. In this case, the elevator should be locked in its current position instead of being allowed to have a free-fall. This locked state is a failure state, but a safe state, unless nothing is done over a long period of time to free the passengers or to restore power.

In the case that the problems cannot be isolated and contained in a local area and accidents do occur, there are usually failure containment measures to contain the damage. For example, the idea of containment walls has been around for ages, to contain such damaging disasters from age-old floods to modern day nuclear melt-downs. What is more, in the unfortunate event of accidents, we need to learn from them and improve our ability to deal with future problems. For example, in aircraft crashes, we try to recover the "black-boxes", and perform analysis to pinpoint possible problems, or hazards, through various analyses techniques and eliminate these hazard sources by modifying designs, procedures, etc., to minimize the probability of future disasters.

In the above discussion, we made two basic assumptions about such highly dependable systems and their usage scenarios:

- **A1.** *Rare event assumption*: Some system failures and accidents are associated with rare events with extremely low probabilities. Therefore, it is impossible to anticipate all these rare events, otherwise our systems would be designed and implemented to deal with them. Consequently, dynamic actions during the operations of the systems are needed to deal with the problems associated with such rare events. These dynamic actions constitute much of the work in fault tolerance and failure containment for highly dependable systems.

- **A2.** *Failure independence assumption*: Different components or subsystems fail independently of one another. Without this assumption, duplication and other safety-assurance techniques, such as use of interlocks, barriers, and protective sub-systems, would not work, or at least would not work as effectively. For example, if all aircraft engines are related in such a way that if one fails, all other fail at the same time, then the use of multiple engines does not reduce the likelihood of failures over a single engine. Similarly, if containment walls give way whenever nuclear melt-down occurs, it does not contribute to accident containment.

Both these basic assumptions will be examines in connection to software fault tolerance and failure containment techniques later in this chapter.

Adoption and adaptation to computers and software

These ideas of duplication and containment have been used in designing and implementing computer hardware, systems, networks, and computing infrastructure. For example, there is typically more than one route between any two points in the computer network, so that communication and/or coordination can still be achieved even if some nodes experience difficulties or are completed shut down, or when some links are broken. In the ideal case, these problems should be transparent to the users so that they will not notice any difference. When this goal is difficult to achieve, we would like to see the system to be kept operational at a reduced performance or capacity, with this reduction managed at an acceptable level. Similarly, the idea of backing up critical data and information has been used ever since the computer has been invented and started to be used in early applications.

The same idea can be adopted to the software domain, leading to the fault tolerance techniques for software QA. On the other hand, software is not usually involved in the safety problems, unless it is used in embedded systems to control physical devices or processes, such as in the case of control software for medical equipment, navigation systems, and nuclear reactor controllers. In the latter case, we also need to examine if various safety techniques for physical systems can be adopted and adapted to work for these software controllers.

Similar to the assumption of physical systems, these few remaining faults may be triggered under rare conditions or unusual dynamic scenarios (Assumption A1) to cause failures or possible accidents, making it unrealistic to attempt to generate the huge number of test cases to cover all these conditions or to perform exhaustive inspection or analysis based on all possible scenarios. Instead, some other means needs to be used to prevent failures by breaking the causal relations between these faults and the resulting failures, thus "tolerating" these faults, or to contain the failures to reduce the resulting damage. Similarly, when duplication software components or executions are involved, we would like to ensure their independence (Assumption A2), so that the overall system reliability or safety can be improved.

Classification of techniques

The above discussion already divided the overall approach to fault tolerance and failure containment categories. The former will tolerate faults and local failures so that no global failures occur. The latter will apply some containment measures after some global failure has occurred. However, sometimes, it would be hard to make a distinction. For example, some fault tolerance techniques often lead to reduced system performance or capacity. Such reductions could fit failure definitions, particularly in real-time systems, when a delay of more than a given threshold is defined to be a failure. Nevertheless, this rough distinction serves some purposes: In the former category of techniques, we focus on keeping the system operational under dynamic problems. In the latter category, we focus on keeping the system safe or reduce the damage while paying little attention to whether the system is operational or not.

Within fault tolerance techniques, we distinguish between duplication and backup. Duplication generally implies that multiple programs are running in parallel, similar to the example of multiple aircraft engines. One such specific technique we will describe in Section 16.3 is call N-version programming or NVP, which uses some kind of consensus from n parallel programs to make the system fault tolerant. On the other hand, backup implies that there is a primary program or dynamic execution, and backup is used when there are

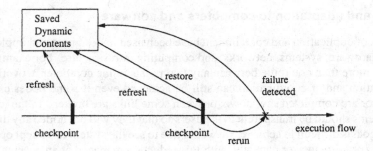

Figure 16.1 Fault tolerance with recovery blocks

some problems or suspected irregularities associated with this primary version. When the backup is provided by the same program, we have the recovery block or checkpointing-and-recovery technique described in Section 16.2. In the case where backup is provide by a different program, if the program has the same functionality, we can consider it as a combination of backup and duplication ideas. However, this backup program is more likely to have somewhat different functionality than the primary program it backs up, for example, with reduced functionality to allow for speedy recovery, or to have general backup procedures that serves multiple purposes. All these and other fault tolerance techniques and related topics are described in much more detail in Lyu (1995b).

Within failure containment techniques, we can focus either on the accident prevention before accidents happen, or focus on damage control or reduction after accidents happen. In the former case, we try to limit the scope and impact of failures so that they do not lead to accidents. In the latter case, we try to reduce the accident damage through various techniques. Both these categories are described in Section 16.4, and related analysis techniques are also covered therein. All these and other failure containment techniques and related topics on software safety and embedded systems are described in much more detail in Leveson (1995).

16.2 FAULT TOLERANCE WITH RECOVERY BLOCKS

With the increasingly faster and faster processors, we may have the luxury of repeating some computational tasks within a prescribed time limit without seriously affecting the system performance. Under this circumstance, we can use recovery blocks to repeatedly establish checkpoints, and repeat certain computational steps when dynamic problems are observed or suspected, as described in this section.

Basic operations of systems using recovery blocks

The use of recovery blocks introduces duplication of software executions so that occasional failures only cause loss of partial computational results but not complete execution failures. For example, the ability to dynamically backup and recover from occasional lost or corrupted transactions is built into many critical databases used in financial, insurance, health care, and other industries. Figure 16.1 illustrates this technique, and depicts the major activities involved:

- Periodic checkpointing and refreshing to save the dynamic contents of software executions. Sometimes this activity can be associated with the completion of some major tasks or occurrence of some significant events, in addition to at the pre-determined time instances.

- Failure detection: This activity is typically associated with the checkpointing activity above. Typically, before a new checkpoint can be established, some consistency check is carried out to see if there is an execution failure or other suspected problems since the last checkpoint. This activity can be event driven as well, such as when triggered by some system anomalies. If a failure is detected or if a problem is suspected, the following two steps are performed before normal activity continues:

    1. Rollback by restoring the saved dynamic contents associated with the latest checkpoint.
    2. Rerun the lost computation.

In using recovery blocks, failures are detected but the underlying faults are not removed. Hopefully the dynamic condition or external disturbance that accompanied the original failure will not repeat, and subsequent rerun of the lost computation can succeed and normal operation can resume. Although this hope may look like wishful thinking on the part of the software designers and system users, some rare dynamic conditions caused by system disturbances do fit into this profile. Therefore, this optimistic technique is more of an enhancement of system robustness under disturbances or unexpected usage environments.

Capability, performance, and other issues

The limited capability for fault tolerance is achieved through fault avoidance due to a different execution path or execution condition that does not involve the faulty code triggered in the first place. In this way, faults are tolerated in the system, or more precisely, faulty code is circumvented with occasional minor delays — a loss of performance tolerable under many circumstances. However, the situation with repeated failures is a real possibility. To reduce the chance of such repeated failures, the system might be re-run with slightly different configurations and conditions to minimize repetition of the exact execution path. A different version of the program that implements the same functionality can be used if it is available. This approach actually combines the ideas of backup and duplication, as mentioned in Section 16.1.

In the case of repeated identical or closely-related failures, the system has to be brought down, or partially incorrect results have to be accepted if operations need to continue. The software faults that caused the runtime problems need to be dealt with off-line. Activities can be carried out to identify and remove the faults. Alternatively, other fault tolerance techniques can be used, such as NVP discussed in Section 16.3.

In the above discussion, we have seen that both the basic assumptions for fault tolerance techniques, names, the rare event assumption (A1) and independence assumption (A2), are necessary for this technique to work. In addition, we assume that there is excess capacity in speed and occasional delays are tolerable. Violation of these assumptions would greatly impact the performance of this technique, because frequent re-runs or repetitions would serious hinder the progress of the computational task carried out. On the other hand, several other factors also affect the performance of these techniques.

One key decision in this technique is the checkpointing frequency: higher frequency leads to higher cost associated with frequent refreshing of the saved dynamic contents,

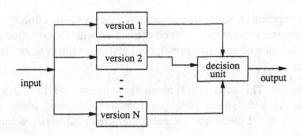

Figure 16.2 Fault tolerance with NVP

while lower frequency leads to longer and more costly recovery. An optimal frequency balances the two and incurs minimal overall cost. Alternative checkpoint strategies might also be used, for example, performing partial checkpointing for only those contents that are more likely to change more frequently than other contents. Therefore, the overall performance could be improved.

Another issue is the maintenance and follow-up activities to normal operations. As we noted before, repeated failures need to be dealt with by taking the system off-line for defect analysis and fixing. However, for normal operations, some information about the re-runs should be recorded and analyzed at a later time, either parallel to system operations or when the system is off-line. The key determination is whether these re-runs are truly due to rare environmental disturbances, or if software faults are to blame. In the latter case, the related software faults need to be located and fixed at the earliest opportunity.

16.3 FAULT TOLERANCE WITH N-VERSION PROGRAMMING

N-version programming (NVP) is another way to tolerate software faults by directly introducing duplications into the software itself (Avižienis, 1995). NVP is generally more suitable than recovery blocks when timely decisions or performance are critical, such as in many real-time control systems, or when software faults, instead of environmental disturbances, are more likely to be the primary sources of problems.

16.3.1 NVP: Basic technique and implementation

The basic technique is illustrated in Figure 16.2 and briefly described below:

- The basic functional units of the software system consist of N parallel independent versions of programs with identical functionality: version 1, version 2, ..., version N.

- The system input is distributed to all the N versions.

- The individual output for each version is fed to a decision unit.

- The decision unit determines the system output using a specific decision algorithm. The most commonly used algorithm is a simple majority vote, but other algorithms are also possible.

The decision algorithm determines the degree of fault tolerance. For example, when the simple majority rule is used, the system output would be the correct one as long as at least half of the versions are operational and produce correct results. In this case, we say that the overall system is fault tolerant up to

$$\frac{N}{2} - 1$$

Other variations to the algorithms, designs, and implementations are also possible, as we discuss next in connection with various other issues about NVP.

Besides the symmetric implementation as depicted in Figure 16.2 and the majority algorithm, various asymmetric implementations or other symmetric implementations are also possible. For example, we might use the asymmetric design and algorithm to designate one version as the primary one and the others as backups. In this case, the backup versions are only considered if some internal or external checking is performed and determined that the result is incorrect. We could also partition the N versions into different subgroups to form a hierarchical implementation. Alternatively, we can also combine NVP with recovery blocks and other fault tolerance ideas to enhance the overall system reliability. In fact, innovative design and configuration of multiple versions of similar programs, together with the related decision algorithm, are a major research area within fault tolerant computing and communication.

The determination of overall system reliability is one major topic in fault tolerance studies (McAllister and Vouk, 1995). System reliability can be determined by the reliability of its individual versions, the decision algorithm, as well as the relationship among these different versions. For example, if all individual versions are highly correlated, then they tend to fail at the same time or under similar operational conditions, thus defeating the whole purpose of multiple versions. Therefore, the most fundamental assumption and the enabling factor in NVP is that faults in different versions are independent (Assumption A2 in Section 16.1).

When different versions are independent, even if there is a fault that causes a local failure in version i, the whole system is likely to function correctly because the other (independent) versions are likely to function correctly under the same dynamic environment. In this way, the causal relation between local faults and system failures is broken for most local faults under most situations, thus improving the quality and reliability of the software system. One of the main research topics in NVP is to ensure that the software versions are as independent as possible so that local faults can be tolerated and the resulting local failures can be contained effectively.

The other assumption for fault tolerance, the rare and unanticipated event assumption (A1), is not directly used in NVP. However, it does affect NVP implementation to a large degree. NVP costs significantly more to implement than a single version, typically by a factor of N or more if we count also the decision unit and the coordination in addition to the N individual versions. Therefore, in actual implementations, we can only afford it for selected critical components or units in a large systems where rare individual failure events that can not be anticipated ahead of time need to be tolerated. For frequent and anticipated events, other solutions are much more effective and economical.

16.3.2 Ensuring version independence

Besides ensuring the quality of the overall NVP scheme and its individual elements, the most important factor to make NVP work reliably is to ensure independence among its different versions. The differences in these different versions are reflected in their different designs and implementations. Since the implementations are constrained by their designs, most of the existing work focuses on design diversities in trying to achieve version independence

(Lyu and Avižienis, 1992). There are several general areas that we can focus on in trying to achieve this diversity:

- People diversity: People of different background and training are more like to produce different solutions. Other factors also include personality types, group or team structure, and related communication structure, etc. All these factors might affect the solution design and implementations.

- Process variations: Different development processes might favor different solutions. For example, the waterfall process might favor design and implementation with a hierarchical structure, while the iterative process is more likely to produce a star structure, with some core function in a central unit and many other utilities connected to it. Therefore, process variations might lead to more diverse design and implementation as well.

- Technology diversity: The use of different software development methods or methodologies, support tools, programming languages, algorithms and data structure, etc., all could contribute to version independence. In addition, different QA techniques and tools also add to the diversity, because each of them works differently to assure product quality.

To implement and integrate these diversity initiatives, some NVP-specific development process is called for. For example, one approach is to use tightly managed communication among the different teams for the different versions, thus achieving version independence through team independence (Avižienis, 1995; Lyu and Avižienis, 1992). Key ideas in this approach include:

- Each version is developed by an independent production team (or P-team), totaling N such P-teams for NVP.

- Controlled communication is carried out through the use of a single specially-trained coordination team (C-team). P-teams communicate with one another through C-team only, but not directly.

- There are mandatory rules (DOs & DON'Ts) that the developers in these teams must follow.

In software development specifically tailored for NVP development, version independence through design and implementation diversity needs to be managed as part of the requirement throughout the process. The overall evaluation and the decision on system acceptance demand evidence of diversity and/or independence, in addition to how the overall system works together.

16.3.3 Applying NVP ideas in other QA activities

The basic ideas in NVP can also be applied to various other QA activities to improve the overall product quality. In fact, the combined use of different QA techniques for most large software systems can itself be considered a fault tolerance feature, with different QA techniques effective at preventing, catching, or containing different kinds of problems. Therefore, the overall system quality and reliability are assured and improved through the combined effort.

In the QA for critical units or components, NVP idea is often directly applied. For example, in Fagan inspection (Fagan, 1976) and other inspection techniques described in Chapter 14, multiple inspectors may be assigned to the same critical inspection object to ensure its quality. As a general extension, this duplication can be provided by multiple inspection teams and coordinated through some mechanisms. Similarly, critical product functions may be tested by multiple individuals and teams to ensure their correct operational behavior. Such duplications go beyond basic coverage or usage criteria for inspection or testing to ensure higher quality for these critical parts.

16.4 FAILURE CONTAINMENT: SAFETY ASSURANCE AND DAMAGE CONTROL

The fault tolerance techniques, when combined with other QA techniques we described so far in this book, can keep the failure occurrence rate to a fairly low level. However, even such low failure rates may not be adequate for some systems where damages associated with failures are substantial, such as embedded control systems for aircraft, nuclear reactors, medical devices, etc. We need to treat different failures differently and focus on those that may lead to accidents or safety problems through the use of related safety assurance and damage control techniques, as described below.

For safety critical systems, the primary concern is our ability to prevent accidents from happening, where an *accident* is defined to be a failure with a severe consequence. The secondary concern is our ability to reduce accident damage in case of accidents. Various specific techniques are used for safety critical systems based on analysis of *hazards*, or logical pre-conditions for accidents. Accident prevention include two generic steps:

1. Analysis of actual or potential accident scenarios with a focus on preconditions, or hazards, for these scenarios. This type of analysis is called *hazard analysis*.

2. Preventive or remedial actions for accident prevention, referred to as *hazard resolution*, to deal with the hazards identified in the above analysis. Generic ways include hazard elimination, hazard reduction, and hazard control.

Each of these steps and the techniques used in them are described below.

16.4.1 Hazard analysis using fault-trees and event-trees

There are several hazard analysis techniques (Aldemir et al., 1994), among which the most commonly used ones are fault-tree and event-tree analyses, which have been adapted to work for software-intensive embedded systems (Dugan, 1995; Leveson, 1995). The basic idea of fault-tree analysis (FTA) can be summarized below:

- The basic analysis tool is logical diagrams called *fault-trees*, which also represent the analysis results. Nodes in a fault-tree represent various events or conditions and are connected through logical connectors, AND, OR, NOT, to represent logical relations among sub-conditions.

- The analysis follows a top-down procedure: starting with the top event and recursively analyzing each event or condition to find out its logical conditions or sub-conditions. The top event is usually associated with an accident and is represented as the root node of the tree.

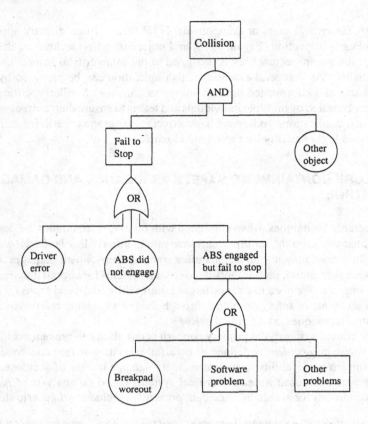

Figure 16.3   Fault-tree analysis (FTA) for an automobile accident

- We stop this recursive procedure at a terminal node under one of several conditions:
  - The current node is well understood, therefore there is no need to analyzed it further.
  - We cannot break a node into its sub-conditions any further (an *atomic* node).
  - We do not have enough information to perform further analysis.
- The terminal nodes are associated with the so-called basic or primary events or conditions represented as circles. The non-terminal nodes in-between are associated with intermediate events or conditions represented as rectangles.

As an example of FTA, consider the collision between an object (representing an obstacle) and an automobile that fails to stop, even though it is equipped with an anti-lock break system (ABS), illustrated in Figure 16.3. ABS contains embedded software used in controlling this safety critical device. In this case, the top event "collision" must involve the automobile in question AND another object. The automobile failed to stop due to three possible conditions, 1) driver error, 2) ABS did not engage, OR 3) ABS engaged but failed to stop. We can carry this analysis further, and find out that certain software functions may be part of the problem, and therefore need to be fixed. Notice that in FTAs, we focus on the controllable events or conditions. For example, driver error, such as incorrect use of ABS, is not analyzed further because we focus on the embedded software problems. On the other hand, the FTA

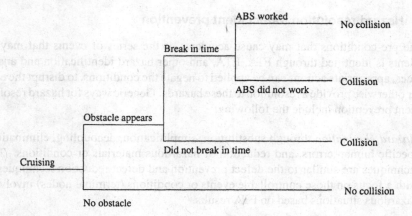

Figure 16.4 Event-tree analysis (ETA) for an automobile accident

in Figure 16.3 can be expanded further to analyze the causes for the software problem or other problems.

In contrast to FTA that extracts the static logical conditions, event-tree analysis, or ETA, focuses on the dynamic aspect of accidents by examining the timing or temporal relations in the series of events that led to accidents. The basic ideas are summarized below:

- An event tree is a temporal cause-effect diagram. We start with the primary event and follow through its subsequent events and consequences over time or stages (simplified or discretized time) until we reach a stage where an accident is encountered.

- Each branch of the event tree represents a specific consequence of a decision, which in turn can be associated with their own subsequent decisions and consequences.

- The main usage of ETA is to recreate accident sequences and/or scenarios, and identify the *critical* paths that lead from the primary events through a sequence of decisions and consequences eventually to an accident. Typically, the events and consequences not related to the critical path are not analyzed further to allow us to focus on system safety and hazard resolution actions that can be guided by ETA.

As an example of ETA, consider the collision scenario above. Figure 16.4 illustrate the ETA for chains of events leading to collisions or no collisions. In this case, while an automobile is cruising, there won't be a collision if no object or obstacle appears. When an obstacle appears, if the driver did not break in time, collision occurs (due to driver error). If the driver did break in time, the collision could be avoided if the ABS is working fine, otherwise we still may have an collision because ABS malfunctioning. We can carry this analysis further, and find out that certain software functions and related events may be part of the accident scenarios, and therefore pin-point the specific software functions and related usage scenario so that the related problems could be fixed.

Besides FTA and ETA, many other analysis techniques can be used for hazard analysis, identification, and related activities, including: safety related checklists and design reviews, hazard indices, risk trees, cause-consequence analysis (CCA), hazard & operability analysis (HAZOP), failure modes and effect analysis (FMEA), etc. (Aldemir et al., 1994; Leveson, 1995).

16.4.2 Hazard resolution for accident prevention

Once the pre-conditions that may cause accidents or the series of events that may lead to accidents is identified through FTA, ETA, and other hazard identification and analysis techniques, appropriate actions can be applied to negate the conditions, to disrupt the event-chain, or otherwise provide a resolution to these hazards. Generic ways for hazard resolution in accident prevention include the following:

- *Hazard elimination* through substitution, simplification, decoupling, elimination of specific human errors, and reduction of hazardous materials or conditions. These techniques are similar to the defect prevention and defect reduction techniques, but with a focus on those controllable events or conditions (terminal nodes) involved in hazardous situations based on FTA results.

- *Hazard reduction* through design for controllability (for example, automatic pressure release in boilers), use of locking devices (for example, hardware/software inter-locks), and failure probability minimization using safety margins and redundancy. These techniques are similar to the fault tolerance techniques, where local failures are contained without leading to system failures. However, the actions are guided by FTA and ETA results to focus on the key events, conditions, and sequences that are potentially related to accidents.

- *Hazard control* through reducing exposure, isolation and containment (for example, barriers between the system and the environment), protection systems (active pro-tection activated in case of hazard), and fail-safe design (passive protection, fail in a safe state without causing further damages). These techniques reduce the severity of failures, therefore weakening the link between failures and accidents.

In the above hazard resolution activities, some specific results from FTA can be used. For example, component replacement could be focused on those parts and areas that are linked through FTA as conditions for accidents. The software components thus identified can be the focus of formal verification activities, in the so called safety verification instead of broad-based formal verification of all the system components. We can also design lock-in, lock-out, and interlock devices, using a mixture of software and hardware technologies, to negate logical relations represented in FTA to prevent related accidents from happening. Similarly, some specific results from ETA can be used in hazard resolution, especially in hazard reduction and hazard control strategies. For example, barriers created between the critical and other paths, as well as other isolation and containment measures, can be applied to break or disrupt the chain of events that can lead to accidents.

16.4.3 Accident analysis and post-accident damage control

Similar to the situation with accident prevention described above, *damage control* also involves accident analyses that guide planned and actual strategies for damage control in the unfortunate event that accidents do happen. However, these analyses are much simpler than hazard analyses, and do not involve searching for intricate pre-conditions and event-chains that lead to the accidents. Instead, accident analyses focus on possible accidents and their consequences or damage areas. Typically the application domain knowledge would be adequate for such analyses, but not implementation details needed for hazard analyses. For example, aircraft accidents involve crashes that lead to loss of lives and property damages, while nuclear reactor accidents typically involve radioactive material causing damages to people's health and the environment.

Once such accident scenario and damage areas are identified, various techniques can be used for damage control, such as through escape routes, safe abandonment of products and materials, and devices for limiting physical damages to equipment or people. These techniques reduce the severity of accidents thus limiting the damage caused by these accidents.

Notice that both hazard control described earlier and damage control here are post-failure activities not generally covered in the QA activities described before. These activities are specific to safety critical systems. On the other hand, many techniques for hazard elimination and reduction can also be used in general systems to reduce fault injection and to tolerate local faults.

16.5 APPLICATION IN HETEROGENEOUS SYSTEMS

As mentioned at the beginning of this chapter, most systems where high dependability and safety are required fall into the heterogeneous or embedded system category. These systems involve software interacting with other physical subsystems, processes, equipments or devices, either as loosely coupled heterogeneous systems, or as embedded systems where software directly monitors or controls its physical surroundings. Fault tolerance and failure containment techniques are generally suitable for such systems, because the significant consequences of failures justify the high cost involved. We next examine this application domain and its environment and give some application examples, mostly based on a previous study of safety assurance for computer-controlled safety-critical systems (CCSCS) (Yih and Tian, 1998).

16.5.1 Modeling and analyzing heterogeneous systems

When we consider software as part of a heterogeneous system, system reliability and dependability issues need to be addressed. *System reliability* deals with hardware and communication/interaction problems, in addition to software problems. Therefore, the system reliability is the probability of failure-free operations for the whole system for a given time period or under a given set of usage scenarios. *System dependability* is a broader concept still, which includes reliability, fault tolerance, safety, etc., all related to how likely or how much a system can be depended upon. It is typically hard to quantify. However, system dependability can generally be represented by the values for its components that can usually be measured quantitatively. Traditional reliability and safety engineering focuses on hardware, identifying actual or potential failures, their causes and related event sequences, and assessing the probabilities for them (Henley and Kumamoto, 1981; Aldemir et al., 1994). Existing work on software reliability also treats software in isolation.

For heterogeneous systems involving computers and related software, the software subsystem and the physical subsystem demonstrate vastly different operational behavior and characteristics. For example, common assumptions for hardware and equipment, such as wear, aging, and decay, are not immediately applicable to software domain. Various models, such as the two-frame model (or TFM) (Yih and Tian, 1998), were developed to analyze such systems.

In TFM, a heterogeneous system, such as a computer-controlled safety-critical system (CCSCS), is divided into a logical subsystem (or logical frame) and a physical subsystem (or physical frame). The logical subsystem corresponds to the computer controller, and

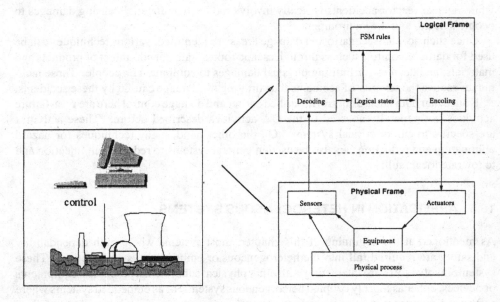

Figure 16.5 Two-frame model for a CCSCS

the physical subsystem is monitored and controlled by the computer controller through sensors and actuators, as graphically illustrated in Figure 16.5. TFM is similar to the "four variable model" (Parnas and Madey, 1995), but the symmetry between the two frames was highlighted instead of treating the software as the center and the physical subsystem as the environment. This perspective also gives us a better way to analyze the similarities and differences between the two frames to ensure and improve their safety. In such a heterogeneous system, failures may involve many different scenarios, including:

- Software failures due to defects in software design and implementation, which can be addressed to a large degree by QA techniques we have described so far in this book.

- Hardware or equipment failures due to wear, decay, or other physical processes, which is the main subject of traditional reliability and safety engineering, and can be largely addressed by related techniques.

- Communication/interface failures due to erroneous interactions among different subsystems or components.

Most computer-related accidents in CCSCS can be traced back to problems in the interface or interactions among the components of the systems, particularly between the computer controller and the surrounding environment (Mackenzie, 1994). Therefore, hazard analyses focusing on the interaction/interface problems can be performed to develop techniques for hazard prevention and safety improvement.

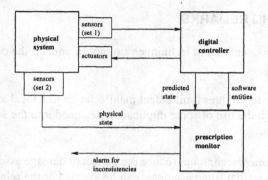

Figure 16.6 Prescription monitor for safety assurance

16.5.2 Prescriptive specifications for safety

In TFM, the commonly noted interface/interaction problems are mostly manifested as frame inconsistency problems. The primary causes for these inconsistencies can be identified to be the fundamental differences between the logical and physical frames, as follows:

- Physical states generally demonstrate regular behavior or form *total functions* according to physical laws; while the *discrete* software states usually form *partial functions*.

- There are typically *invariants* or *limits* reflecting physical laws, which, when implemented in software, may be violated or surpassed in failure situations.

However, because of the ultimate flexibility offered by software, if we could derive some *prescriptive specifications* as maintainable formal assertions for the logical frame, we can effectively keep the logical frame consistent with its physical frame, thus preventing various hazardous conditions from occurring. The logical subsystem could be enhanced to include a *prescription monitor*, as illustrated in Figure 16.6. The prescription monitor takes input from both the logical and physical subsystems, automatically checks prescriptive specifications to assure system integrity, and sounds alarms or carries out emergency actions if any of these assertions is violated.

A series of experiments was conducted to evaluate the effectiveness of this technique. based on report of actual scenarios of a nuclear accident. Nineteen hazard situations were tested in the simulated nuclear reactor control system, covering a wide variety of errors representative of realistic situations. In all the 19 instances, errors have been successfully detected on the spot by checking the prescriptive specifications developed above.

The approach above can be interpreted as using formal methods, in particular model checking, on CCSCS. However, system modeling and hazard analysis play a very important role in identifying the areas to focus, possible prescriptive specification, as well as the checking of these properties. This approach can be considered as a specific adaptation of the comprehensive approach in (Leveson, 1995) where hazard analysis and identification techniques are used throughout the development process for embedded software in CCSCS. This is in contrast to the current practice of applying formal verification techniques that generally focused on internal logical errors, which, as indicated above, are not the main sources of hazard for CCSCS.

16.6 CONCLUDING REMARKS

To summarize, defect containment techniques attempt to contain the defects through two generic means:

- *Fault tolerance* techniques limit defect manifestation to a local area to avoid global failures, through the use of some duplication designed into the software systems or their operations.

- *Failure containment* techniques reduce the impact or damage associated with certain system failures so that some accidents can be avoided or the related damage can be minimized. Accidents are a subset of failures with severe consequences, and the pre-conditions to such accidents are called hazards. Most of the failure containment activities are associated with safety-critical systems, where the main concerns are for the system to be as safe or to be as accident free as possible. Hazard analysis and resolution play an important role in identifying hazards and dealing with them to contain failures related to potential accidents, thus ensuring system safety.

Because of the duplications and other expensive mechanisms used, such as interlocks, barriers, and protective systems, both these variations of defect containment strategies are more costly than other QA techniques we covered in this book. In addition, the problem analyses for fault tolerance and hazard analyses for safety assurance require specialized expertise, extensive data that could be difficulty or expensive to collect, and substantial time and effort to perform. Consequently, these QA alternatives can only be used in limited settings and applied to critical components or functions for systems where stoppage in operation can be very costly or certain failures may be associated with catastrophic consequences. As for other non-critical components and functions, other QA alternatives we covered earlier in this book should be used to reduce the overall system development and operational cost.

Problems

16.1 What is the difference between reliability and safety?

16.2 What is the impact of fault tolerance on reliability and safety?

16.3 Compare the operational implementation of recovery blocks and common backup-and-recovery for your data or information on your PCs.

16.4 The fault tolerance capability defines how many faults can be tolerated. For specific situations, we might design or select different appropriate decision algorithm to make the system more fault tolerant. (Sometimes backup might be more meaningful than duplication.) Analyze the fault tolerance capability for the following situations with NVP:
  a) no problem detection (normal case we covered in Section 16.3),
  b) accurate detection of local problems,
  c) accurate detection and correction of local problems.

16.5 Answer the following questions about NVP:
  a) Would NVP work if you use N identical software copies?
  b) How would the availability of parallel and distributed processing affect NVP? What if you only have a single-processor machine?

c) NVP has not been as widely used as hardware duplications for highly dependable or critical systems. Why?

16.6   In your view, would CBSE (component-based software engineering) help make NVP more popular or less popular? Why?

16.7   Define the terms and concepts: accident, hazard, hazard analysis, fault tree, event tree.

16.8   What are the similarities and differences between decision trees and fault trees or event trees?

16.9   Find some problem, defect, or accident report, and try to perform a fault-tree analysis and an event-tree analysis on it.

16.10   Of the different safety assurance strategies described in this chapter, which ones are applicable to the systems you are working on?

CHAPTER 17

COMPARING QUALITY ASSURANCE TECHNIQUES AND ACTIVITIES

In this chapter, we compare the different quality assurance (QA) techniques and activities by examining their cost, applicability under different environments and development phases, and effectiveness in dealing with different types of problems. Based on this comparison, we also provide some general recommendations. Notice that all the QA techniques and activities covered in both Part II (testing) and Part III (QA alternatives other than testing) are compared here.

17.1 GENERAL QUESTIONS: COST, BENEFIT, AND ENVIRONMENT

Broadly speaking, a comparison of QA alternatives, together with related techniques and activities, is a cost–benefit analysis under the overall environment for software development or long-term maintenance. Consequently, the questions and comparison criteria can be classified into three broad categories of cost, benefit, and environment.

Questions and criteria related to environment

The main question is the applicability of specific QA alternatives and related activities and techniques to specific development and maintenance environments. We can first divide our examination of the applicability question into two general environments: 1) development environment, and 2) maintenance environment, which includes operational support and software maintenance activities.

Most of the QA alternatives have a development focus, although some can be used in software maintenance as well. All the QA alternatives covered so far in this book are applicable to software development. However, the applicability to software maintenance may vary, as follows:

- Defect prevention techniques are typically not applicable to the software maintenance process, although lessons learned from related activities can be used and package for future defect prevention activities.

- Inspection, formal verification, and testing can be applied to a very limited degree to software maintenance process. For example, when a problem is reported by some customers, we can perform related inspection, verification, or testing activities to locate the problem, as well as to ensure that the fix indeed would correct the problem.

- Defect containment alternatives, such as fault tolerance and failure containment, apply to software in operation. Therefore, they can also be applied to the software maintenance process. However, as noted in Chapter 16, the design and implementation of these features are supposed to be completed during the development processes. The focus during the software maintenance process is the support for normal operations and damage reduction, but not fixing problems or correcting the underlying software product.

Notice that in the above discussions, we focused on the corrective maintenance. For the other types of maintenance, such as adaptive and perfective maintenance, the adaptations to new application environment or the product improvements to make it more effective or more efficient, share many things in common with product development. Consequently, the applicability of different QA alternatives to adaptive and perfective maintenance activities is similar to their applicability to software development.

Once we confirmed the general applicability of all the QA alternatives to software development environment, we can further examine their applicability to different development processes or to different product domains or market segments. In addition, we can examine the kind of product artifacts these QA alternatives are applied to, or what the objects of related activities are, and the influence of different people (human and organizational) environment. One key question that we will focus on is the timeline or project phases/sub-phases, because of their relation to both the effectiveness and cost, with correcting problems earlier producing far more benefit and incurring far less cost than correcting them later. These and other specific questions are examined in Section 17.2.

Questions and criteria related to effectiveness or benefit

As discussed in Part I of this book, the general benefit of performing the various QA activities is to ensure the quality of software systems. Consequently, the comparison of individual QA alternatives can be made on how effectively each of them can help us achieve this general goal. However, as also noted in the previous chapters in both Part II and Part III, these different QA alternative address the software quality problems from different perspectives, dealing with different problems, and can be used in complementary ways in a concerted strategy to ensure software quality. The flip side of the argument is that each QA alternative exists for its own reasons, where it might be the most effective or cost-effective under certain situations. Otherwise, there is no real reason for it to exist. Therefore, a more meaningful comparison is their effectiveness under different situations and environments instead of effectiveness in general.

As we outlined in Chapter 3, different QA alternatives can be treated as different ways to deal with defects. Therefore, we can examine the effectiveness of different QA alternatives by examining the qualitative and quantitative information regarding defects under different environments, as follows:

- *Defect perspective:* Is the QA technique dealing with errors, faults, or failures? This question can be broken down further with the execution/observation of the specific QA activities and the follow-up actions, where different defect perspectives may be taken. For example, during testing, failures are observed, which lead to follow-up actions to locate and fix the faults that caused these observed failures.

- *Problem types:* Closely related to different defect perspectives are the problem or defect types. For example, dynamic or timing problems are typically associated with some interface or interaction among different parts of the software products, which might be more easily detected through testing than through inspection. On the other hand, logical and static problems may be more cost-effectively detected through inspection.

- *Defect levels and pervasiveness:* Different QA techniques may be suitable for different defect levels or pervasiveness. For example, if defects are pervasive in the system, systematic inspection might be more appropriate than testing because inspection can continue after some defects are detected, unlike in the case of testing, which often needs to be stopped once a failure is observed.

- *Constructive information and guidance for quality improvement:* Ideally, we would like to have different QA alternatives to provide as much information as possible to help us deal with the problems observed and to improve quality for the current and future products. For example, in inspection, not only the specific problem can be identified for immediate defect removal, but sometimes systematic problem patterns can be detected, leading to process changes or focused remedial actions aimed at preventing similar problems in the future.

We will examine individual QA alternatives with respect to the above questions in Section 17.3.

Questions and criteria related to cost

If the total cost can be calculated for each QA alternative, then it can be used together with the benefit assessment to select appropriate ones for a specific environment. The direct cost for carrying out the planned QA activities typically involves the time and effort of the software professionals who perform related activities and the consumption of other resources such as computer systems and supporting facilities. In addition, there are also indirect costs, such as training project participants, acquisition and support for related software tools, meeting time and other overhead. All these costs should be considered in our decision to choose appropriate QA alternatives.

There are several factors affecting the above total cost. Sometimes it is easier and more straightforward to deal with these factors instead of dealing with the cost directly, because some of these factor are more closely related to individual QA alternatives. Some key factors include:

- *Simplicity* of the techniques associated with the specific QA alternatives. A simple technique is generally easy to understand, easy to use, easy to perform, and more likely to be supported by existing tools. Minimal amount of training is needed before a software quality professional can learn and master the technique. Therefore, technique simplicity will affect the total cost of the selected QA alternative. For example, inspection is much simpler than formal verification, thus costing significantly less to perform.

- *Availability of tool support* also has a significant influence on the cost of specific QA alternatives. This is particularly true for our software and IT industries, where the share of cost of professionals' time dominant other material cost. Consequently, availability and affordability of software tool support is an important issue, because such automated support would save software professionals' valuable time and allow them to perform other tasks that only they can do best.

Other general questions and observations

If the above factors affecting the choice of appropriate QA alternatives can be characterized and quantified, then the choice is reduced to a mathematical optimization problem in the form of optimizing some form of cost–benefit objective functions under the constraints imposed by the environment. However, the benefit is typically hard to quantify in monetary terms, although sometimes it can be quantified to some degree in terms of defect count or density (#defects/unit). Even on the cost side, it is typically easier to quantify the total time or effort instead of the monetary amount. Therefore, it would be hard to formulate the choice of different QA alternatives as a mathematical optimization problem, although the general ideas and techniques would certainly help.

There are also questions and criteria related to more than one of the above areas. For example, the early applicability and availability of a QA techniques is not only related to the general applicability, but also to cost and benefit, because problems found late in development are much harder and cost significantly more to fix. In addition, a defect remaining in the software system — what we call a *dormant* defect — may also lead to the injection of other related defects. And the longer it stays in the system, the more likely the reasons for its injection in the first place get obscured. Therefore, the effectiveness comparison needs to be re-adjusted accordingly. For example, a 10% reduction of defect injection rate might be more significant than a 10% increase of defect detection rate.

Similarly, many questions we posed as related to cost and benefit also have a strong applicability implications or are strongly influenced by the overall application environment. For example, defect perspective may be heavily influenced by the product type and the overall market expectations. As a concrete example, a user-oriented or user-centered software product, such as graphical user interface (GUI) products and various PC-based utilities or web-based applications, would favor user-oriented defect perspectives. Validation activities involving actual usage scenarios, such as through usage-based statistical testing, are more likely to be useful in this situation than verification activities aimed at internal implementations, such as formal verification of individual units in isolation. However, each question we posed above typically has a primary affiliation to one of the three categories, cost, benefit, and environment, and would be examined accordingly.

In subsequent detailed comparisons, we will examine each question listed above as well as some related questions for each of the following QA alternatives individually:

- testing
- defect prevention

Table 17.1 Objects of QA alternatives

QA Alternative	Object
testing	(executable) code
defect prevention	(implementation activities)
inspection	design, code, and other software artifacts
formal verification	design/code with formal specification
fault tolerance	operational software system
failure containment	system with potential accidents

- inspection

- formal verification

- fault tolerance

- failure containment

Notice that the contents of the above list are slightly different from the list of chapters in Part III. Besides the addition of testing covered in Part II, fault tolerance and failure containment are listed separately due to their individual differences. In addition, we isolate out formal verification from formal specification, with the latter treated as part of the defect prevention activities. Several related topics, such as model checking, dynamic analysis, and static analysis, are treated the same way as the QA technique they are closest to, that is, formal verification, testing, and inspection, respectively, in subsequent discussions.

17.2 APPLICABILITY TO DIFFERENT ENVIRONMENTS

Our comparison of applicability concentrates on the development process, related activities and phases, and the general project environment.

Artifacts as objects

Table 17.1 lists the main objects of different QA alternatives and related activities. Notice that all of them are applied to some specific and concrete artifacts, with the exception of defect prevention that applies to implementation activities in general with a focus on human actions and conceptual mistakes. By extension, defect prevention also applies to all the artifacts involved in the implementation activities, including conceptual models, product domain knowledge, development process and technology knowledge, requirement and specification documents, designs, code, test plans, etc. However, the focus is on the activities that might be related to the injection of software faults into the system, and their related causes in human knowledge base.

In addition to the primary objects listed in Table 17.1, some secondary objects might also be involved. For example, fault tolerance and failure containment also involve the whole development process and related artifacts in the design and implementation of fault tolerance and failure containment features, in addition to their focus on the operational support of such systems.

Table 17.2 Development activities where different QA alternatives are applicable

QA Alternative	Development Activity/Phase
testing	testing phase and after
defect prevention	implementation (req/spec/design/coding)
inspection	all
formal verification	design/coding
fault tolerance	in-field operation
failure containment	in-field operation

Products, processes, activities/phases

Generally speaking, all QA alternatives can be potentially applied to all kinds of products. However, for different products or market segments, some might be more appropriate while others less so. For example, fault tolerance and failure containment are appropriate for market segments where high dependability and safety are major concerns, while they may be too costly for some low-cost entertainment software. The applicability of different QA alternatives to different products or market environments is closely related to defect or quality perspectives and related expectations as characterized by defect levels, which we examine in Section 17.3. It is also closely related to the cost issues examined in Section 17.4.

As discussed in Chapter 4, all QA alternatives can be applied to all variations of development processes. We can refine this to individual activities and individual QA alternatives, as summarized in Table 17.2. Notice that we generally follow the sequence of activities in the commonly used waterfall development process. Although the individual activities can be organized differently to form other development processes, this would not adversely affect the applicability of different QA alternatives to them.

Once again, fault tolerance and failure containment features need the support of other QA alternatives during their design, implementation, and testing phases. In addition, individual QA alternatives may be applied to some other seeondary phases in addition to the ones listed above, such as defect prevention used in limited scope during testing, particularly during defect fixing to reduce the injection of new defects while fixing existing ones.

Required participant expertise

The factor of people's expertise, including people's prior education, skill, experience, and on-job training, affects the applicability of specific QA techniques. This factor also affects the overall cost directly, because a good fit between people's expertise and the specific QA activities to be performed would incur little additional cost beyond the professionals' time. In addition, it also affects the overall effectiveness indirectly, because people with appropriate expertise are more likely to perform relevant tasks well.

A direct measure of people's expertise that affects the applicability and cost is the level of education and training required to gain the expertise to competently perform the specific QA activities. This includes:

- the specific knowledge regarding the specific QA alternatives and related techniques;

- the background knowledge as prerequisites.

Table 17.3   Required expertise and background knowledge for people to perform different QA alternatives

QA Alternative	Expertise Level	Background Knowledge
testing	low – high	
defect prevention	medium – high	
inspection	low – medium	
formal verification	high	formal training
fault tolerance	high	dynamic systems
failure containment	high	safety, embedded systems

In Table 17.3 we summarize both the main specific background knowledge required and the overall level of education and training effort required to gain the expertise.

Notice that in Table 17.3 we omitted the specific knowledge for each QA alternative because it is implied. In addition, we omitted the general knowledge of computer science and software engineering, which is assumed for the readers of this book, as outlined in Chapter 1.

Also worth noting is that the expertise level for some QA alternatives is given as broader ranges instead of individual levels, because some of them cover a wide spectrum of techniques which require different levels of expertise. For example, informal testing and checklist-based testing requires little in terms of formal training, while formal structural testing and usage-based statistical testing require significantly more effort in training to gain the expertise. Defect prevention typically requires good knowledge of the application domain, development methodologies and processes, tools etc., to be effective, thus requiring medium to high levels of expertise. On the other hand, inspection training is typically less time consuming, with many professional programs or training courses for inspection that can be mastered in a few days. On the higher end, formal verification, fault tolerance, and failure containment require more effort in education and training before project participants can effectively applied the related techniques.

17.3 EFFECTIVENESS COMPARISON

We next compare different QA alternatives by examining the specific perspectives of defect they are dealing with, what kind of problems they are good at addressing, their suitability to different defect levels and pervasiveness, and their ability to provide additional information for quality improvement.

17.3.1 Defect perspective

Among the different defect related perspectives and concepts, we can examine the QA alternatives by examining whether they are dealing with error sources, errors, faults, failures, or accidents. This examination can be broken down further into two parts:

- *Detection or observation* of specific problems from specific defect perspectives during the performance of specific QA activities.

- *Types of follow-up actions* that deal with the observed or detected problems in specific ways as examined from the defect perspectives.

Table 17.4   Defect observed and dealt with by different QA alternatives

QA Alternative	Defect Perspective	
	At Observation	At Follow-up (& Action)
testing	failures	fault removal
defect prevention	errors & error sources	reduced fault injection
inspection	faults	fault removal
formal verification	(absence of) faults	fault absence verified
fault tolerance	local failures	global failures avoided
failure containment	accidents	hazards resolution & damage reduction

Table 17.5   Main problem types dealt with by different QA alternatives

QA Alternative	Problem Types
testing	dynamic failures & related faults
defect prevention	systematic errors or conceptual mistakes
inspection	static & localized faults
formal verification	logical faults, indirectly
fault tolerance	operational failures in small areas
failure containment	accidents and related hazards

Sometimes, they may be dealing with the same defect perspective, such as faults that are directly detected and removed in inspection. In other cases, they may be dealing with different defect perspectives, linked through some analysis activities in between. For example, testing detects failures during execution, and additional analyses are performed based on information recorded during the failed executions to locate and remove the underlying faults that caused the failures. Table 17.4 summarizes the perspectives or types of defects observed and dealt with by individual QA alternatives. To make the follow-up defect perspective more meaningful, we also include the general follow-up actions and results for each QA alternative.

17.3.2   Problem types

Different QA alternative might be effective for different types of problems, including dealing with different perspectives of defects, ranging from different errors and error sources, various types of faults, and failures of different severity and other characteristics. Table 17.5 summarizes the different problem types each QA alternative is effective in dealing with.

Defect prevention works to block some errors or to remove error sources to prevent the injection of related faults. Therefore, it is generally good at dealing with conceptual mistakes made by software designers and programmers. Once such conceptual mistakes can be identified as error sources, they can be effectively eliminated. Some systematic problems can also be addressed by defect prevention techniques by using certain tools, processes, standards, technologies, etc., to block the errors that are related to fault injections. These problem types are also related to the pervasive, systematic problems we discuss below in connection to defect levels.

One key difference between inspection and testing is the way faults are identified: inspection identifies them directly by examining the software artifact, while failures are observed during testing and related faults are identified later by utilizing the recorded execution information. This key difference leads to the different types of faults commonly detected using these two techniques: Inspection is usually good at detecting static and localized faults which are often related to some common conceptual mistakes, while testing is good at detecting dynamic faults involving multiple components in interactions. The reasons behind this difference in detected defects can be explained by the following differences between the two types of QA alternatives:

- Inspection involves static examination while testing involves dynamic executions. Therefore, static problems are more likely to be found during inspection, while dynamic problems are more likely to be found during testing.

- It is hard for human inspectors to keep track of multiple components and complicated interactions over time, while the same task may not be such a difficult one for computers. Therefore, testing is generally better at detecting interaction problems involving multiple components.

- Human inspectors can focus on a small area and perform in-depth analysis, leading to effective detection of localized faults. In addition, in-depth analyses can also be used to identify conceptual problems for related defect prevention — a topic we examine further in connection to the comparison of constructive information provided by different QA alternatives later in this section.

Formal verification deals with logical (or mathematical) correctness, and can be interpreted as extremely formalized inspection. Therefore, it shares some of the characteristics of inspection in dealing with static and logical problems. However, such problems are dealt with indirectly, because the correctness verification instead of fault detection is the focus. Problem identification is only a side-effect of failing to produce a correctness proof. However, in model checking, an important variation of formal verification we covered in Chapter 15, this ability to identify problems is enhanced through the use of counterexamples.

Fault tolerance and failure containment are designed to work with dynamic operational problems that may lead to global failures or accidents. Fault tolerance techniques are good at isolating faults to only cause local failures but not global ones, while failure containment works to contain failures that may lead to accidents by dealing with hazards or reducing damage related to accidents.

17.3.3 Defect level and pervasiveness

Different QA techniques may be suitable for different defect levels or pervasiveness. Table 17.6 summarizes the defect levels each individual QA alternative is suitable for, with more discussions presented below.

In general, if systematic problems exist in an organization and the related products, preventive action is the most effective way to deal with them. Such systematic problems are generally associated with common failures traceable to common faults, and these common faults can be traced in turn to some common errors through causal analysis. As pointed out in Humphrey (1995):

> "While detecting and fixing defects is critically important, it is an inherently defensive strategy. To make significant quality improvements, you should identify the causes of these defects and take steps to eliminate them."

Table 17.6   Defect levels where different QA alternatives are suitable

QA Alternative	Defect Level	
testing	low – medium	
defect prevention	low – high	(particularly pervasive problems)
inspection	medium – high	
formal verification	low	
fault tolerance	low	
failure containment	lowest	

On the other hand, sporadic problems can generally be dealt with by other QA alternatives.

For existing products with relatively high defect levels or with many common faults, inspection is most likely to be more effective than testing, because inspection can continue after the initial fault is detected, but further testing is often blocked or partially blocked once a fault is encountered and a failure is observed. In addition, when defect levels are high, execution of most test cases will result in failure observations, and the subsequent effort to locate and remove the underlying faults is similar to that for inspection. Analysis of existing high-defect projects commonly conducted in conjunction with inspection can often point to systematic problems. Such systematic problems can be most effectively addressed by defect prevention activities in successor projects.

A proof of correctness or a formal verification can only be produced if the program is fault-free with respect to its formal specifications. When verification cannot be successfully completed, further analysis can often reveal accidental logical or functional faults. However, this is not an effective method for fault detection because of the substantial effort involved in the failed verification attempt. Therefore, formal verification does not work for software with high defect levels. Fortunately, the use of formal methods, with formal specification focusing on error source elimination and formal verification focusing on verifying the conformance in designs and code, generally results in low defect levels.

Fault tolerance techniques generally involve the observations of dynamic local failures and the tolerance of the related faults, but not the identification and removal of these faults. These techniques only work when defect levels are very low, because multiple fault encounters or frequent failures cannot be effectively tolerated. Therefore, other QA alternatives need to be used to reduce the defects to a very low level before fault tolerance techniques can be used to further reduce the probability of system failures.

On the other hand, many software safety assurance techniques attempt to weaken the link between failures and accidents or reduce the damage associated with accidents. The focus of these activities is the post-failure accidents and the related hazard analysis and resolution. Defect levels are expected to be extremely low, because these expensive techniques are generally applied as the last guard against system safety problems after all relevant traditional QA activities have been performed already.

17.3.4   Result interpretation and constructive information

Ease of result interpretation plays an important role in the application of specific QA techniques. A good understanding of the results is a precondition to follow-up actions. For example, both inspection and testing are aimed at defect removal. However, inspection results are much easier to interpret and can be used directly for defect removal. Testing results

Table 17.7   Ease of result interpretation for different QA alternatives and amount of constructive information/measurements

QA Alternative	Result Interpretation	Information/Measurement
testing	moderate	executions & failures
defect prevention	(intangible)	experience
inspection	easy	faults, already located
formal verification	hard	fault absence verified
fault tolerance	hard	(unanticipated) environments/usages
failure containment	hard	accident scenarios and hazards

need to be analyzed by experienced software professionals to locate the faults that caused the failures observed during testing, and only then can these faults be removed. In addition, re-verification of defect removal is also more complicated in testing than in inspection. Additional testing effort in the form of re-runs is typically involved, while re-inspection are less likely to be required and, even if required, it would be much simpler.

On the other hand, result interpretation for formal verification, fault tolerance, and failure containment is harder than that for inspection and testing. Sometimes, a significant amount of effort is needed to analyze these results to support follow-up actions. For example, in a fault tolerant system using recovery blocks, repeated failures need to be dealt with off-line by analyzing the dynamic records. Much information related to unanticipated environment and usage not covered in the pre-planned testing activities may be included in these records. Similarly, failure containment results typically need additional analysis support such as those described in Chapter 16. The difficulties with interpreting formal verification results usually involve the formalism used, which requires formal training not as readily available to software practitioners as other QA alternatives.

In comparison, defect prevention produces results in the form of reduced fault injection, which is harder to quantify or visualize, thus somewhat intangible or invisible. However, we do not usually associate direct follow-up action with them, except packaging the experience for future projects. Therefore, the difficulty with interpreting defect prevention results is less of an issue.

Table 17.7 summarizes the above comparison of result interpretation for different QA alternatives. In addition to easy result interpretation, we would like to have different QA alternatives to provide as much information as possible to help us improve quality for the current and future products. Consequently, such additional information and related measurement data are also summarized in Table 17.7. As discussed above, this information and data can be used in direct follow-up activities after the execution of selected QA activities. More detailed description of these measurement data and their usage to provide quality assessment and improvement is given in Part IV, and particularly in Chapter 18.

17.4 COST COMPARISON

Testing is among the standard activities that make up the whole software development process, regardless of the process choice or the product type. Therefore, the cost of other QA alternatives is examined below using testing as the baseline for comparison.

Cost factors

Most traditional QA activities, such as testing and inspection, focus on defect detection and removal. The cost can then be directly related to the effort in detecting and fixing the problems. Another part of cost not commonly considered is the cost of down-stream damage caused by dormant defects, or those who escaped the collection of QA activities. However, this cost is negatively correlated with the effectiveness of the different QA techniques we discussed above, particularly the quality levels at the exit after the application of a collection of QA techniques. Therefore we focus on the cost of defect detection and removal in this section.

Another complication to this cost evaluation and comparison is the defect prevention techniques, which prevent the injection of certain faults by spending valuable resources up-stream to block errors or to remove error sources. As discussed in the previous section, this reduction in defect injection is hard to quantify. Therefore, we focus on the cost related to the effort to prevent fault injection, instead the cost of down-stream cost of poor quality.

For the cases of fault tolerance and failure containment, the cost includes three parts:

- *Operational cost* of having specific mechanisms in the operational systems, which may slow down the overall system, reduce the system capacity, or negatively affect other performance measures. For example, repeating failed executions in the fault tolerance implementation using recovery blocks slows down normal processing.

- *Implementation cost* to design, implement, and assure selected features and mechanisms, such as backups and redundancies.

- *Failure or accident cost*, which is similar to the dormant defect cost considered above for defect prevention and defect reduction techniques.

Among the three, failure/accident cost need to be balanced against the other two to justify spending valuable resources to implement and operate these fault tolerance and failure containment mechanisms. On the other hand, operational cost in the form of reduced performance or capacity is typically tolerable to the customers and users. Therefore, we focus on the implementation cost when we consider the cost for fault tolerance and failure containment techniques.

Cost comparison for specific QA alternatives

In general, the longer a fault remains in a software system, the higher the total cost (more than linear increase) associated with fixing the related problems (Boehm, 1981; Humphrey, 1995). In addition to fixing the original fault, the problems that need to be resolved include the failures caused by the original fault, as well as other related faults which may be injected in a chain reaction because of the presence of the original fault, for example, in a module that needs to interface with the module containing the original fault. Therefore, fixing problems early in the development process, or even better, preventing the injection of faults through error removal, is generally much more cost-effective than dealing with the problems later in other QA activities.

Unlike testing, which can only be performed after the software system is at least partially implemented, inspection can be performed throughout the software development process and on almost any software artifact. The cost for conducting different variations of inspection ranges from very low for informal reviews to that comparable to testing for

Table 17.8 Cost comparison for different QA alternatives

QA Alternative	Cost	
testing	medium	(low − high)
defect prevention	low	
inspection	low − medium	
formal verification	high	
fault tolerance	high	
failure containment	highest	

formal inspections. According to some empirical data (Gilb and Graham, 1993), inspection typically brings in a return-on-investment (ROI) ratio of around 10-to-1. This effect is particularly strong in the earlier phases of software development.

Formal verification can be viewed as an extremely formal form of inspection where all the elements of the design or the code are formally verified. As mentioned before, the proof of correctness for a program or a design is typically one order of magnitude longer than the program or the design itself. Therefore, such human intensive proofs cost significantly more than most inspections, and usually cost more than testing.

Fault tolerance techniques cost significantly more to implement due to the built-in duplications. Safety assurance activities cost even more because of all the associated actions taken to address both pre-failure and post-failure issues to ensure not only low probability of failure, but also to limit the failure consequences and damages. However, for safety critical applications, the associated high cost is usually justified.

Table 17.8 summarizes the cost comparison presented above. Notice that we used testing, the most widely performed QA activity, as the baseline of comparison and set its cost as medium. However, different forms of testing have significantly different costs, as represented by the general range in Table 17.8. A careful cost–benefit analysis needs to be performed based on historical data to choose the appropriate QA alternatives for different types of software products.

17.5 COMPARISON SUMMARY AND RECOMMENDATIONS

Table 17.9 summarizes the above comparisons in three categories: applicability, effectiveness, and cost. Among the three, only the cost comparison is directly taken from Table 17.8. The other two are summarized from many factors related to applicability and effectiveness as presented above. For the applicability comparison, we focus on the major applicability limits for individual QA alternatives. For effectiveness comparison, we focus on problem type, level, and defect perspective, all summarized in one short phrase for each QA alternative.

Based on the comparison and analysis presented so far, we make the following general recommendations:

- In general, a concerted effort is necessary with many different QA activities to be used in an integrated fashion to effectively and efficiently deal with defects and ensure product quality.

- Defect prevention greatly reduces the chance of fault injections. Therefore, such preventive actions should be an integral part of any QA plan. Causal analyses covered

Table 17.9   General comparison for different QA alternatives

QA Alternative	Applicability	Effectiveness	Cost
testing	code	occasional failures	medium
defect prevention	known causes	systematic problems	low
inspection	s/w artifacts	scattered faults	low – medium
formal verification	formal spec.	fault absence	high
fault tolerance	duplication	rare-cond. failures	high
failure containment	known hazards	rare-cond. accidents	highest

in Chapter 20 can be performed to identify systematic problems and select specific preventive actions to deal with the identified problems.

- Inspection and testing are applicable to different situations, and effective for different defect types at different defect levels. Therefore, inspection can be performed first to lower defect levels by directly detecting and removing many localized and static faults, then testing can be performed to remove the remaining faults related to dynamic scenarios and interactions. To maximize the benefit-to-cost ratio, various risk identification techniques covered in Chapter 21 can be used to focus inspection and testing effort on identified high-risk product components.

- Software safety assurance (especially hazard and damage control), fault tolerance, and formal verification techniques cost significantly more to implement than traditional QA techniques. However, if consequence of failures is severe and potential damage is high, they can be used to further reduce the failure probability, or to reduce the accident probability or severity.

The comparison of the applicability, effectiveness, and cost of these QA alternatives in this chapter can help software professionals choose appropriate QA alternatives and related techniques, and tailor or integrate them for specific applications. Together with the measurement and analysis activities described in Part IV, they can help us arrive at an optimal strategy for software QA and achieve quantifiable quality improvement.

Problems

17.1   In software engineering literature, there are various studies comparing different QA alternatives and techniques based on empirical data. Scan through some recent publications and read some articles on this topic, and compare their results with the general comparisons described in this chapter.

17.2   Most empirical studies mentioned above typically compare one QA alternative to another (for example, inspection vs. testing), or compare different techniques within a general category (for example, different inspection processes or techniques). Can you replicate some of these studies in your work?

17.3   Can you use the comparison questions listed in this chapter to compare individual testing techniques?

17.4   How would the applicability of different QA alternatives be different when other software processes (non-waterfall ones) are used?

17.5   Based on what we have covered so far in this book, list the specific background knowledge for individual QA alternatives.

17.6   Compare both the entry and exit levels of quality for individual QA alternatives. That is, what is the defect level *before* and *after* applying these specific QA alternatives.

17.7   Can your relate the difficulty level of result interpretation to the required expertise to perform a specific QA activity?

17.8   Consider the specific application environment in your organization, how would different QA alternatives compare? In addition, is cost a critical factor in your market segment? How would it affect the choice of different QA alternatives for your products?

17.9   With the overall technology change and development, would the comparison results we discussed in this chapter be different? How? Give some specific examples.

PART IV

QUANTIFIABLE QUALITY IMPROVEMENT

Our focus in Part IV is quantifiable quality improvement, which includes two basic elements:

- *Quantification* of quality through quantitative measurements and models so that the quantified quality assessment results can be compared to the pre-set quality goals for quality and process management.

- Quality *improvement* through analyses and follow-up activities by identifying quality improvement possibilities, providing feedback, and initiating follow-up actions.

We start this part with a general description of the feedback loop and all the activities involved in quantifiable quality improvement in Chapter 18. It is followed by a general description of the models and measurements that can be used for these purposes in Chapter 19. Finally, we describe the major types of analyses and models, including defect analysis, risk analysis and identification, and software reliability engineering in Chapters 20, 21, and 22, respectively.

CHAPTER 18

FEEDBACK LOOP AND ACTIVITIES FOR QUANTIFIABLE QUALITY IMPROVEMENT

To support quantifiable quality improvement, various parallel and follow-up activities to the main quality assurance (QA) activities are needed, including:

- Monitoring the specific QA activities and the overall software development or maintenance activities, and extracting relevant measurement data.

- Analyzing the data collected above for quality quantification and identification of quality improvement opportunities.

- Providing feedback to the QA and development/maintenance activities and carrying out follow-up actions based on the analysis results above.

These activities also close the quality engineering feedback loop in Figure 5.1 and refine it into Figure 18.1:

- The single measurement source in Figure 5.1 is expanded in Figure 18.1 to include:
  - *in-process measurements* from the QA activities as well as the related development/maintenance activities;
  - *environmental measurements* about the overall project environment and *external measurements* beyond the project scope.

- The quality assessment and improvement box in Figure 5.1 is significantly enlarged in Figure 18.1 to depict the various analysis and modeling activities for quantifiable quality improvement.

303

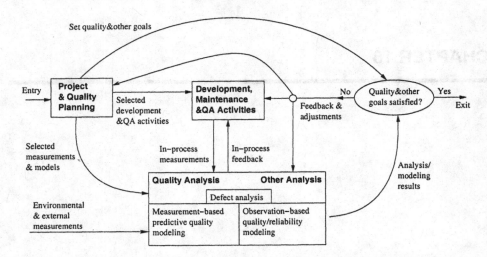

Figure 18.1 Refined quality engineering process: Measurement, analysis, and feedback for quantifiable quality improvement

- In addition to the important use of analysis and modeling results for the product release decision in Figure 5.1, some short-term direct feedback is added from the analysis box to the activity box in Figure 18.1.

All the important issues related to these activities, measurements, analyses, and feedback are discussed in subsequent sections.

18.1 QA MONITORING AND MEASUREMENT

The primary purpose of QA monitoring is to ensure proper execution of the planned QA activities through the use of various measurements. These measurements also provide the data input to subsequent analysis and modeling activities. We next examine these measurements and their roles in quantifiable quality improvement.

18.1.1 Direct vs. indirect quality measurements

As discussed in Part-I, the correctness aspect of quality can often be *directly* derived from its definition or related to various defect measurements. For example, how likely a system is going to fail is captured by its reliability and related measurements. Alternatively, defect measurements for a product, such as total fault count, can also be used to characterize its quality. External data from industry and related quality models can also be used to provide a rough estimate of product quality without actually measuring it, as described in Chapter 19. However, such rough estimates can only serve as the starting point for some quality planning or related activities before actual measurement data from the project in question become available.

Measuring quality directly would typically require that we measure the results of individual QA activities and related defects. Result and defect measurements can sometimes be used in isolation (that is, without relating to other measurements) in QA monitoring. For example, many software development organizations track their QA activities by the discovered defects so far, with an implicit understanding of how these discovered defects represent the share of total defects. The total number of defects can be estimated by various software estimation techniques. These direct quality measurements may be used in isolation in selected quality models as well, as described in Chapter 19.

Under most circumstances, these direct quality measurements need to be used in conjunction with other indirect measurements in quality modeling to monitor the QA and software processes and provide feedback to them. For example, even in the above example of QA monitoring by tracking the number of discovered defects, we need some time or activity measurements, such as days or execution hours spent in testing. These measurements would give us a general idea of not only where we are in the proportion of defects discovered, but also in project schedule.

In addition, various direct quality measurements need other indirect quality measurements as well. For example, the measurement of reliability, which is defined to be the probability of failure free operations of a software system for a specific time period or for a given set of input under a specific environment (Musa et al., 1987; Lyu, 1995a; Tian, 1995), requires us to measure time or input and characterize the environment, in addition to measuring failures.

More importantly, most of the result and defect measurements can only become available in the later part of the software development process. In addition, fixing problems at late stages may not be cost effective, because the longer a defect stays dormant in a system, the more harm it is likely to cause and the more difficult to fix (Boehm, 1991). Consequently, there is a strong need for us to use other early indicators and related quality models to provide early quality predictions. These indirect quality indicators can generally be measured by the *environmental*, *product internal*, and *activity* measurements.

Most of these direct and indirect quality measurements can be obtained from the QA activities or from the overall software development or maintenance processes. Therefore, they are classified as *in-process* measurements, as depicted in Figure 18.1. However, the overall project environment shouldn't be affected much by the exact process dynamics or the specific QA activities. Similarly, various external measurements and models might also be used in providing rough quality estimates for the current project. These environmental and external measurements are depicted as from data sources different from the in-process measurements in Figure 18.1.

To ensure proper collection and usage of various measurement data, we need to pay special attention to the following:

- *Consistent interpretation and tracking*: For defects, we need to distinguish execution failures, internal faults, and errors in human actions. The specific problems need to be counted and tracked consistently. Similarly, other measurements also require us to maintain consistent interpretation.

- *Timely defect and data reporting*: Because these measurements are used to monitor and control software projects, we must ensure timely reporting of defects and other dynamic measurements to keep the information current.

- *Proper data granularity*: Different quality analyses and models might require data at different levels of granularity. We will examine this aspect further in connection with models for quality assessment and improvement in Chapter 19.

The data collection also needs some process and implementation support, which is described in Section 18.4.

18.1.2   Direct quality measurements: Result and defect measurements

As described in Part II and Part III, an important part of any QA activity is to analyze the results from individual activities, to handle the problems, and to follow up on them. For example, the result of the execution of a selected test case needs to be checked to see if it conforms to the user expectation or product specification. In case of non-conformance, we need to decide if the deviation can be counted as a failure. If it is deemed to be a failure, then a defect record is opened, and all the rules and regulations of the defect handling process apply to this reported defect. For defect resolution, the underlying fault that caused the failure observed in testing needs to be located and fixed. In case a decision is made not to count it as a defect, to defer the fix, etc., proper rules for defect handling need to be followed. The details about defect handling were described in Chapter 4.

At the minimum, each defect will be uniquely identified to facilitate its tracking and resolution. Various other specific information about the discovered defects can be recorded and updated through the defect handling process, including:

- Circumstantial information about the defect discovery. For example, the exact thing that a tester was doing when this failure was triggered might provide valuable information for the responsible developers or "code owners" to analyze the problem and fix the underlying faults that caused the observed failure.

- Exact location of the faults fixed in response to an observed failure, or the location of the fault directly detected through inspection or other QA activities.

Each of these discovered defects can then be counted and relevant information about it can be used, in combination with other information about the project, in analyses using various quality assessment models described in Chapter 19. Such models provide us with quality assessments, such as defect density and distribution, current product reliability, the progress information of the QA activities, or other results. Additional information about these defects, such as defect type, severity, types of fix applied, etc., often needs to be collected for additional analyses that promise more valuable feedback. Details about such additional information and its usage in quality assessment and improvement are included in Chapter 20.

18.1.3   Indirect quality measurements: Environmental, product internal, and activity measurements

Environmental measurements can be associated with the general characteristics of the process, product and people, or the software product's *domain* (Prahalad and Krishnan, 1999), in the following hierarchy:

- The *process characteristics* include:

  - the process used: waterfall, iterative, spiral, etc.,

  - activities and their relationships,

  - specific development techniques used, etc.

- *People characteristics* include:

  - skills and experience,

  - roles and responsibilities,
  - organizational and team structure, etc.
- *Product characteristics* include:

  - general expectations of the target users,
  - high-level product functionality,
  - market environment for the product,
  - specific hardware/software configuration, etc.

Environmental measurements are typically rough categorical measurements instead of quantitative or numerical measurements. They specify a general category a product belongs to, a specific process used, or a group of people involved. Associating numbers to them does not usually add new information. In fact, it often obscures the main information provided. Environmental measurements are mainly used to characterize the current product and its market segment. This characterization can often provide the basis for some general extrapolation based on industrial averages, market segmentation, or product history. Sometimes, various models make assumptions about the overall environment. These assumptions need to be validated before actually analyses using these models can be performed.

Product internal measurements characterize various product internal attributes of selected software artifacts (Fenton and Pfleeger, 1996). This category is the most studied and most well understood in the software engineering community. These measurements can be characterized by the following:

- *Software artifacts* being measured, including software requirement specifications, designs, program code, test cases, related documents, and other software artifacts.

- *Product (internal) attributes* being measured, including control (for example, control flow paths), data (for example, operand count), and presentation (for example, different indentation rules used).

- *Measurement of structures*: Different attributes of the software artifacts may be treated as an unstructured heap of symbols (for example, raw count such as LOC – line of code), or as syntactical structures (for example, various control flow path measurements (Fenton and Pfleeger, 1996)), or even as interconnected semantic entities (for example, context-sensitive measures such as live data definitions (Tai, 1984)).

Most product internal measurements are available before testing, with many available in requirement and design phases, while most direct quality measurements cannot be obtained early. Because of this, product internal measurements are often used in various models to provide early assessments of product quality and to identify problematic areas for focused quality improvement.

Activity measurements directly measure specific software development and maintenance activities and the associated effort, time, and other resources. Many of these measurements involve dynamic measurement, which is in contrast to the mostly static product internal and environmental measurements above. Activity measurement can be done at different levels of granularity:

- *Coarse-grain* activity measurements for the whole project. For example, total effort and cycle-time can be used in various models for overall quality assessment and project release decisions.

- *Medium-grain* activity measurements for individual development phases, sub-phases, or time periods such as weeks or months. For example, defect profiles over development phases are commonly used in various models for quality assessment, resource allocation, and project management.

- *Fine-grain* activity measurements for individual activities. For example, test workload assessments for individual test cases are used in various reliability models to provide valuable feedback to the software development process and QA activities, as described in Chapter 22.

18.2 IMMEDIATE FOLLOW-UP ACTIONS AND FEEDBACK

Although some analyses are typically needed to provide feedback and drive follow-up actions, a few feedback or follow-up actions can be provided or carried out immediately for timely feedback and adjustment without further analysis. The most obvious and most immediate follow-up action to defect discovery is defect fixing, which is usually considered part of the QA activities themselves. Once a defect fix is attempted, usually re-verification is carried out to certify the defect fix before it is declared as "fixed", as described in the defect handling process in Chapter 4.

The action of defect fixing may also have various implicit impacts on the QA activities. For example, during Gilb inspection covered in Chapter 14, a step called process brainstorming is performed to identify defect causes and problem areas and to formulate quality and process improvement plans. Therefore, the subsequent steps in the inspection process, as well as the subsequent inspections, would be affected by this immediate feedback.

Another concrete example of this impact on QA activities is in the testing activity planning and execution. For the testing of many large software systems, such as the system testing of IBM's commercial software products (Tian, 1998), test activity adjustment according to defect discovery is quite common, as follows:

- The testing team usually suspends activities related to the testing scenarios that have triggered the defect and continues with others. This approach reduces the chance of repeatedly finding duplicate defects that provide little additional information for defect removal or quality improvement. The same change of areas of testing also contributes to good testing efficiency.

- When an integrated fix for the reported defect arrives from the development team, the failing scenario is rerun and the testing process continues.

This adjustment to testing activities also has an impact on the suitability of model used to analyze product reliability, as discussed in Chapter 22.

The overall results of a QA activity can often be directly measured, and sometimes used for immediate follow-up actions. For example, in multi-phase inspection, process termination might be influenced by the number of defects found in an inspection phase: When it is under a certain threshold, inspection can stop; otherwise another inspection phase is carried out. Similarly, testing sub-phases, and decision of which sub-area to test, may well be influenced by the direct results of the previous testing sub-phase or sub-area.

Other indirect quality measurements can also be used to provide immediate feedback and lead to appropriate adjustments to the QA activities and the overall development process. Among the three sub-types of indirect quality measurements, environmental measurements are the most stable over time, and therefore are less likely to be used for immediate feedback. Unlike the "in-process" product internal and activity measurements in Figure 18.1, these measurements reflect the overall development environments instead of the dynamic information about the project in progress.

Product internal measurements should be fairly stable during the later part of development, when the code base is stable. After "code freeze", major additions or changes to the code base are prohibited, except for changes in response to discovered defects. Therefore, these measurements are less likely to be used for immediate feedback during late part of development or during software maintenance activities. However, during the early part of development, product-internal measurements may be used for immediate feedback and follow-up actions. For example, extremely high complexity of product components, such as tight coupling among different modules, may be an indication of improper design. Such problems may need to be modified as early as possible, by changing the design to de-couple the modules in this example, to avoid later and more costly changes that would require discarding many of the lower-level designs and code in those affected modules. Notice that in this case, we implicitly assume a "norm" of module complexity so that exceptions (extremely high complexity, in this case) can be detected. Therefore, we are in effect using external input to provide feedback.

Activity measurements are the most dynamic, and can be updated in a timely fashion and used to track the progress of QA and development activities, and make initial suggestions for the adjustments to the project schedule, resource allocation, etc. Here, again, we implicitly assume that there are plans and norms that we can compare against to provide such immediate feedback. However, typically, formal adjustments and major decisions need further justification and support from additional analyses, as discussed below.

18.3   ANALYSES AND FOLLOW-UP ACTIONS

The analysis and modeling activities provide feedback to the QA activities and the overall software development/maintenance process, and serve as the basis for follow-up activities. There is a tight connection between the types of analyses performed and the feedback and follow-up activities in response to the specific analysis results. Therefore, we examine them together, linking specific analyses to specific feedback and follow-up actions.

18.3.1   Analyses for product release decisions

The most important use of analysis and modeling results is to provide input for making product release decisions, which is shown prominently in Figure 18.1, in the question: "Quality & other goals satisfied?". In general, comparing quality assessment results from selected models to pre-set quality goals can help us make product release decisions. Various other factors, such as project schedule, resource utilization, market environment, competitive pressure, prior plans and announcements, etc., all play an important role in these decisions. There are two basic ways to make product release decisions:

- *Decisions without explicit quality assessment*, which may take three general forms:

    - *Implicit quality assessments*, such as completion of planned test activities, can be used as exit criteria, which implicitly assumes the effectiveness of the testing activities.

- *Indirect quality assessments*, such as achieving certain test coverage goals, can be used as exit criteria, which implicitly equates coverage levels to reliability levels.

- *Other factors*, such as project schedule, cost, and resource utilization, can sometimes be used as exit criteria.

- *Decisions based on explicit quality assessments*: Two types of quality assessments exist depending on the two major quality perspectives described in Chapter 2:

  - *Failure-related quality assessments* from a customer's or external perspective, such as various reliability measures and impact assessments.

  - *Fault-related quality assessments* from a developer's or internal perspective, such as defect density and count estimates for latent defects.

The most direct and obvious use of quality assessments for product release decisions is the use of various reliability assessments. Reliability is a measure of quality directly meaningful to customers and users. The basic idea is to set reliability goals in the quality planning activity during product planning and requirement analysis early in the software development process, and later on to compare the reliability assessment based on testing data to see if this preset goal has been reached. If so, the product can be released. Otherwise, testing needs to continue and product release needs to be deferred. Various models exist today to provide reliability assessments and improvement based on data from testing, as described in Chapter 22.

Besides reliability, other failure-based quality assessments can also be used for product release decisions. For example, for safety critical systems, the focus is not on all the failures, but only on those with severe consequences. Therefore, failure impact analysis may be used as a product release criterion. For example, the product can be released if the worst-case damage is limited to a preset amount. Sometimes, a composite release criterion, such as reliability goal for the general problems combined with worst-case damage limit, can be used.

Many companies use internal defect information to build quality models and use the related results for product release decisions. Such usage was particularly prevalent before software reliability engineering becomes widely used in industry. For example, defect profile based on past projects from the same organization can be used to put the current defect measurement into perspective, and to estimate the latent defects, or the remaining faults still in the systems that are likely to cause problems to users. Product release criterion can then be based on a threshold of such estimated latent defects. The advantage of such release criteria is the availability of internal product and defect data that can be used to make such decisions. The disadvantage is the tenuous connection between such quality estimates and quality as perceived by target customers and users. Although there is generally a positive correlation between the two, a functional mapping from such faults to failures and reliability simply does not exist.

On the other hand, acceptance testing is typically the last major QA activity carried out before product release, no matter what kind of development process is followed. Naturally, quality analysis results based on this activity can be used as part of the input for product release decisions. In addition, product release decisions are generally accompanied by some forms of final reviews that focus on quality or other factors mentioned above. The quality reviews typically include: conformance to certain standards, presence or absence of major functions or features, match or mismatch between the overall quality levels and users' quality expectations. With the general connection of acceptance testing as the last major QA activity, the product release decision is closely linked to the question: "When to stop testing?" that we have already addressed in Chapter 6.

Based on the above discussion and the analysis of exit criteria for different types of testing in Chapter 6, the product release decision can be made as follows:

- If quality measurements directly meaningful to target customers are available, such as reliability, safety, and other failure-based measurements, they should be used as the primary criterion for product release. Explicit quality analysis and modeling based on various measurement data are required to support such product release decisions.

- When the above are not available because of lack of data or other difficulties, internal quality assessments, such as various internal defects and fault-based measurements, can be used.

- In the absence of any direct quality assessments, coverage-based product release criteria are probably the best we can hope for. Consequently, they are the most commonly used product release criteria based on indirect or implicit quality assessment.

- When none of the above is available, we can use the completion of certain QA activities or other factors as the last resort to make product release decisions.

18.3.2   Analyses for other project management decisions

Termination criteria for various QA activities, or sometime for general software development activities, can also be based on analysis results from various quality assessment models. The product release decision discussed above can be treated as a special case of these termination criteria where the termination of the last testing sub-phase is accompanied by the product release. Different concerns of different sub-phases might induce certain changes to the corresponding termination criteria:

- In later sub-phases of testing, such as system testing, beta testing, integration testing, etc., the focus is typically on the overall operation of the software system from the users' perspective. Therefore, when we make test termination decisions, little or no adjustment is needed to use the analysis and modeling results for product release discussed above.

- In earlier sub-phases of testing, such as in unit and component testing, the focus is on the internal implementation of a product subpart. In addition, the complete system may not be operational yet. The overall system reliability from a users' perspective may not be defined nor can it be assessed. Therefore, criteria based on test coverage, internal defects, or even just schedule and resources, could be more easily justified.

The termination criteria for other early QA activities, such as inspection of design and code, have more similarities to earlier sub-phases of testing than to later ones. Most likely some criteria based on internal assessments can be adopted, such as completion of planned activities, coverage, and occasionally modeling results based on internal defects. For example, exit criterion for inspection is typically completion of planned objects to inspect. This completion usually represents certain levels of coverage that are determined in the planning stage for inspection.

The quality assessment and modeling results can also be used to support various other management decisions, primarily in the following areas:

- *Schedule adjustment*: This decision is probably the one most closely identified with product release or phase/sub-phase termination decisions. When there is a mismatch between a product's quality progress and project schedule, adjustment is called for. The quality assessment results typically will indicate when the quality goal will be satisfied. This input can be used to delay (more often) or speed up (less often) the project schedule.

- *Resource allocation and adjustment*: Similar to the above, if a project is behind schedule or ahead of schedule, resource allocation decisions may be made to try to compensate for it by adding or removing certain resources, although the impact of this is limited (Brooks, 1995). When such analysis results are available for subparts of projects, then re-allocation of planned resources among those different subparts may be a good idea, so that high-risk or problematic areas can receive more attention and the overall product quality can be improved in the most cost-effective way. This topic is discussed in conjunction with various risk identification techniques needed to support such resource allocation decisions in Chapter 21.

- *Planning for post-release product support*: Sometimes, product release decisions are made regardless of the current quality level. For example, a product might be released due to competitive pressure, or to capture market share even if the preset quality goals have not been achieved yet. Under such circumstances, the quality analysis results can be used to plan for anticipated increase for post-release product support. Similarly, if we have information about problematic areas, we can also better plan for post-release product support, for example, to allocate more support personnel to potentially problematic areas.

- *Planning for future products* can be based on an assessment of quality strength and weakness of the current product, or a comparison between this and other competitive products.

18.3.3   Other feedback and follow-up actions

The analysis and modeling activities can also provide feedback to themselves, although mostly indirectly. For example, if the analysis results are not usable by the upper management to make product release decisions, it might be an indication that inappropriate models and measures are used. As a concrete example, suppose only reliability is assessed and managed during the development of a mass-market end-user product without paying attention to usability, the upper management may totally disregard the quality modeling results and base their product release decision on other evidence. In this case, if the problem was discovered early, new quality measurements and models might be adopted to assess the usability or other aspects of product quality.

A less drastic adjustment is usually called for, because the major concerns, such as in the usability vs. reliability focus in the example above, should have been addressed in the quality planning stage already. One concrete example of this is the application of software reliability engineering in IBM Software Solutions Toronto Laboratory (Tian et al., 1995) summarized below:

- At the beginning of the project, the commonly recommended time measurement for reliability analysis, CPU execution time (Musa et al., 1987), was selected as the primary time measurement for reliability analysis and modeling.

- As time goes on, it was discovered that the modeling results based on this time measurement were not stable for this kind of products due to some specific product characteristics.

- Additional analysis was performed to identify other alternative time measurements. Test run count was found to provide more stable modeling results and was adopted.

Follow-up studies also identified other appropriate time measurements, such as transactions processed, and combined timing information with input information to identify problematic areas for focused reliability improvement (Tian, 1995; Tian and Palma, 1997; Tian and Palma, 1998). The models used, analyses performed, and the overall results from this series of studies are described in Chapter 22.

Longer-term and broader-scope follow-up activities are those carried out over more than a few months and beyond the scope of the current project. Such activities can be supported by the analysis and modeling activities described above, the overall experience of the current project, and an overall analysis of the quality engineering process for the current project. The follow-up and improvement can be concentrated in three major areas:

- *Future product quality improvement*: This is similar to the above feedback and follow-up activities, but with the added hindsight. Better quality planning can be formulated based on the experience of the current project, both in terms of goal setting and the selection of the overall QA strategies. The concrete results from the current project would allow us to set more realistic quality goals. The experience with specific QA strategies would allow us to select effective QA techniques, proper measurements, and analysis models for use in future projects, and to execute the plans more smoothly.

- *Process quality improvement*: This improvement can be achieved in two general areas, the quality engineering process itself and the general software engineering process. The former can be based on the experience with carrying out the current quality engineering process, while the latter would also benefit greatly from alternative experience using other development processes to develop similar products. Therefore, a comparative assessment can be made, and new processes, or new process elements, can be adopted or adapted to work better for future projects.

- *People quality improvement*: A more intangible benefit is the experience gained by people in many areas, including domain knowledge of the specific product, software process and technology experience, and quality engineering knowledge. Their experience can be packaged to ensure effective transfer of the collective knowledge and experience, or the so-called institutional memory, to new project personnel. In addition, specific shortcomings can be identified for further education and training for the current project personnel.

18.4 IMPLEMENTATION, INTEGRATION, AND TOOL SUPPORT

All the activities described above need to be implemented as part of the overall quality engineering activities, supported by various automated tools to allow for an effective and efficient implementation, and integrated into the quality engineering process.

18.4.1 Feedback loop: Implementation and integration

As described in Chapter 5, the quality engineering process connects the main QA activities in the center with the quality planning activities at the beginning and the measurement and analysis activities as the parallel and follow-up activities. The measurement and analysis activities monitor the QA activities as well as the overall development activities, and provide feedback to them and serve as the basis for follow-up actions. From the operational view, these measurement and analysis activities complete the feedback loop and play a central role in the quality engineering process. We next identify specific feedback loop passages by examining 1) the specific measurements used as input to various analyses; and 2) specific feedback produced as output from them.

As described in Section 18.1, the direct quality measurements include results and defect measurements, and the indirect quality measurements include activity, product internal, and environmental measurements. We need to enlarge the input sources for measurements to include all the sources to provide these four sub-types of direct and indirect quality measurements:

1. *Results and defect measurements*: The main source of this data input is the QA activities themselves, probably through the use of defect tracking tools.

2. *Activity measurements*: Both the QA activities as well as the general development activities are measured here.

3. *Product internal measurements*: The main source of this data input is the current product under development instead of the QA activities. However, the current product is directly affected by the development process and so is its measurement values.

4. *Environmental measurements*: The main source of this data input is the overall project environment instead of the QA activities.

The first three above are from QA/development/maintenance activities and processes. Therefore, they are classified as in-process measurements. The environmental measurements are not from these processes or activities, similar to some external measurements that might be used for comparison or for rough quality estimates.

On the analysis and modeling output side, different kinds of feedback include immediate feedback without performing analyses, and other short- to long-term feedback based on analysis and modeling results. In fact, the frequency of feedback as well as the feedback passages are both affected by the "term" of the feedback, which we arrange in the following spectrum in increasing duration:

- *Immediate feedback*: Such feedback can be provided without going through analysis or modeling on collected data. Therefore, it can be provided immediately and frequently. The time duration and the associated frequency are typically in the range of a few days to at most (and rarely) a few weeks. The data are typically the results and defect data, as well as some activity data, and the data sources are likely to be from the QA activities themselves.

- *Short-term or sub-project level feedback*: Most of the feedback and follow-up activities are at this time duration or at the sub-project level, such as termination of project phases or sub-phases and transition to the next one, schedule and resource adjustments, staffing buildup, etc. These activities are typically within a sub-part or

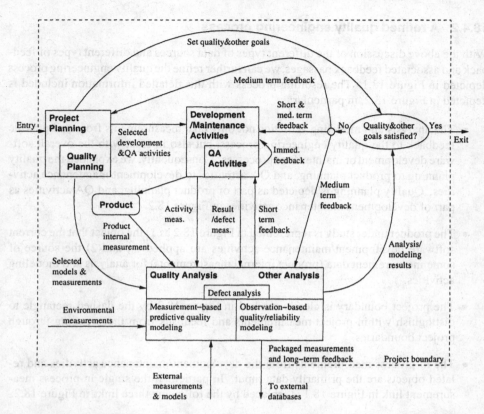

Figure 18.2 Further refined quality engineering process with detailed measurement sources and feedback paths

sub-phase of a project, but not at the overall project level. The typical frequency is the weekly status report and adjustments, or sometimes up to a few months at most in duration. All types of measurement data are used and analyzed for these feedback and follow-up activities.

- *Medium-term or project level feedback*: The most important feedback and decision associated with this category is the product release decision. Other types of feedback and follow-up activities include adjustments to overall project schedule, quality goals, etc. The data are accumulated over the project, especially in the latest part of the project, usually for durations of more than a few weeks and sometimes over a year. All types of measurement data are used and analyzed for this kind of feedback and follow-up activities.

- *Long-term feedback*: Unlike the medium-term feedback that is still limited to within a single project, the long-term feedback is aimed at overall organizational improvement over many projects and many years. Although all types of measurement data may be used for this purpose, typically only those at the coarse granularity are commonly used. We will explore this issue further in connection with some coarse-grain quality models in Chapter 19.

18.4.2   A refined quality engineering process

With the above discussion of the different types of data sources and different types of feedback and associated feedback passages, we can further refine the quality engineering process depicted in Figure 18.1. .The resulting process with this detailed information included is depicted in Figure 18.2, in particular:

- The analysis and modeling activities not only take measurements from and provide feedback to the quality engineering process, but also interact with the overall software development or maintenance processes. Consequently, we expanded the quality planning to product planning, and QA activities to development/maintenance activities. Quality planning is depicted as part of product planning, and QA activities as part of development/maintenance activities in Figure 18.2.

- The product under study is represented in Figure 18.2 as 1) the object that the current software development/maintenance activities are applied to, and 2) the source of some measurement data (product internal measurements) for analysis and modeling activities.

- The project boundary is clearly marked in Figure 18.2 by the dashed rectangle to distinguish within-project measurements and feedback from those cutting through project boundaries.

- The in-process measurements from the development/maintenance activities and related objects are the primarily data input. In particular, the single in-process measurement link in Figure 18.1 is replaced by the following three links in Figure 18.2:

  - Results and defects measurements are primarily from QA activities and are depicted by a link from QA activities to analysis/modeling activities.

  - Activity measurements are depicted by a link from the overall development/-maintenance activities to analysis/modeling activities.

  - The link from the product to analysis/modeling activities depicts product internal measurements.

- In addition, other measurement data and related sources are also depicted in Figure 18.2:

  - Environmental measurements are depicted as from within the project boundary but not from the (in-process measurement) sources above.

  - External data input and related modeling results from industry, existing research, etc., may also be used in the quality engineering process. This is also depicted in Figure 18.2 as from beyond this single project boundary.

- All types of feedback are depicted explicitly in Figure 18.2 by individual feedback paths, including immediate, short-term, medium-term, and long-term feedback paths:

  - Immediate feedback is depicted as a short loop from QA activities directly back to the enclosing development/maintenance activities.

  - Short-term feedback is depicted as directly coming from analysis and modeling activities to development/maintenance activities. Some specific short-term feedback can also be provided from the above sources and destinations by way of examining the product release question ("Quality and other goals satisfied?").

- Medium-term feedback is depicted as based on measurement and modeling results examined in connection to the product release question. The destinations of this feedback are project planning, development/maintenance activities, and analysis and modeling activities.

- Long-term feedback is typically beyond the scope of a single project. Therefore, it is explicitly depicted as going beyond project boundary in Figure 18.2. Relevant results can be accumulated into some company-wide, industry-wide, or even global databases and general quality models, such as discussed in Chapter 19, for use as external input in future projects.

18.4.3 Tool support: Strategy, implementation, and integration

All the above measurement, analysis, and feedback activities need to be supported by various automated tools to allow for an effective and efficient implementation. Three classes of tools are needed to support these activities:

- *Data gathering tools*: These tools support gathering of both direct and indirect quality measurements and feed the analysis tools with the raw data:

  - Direct quality measurements, such as defect information, can be gathered using various defect tracking tools.

  - Indirect quality measurements can be gathered using code measurement tools that take source programs as input and produce code metrics data as output, test logging tools that capture test activity and input information, and project databases for environmental measurements.

- *Analysis tools*: These tools help us perform data processing, analysis, and modeling:

  - Various models can be used to analyze the collected data with the support of these tools.

  - The raw measurement data often need to be processed before model fitting, and the modeling results often need to be transformed to examine various entities of interest. These additional data processing tasks are also supported by these analysis tools.

- *Presentation tools*: These tools help us examine the analysis results and present them to the interested parties so that appropriate actions can be taken to improve quality. Appropriate presentation tools need to be selected or constructed to make the interpretation of analysis results easy and to support exploration of alternatives.

Unfortunately, there is no single tool that satisfies all the needs for data collection, analysis, and presentation. One option is to construct a comprehensive tool to satisfy all our needs. However, this solution is impractical because of the significant effort required. It is also wasteful because many individual tools are commonly used to support various activities within software development organizations. As a viable alternative, a collection of loosely integrated tools can be used. Existing tools can be adapted to support some of our individual needs. Some special purpose tools can be constructed for specific applications where no appropriate tool existed. In general, the choice of tools depends on their internal characteristics and external constraints. Several important issues need to be considered:

- *Functionality and availability*: Are there software tools with the desired functionality? If some functionality is not supported by any existing tool, some specialized tools need to be constructed.

- *Usability*: Is the tool easy to use? The platform on which the tool runs and end user preferences also need to be considered.

- *Flexibility*: Is the tool prepackaged or flexible (programmable)? Tools often need to be modified to fit different needs.

- *Integration*: Can these tools be integrated to work together toward the common goals? This is particularly important when multiple tools are going to be used.

The issues of tool support are common problems faced by many large software development organizations, who usually adopted their own strategies. For example, to support the measurement, analysis, and feedback for the development and testing of various large commercial software products, a particular strategy depicted in Figure 18.3 was adopted by the IBM Toronto Laboratory (Tian et al., 1997). Key characteristics of this tool support strategy include:

- *Overall strategy*: To accommodate the diverse software measurement environments and data sources, and to support different analyses and usages of the analysis results, a comprehensive suite of tools, both those from within IBM and external ones, were used for data gathering, analysis, and result presentation. In Figure 18.3, each tool is shown graphically as a rectangle, with its name identified in boldface and its main functions listed. The sources for the data capturing tools and the reports produced by the presentation tools are shown in ovals. The interconnections (directed links) show the information flow among the different tools, data sources, and reports.

- *Data gathering tools*: The development and test groups used existing IBM tools to track various data. CMVC (Configuration Management/Version Control, an IBM product) and IDSS (Integrated Development Support System, an IBM internal tool) were used to record and track defect data. Home-grown applications, such as TestLog and SlaveDriver, were used to provide manual or semi-automatic data recording of test cases and execution information, under access control and automated consistency checking. These tools were also used, with minor modifications, to gather defect and test data. Product internal data defined on source programs were computed in two ways: 1) using REFINE[1] and related utilities based on some earlier work on program understanding analysis (Buss and Henshaw, 1992), or 2) using W-Analyzer, a specifically constructed set of utilities, to analyze the intermediate code (W-code) generated by the compilers (Tian and Troster, 1998).

- *Analysis tools*: The analyses techniques used for these projects included reliability growth modeling, integrated test data analysis using tree-based models, and predictive modeling linking code metrics to quality data. A commercial tool S-PLUS[2] was used

[1]REFINE is a trademark of Reasoning Systems Inc.
[2]S-PLUS is a trademark of Mathsoft, Inc.

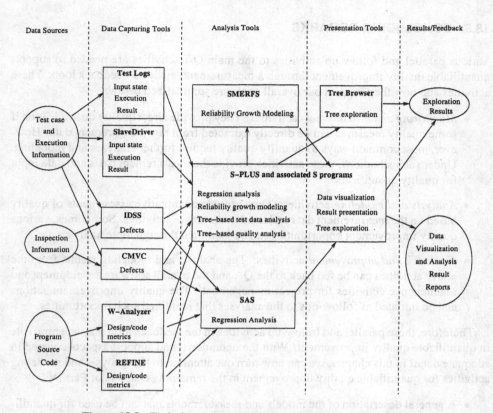

Figure 18.3 Tools for quality measurement, analysis, and feedback

to support tree-based modeling, data analysis, and several commonly used SRGMs. Another external tool, SMERFS (Farr and Smith, 1991), was used for additional SRGMs when necessary. The statistical analysis tool SAS[3] was also used for various statistical analyses of the measurement data.

- *Presentation tools*: Many of the data collection and analysis tools discussed above do not have good user interfaces or presentation facilities, nor are they always available on the desired platforms. Various new utilities were developed within S-PLUS to support visual and graphical presentation techniques. TreeBrowser, a new tool on the OS/2 and AIX platforms was also developed for interactive exploration of the analysis results (Troster and Tian, 1996).

- *Tool integration*: Integration of tools were achieved by: 1) adopting external rules for data contents and formats to ensure inter-operability of tools, 2) using common tools for multiple purposes, and 3) using other utility programs that convert data for interoperability of tools.

---

[3]SAS is a trademark of the SAS Institute Inc.

18.5 CONCLUDING REMARKS

Various parallel and follow-up activities to the main QA activities are needed to support quantifiable quality improvement through a measurement–analysis–feedback loop. These activities and how they support our overall goals are summarized below:

- *Monitoring and measurement* activities: They provide direct quality quantification if some quality measures can be directly extracted from raw measurement data. However, most common ways to quantify quality require further analyses and modeling. Under such situations, these activities provide the measurement basis and data input for quality quantification.

- *Analysis and modeling* activities: They provide quantitative assessments of quality based on the measurement data collected in the above activities. Sometimes, various quality improvement opportunities can be identified through these analyses.

- *Feedback and improvement* activities: The analysis and modeling results from the above activities can be fed back to the QA and the overall software development and maintenance activities for project management. The quality improvement actions can be initiated as follow-ups to the analyses that identified such opportunities.

Therefore, these parallel and follow-up activities in the feedback loop play a central role in quantifiable quality improvement. With the operational and support aspects covered in adequate detail in this chapter, we can now turn our attention to the analysis and modeling activities for quantifiable quality improvement in the remaining chapters of Part IV:

- A general description of the models and measurements that can be used for quantifiable quality improvement is presented in Chapter 19.

- The major types of analyses and models, including defect analysis, risk analysis and identification, and software reliability engineering, are described in Chapters 20, 21, and 22, respectively.

Problems

18.1 Examine the activities described in this chapter, and classify them into the three categories: pre-QA, parallel to QA, post-QA.

18.2 Many of the above activities last over a period of time. Repeat the above question to identify the start and finish time of each activity, or draw a rough activity profile (similar to Figure 5.3 in Chapter 5).

18.3 Measurement data were classified in this chapter by what they measure (direct vs. indirect quality) or by where they come from (data sources). Provide a mapping between these two classification schemes.

18.4 Can you think of other classification schemes for (quality-related) measurement data? What is the classification scheme for software measurements in your organization? Can you map them to our classification schemes in this chapter?

18.5 In actual collection of measurement data, there are many practical problems and obstacles. For example, detailed discussions of such problems related to reliability measurement and modeling are included in Musa et al. (1987). Particularly relevant to this chapter is the discussion on failure determination, timing and activity measurement. Examine some of your practical measurement implementation problems, and propose/describe appropriate solutions to them.

18.6 We have examined many different data usages and feedback paths. Draw a feedback loop for each of them separately.

18.7 What are the measurement and analysis tools used in your organization? Compare them to that in Figure 18.3.

CHAPTER 19

QUALITY MODELS AND MEASUREMENTS

The primary purpose of the measurement and analysis activities is to provide feedback and useful information to manage software quality, the quality engineering process, and the overall software development/maintenance process and activities. The feedback and information provided are based on the analysis results using various models on the data collected from the quality assurance (QA) and the general development activities. In this chapter, we examine and classify these models, relate them to the required measurements, compare the different models, and outline a general strategy to select appropriate models and measurements to satisfy specific quality assessment and improvement goals under specific application environments. A preliminary survey (Tian, 2004) is expanded in this chapter with more details and examples based on actual scenarios from software testing in IBM (Tian, 1998).

19.1 MODELS FOR QUALITY ASSESSMENT

We define quality assessment models as analytical models that provide quantitative assessment of selected quality characteristics or sub-characteristics based on measurement data from software projects. Such models can help us obtain an objective assessment of our current product quality, in contrast to the often unreliable subjective assessment based on personal judgment or imprecise qualitative assessment. When applied over time, these models can provide us with an accurate prediction of the future quality, which can be used to help us make project scheduling, resource allocation, and other management decisions.

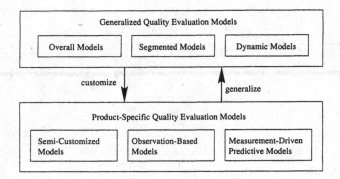

Figure 19.1   Classification of quality assessment models

In addition, some models can also help us identify problematic areas so that appropriate remedial actions can be applied for quality and process improvement.

The existence of a defect indicates non-conformance to specific specification items. Therefore, various defect measurements, such as defect density (Kan, 2002), can be used as *direct* indicators of quality. Sometimes, the correctness aspect of quality can be measured and derived *directly* from its definitions. For example, reliability can be defined as probability of failure-free operations for a specific period or input set and measured accordingly (Musa et al., 1987; Lyu, 1995a; Tian, 1995). Once such direct quality data are gathered, we can use them in corresponding models to evaluate product quality defined accordingly. However, as noted in the above reliability assessment, some measure of time or input set is needed in addition to the direct quality measurement.

As described in the previous chapter, quality and correctness are also affected by various product internal attributes, the interaction between software products and their users, and the general characteristics of the product, the development process, and the overall environment. In addition, direct quality measurements can only be measured with accuracy towards the end of software development, while various indirect quality measurements can be available much earlier and provide the basis for early quality predictions. As a result, we also need to monitor these *indirect* quality measurements and analyze them using various quality assessment models, so that we can assure and improve quality by controlling these indirect entities, particularly in the early part of software development process.

When interpreted under this context, quality assessment models provide direct quality assessment results using various direct or indirect quality measurements. Depending on whether product-specific measurements and results are used and provided, we can classify existing quality assessment models into two broad categories: *generalized* models and *product-specific* models, as depicted in Figure 19.1, with detailed descriptions in subsequent sections.

19.2   GENERALIZED MODELS

Many existing models provide rough estimates of product quality in the form of industrial averages or general trends for a wide variety of application environments with little or no project-specific data required. We call these models generalized quality assessment models, or *generalized models* for short. There are three subcategories of generalized models:

- An *overall model* provides a single estimate of overall product quality.

- A *segmented model* provides different quality estimates for different industrial segments.

- A *dynamic model* provides quality trend or distribution over time or development phases.

We next examine each subtype in turn and give some examples.

Overall models

Overall quality models are the most general subtype of generalized quality models, which provide a rough estimate of product quality without requiring any product specific measurement or even a general characterization of the product segment. Because of this general nature, such models only provide a very rough estimate of product quality. However, if some additional information is available about the product under study, better quality estimated can be provided by alternative models.

As an example of overall models, defect density can be defined as:

$$\text{defect density} = \frac{\text{total defects}}{\text{product size}},$$

where the product size is often measured by the lines of code (LOC), function points, etc. (Kan, 2002). This model would lump all products together, and provide a *single* defect density estimate based on all observed defects for all products. Various product sizing models can also be used in conjunction with defect density to estimate the total defects for a given product.

An overall model can also be an abstraction of the commonly observed facts about quality generally true over all kinds of application domains or product segments. One example of this is the uneven distribution of defects summarized in the so-called 80:20 rule, which states that 80% of the defects are concentrated in 20% of the product modules or components. Similarly, various general observations about software defect (Boehm and Basili, 2001), software risk (Boehm, 1991), and the general linkage between process maturity (CMM level) and quality (Humphrey, 1989; Paulk et al., 1995), can also be considered as examples of overall quality models.

Segmented models

If some general information about the product under study is available, we can use segmented models instead of overall models to get a better quality estimate. For example, the above defect density model can be refined into a segmented model if we use market segmentation to group products and provide different defect density estimates accordingly. Similarly, sizing models tailored for different product segments can be used with such defect density models to estimate the total defects for a given product.

Table 19.1 gives another example of segmented models, based on empirical data (Leveson, 1995; Lyu, 1995a), which estimates reliability levels for different product segments. There are three products segments: 1) safety-critical software, such as control software for medical devices or nuclear reactors, 2) commercial software, such as telecommunication software and business applications, and 3) auxiliary software, such as computer games and other low-cost PC software. The reliability level is measured by the failure rate, or the average number of failures per operating hour.

Table 19.1   A segmented model for reliability level estimation

Product Type	Failure Rate (per hour)	Reliability Level
safety-critical software	$< 10^{-7}$	ultra-high
commercial software	10^{-3} to 10^{-7}	moderate
auxiliary software	$> 10^{-3}$	low

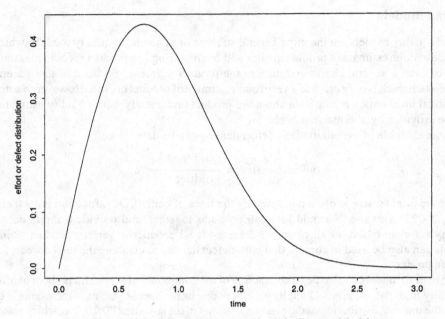

Figure 19.2   Effort or defect profile in the Putnam Model

Dynamic models

As a subset of generalized models, the *dynamic* models provide information about quality over time or development phases. For example, a general profile of defect distribution over different development phases can be considered a quality model of this type.

Alternatively, fine grain dynamic models may measure the precise time instead of the rough time corresponding to development phases. The most well-known model in this category is the Putnam model (Putnam, 1978), that generalizes empirical effort and defect profiles over time into a Rayleigh curve. Figure 19.2 gives an example of such an profile, with failure rate

$$r = 2Bate^{-at^2}$$

or, equivalently, with cumulative failures $F = B(1 - e^{-at^2})$. It is used to estimate defects from a specific development phase in Example A (Section 19.6).

Various other general observations about systems dynamic behavior related to defects or quality can also be considered as examples of dynamic models. For example, the overall expectation of reliability growth during product testing and defect removal commonly assumed in software reliability engineering (Musa et al., 1987; Lyu, 1995a) can be considered a generalized dynamic model.

Table 19.2   DRM (defect removal model): defect distribution for previous releases of a product

Requirement	Design	Coding	Testing	Support
5%	10%	35%	40%	10%

Sometimes, dynamic models and segmented models can be combined to give us segmented dynamic models. For example, if general defect or reliability patterns emerge for a product segment, we can use these new patterns to better estimate the defect or reliability dynamics for this product segment instead of using the general dynamic models for it.

19.3   PRODUCT-SPECIFIC MODELS

Product-specific quality assessment models, or *product-specific models* for short, provide more precise quality assessments using product-specific data. They can be further divided into three sub-categories:

- *Semi-customized models* extrapolate product history to predict quality for the current project.

- *Observation-based models* estimate quality based on observations from the current project.

- *Measurement-driven predictive models* establish predictive relations between various early measurements and product quality, and use them for QA and improvement.

We next examine each subtype in turn and give some examples.

Semi-customized models

Semi-customized models make use of general characteristics and historical information about the product, process, or environment, to provide quality extrapolations. For example, various defect removal models (DRMs) commonly used in industry (Kan, 2002), such as the one in Table 19.2, provide a defect distribution profile over development phases based on previous releases of the same product. The difference between this DRM and the general defect profile we mentioned in the above generalized dynamic models is that it is based on the previous releases of the same product instead of a general profile for all available products. Consequently, the use of this relevant local information can help provide more accurate quality estimates.

The information from these semi-customized models can be directly used to predict defect distribution for the current release. For example, with the DRM in Table 19.2, if we have found 20 design defects in the current product, we can predict that the total defects will be around $20/10\% = 200$.

A more detailed semi-customized model is the defect dynamics model and orthogonal defect classification (ODC) model (Chillarege et al., 1992), both of which will be introduced in Chapter 20. In these models, more detailed information about defects are profiled by individual phases where they were injected, where they were discovered, and by categories according to a systematic classification scheme. Such models can help developers and testers focus on high-defect areas for timely and cost-effective problem resolution and quality improvement.

Observation-based models

Observation-based models relate observations of the software system behavior to information about related activities to provide more precise quality assessments. Examples of such models include various software reliability growth models (SRGMs) (Lyu, 1995a), where observed failures and associated time intervals are fitted to SRGMs to evaluate product reliability. For example, in the Goel-Okumoto SRGM (Goel and Okumoto, 1979), the relationship between the expected number of failures $m(t)$ and testing time t is given by the function:

$$m(t) = N(1 - e^{-bt}).$$

N and b are model parameters that can be estimated from the observation data.

Unlike generalized models that use industrial averages and semi-customized models that use historical data, observation-based models usually only use data from the current project. For example, SRGMs only need the failure and time data from the current project to make their reliability assessments. Details about these models are covered in Chapter 22.

Measurement-driven predictive models

Measurement-driven predictive models establish predictive relations between quality and other measurements based on historical data, provide early predictions of quality, and identify problems early so that timely actions can be taken to improve product quality. Various statistical analysis techniques and learning algorithms can be used to establish such predictive relations (Tian, 2000), which are covered in Chapter 21.

Once such predictive relations are established, we can affect the development process by using them to identify high-risk areas for focused remedial actions. For example, tree-based models were used to analyze the relationship between defect fixes (DF) and various design and code measurements for two IBM software products LS and NS (Tian and Troster, 1998). Table 19.3 lists subsets of modules with the highest DF per module. The analysis results indicated that the high-defect modules of legacy products such as LS are associated with numerous changes and high data complexity, while high-defect modules for new products such as NS are associated with complex design and control structures. Various development teams have since used these predictive relations to focus their inspection effort on a few selected modules to effectively utilize limited resources.

19.4 MODEL COMPARISON AND INTERCONNECTIONS

Different types of quality assessment models and their relations can be compared by looking at their ability to provide useful information, their applicability to different project environments, and their inter-connections. Specifically, we can compare the following:

- *Usefulness* of the modeling results, in terms of how *accurate* the quality estimates are and the *applicability* of the models to different environments.

- Model *inter-connections*, which can be examined in two opposite directions:

Table 19.3 High-defect modules for two products identified by tree-based modeling

Product	Subset	#Modules	Mean-DF
LS	lrrr	16	9.81
	rlr	53	10.74
	rr	17	22.18
	whole product	1296	1.8
NS	rlll	8	55.0
	rr	5	77.0
	whole product	995	7.9

Table 19.4 Summary of quality assessment models and their applications

Model Type	Sub-Type	Primary Result	Applicability
generalized models		rough quality estimates	all or by industry
	overall	overall product quality	across industries
	segmented	industry-specific quality	within an industry
	dynamic	quality trend over time	trend in all
product-specific quality models		better quality estimates	specific product
	semi-customized	quality extrapolation	prev→cur release
	observation-based	quality assessments	current product
	measurement-driven	quality predictions	both above

- *Customization* of generalized quality models to provide better quality estimates when product-specific information is available.

- *Generalization* of product-specific models when enough empirical evidence from different products or projects is accumulated.

Table 19.4 summarizes the primary results and applicability for all the model types and sub-types. The usefulness of a model mainly depends on two factors:

- Is it applicable to the specific development environment and the specific product under development or maintenance?

- If so, how accurate the model is in its quality estimates?

Then, this usefulness can be weighted against its cost, in particular, the cost of collecting the required measurement data, which is typically the dominant part of the modeling cost.

Generalized models provide rough quality estimates based on empirical data from industry. Product-specific models provide more precise quality assessments using product-specific measurements. However, generalized models are more widely applicable and less expensive to use than product-specific models, because they do not require product-specific measurements.

Consequently, generalized models may be more useful in the product planning stage, and in the early phases of product development, when most product-specific data are unavailable. One exception to this general rule is when there exist historical data for the previous releases of the current product. Semi-customized models can be used to provide better estimates under this situation. However, under most circumstances, these historical data are not expected to be complete and cover all aspects of product quality. Therefore, generalized models can still be used to complement semi-customized models.

As development or maintenance activities progress, more measurement data can be collected and various detailed quality models in the category of product-specific models, such as observation-based models and measurement-based predictive models, can be used to better manage the QA activities as well as the overall software development or maintenance processes. We will see some examples about the different concerns at different stages of software development, and the selection of different quality models in Section 19.6.

As we have already seen in the above examples of different quality models, there are generally counterparts in generalized models to product-specific models, and vice versa. We can obtain corresponding product-specific models by customizing generalized models using the product-specific data and results. In the other direction, we can generalize product-specific models if enough empirical evidence from a wide variety of products and their related product-specific quality models is available.

In the direction of model customization, various generalized models can be customized into corresponding product-specific ones depending on the kind of measurement data and analysis results available. For example, if defect and size data for previous releases are available, the overall defect profile, a generalized quality model, can be customized into defect removal model (DRM), a semi-customized one. The resulting model, DRM, can be used to extrapolate past defect densities into quality estimates for the current project. This issue is examined further in connection with model data requirements in Section 19.5.

Product-specific models can be generalized into corresponding generalized models if modeling results from a wide variety of projects form a general pattern. For example, if reliability data and modeling results are available for many products, they can be generalized into an overall model similar to the overall defect density model, to a segmented model similar to that in Table 19.1, or to a general reliability profile of expected shapes and reliability growth.

19.5 DATA REQUIREMENTS AND MEASUREMENT

Different types of quality assessment models have different data requirements. All models discussed above make use of *direct* quality measurements. Many of them also make heavy use of other *indirect* quality measurements for quality assessment, mostly in-process measurements, but also some environmental or external measurements. These measurements were described in Chapter 18. What we would like to do next is to make the connection between specific models and the specific measurements required. This connection can be examined in two directions, tracing the model requirements back to specific measurements (backward tracing or backtracking), and measurement support for different models (forward linkage).

We first examine the different kinds of data measurements required by different models, with the quality models as the driving force.

- *Generalized models* are based on industrial averages and general profiles for all the products or for a specific product segment. Therefore, no measurement data from the current project is needed directly. However, measurements taken at the current project can be accumulated into the empirical base to calibrate these models for future applications.

Table 19.5 Summary of measurements required by different quality models

Model Type	Sub-Type	Measurement Data
generalized		industrial averages
	overall	average: all industries Section 19.2
	segmented	average: own industry Table 19.1
	dynamic	trend: all industries
product-specific		product-specific data
	semi-customized	rough historical data Table 19.2
	obser.-based	current observations
	meas.-driven	current & historical data

- *Product-specific models* use product specific measurement data to make better quality assessments and predictions, which are given in the form of values or ranges of selected direct quality measurements. The different sub-types use different indirect quality measurements to make such quality assessments or predictions, as described below:

  - *Measurement-driven models* attempt to establish predictive relations between direct quality measurements and other early measurements. All three types of indirect quality measurements, especially those available early in the software development process, are used as primary measurements in these models.

  - *Semi-customized models* use environmental measurements to characterize the current project and extrapolate quality estimates from previous product releases. Sometimes, they also use coarse-grain activity measurements.

  - *Observation-based models* relate direct quality measurements to activity measurements, with the environmental characteristics implicitly assumed.

These measurement data requirements for different models are summarized in Table 19.5. We next examine the different quality models that are supported by different kinds of data measurements, with the quality measurement as the driving force.

- Both *direct and indirect quality measurements* from industry form the empirical basis for generalized models to provide quality estimates for the current project before it is completed or even before it is started, although they are not used directly in generalized models.

- *Direct quality measurements* are used in all the product-specific models: as product-specific extrapolations in semi-customized models, related to development activities in observation-based models, or predicted by various early measurements in measurement-driven models.

- *Environmental measurements* are mainly used in semi-customized models to characterize the current product and its predecessors so that direct extrapolations can be made. They are often implicitly assumed, but not directly used, in generalized and observation-based models to evaluate quality. Some of the environmental measurements, especially those available early, are used in measurement-driven predictive models.

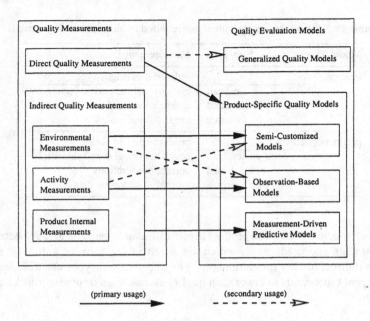

Figure 19.3   Relating measurements to quality assessment models

- *Product internal measurements* are often used in measurement-driven predictive models to provide early assessments of product quality and to identify problematic areas for focused quality improvement. The main reason for this is their early availability, with most product internal measurements available before testing, and many available in requirement and design phases. In contrast, most direct quality measurements cannot be obtained early or predicted with accuracy using other models.

- *Activity measurements* can be used in various models to predict quality from QA and development activities. Coarse-grain activity measurements can be used in semi-customized models, for example, defect data grouped by development phases and sub-phases can be used to predict defect profile over time. Fine-grain activity measurements can be used in observation-based models, for example, test runs and workloads can be used in various software reliability growth models to assess and predict product reliability.

Notice that direct quality measurements can sometimes be used in isolation (that is, without relating to other measurements) in generalized models. For example, we can use average defect density from industry to estimate quality for the current product before it starts. Nevertheless, direct quality measurements are mostly used in conjunction with various indirect quality measurements in product-specific models, because these product-specific data are typically those about the product itself, the product environment, and specific activities carried out in the product development.

The relationships between quality assessment models and measurements can be summarized in Figure 19.3. A solid line depicts primary usage and a dotted line depicts secondary usage. Some key points are summarized below:

- The usage of measurement data in generalized models is depicted as a secondary one, because they are not used directly in these models but rather indirectly through the accumulated data as the basis for future adjustment to these models.

- Direct quality measurements are used as primary measurements in all the product-specific models.

- All three types of indirect quality measurements that are available early in the software development process are used as primary measurements in measurement-driven models.

- Environmental measurements are primarily used in semi-customized models.

- Activity measurements are used directly, thus depicted as a primary usage, to predict quality in observation-based models.

- When some measurements are used indirectly in some models, or used occasionally but not always, the specific usage is depicted as a secondary one. For example, coarse-grain activity measurements are used sometimes in semi-customized models, and environmental characteristics are implicitly assumed (but not directly used) in observation-based models.

19.6 SELECTING MEASUREMENTS AND MODELS

Based on the characteristics of quality assessment models and the relationships between these models and relevant measurements discussed above, we next outline an approach for measurement and model selection, and illustrate it with some practical examples.

Selection guidelines and a recommended procedure

A goal-oriented approach for software measurement and continuous improvement called GQM-paradigm (Basili and Rombach, 1988) has been successfully used in various practical applications (van Solingen and Berghout, 1999), which was described in Chapter 13 in connection to defect prevention and process improvement. An approach for selecting quality assessment models and measurements was developed under the guidance of GQM-paradigm, while making use of analysis results above (Tian, 2004). Using this approach, we can follow the following three steps to set quality goals and select appropriate models and measurements:

Step 1. *Set specific quality goals.* For example, if we are concerned with problem-free services, reliability measurement and improvement should be the goal. This step restricts the "G" in the GQM-paradigm to specific quality goals instead of general measurement goals.

Step 2. *Choose specific quality assessment models* that can answer our questions and concerns about the quality goals under the constraints of the application environment. For example, if we need precise reliability estimates, we can consider using SRGMs. This step roughly corresponds to "Q" in the GQM-paradigm, but the model classification scheme in this chapter is used to select appropriate quality assessment models.

Step 3. *Choose appropriate measurements* based on the model data requirements. For example, we can take failure and test execution time measurements in order to evaluate product reliability using SRGMs. This step roughly corresponds to "M" in the GQM-paradigm, but the model-data relations summarized in Figure 19.3 are used to select appropriate measurements.

We next consider actual scenarios during the testing of several large commercial software systems developed in IBM (Tian, 1998) to illustrate the use of this approach. These systems include relational data base products, compilers, and computing environments, for platforms ranging from mainframes to PCs. They can be characterized by their large size, usually exceeding several hundred thousand lines of source code, high complexity, diverse functionality, and components developed over a long period of time. The overall testing effort usually lasts from over several months to more than a year.

Example A. Rough quality estimates

Before testing phase started, a rough defect estimate was needed for project planning. Such rough estimates for a single development phase can be easily obtained using dynamic generalized models based on empirical trend data from industry. Therefore, the Putnam model (Putnam, 1978) was selected to estimate testing defects. This decision was also influenced by the previous positive experience using the Putnam model and related tools for software estimation in several projects within the lab.

For new releases of existing products, more precise quality estimates can be obtained if the large amount of historical defect data routinely collected in IBM can be used with selected semi-customized models. Therefore, these data were also extracted and used in the semi-customized defect removal models (DRMs) (Kan, 2002) to estimate testing defects for these new releases, and used to calibrate the Putnam models above.

One of the projects studied was also used as a pilot for ODC deployment (Chillarege et al., 1992). Therefore, defect information according to ODC scheme were collected during testing and an ODC defect profile was built to further analyze the data. This ODC defect profile can also be used as a semi-customized model for successor projects. The details about this application are described in Chapter 20.

Example B. Reliability assessment

Once the system testing started, the focus was shifted to providing more precise quality assessments. Because this phase is the last one before the product is released to the customers, measuring product reliability under a simulated customer usage environment and meeting a specific customer reliability target were established as primary goals. After examining the match between the testing environment and the reliability model assumptions, several software reliability growth models (SRGMs) were selected from the category of observation-based models.

SRGMs require measurement of failures and related time intervals, and assume that the elapsed time must reflect software usage (Goel, 1985). To account for the vast variations in test workload for these IBM products, the detailed workload measure, cumulative transactions were chosen as the usage time measurement despite its relatively higher measurement cost. Figure 19.4 plots cumulative failures vs. cumulative transactions, and the fitted Goel-Okumoto SRGM (Goel and Okumoto, 1979). As seen in Figure 19.4 and quantified earlier (Tian, 1998), this model fits the observations fairly well, and provides good assessments

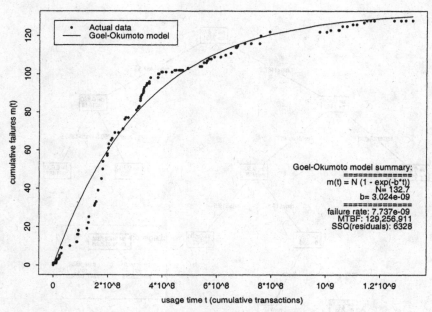

Figure 19.4   A fitted SRGM for an IBM product

and predictions of the product reliability. This and other applications of software reliability engineering, as well as its overall context, are described in detail in Chapter 22.

Example C. Process/reliability improvement

Realizing that fault distribution within a software product and the chance for encountering failures for a given set of operations are not uniform, an attempt was made to identify high-risk areas in order to meet the pre-set goal of cost-effective reliability improvement in a later project. Tree-based reliability models (TBRMs) developed earlier under similar settings (Tian, 1995) were selected from the category of measurement-driven predictive models, attempting to identify and correct problems early in testing.

Similar to other measurement-driven predictive models, TBRMs require the use of external result data as our direct quality measurement and various other early measurements such as time, input state and personnel. Figure 19.5 presents a TBRM for an IBM product, with all the data attributes shown in *italic* in Table 19.6. Such TBRMs can help us identify groups of test runs with particularly low success rates for focused remedial actions. The active use of these TBRMs resulted in much improved product reliability as compared to earlier products where no such measurement-driven predictive models were used (Tian, 1998). This modeling technique and its applications are described in Chapters 21 and 22.

19.7   CONCLUDING REMARKS

There is a strong need for practical guidance to help software practitioners select appropriate models and measurements for various QA and improvement initiatives. In this chapter, we

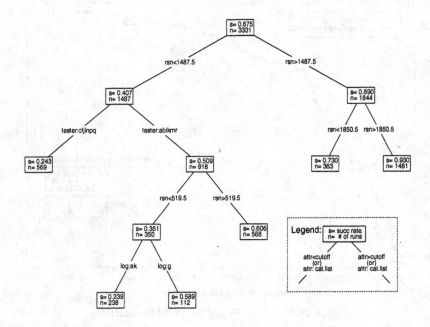

Figure 19.5 A tree-based reliability model (TBRM) for an IBM product

Table 19.6 Data attributes used in Figure 19.5

Timing: calendar date (*year, month, day*), *tday* (cumulative testing days since the start of testing), and *rsn* (run sequence number, uniquely identifies a run in the execution sequence).

Input state: *SC* (scenario class), *SN* (scenario number), *log* (corresponding to a sub-product with a separate test log) and *tester*.

Result: *result* indicator of the test run, with 1 indicating success and 0 indicating failure.

---

compared and classified different models that can be used to evaluate the correctness aspect of quality into the following hierarchical framework:

- *Generalized models* that provide rough quality estimates without requiring product-specific data. The sub-categories include:

  - *Overall models* that provide the same quality estimates for all products.
  - *Segmented models* that provide different estimates for different product segments.
  - *Dynamic models* that provide quality profiles along the timeline.

- *Product-specific models* that provide better quality assessments and predictions based on product-specific data. The sub-categories include:

- *Semi-customized models*, which use coarse-granularity product data for quality extrapolation from previous releases to current release of the product.
- *Observation-based models*, which use fine-granularity activity data for progress tracking and quality assessments.
- *Measurement-based predictive models*, which use early-available data to predict quality ahead of time and to improve product quality.

We also examined data requirements for these models individually, and introduced an approach to select quality assessment models and measurements designed under the guidance of the GQM-paradigm (Basili and Rombach, 1988). The successful applications of this approach in the testing of several IBM software products demonstrated its apparent applicability and usefulness.

With this overall framework to select different quality models and the required measurements for quality quantification and improvement, we can now turn our attention to some important models and analysis techniques. In the rest of Part III, we describe various defect analysis models in Chapter 20, risk identification models in Chapter 21, and software reliability models in Chapter 22.

Problems

19.1   Many models for quality assessment can also be used for effort estimation or prediction, such as the Putnam model we discussed in this chapter. Can you find some examples of such cross-usage for every category and sub-category of quality assessment models in Figure 19.1?

19.2   When you use defect density models, should you count unique defects or all defects? Briefly justify yourself.

19.3   Segmented models play an important role in software estimation, particularly at the beginning of a software project. Why?

19.4   Compare the Putnam model with our quality engineering effort profile in Figure 5.3 (Chapter 5), and discuss the similarities and differences.

19.5   Observation-based models are often used as or with control charts to track project progress. Outline the approach to project progress tracking in your organization, and discuss how observation-based models can be integrated into progress tracking in your project.

19.6   Why is "predictive" quality important in the measurement-drive predictive models?

19.7   For the example models given in this chapter, can you generalize or customize them into a different model in the opposite category? Select one model and generalize it, and select another model and specialize it.

19.8   List all the quality assessment models used in your organization, examine their usage, and suggest some improvement actions.

CHAPTER 20

DEFECT CLASSIFICATION AND ANALYSIS

Analyses of discovered defects and related information from quality assurance (QA) activities can help both developers and testers to detect and remove *potential* defects, and help other project personnel to improve the development process, to prevent injection of *similar* defects and to manage risk better by planning early for product support and services. The defect data are typically collected from the main QA activities. Some additional details regarding the defects may need to be collected during this process or extracted from some system records to provide better quality assessments, predictions, or identification of problematic areas. We next discuss these topics, and illustrate them through several case studies analyzing defects from system testing for some IBM products, and web-related defects for www.seas.smu.edu, the official web site for the School of Engineering and Applied Science, Southern Methodist University (SMU/SEAS).

20.1 GENERAL TYPES OF DEFECT ANALYSES

Once a defect is discovered, various individual analyses can be performed. When defect data are accumulated over time, collective analyses can be performed. Although these two forms of analysis have different focuses, the questions asked during the analyses are similar, including:

- *What?* The identification and classification of the discovered defects can be performed to identify what they are and classify them by some consistent scheme. This topic is the focus of this chapter, which is discussed in all subsequent sections.

- *Where?* Where was the defect found or discovered? This information can be used to provide valuable feedback to the development process through defect distribution analysis.

- *When?* The identification of the exact time or associated development phase or sub-phase when a defect is injected and when it is discovered is important, because it provides information to analyze the overall defect trend and serves as the basis for quality prediction into the future. This topic is discussed later in this section, and fine-grain defect timing analysis is covered in Chapter 22 as part of software reliability engineering.

- *Pre- or post-release?* An important extension to the "when" question is whether a defect is a pre-release defect or a post-release defect, sometimes labeled as an in-development (or in-process) or an in-field defect, respectively. Although the in-field defects are the ones experienced by actual customers or users, and should receive adequate attention, the scarcity of post-release data and business-sensitive information they might contain leave most existing software engineering research with the use of pre-release defect data only. This issue is discussed in relation to specific topics throughout this chapter.

- *How and Why?* How was the defect injected into the software, and why? These two questions are closely related, both pertaining to the cause of the discovered defects.

Notice that all the analyses listed above are applied to defect information as the primary target or focus. However, other information and measurements related to defect information are often needed in these analyses, although sometimes used implicitly. Each of these analyses, defect distribution, trend, and causal analyses, for the overall defect data are described below.

20.1.1   Defect distribution analysis

Defect distribution analyses can help us answer the *what* and *where* questions above. In answering the *what* question, we can find out the distribution of defects over different defect types, and if certain defect types are associated with an overwhelming share of the overall defects. If the latter is confirmed to be true, the identification of these dominant defect types can help us select appropriate remedial or corrective actions to effectively address the problems and improve product quality. Similarly, in answering the *where* question, we can find out the distribution of defects over different areas or product components, and if there are certain areas that are associated with an overwhelming share of the overall defects. If the latter is confirmed to be true, the identification of these high-defect areas can help us focus our remedial or corrective actions to effectively improve product quality.

The defect distribution analyses typically deal with faults or defect fixes instead of failures or errors we defined in Chapter 2. "Defect fixes" is typically used if actual fixing of discovered problem took place before defect analyses were performed, while "faults" can be used as long as it is identified (but not necessarily fixed already). Defect fixes, labeled DF in this book, are in response to observed failures during testing or to discoveries of other problems during development or operation. We selected defect fixes instead of raw defect counts because much of the defect propagation information is captured in the former but not in the latter. Defect propagation is affected by the system structure, the interconnection among different components, and product evolution. DF can be identified

Table 20.1   Common error types and error distribution for SMU/SEAS

Error Type	Description	Number of Errors
A	permission denied	2079
B	no such file or directory	14
C	stale NFS file handle	4
D	client denied by server configuration	2
E	file does not exist	28631
F	invalid method in request	0
G	invalid URL in request connection	1
H	mod_mime_magic	1
I	request failed	1
J	script not found or unable to start	27
K	connection reset by peer	0
all types		30760

with specific modules, therefore permitting analysis and modeling using various software metrics defined on modules. Both the pre-release and post-release defect data can be analyzed and compared.

What: Distribution over defect types

For different product types or different application domains, the answer to the "what" question can be analyzed by examining the defect types defined accordingly. For example, the type of problems can be directly related to quality attributes, such as CUPRIMDS (capability, usability, performance, reliability, installation, maintenance, documentation, and service) used by IBM for their software products (Kan, 2002). Other information regarding the discovered defects can also be used to answer the "what" questions, as we describe late in connection with defect classification and analysis in Sections 20.2 and 20.3.

As a concrete example, consider the defects for web-based applications. Using the terminology commonly adopted for WWW, the defects are actually operational failures labeled as web errors and recorded in web server error logs. For the www.seas.smu.edu web site, a total of 30760 errors were recorded for the 26 days covered by the web server logs (Kallepalli and Tian, 2001). The distribution of these errors by error types was summarized in Table 20.1. The first and immediate observation we can make from this distribution analysis is the highly uneven distribution of web errors (or defects in our terminology) over the different error types:

- The most dominant error type is type E, "file does not exist", which accounts for 93.08% of all the errors recorded.

- Type A errors, "permission denied", account for 6.76% of the total errors.

- All the rest 9 error types account for only 0.16%, a truly negligible share of the total.

Because of this overwhelming share of type E errors, subsequent studies were focused on this error type to assess and improve the quality for this web site.

Table 20.2 Characterizing web errors by file types

Type	Errors	%
.gif	12489	43.62
.class	4913	17.16
directory	4425	15.46
.html	3656	12.77
.jpg	1323	4.62
other	394	1.38
All	28631	100

Table 20.3 Distribution of DF for a commercial product LS

DF=	0	1	2	3	4	5	6	7	8	9	10~19	20~37	all
module #	771	174	102	63	31	29	23	25	16	7	50	14	1295
%	58.8	13.4	7.9	4.9	2.4	2.2	1.8	1.9	1.2	0.5	3.9	1.1	100
DF sum	0	174	204	189	124	145	138	175	128	63	673	417	2367
%	0	7.4	8.6	8.0	5.2	6.1	5.8	7.4	5.0	2.7	28.4	17.6	100

Where: Distribution over defect locations

When the defects are located, we can answer the "where" question. As an example to address the *where* question by distribution analysis, further analysis for the above web site was performed (Li and Tian, 2003). Since the missing files (Type E errors) are the main defect type, the question worthy of examination is: "What kind of files are missing?" The results are summarized in Table 20.2. Of the more than 100 different file types, the top five accounted for more than 98% of all the missing files. The identification of these missing file types, in connection with their access information, could lead to more focused web site maintenance effort to fix problems and improve web reliability.

The most common type of distribution analyses to answer the *where* question is in connection with product components, such in the study of two IBM products LS and NS (Tian and Troster, 1998). Tables 20.3 and 20.4 summarize DF (defect fixes) distribution for LS and NS, respectively, giving the numbers and percentages of modules with given numbers of DF. Although high-defect modules are relatively few, they represent an overwhelming share of observed problems. For example, in LS, only 19.2% (248) of the modules have more than 2 DF (DF > 2), but they represent 84.0% (1989) of the total DF; while 58.8% of the modules are defect free. In NS, 20.5% (204) of the modules have more than 10 defect fixes, but represent 59.5% (4653) of the total fixes. This kind of uneven distribution is generally true for most software systems (Boehm and Basili, 2001).

General observations about defect distribution

Notice that in the above analysis, the generally uneven distribution of defects over types, areas, or product components points to the importance of focusing on the identification and strengthening of specific areas for focused quality improvement initiatives. Similar

Table 20.4 Distribution of DF for a commercial product NS

DF=	0	1	2	3	4	5	6	7	8	9	10-19	20-49	>50	all
module #	23	131	112	120	99	94	68	50	38	32	147	68	13	995
%	2.3	13.2	11.3	12.1	9.9	9.4	6.8	5.0	3.8	3.2	14.8	6.8	1.3	100
DF sum	0	131	224	360	396	470	408	350	304	288	2109	2040	910	7824
%	1.67	2.86	4.60	5.06	6.01	5.21	4.47	3.89	3.68	3.07	26.96	26.07	11.63	100

observations about uneven distributions by other defect attributes, such as severity, fix type, functionality, usage scenarios, etc., have also shown to be true (Chillarege et al., 1992).

However, under most circumstances, we cannot wait until such defects are discovered and such uneven defect distribution has been confirmed to take actions. Instead, we need to find some way to identify such high-risk or potentially high-defect areas based on historical data. Applicable risk identification techniques and related issues are described in Chapter 21.

20.1.2   Defect trend analysis and defect dynamics model

Most of the defect data contains some timing information. At a minimum, the discovered defect is classified as either pre-release or post-release. This information can be used to give us a general picture of the defect trend. When used with appropriate models, these data can provide us with the basis for prediction into the future.

Sometimes, timing information for individual defects corresponds to some rough information about the development phases or sub-phases recorded in relevant defect records. When such information is available, we can examine the defect distribution over these phases or sub-phases, much like the distribution analysis described above, but with phases or sub-phases along some timeline. The defect removal model in the previous chapter can be considered an example of such a trend analysis.

If the information about defect injection time is available, it can be used to augment the defect removal models into the so called *defect dynamics model*, where both the injection and removal of defects are tracked by development phases. This model is often represented as a matrix, such as in Table 20.5, with the rows corresponding to defect injections in each phase, and column corresponding to defect removals in each phase. The inner matrix is always an upper triangular matrix because the removal of a defect is always after its injection. The last row, summing up all the defects removed in different phases, actually gives us a defect removal model similar to the one given in the previous chapter. The last column, summing up all the defects injected in different phases, gives us information about where the major defect sources are in terms of when they are injected.

However, the cost of each defect injected in phase X and removed in phase Y is not uniform. Typically, the cost increases substantially with the increase of the distance between X and Y, or the number of phases when a defect lies dormant. Because a dormant defect might trigger the injection of other related defects, and the further away a defect is removed from when it is injected, the harder it gets to remove it because of all the intermediate decisions and actions applied that obscure the linkage between causes and effects. Consequently, the focus of defect dynamics models is typically on the off-diagonal ones, or those out-of-phase defect removals. In addition, when the post-release defect data are available, they deserve more attention as well, because these defects are the ones that escaped the software QA

Table 20.5   A sample defect dynamics model

Injection Phase	Removal Phase						
	req.	spec.	design	coding	testing	post-rel	all phases
requirement	10	22	8	0	5	2	47
specification		10	20	2	0	1	33
design			52	120	32	5	209
coding				198	320	46	564
testing					58	7	65
post-release						2	2
all phases	10	32	80	320	415	63	920

process to cause real damage to the customers and users. They also harm the development organizations' reputation and may lead to product liability problems.

When precise time information about the defect discoveries is available, it can be used in various models of greater precision to provide finer-grain or better quality predictions. For example, the Putnam model (Putnam, 1978) described in the previous chapter is an example of such a model. Various software reliability growth models (SRGMs) to be described in Chapter 22 can also be considered examples of fine-grain defect trend models. However, typically other measurement data, such as testing or usage activities, are needed for analyses with SRGMs. On the other hand, precise defect injection time information is typically impossible to obtain, depriving us of the fine-grain defect injection or defect dynamics models.

20.1.3   Defect causal analysis

Defect causal analysis can usually take two forms: logical analysis and statistical analysis. Logical analysis is a deterministic analysis that examines the logical link between the effects and the corresponding causes, and establishes general causal relations. Statistical analysis is a probabilistic analysis that examines the statistical link between causes and effects and deduces the probable causal relations between the two.

The effects in the defect causal analysis can be either the observed failures or discovered (or fixed) faults, and the corresponding causes are the faults that caused the failures or the errors that caused the injection of the faults, respectively. The causal relations between faults and failures typically are determined by the developers or code owners who fix the code or design in response to failure observations during testing, inspection, or normal operational usage, as part of the normal development process where defects are fixed. The causal relations between errors and faults are typically determined through dedicated defect causal analysis beyond the normal development process. This kind of defect causal analysis, particularly its logical instead of the statistical variation, is also referred to as root cause analysis in literature.

Root cause analysis is human intensive, and should be performed by experts with thorough knowledge about the product, the development process, the application domain, and the general environment. Sometimes, it can be integrated into the development or specific QA process. For example, in the Gilb inspection (Gilb and Graham, 1993) described in Chapter 14, a phase called process brainstorming is added between inspection meetings and follow-up actions. This process brainstorming is essentially a root cause analysis. Sometimes, root cause analysis can be performed selectively, for example, for all the critical defects.

Statistical analysis is based on empirical evidence collected either locally or from other similar projects. These empirical data can be fed to various models to establish the predictive relations between causes and effects. Once such causal relations are established, appropriate QA activities can then be selected and applied for fault or error removal. This kind of analyses employ various statistical models. For example, the simplest of such models is correlation analysis, which is often performed between defects and product internal measurements. For example, we may find that for a product, the number of defects per module may be closely correlated to module control flow complexity. Then we can conclude that high control flow complexity is probably the cause for the modules to have high defect, and focus our attention on the high-complexity modules in our QA activities even before defects are discovered. This risk focus, or focus on high-risk or potentially high-defect areas or product components, is the primary usage of statistical defect causal analysis. Various statistical analysis techniques for this purpose will be described in Chapter 21.

20.2 DEFECT CLASSIFICATION AND ODC

When problems are encountered during operational use of a software or during development, various detailed information can be collected and recorded regarding the problems or the defects. Some part of this information is usually derived from explicit or implicit root cause analysis. Such information can be organized in a systematic way for further analyses, and the analysis results promise more valuable and specific feedback that pinpoint specific problematic areas for focused problem resolution and quality improvement. These analyses typically use statistical models. However, the causal analysis for individual defects and the statistical analysis for the collective defect data are typically used disjointly.

The systematic classification and analysis of defect data bridge the gap between causal analysis and statistical quality control, and provide valuable in-process feedback to the development or maintenance process and help assure and improve product quality. Orthogonal defect classification, or ODC, developed initially at IBM (Chillarege et al., 1992), is the most influential among general frameworks for software defect classification and analysis. ODC has been successfully used in various industrial applications, to identify problematic areas, and to improve overall software product quality (Bhandari et al., 1993; Chaar et al., 1993; Tian and Henshaw, 1994).

20.2.1 ODC concepts

ODC has a rich and extensive category of defect attributes, stemming from both the failure view and the fault view. The attributes related to the former are typically completed by software testers or inspectors who initially observed problems and opened defect reports; while those related to the latter are typically completed by the software developers or system maintenance personnel who fixed the reported problems and updated the corresponding defect reports. The defect attributes are organized in the following hierarchy:

- Key defect attributes from the failure view and information collected at defect discovery include:

    - Defect impact, with attribute values covering functionality, reliability, etc.

- Defect trigger, with attribute values corresponding to the specific types of testing or inspection activities or scenarios that triggered the defect detection.
- Defect severity, with commonly used attribute values: critical, major, minor, or some numerical scale.

- Key information from the fault view collected at defect fixing includes:

  - Defect type, with attribute values: function, interface, algorithm, timing, etc.
  - Number of lines changed for the fixing.

- Some additional causal analyses might be carried out, and the related results also yield defect information and related attributes, such as:

  - Defect source, with attribute values: vendor code, new code, base code, etc.
  - Where the defect was injected, located to subsystems, modules, or components.
  - When the defect was injected, typically identified with the development phase.

A complete description of these defect attributes and related values can be found in Chillarege et al. (1992).

20.2.2   Defect classification using ODC: A comprehensive example

In an earlier study of defect classification and analysis for some relational database products from IBM (Tian and Henshaw, 1994), various defect attribute data according to ODC were collected in the system testing stage. Under this environment, once a defect is detected, a formal report (called Problem Tracking Report or PTR in IBM) is recorded and tracked until its final resolution. Various tools originally used to track defect reports were augmented to collect additional defect information related to ODC. Table 20.6 lists the defect attributes and pre-defined categories of possible values for each attribute.

The information, provided by testers at defect discovery, includes defect *impact*, *trigger*, *severity*, and defect detection time identified with *week*:

- Defect impact is based on the answers to the question: "If this defect is not fixed, how will it impact the customer?" Pre-defined impact categories (possible answers) include performance, reliability, etc.

- Defect trigger categories closely resemble test scenario classes used for managing the testing process for this product. In fact, more detailed information is available using the hierarchical test case organization recorded in the test execution data we described in Table 7.1 (Chapter 7).

- Defect severity can be 1 (critical problem), 2 (major problem), 3 (minor problem), and 4 (minor inconvenience).

- The week when the defect is detected, counted from the start of the project.

The information collected at defect fixing pertains to the actions taken by the developers to locate, identify and correct the faults that caused detected failures:

- Fix type: fix to design, code, etc.

Table 20.6 Some defect attributes and values for an IBM product

Label	Name	Possible Values or Categories & Labels
imp	impact	c=capability, im=implementation, in=installation, ma=maintenance, mi=migration, p=performance, r=reliability, sec=security, ser=service, std=standard, u=usability
trig	trigger	i=installation, m=migration, s=stress, b=backup, c=communications, f=file i/o, co=coexistence, e=exception, hc=h/w config., sc=s/w config., a=ad-hoc, ss=startup/shutdown, o=normal operation
sev	severity	range from 1 (highest) to 4 (lowest) in severity
wk	week	week detected, counted from the start of the project
ftype	fix type	o=other product, s=specification, hld=high-level design, lld=low-level design, c=code, b=build process
act	action	a=add, d=delete, c=change
src	code source	b=base, v=vendor, n=new, c=changed, i=incremental (added to old), s=scaffolded, p=previous defect fix
inj	phase injected	p=previous release, s=specification, hld=high-level design, lld=low-level design, c=coding, ut=unit test, ft=function test, st=system test, d=customer usage

- Number of lines changed for the fixing. (Not shown in Table 20.6 because the values for this defect attribute are obvious.)

- Fix action: adding, deleting, or changing to design or code.

Some simple causal analyses were performed by the developers when they fix the reported defects, leading to the following causal analysis results recorded in the ODC data:

- Defect source: vendor code, new code, base code, etc.

- The development phase when the defect was injected: previous release or waterfall-like development phases in the current release.

20.2.3 Adapting ODC to analyze web errors

For web-based applications, ODC-like defect classification can be defined and relevant defect data can be extracted from existing web server logs for analysis (Ma and Tian, 2003). The availability of such information in web logs is a significant advantage for this situation over traditional applications of ODC, where data collection is always a big hurdle that requires developers and testers to devote substantial time to analyze the defects and report the findings. Among the various ODC attributes, the following can be adapted for web problem analysis:

- Defect *impact* corresponds to web error type, which indicates what problem was experienced by web users. It can be analyzed directly based on information extracted from the error logs or from response code used in web access logs (Kallepalli and Tian, 2001).

- Defect *trigger* corresponds to specific usage sequences or referrals that lead to problems recorded in the error logs. It can be analyzed by examining the referral pair information that can be extracted from the access logs (Ma and Tian, 2003).

- Defect *source* corresponds to specific files or file types that need to be changed, added, or removed to fix problems recorded in the error logs. It can be analyzed by examining both the specific errors and referral pairs.

Various other attributes can also be adopted or adapted from the original ODC attributes through a close examination of the web environment and data availability. Such adaptation to different environments can help people analyze problems or issues of concern to them and fulfill different purposes. As an additional example, ODC has been adapted to help with ongoing requirement discovery in high-integrity systems (Lutz and Mikulski, 2004).

20.3 DEFECT ANALYSIS FOR CLASSIFIED DATA

Various techniques can be applied to analyze the classified data. The most obvious and most straightforward analyses are to apply defect distribution and trend analyses we described in Section 20.1 for unclassified defect data directly on classified data. In ODC terminology, this is called one-way analysis, because it examines one attribute at a time, either its overall distribution or its trend over time. Two-way analysis can be used to examine the cross-interaction of two attributes (Bhandari et al., 1993). Higher-order analysis is also possible, such as using tree-based modeling on all the ODC attributes (Tian and Henshaw, 1994).

One fundamental assumption in all these analyses is that there exists an expected defect profile. The actual analysis results are supposedly compared to this profile, ranked by their differences to identify anomalies, or the ones with the greatest differences. These identified anomalies are analyzed by development personnel to see if they are expected; if not, some corrective actions need to be initiated to deal with the problems. However, under many application environments, such a profile does not exist. What is suggested is to use uniform distribution as the starting point, and gradually build such a defect profile for future use.

20.3.1 One-way analysis: Analyzing a single defect attribute

For each defect attribute, the overall distribution of its values can be examined. For example, Figure 20.1 gives the defect impact attribute distribution for the IBM product discussed in the previous section. The analysis shows that the distribution of defects among the different defect impact areas is very non-homogeneous. Expectedly, the largest proportion of defects is the reliability defects, representing 196 out of 474 overall failures, or 41% of the total share. The main reason is that the system testing is mainly concerned with the overall working and robustness of the product (that is, conformance to functional specifications).

As another example, Table 20.1 gives us the overall distribution of the defect attribute error type for the web site www.seas.smu.edu. The overwhelming share of type E errors became the primary focus of follow-up studies on web defect analysis and quality improvement.

When similar distribution data are available over time or different development phases, we can trace them to perform defect trend analysis. This analysis can be performed individually. For example, Figure 20.2 gives us the trend of type E errors for the SMU/SEAS

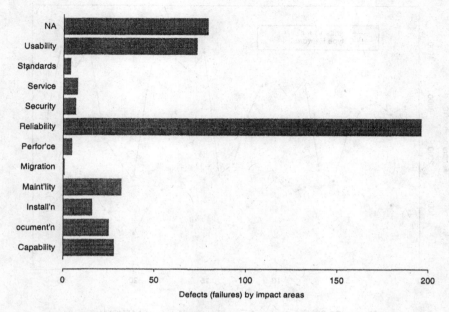

Figure 20.1   One-way analysis of defect impact for an IBM product

web site over 26 days, with each day as a data point. Further analysis was performed to explain this profile by relating it to the number of daily hits (Kallepalli and Tian, 2001), also plotted in Figure 20.2. A clearly synchronized pattern is detected. This synchronized pattern can be captured by the input domain reliability model, such as the Nelson model (Nelson, 1978), to give us an estimate of the overall reliability under normal operational environment for this web site as $R = 0.962$ (or 96.2% reliable). Some additional details about this operational reliability analysis are presented in Chapter 22.

20.3.2 Two-way and multi-way analysis: Examining cross-interactions

Two-way analysis examines the interaction between two attributes, and can be applied to all the attributes in pair-wise fashion. The simplest form of two-way analysis is the conditional analysis of an individual attribute under the condition of another attribute taking a specific value. For example, in the web error analysis example above for the SMU/SEAS web site, Table 20.2 gives the type E error distribution by file type. This can be interpreted as a two-way analysis for the two attributes: error type (type E as the condition here), and missing file type.

When such conditional distribution analysis is carried out for every attribution values used as conditions, we get the full fledged two-way analysis. For example, Table 20.7 gives the two-way analysis results for the IBM product in the example above, with the defect attributes impact and severity examined together. Usability problems are the second most observed failure types (defect impact), second only to reliability problems, most of them are low in severity (severity 3 and 4). However, there are 27 critical reliability problems (severity 1). Therefore, this two-way analysis clearly demonstrated the need to focus on reliability problems at this stage of software development.

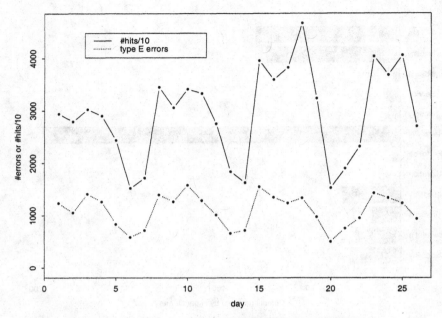

Figure 20.2   Error (type E) and hit profiles for SMU/SEAS

Following the general progression above from one-way analysis to two-way analysis, we can have general multi-way analysis. However, such analysis results are too numerous to track because of the combinatorial explosion of the multiple attributes, making it almost impossible to interpret and use the results for practical purposes. One way to cut down such combinatorial explosions is through the tree-based modeling technique to be described in Chapter 21. Our multi-way analysis for ODC data using tree-based modeling is also presented there.

20.4   CONCLUDING REMARKS

Analyses of discovered defects and related information can help both developers and testers to detect and remove *potential* defects, and help other project personnel to improve the development process, to prevent injection of *similar* defects, and to manage risk better by planning early for product support and services. As described in this chapter, these defect analyses can be performed at different levels of granularity and using different techniques:

- Overall defect distribution and trend analyses can give us an overall picture of product quality as well as some general areas for focused quality improvement.

- Defect causal analysis can help us identify causes of execution failures or internal faults and help initiate quality improvement actions. It can also provide valuable data for various additional analyses.

- Detailed classification and analysis of defect data, such as through ODC (orthogonal defect classification), can help us obtain more detailed information regarding potentially problematic areas to provide more specific and more valuable feedback to the software development or maintenance process for focused quality improvement.

Table 20.7 Two-way analysis results: Interaction between impact and severity

Impact	Severity			
	1	2	3	4
Capability	2	12	13	1
Documentation	0	1	14	10
Installability	0	6	6	4
Maintainability	0	6	19	7
Migration	0	0	0	1
Performance	1	1	3	0
Reliability	27	96	66	7
Security	1	3	3	0
Service	0	0	4	4
Standards	0	1	2	1
Usability	0	10	44	19

No matter at what level we are performing the defect analysis, the general observation is that defects are typically concentrated in some specific areas instead of spread out evenly. Therefore, there is a strong need for analysis techniques and models that can help us identify these "high-risk" areas that are more likely to contain concentrated defects. We turn our attention to such risk identification techniques and related models in the next chapter.

Problems

20.1 What kind of analyses can be performed on the defect data?

20.2 One of the primary reasons for many measurement programs to fail is that most of the collected measurement data are never used. Defect data are typically an essential part of such data. The collection of these data takes time, effort, and money. If not used, the cost is just pure cost, not associated with any benefit. How would you change the situation?

20.3 Perform some defect distribution analyses based on data from your organization or data reported in literature. Is the 80:20 rule valid here?

20.4 Perform some defect trend analyses based on data from your organization or data reported in literature. Pay special attention to time measurement: Is idle time counted or only activity time? Is the granularity proper?

20.5 Perform some defect causal analyses based on data from your organization. (Data from literature would probably not be usable for this, because you probably don't have needed information to determine the causes.)

20.6 Is ODC adaptable to your development environment? If yes, list your defect attributes and attribute values. If not, justify yourself.

20.7 Can you suggest some more defect attributes for web applications and related problems? Pay special attention to how to obtain the information for the attributes you define.

20.8 Try a three-way or four-way analysis to see how difficult it is.

CHAPTER 21

RISK IDENTIFICATION FOR QUANTIFIABLE QUALITY IMPROVEMENT

This chapter describes and compares risk identification techniques that can be used to identify high-risk (low-quality) areas for focused quality improvement. Each technique is briefly described and illustrated with practical application examples from industrial or governmental projects. The techniques are compared using several criteria, including simplicity, accuracy and stability of results, ease of result interpretation, and utility in guiding quality assurance and improvement. A comprehensive example using a specific risk identification technique to analyze defect data classified according to ODC (Chapter 20) is also included.

21.1 BASIC IDEAS AND CONCEPTS

As described in Chapter 2, a *defect* generally refers to a problem in the software, which may lead to undesirable consequences for both the software development/maintenance organizations and the software users. The potential for such undesirable consequences, including schedule delays, cost overruns, and highly defective software products, is usually referred to as *risk*. Various statistical analyses and learning algorithm based techniques have been developed or adopted to identify and reduce such risks.

On the other hand, fault distribution is highly uneven for most software products, regardless of their size, functionality, implementation language, and other characteristics. Much empirical evidence has accumulated over the years to support the so-called 80:20 rule, which states that about 20% of the software components are responsible for about 80% of the problems (Porter and Selby, 1990; Tian and Troster, 1998; Boehm and Basili, 2001), as also demonstrated by various defect distribution and analysis examples in the previous chapter. These problematic components represent high risks to both the software development/maintenance organizations and software users. Therefore, there is a great need for risk identification techniques to analyze these measurement data so that inspection, testing, and other quality assurance activities can be more effectively focused on those potentially high-defect components.

Similar concepts about risk related to other entities of concern, such as schedule, cost, or reliability related risk can also be defined (Boehm, 1991). As we will describe in Chapter 22, reliability problems and related risk can be addressed through the use of appropriate risk identification techniques to identify low-reliability areas for focused reliability improvement.

To measure and characterize these high-risk or potentially high-defect modules, various software metrics can be used to capture information about software design, code, size, change history, etc. (Fenton and Pfleeger, 1996), as well as other product or process characteristics we described in Chapter 18. Once the measurement data are collected from existing project databases or calculated using measurement tools, various techniques can then be employed to analyze the data in order to identify high-risk modules. The basic idea of risk identification is to use predictive modeling to focus on the high-risk areas, as follows:

- First, we need to establish a predictive relationship between project metrics and actual product defects based on historical data.

- Then, this established predictive relation is used to predict potential defects for the new project or new product release once the project metrics data become available, but before actual defects are observed in the new project or product release.

- In the above prediction, the focus is on the high-risk or the potentially high-defect modules or components.

Following the discussion in Chapter 20, we primarily use DF, or defect fixes as our defect measurement in this chapter, and relate it to other project measurements through measurement-based predictive models covered in Chapter 19, particularly those tailored for risk identification and analyses.

Like any other statistical technique, these risk identification techniques cannot establish proof of a causal relationship. However, they can provide some strong evidence that there may be a causal relationship in an observed effect. By extracting the specific characteristics of existing high-defect modules, these analyses can help software professionals identify new modules demonstrating similar measurement characteristics and take early actions to reduce risks or prevent potential problems. Appropriate risk identification techniques can be selected to fit specific application environments in order to identify high-risk software components for focused inspection and testing.

A preliminary survey of these risk identification techniques and their comparison can be found in Tian (2000), including: traditional statistical analysis techniques, principal component analysis and discriminant analysis, neural networks, tree-based modeling, pattern matching techniques, and learning algorithms. In this chapter, these techniques are described and illustrated with practical examples from industrial and governmental projects. Data, models, and analysis results presented in this chapter are extracted from several commercial software products from IBM (Tian, 1995; Khoshgoftaar and Szabo, 1996; Tian and Troster, 1998), governmental projects from NASA (Porter and Selby, 1990; Briand et al.,

1993), as well as software systems used in aerospace, medical, and telecommunication industries (Munson and Khoshgoftaar, 1992; Khoshgoftaar et al., 1996; Tian et al., 2001).

In addition, we compare these risk identification techniques according to several criteria, including: accuracy, simplicity, early availability and stability, ease of result interpretation, constructive information and guidance for quality improvement, and availability of tool support. We conclude the chapter with our recommendation for an integrated life-cycle approach where selected techniques can be used effectively through software development for quality assurance and improvement.

21.2 TRADITIONAL STATISTICAL ANALYSIS TECHNIQUES

Various traditional statistical analysis techniques (Venables and Ripley, 1994) can be used to understand the general relations between defects and various other software measurement data. These statistical relations and the general understanding can be used to a limited degree to identify high-defect modules.

Correlation analysis

The statistical correlation between two random variables x and y can be captured by the (linear) correlation coefficient $c(x, y)$, which ranges between -1 and 1. A positive correlation indicates that the two variables are generally moving in the same direction (for example, a larger x is usually accompanied by a larger y); while a negative correlation indicates the opposite. The closer to 1 the absolute value $|c(x, y)|$ is, the more tightly correlated x and y are. Because software measurement data are often skewed, such as in Table 20.3, where many modules contain few DF while a few modules contain many, rank correlations are often calculated in addition to the linear correlations.

If the observed defects are highly correlated to a software metric, we can then identify those modules with larger (or smaller, if negatively correlated) values of the given metric as high-defect modules. However, DF-metric correlations are generally low (Card and Glass, 1990; Fenton and Pfleeger, 1996), which limits our ability to predict high-defect modules based on metrics data. For example, the highest DF-metric correlation is 0.731, between DF and CSI(changed source instructions or changed lines of code), for the product LS (Tian and Troster, 1998).

Linear regression models

Linear regression models express a selected random variable y, referred to as the dependent variable, as a linear combination of n other random variables, $x_1, x_2, \ldots, x_n$, referred to as independent variables, in the form of:

$$y = \alpha_0 + \alpha_1\, x_1 + \alpha_2\, x_2 + \ldots + \alpha_n\, x_n + \epsilon,$$

where ϵ is the error term, and parameters $\alpha_0, \alpha_1, \ldots, \alpha_n$ can be estimated from the observation data. Because of the data skew, logarithmic transformation of data can also be used, yielding a log-linear regression.

When regression models are fitted to defect and metrics data, DF can be expressed as a linear or log-linear function of other metrics. The correlation coefficient between the observed defects and the fitted linear or log-linear models, or the square root of the corresponding multiple R-squared value, can be interpreted in similar ways as for DF-metric correlations. However, these corrections are 0.767 and 0.789 respectively for the product LS (Tian and Troster, 1998), — only slightly higher than correlations between DF and the individual metrics. Similar patterns were also observed in studies of other products. In general, linear or log-linear regression models suffer from similar shortcomings as correlation analysis models, and do not perform well in predicting high-defect modules. In addition, parameter estimates for these models are usually unstable due to high correlation in the metrics data.

Other models and general observations

Various other traditional statistical analysis techniques, such as non-linear regression models, generalized additive models, logistic regression models, etc. (Venables and Ripley, 1994), can also be used to identify high-defect modules. Another alternative to use traditional statistical models on these skewed measurement data is to perform data transformation before modeling. For example, logarithmic transformation is a commonly used technique to deal with data skewed towards the lower end (those with just a few data points at the higher end). But to overcome the undefined values for $\log 0$, which may even be the majority of data point, such as the 58.8% modules with 0 defects in Table 20.3, alternative transformations such as $y = \log(x + 1)$ to transform original data x to transformed data y. However, such transformations obscure the relationship between different entities and make result interpretation harder.

In general, all the above models suffer from similar limitations as correlation and linear regression models described earlier. The key problem is the data treatment: data from the majority of low-defect modules dominate these statistical results, which contain little information about high-defect modules. To overcome these limitations, alternative analysis techniques need to be used, as described below.

21.3 NEW TECHNIQUES FOR RISK IDENTIFICATION

Recently, various new techniques have been developed or adapted for risk identification purposes, including classification and analysis techniques based on statistical analysis, learning, and pattern matching. We next describe these techniques and illustrate how they can be used to identify high-defect modules.

21.3.1 Principal component and discriminant analyses

Principal component analysis and discriminant analysis are useful statistical techniques for multivariate data (Venables and Ripley, 1994). The former reduces multivariate data into a few orthogonal dimensions; while the latter classifies these data points into several mutually exclusive groups. These analysis techniques are especially useful when there are a large number of correlated variables in the collected data. Software metrics data fit into this scenario, where many closely related metrics exist to measure design, size, and complexity of the data and control structures in the code (therefore, the measurement results are correlated, too).

The principal components are formed by linear combinations of the original data variables to form an orthogonal set of variables that are statistically uncorrelated. If the original data with n variables are linearly independent (that is, none of the variables can be expressed

Table 21.1 Principal components for a commercial product

	pc1	pc2	pc3	pc4
eigenvalue λ_i	2.352	1.296	1.042	0.711
% of variance	55.3%	16.8%	10.8%	5.1%
cumulative % of variance	55.3%	72.1%	82.9%	88.0%

as linear combinations of other variables), then their covariance matrix, Σ, an $n \times n$ matrix, can be expressed as its eigendecomposition,

$$\Sigma = C^T \Lambda C,$$

where Λ is a diagonal matrix with eigenvalues λ_i, $i = 1, 2, \ldots, n$, in decreasing order (representing decreasing importance). The original measurement data matrix Z can be transformed into the corresponding principal-component data matrix D using a transformation function also defined by the eigenvalues.

Table 21.1 gives the first 4 principal components (pc1 $\sim$ pc4) for the product NS (Tian and Troster, 1998), where the original data contain 11 variables (for 11 different metrics for modules in NS). Among the principal components, pc1 $\sim$ pc4 explain 88% of the total variance. As a result, the original data can be reduced to these four principal components, without much loss of information.

Once a few important principal components are extracted, they can be used in various models to identify high-defect modules. For example, selected principal components were used with discriminant analysis to classify software modules into *fault-prone* and *other* ones for software systems used in aerospace, medical, and telecommunication industries (Munson and Khoshgoftaar, 1992; Khoshgoftaar et al., 1996). The models using principal components have several advantages over similar models using the original (raw) data: The models are simpler because fewer independent variables are used. The parameter estimates are also more stable due to the orthogonality among the principal components.

Discriminant analysis is a statistical analysis technique that classifies multivariate data points or entities, such as software modules characterized by different metrics, into mutually exclusive groups. This classification is done by using a discriminant function to assign data points to one of the groups while minimizing within group differences. For example, a discriminant function defined on selected principal components was derived to separate fault-prone software modules from the rest for some telecommunication software developed in Nortel (Khoshgoftaar et al., 1996):

- Assign d_i to G_1, if

$$\frac{f_1(d_i)}{f_2(d_i)} > \frac{\pi_2}{\pi_1},$$

where the entities are defined as:

- d_i is the i-th modules principal-component values (i-th row of the D matrix above).

- G_1 and G_2 are mutually exclusive classes representing normal (not fault-prone) and fault-prone modules respectively.

- π_k is the prior probability of membership in G_k.

- $f_k(d_i)$ gives the probability that d_i is in G_k.

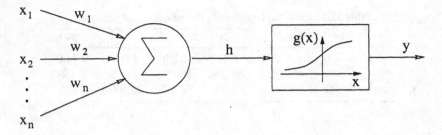

Figure 21.1 Processing model of a neuron

- Otherwise, assign d_i to G_2.

These applications have yielded fairly accurate results for grouping modules in the current project, with misclassification rate at about 1%, and for predictions into the future, with misclassification at 22.6% or 31.1% for the two models used in Khoshgoftaar et al. (1996)..

21.3.2 Artificial neural networks and learning algorithms

Artificial neural networks are based on learning algorithms inspired by biological neural networks, and can be used to solve various challenging problems, including pattern classification, categorization, approximation, etc. (Jain et al., 1996). Processing of an individual neuron is depicted by Figure 21.1, with:

$$h = \sum_{i=1}^{n} w_i x_i \quad \text{and} \quad y = g(h),$$

where x_1, x_2, $\ldots$, x_n are the input, w_1, w_2, $\ldots$, w_n the input weights, g the activation function, and y the output. The commonly used activation functions include threshold, piecewise linear, sigmoid, and Gaussian. Sigmoid function depicted in Figure 21.1 and used in Khoshgoftaar and Szabo (1996) is defined by:

$$g(x) = \frac{1}{1 + e^{-\beta x}}.$$

An artificial neural network is formed by connecting individual neurons in a specific network architecture.

When an artificial neural network is applied to a given data set, an iterative learning procedure can be followed to minimize the network error, or the difference between the predicted and actual output. This can be achieved by following various learning algorithms to adjust the weights at individual neurons. One of the most widely used such algorithms is backward propagation, summarized in Figure 21.2.

Recently, artificial neural network models were used to identify high-defect modules for some system software (Kernel.1, Kernel.2, and Kernel.3) developed in IBM (Khoshgoftaar and Szabo, 1996). Both the raw data and the principal component data from Kernel.1 were used as input to the models, starting with a small number (20) of hidden layer neurons and gradually adding more neurons until the model converge. 40 hidden layer neurons were needed for the model with raw data as input to converge; while only 24 were needed for the principal component data. In addition, as show in Table 21.2, once they were

0. *Initialization:* Initialize the weights to small random values.

1. *Overall control:* Repeat steps 2 ~ 6 until the error in the output layer is below a pre-specified threshold or a maximum number of iterations is reached.

2. Randomly choose an input.

3. Propagate the signal forward through the network.

4. Compute the errors in the output layer.

5. Compute the deltas for the preceding layers by propagating the errors backward.

6. Update the weights based on these deltas.

Figure 21.2 Backward propagation algorithm for artificial neural networks

Table 21.2 Predicting defects using artificial neural networks

System	Model Data	Output Error			
		mean	std.dev	min.	max.
Kernel.2	raw	11.4	6.6	0.19	32.8
	principal components	7.1	5.6	0.05	42.8
Kernel.3	raw	11.0	6.3	0.12	31.6
	principal components	4.7	4.1	0.02	26.2

applied to Kernel.2 and Kernel.3, the model based on principal components outperformed the one based on raw data by a significant margin. The combination of principal component analysis and neural networks also outperformed linear regression models (Khoshgoftaar et al., 1996). This combination offers an effective and efficient (takes less time to train the model with relatively fewer neurons) alternative to identify high-defect modules for quality improvement.

21.3.3 Data partitions and tree-based modeling

In general, different modules of a large software system may possess quite different characteristics because of the diverse functionalities, program sources, and evolution paths. Sometimes, it is not the particular values but specific ranges that have practical significance. Arguably, such data are more properly handled if they are partitioned, and analyzed separately to accommodate for the qualitative differences among the partitioned subsets. In this way, high-defect modules with different characteristics for different partitions can be identified, and different actions can be carried out to correct the problems.

Tree-based modeling (Clark and Pregibon, 1993) is a statistical analysis technique that handles data partitions and related analysis. The model construction involves the data set being recursively partitioned, using split conditions defined on selected predictors (or independent variables), into smaller subsets with increasing homogeneity of response (or dependent variable) values. The binary partitioning algorithm, supported by the commercial software tool S-PLUS is summarized in Figure 21.3. Each subset of data associated with a

0. *Initialization.* Set the list, Slist, to contain only the complete data set as its singleton element. Select the size and homogeneity thresholds T_s and T_h for the algorithm.

1. *Overall control.* Repeatedly remove a data set from Slist and execute step 2 until Slist becomes empty.

2. *Size test.* If $|S| < T_s$, stop; otherwise, execute steps 3 through 6. $|S|$ is the number of data points in set S.

3. *Defining binary partitions.* A binary partition divides S into two subsets using a *split condition* defined on a specific predictor p. For numerical p, it can be defined with a cutoff value c: Data points with $p < c$ form one subset (S_1) and those with $p \geq c$ form another subset (S_2). If p is a categorical variable, a binary partition is a unique grouping of all its category values into two mutually exclusive subsets S_1 and S_2.

4. *Computing predicted responses and prediction deviances.* The predicted response value $v(S)$ for a set S is the average over the set; that is, $v(S) = \frac{1}{|S|} \sum_{i \in S} (v_i)$; and the prediction deviance is $D(S) = \sum_{i \in S} (v_i - v(S))^2$, where v_i is the response value for data point i.

5. *Selecting the optimal partition.* Among all the possible partitions (all predictors with all associated cutoffs or binary groupings), the one that minimizes the deviance of the partitioned subsets is selected; that is, the partition with minimized $D(S_1) + D(S_2)$ is selected.

6. *Homogeneity test:* Stop if $\left(1 - \frac{D(S_1) + D(S_2)}{D(S)}\right) \leq T_h$ (that is, stop if there is no substantial gain in prediction accuracy in further partitioning); otherwise, append S_1 and S_2 to *Slist*.

Figure 21.3   Algorithm for tree-based model construction

tree node is uniquely described by the path and associated split conditions from the root to it. The results presented in such forms are natural to the decision process and, consequently, are easy to interpret and easy to use. The characterization of individual nodes and associated data subsets can also help us understand subsets of high-defect modules, and therefore can be used to guide remedial actions focused on those identified modules and on modules demonstrating similar characteristics in related products.

Tree based models were first used in Porter and Selby (1990) to analyze data from NASA Software Engineering Laboratory, where various software metrics data were used to predict project effort and to identify high-risk areas for focused remedial actions. Recently, it was used to identify high-defect modules for several commercial software products (Tian and Troster, 1998). Figure 21.4 shows a tree-based model constructed for NS, one of these products, relating DF to 11 other design, size, and complexity metrics. The specific metrics selected by the tree construction algorithm include:

- HLSC, or high-level structural complexity (Card and Glass, 1990), a design complexity metric reflecting the number of external function calls.

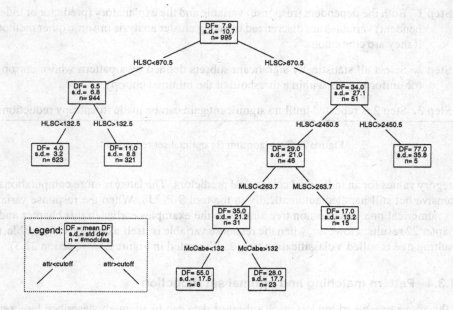

Figure 21.4 Tree-based defect model for a commercial product

Table 21.3 Characterizing high-defect modules for a commercial product

Node:	Split Conditions/Subset Characteristics	#Modules	Predicted-DF
rlll:	$870.5 < $ HLSC $ < 2450.5$, MLSC < 263.7, McCabe < 132	8	55.0
rr:	HLSC > 2450.5	5	77.0

- MLSC, or module-level structural complexity (Card and Glass, 1990), a design complexity metric reflecting the number of internal function calls within the module.

- McCabe, or McCabe's cyclomatic complexity (McCabe, 1976), a program complexity metric defined to be the number of independent control flow paths for a given program.

The subsets with extremely high DF can be easily identified as those associated with leaf nodes "rlll" and "rr" in Figure 21.4. Each node is labeled by the series of decisions, "l" for a left branching, "r" for a right branching, from the tree root to the specific node. Table 21.3 summarizes the data subsets associated with these nodes, characterized by the chains of split conditions. The identification of these high-defect modules and their characterization can lead to focused remedial actions directed at such modules. These and other results were used by the development teams to guide their selective software inspection effort for cost-effective quality assurance and improvement.

As noted in Figure 21.3, tree-based modeling can handle categorical data or combined categorical and numerical data seamlessly — a unique advantage among all the risk identification techniques covered in this chapter. The treatment of these different types of data as predictor variables is similar except in defining binary partitions in the algorithm in Figure 21.3: cut off using "<" for an individual numerical predictor and binary grouping of its

---

Step 1. Both the dependent (response) variable and the explanatory (predictor or independent) variables are discretized by using cluster analysis or some other method if they are continuous.

Step 2. Select all statistically significant subsets defined by a pattern whose entropy (or uniformity) is within a threshold of the minimal entropy.

Step 3. Step 2 is repeated until no significant gain can be made in entropy reduction.

Figure 21.5   Algorithm for optimal set reduction

category values for an individual categorical predictors. The latter is more computationally intensive but still handled automatically in the tool S-PLUS. When the response variable is a numerical one, a regression tree similar to the examples earlier in this chapter and in Chapter 22 results. However, when the response variable is itself a categorical variable, the resulting tree is called a classification tree, as illustrated in Figure 21.7 (Section 21.5).

21.3.4   Pattern matching and optimal set reduction

In the above tree-based models, each subset of data can be uniquely described by a set of split conditions. Therefore, the data subset can be viewed as following a unique "pattern". However, many commonly defined patterns in practical applications do not have to be mutually exclusive, and they can be used in combination and in parallel to identify problematic areas. This kind of analysis can be carried out using a pattern matching technique called optimal set reduction (Briand et al., 1993).

The model construction for optimal set reduction can be summarized by the recursive algorithm in Figure 21.5. The *pattern* for a subset is defined by a condition on an explanatory (independent) variable, similar to the split conditions in tree-based models. The *entropy* is defined on the dependent variable values, capturing the uniformity of a subset. For example, for a subset of data, S, all mildly changed modules (subset S_1, characterized by the pattern: $1 \leq$ CSI ≤ 10, where CSI is the changed lines of code) are likely to have high defects (DF > 5, which defines the high-defect class). All modules with high data content (subset S_2, characterized by the pattern: operand-count > 50) are also likely to have high defects. Then, S_1 and S_2 can be extracted from S in parallel, because of the low entropy for these subsets (most of these modules are high-defect modules). Notice that these subsets may overlap, yielding a general graph instead of a tree structure, as illustrated by Figure 21.6.

Optimal set reduction was recently used to analyze various project effort and metrics data from NASA Software Engineering Laboratory, and to identify high-risk (high-effort) modules (Briand et al., 1993). It performed better (with 92.11% accuracy) than various other techniques, including classification trees, logistic regression without principal component, logistic regression with principal component (with 83.33%, 76.56%, and 80.00% accuracy, respectively). In addition, the combination of patterns for high-risk modules was also identified by the modeling result, which can be used to guide focused remedial actions.

21.4   COMPARISONS AND INTEGRATION

Similar to the cost–benefit analysis under different application environments for different quality assurance techniques in Chapter 17, we can compare the cost and benefit of individual

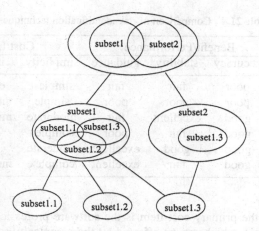

Figure 21.6 Example hierarchy for optimal set reduction

risk identification techniques. On the benefit side, the primary criteria include accuracy of the specific risk identification technique, the early availability of risk identification results and the related stability, and constructive information or guidance for quality improvement. These issues are individually examined below:

- *Accuracy* of analysis results can be measured by the difference (error) between predicted and actual results. The standard deviation of error can be used to measure accuracy for models with numerical response (for example, defect count), and proportion of misclassification for those with categorical response (for example, high-defect vs. low-defect). Since the data and applications are from diverse sources, only a qualitative comparison of result accuracy is possible here. In general, new techniques for risk identification discussed in Section 21.3 perform much better than traditional statistical techniques discussed in Section 21.2.

- *Early availability and stability:* There is a strong need for early modeling results, because problems found late in development are much harder and cost significantly more to fix. Ideally, models could be fitted to observations early and remain fairly stable so that timely and consistent remedial actions can be applied. All the techniques discussed in this chapter can be used early, but their stability differs considerably: Linear regression models are usually highly unstable due to high correlation in the metrics data, while models using principal component analysis are much more stable. On the other hand, techniques depending on data ranges (for example, tree-based modeling and optimal set reduction) are more likely to be stable than those depending on numerical values (for example, traditional statistical models).

- *Constructive information and guidance for quality improvement:* Tree-based models and optimal set reduction can characterize identified high-defect modules by their split conditions or patterns defined by certain metrics values or ranges. Such constructive information can be used to guide quality improvement activities. For example, if the identified high-defect subset of modules are characterized by numerous changes and high data contents, this information can be used in several ways: to minimize change for such modules, to reduce data contents by restructuring the modules, or to take extra precautions toward these modules.

Table 21.4   Comparison of risk identification techniques

Technique	Benefit/Performance			Cost/Usability		
	accuracy	stability	guidance	simplicity	interp.	tool sup.
correlation	poor	fair	fair	simplest	easiest	wide
regression	poor	poor	poor	simple	moderate	wide
discriminant	good	excellent	fair	moderate	moderate	moderate
neural net.	good	fair	poor	complex	hard	moderate
tree-based model	good	good	excellent	moderate	easy	moderate
opt. set reduction	good	fair	excellent	complex	moderate	limited

On the cost side, the primary cost item is the software professionals' time spent on performing the analysis, which can be affected by the complexity (or simplicity) of the technique itself and available tool support. Similarly, ease of result interpretation also affect the cost because of the possible time required not only to interpret the analysis results, but also to convince developers, tester, and managers to initiate follow-up activities for quality improvement. These issues are considered individually below:

- *Simplicity* of the analysis technique has many ramifications. A simple technique is generally easy to understand, easy to use, easy (and less costly) to perform on a given set of data, and is more likely to be supported by existing tools. Minimal amount of training is needed before a software quality professional can learn and master the technique. Among the risk identification techniques, correlation and regression analyses are simple statistical techniques, while others are more complex, with artificial neural networks (multiple parallel, hidden neurons) and optimal set reduction (overlapping subsets extracted in parallel) among the most complex.

- *Ease of result interpretation* plays an important role in model applications. A good understanding of the analysis results is a precondition to follow-up actions. For example, tree-based models present results in a form similar to decision trees commonly used in project management. Therefore, the results are easy to interpret and easy to use. On the other extreme, artificial neuron networks employ multiple hidden layer neurons and give the result as if from a "black-box", making result interpretation hard.

- *Availability of tool support* also has a significant influence on the practical applications of specific techniques. Traditional statistical analysis techniques covered in Section 21.2 are supported by many statistical packages. Some modern statistical packages also support principal component analysis, discriminant analysis, and tree-based modeling. However, special tools are needed to support artificial neural networks (several such tools are available) and optimal set reduction (a tool developed at the University of Maryland).

Table 21.4 summarizes our comparison of the risk identification techniques. Notice that principal component analysis is not listed as a separate entry, but rather included as part of discriminant analysis.

Like any other analysis techniques, the risk identification techniques are only a tool to provide us with evidence or symptoms of existing problems. The ultimate responsibility to use the analysis results and to make changes lies with the development teams and their managers. Tree-based modeling technique seems to combine many good qualities appropriate for this kind of applications: It is conceptually simple, and is supported by a commercial tool S-PLUS. It provides accurate and stable results, and excellent constructive information, both in a consistent and uniform structure (tree) intuitive to the decision process. Therefore, tree-based modeling is an excellent candidate that can be used effectively to solicit changes and remedial actions from developers and managers. The analysis results and remedial action plans can often be cross-validated by other techniques, taking advantage of their individual strengths.

To facilitate practical applications of selected risk identification techniques, the analysis and follow-up activities need to be integrated into and carried out throughout the existing software development process. Such an integrated approach can be used to track quality changes and to identify and characterize problematic areas for focused remedial actions. This approach can be implemented in several stages: Initially, the analyses can be handled off-line by a dedicated quality analyst to minimize disruption to existing processes and to provide timely feedback. Thereafter, the analysis activities can be gradually automated, so that minimal effort is needed by the project teams to produce analysis results for remedial actions.

All the data and examples presented so far in this chapter are based on software artifacts, for example, defects and metrics data associated with specific software modules. However, similar risk identification techniques can also be applied to process or activity based data. For example, tree based modeling was used to link test results (successful vs. failed executions) to various timing and input state information for several IBM software products (Tian, 1995). The modeling results were used to identify clusters of test executions associated with abnormally high failures for focused remedial actions, which lead to significantly higher quality for these products as compared to earlier products. Similar analyses can also be performed on inspection data typically gathered in the earlier phases of software development. Each individual inspection can be treated as a data point, with all the circumstantial information associated with the inspection, such as components inspected, inspection method used, inspectors and time spent, as predictors, to build similar tree-based models to identify high-defect areas for focused quality improvement.

21.5 RISK IDENTIFICATION FOR CLASSIFIED DEFECT DATA

For classified defect data using ODC in Chapter 20, various analyses can be performed, such as the one-way and two-way analysis. However, the combinatorial explosion renders it impossible to perform multi-way analyses indiscriminately. We next examine the use of tree-based models to analyze such classified data and perform multi-way analysis, and illustrate it with examples for an IBM database product (Tian and Henshaw, 1994).

Defect impact analysis using TBM

For TBM analysis, we need to first select the response variable, and then examine its relationship to other variables used as predictor variables. In effect, we are performing 1-to-N analysis instead of isolated one-way analysis or the 1-to-1 two-way analysis. This 1-to-N analysis can be repeated for other variables if we select them as the response variable in individual analyses.

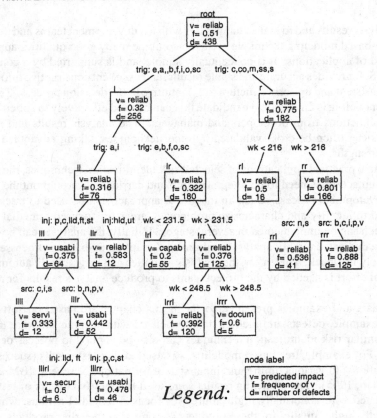

Figure 21.7 Predictions of defect impact for an IBM product

Defect impact is a classification of the defect itself, while all other defect attributes capture circumstantial information associated with the defect discovery and fixing. With the increased focus on customers in today's competitive environment, understanding of defect impact to customers takes on an increased importance. As a result, tree-based models to study the link between defect impact and other attributes would be of interests to project personnel, so that they can understand the linkage and devise appropriate corrective and preventive actions. The specific attributes used in the tree-based models were listed in Table 20.6.

Figure 21.7 shows the classification tree constructed for defect impact analysis. 438 defect entries and related ODC information were used after screening out data points with missing data. At each node (corresponding to a set of defects), the predicted defect impact v is the most frequently cited category by the testers for this set of defects. The analysis shows that the distribution of defects (defect impacts) is very non-homogeneous, and the relationship to other ODC attributes is highly nonlinear.

Detailed information associated with each tree node can be shown in stack-up barplot such as in Figure 21.8, where the vertical bar sequence of different shades represents the distribution of defect impact at this node. For example, the overall defect impact distribution among the impact areas is presented in the middle histogram stack in Figure 21.8. The left and right bars represent the defect impact distributions at nodes 1 and r of Figure 21.7 respectively.

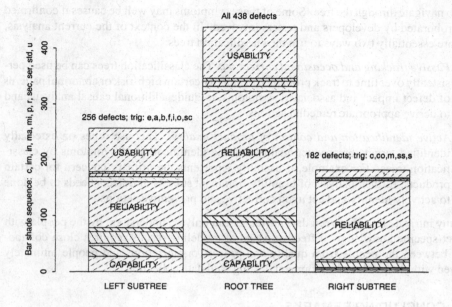

Figure 21.8 Defect impact distributions for an IBM product

Interpretation and usage of the analysis results

The primary partition for the defect impact is the defect trigger. After the partition, the reliability related defects become overwhelmingly dominant for the defects triggered by test cases from communication, coexistence, migration, stress, startup/shutdown scenario classes (trig: c,co,m,s,ss, see Table 20.6 in Chapter 20). For defects triggered by test cases from other scenario classes, although reliability remains a major problem (82 or 32% of the 256 defects), there is a disproportionate number of usability defects (78 or 30% of the 256 defects). The visual representation of this result in Figure 21.8 makes the impact of the primary partition obvious.

In the right sub-tree (rooted at node r), reliability impact is consistently predicted, although with different levels of f, which represents to some degree the confidence of the prediction. In the left sub-tree (rooted at node 1), several other defect types are identified as the dominant defects in certain subsets. For example, usability defects are mostly triggered by testing scenarios of the ad-hoc and installation types. The defects were injected to base, new, refixed and vendor codes in the phases of coding, previous release, and system testing. This result can lead to a focused effort on the identified phases and types of code to remove the usability defects and enhanced test cases to thoroughly test for usability.

In part of the left sub-tree, data sets were partitioned into significantly smaller subsets to identify certain dominating defect impacts. For example, security defects dominate among the six defects associated with node 111r1, and documentation defects dominate among the five defects associated with node 1rrr. In practical application, the information presented should only be used with both the set size d and frequency f in mind. Greater values for both f and d provide stronger evidence than smaller f or d.

The subsets of defects where certain impacts dominate can be easily identified in classification trees, together with their associated symptoms, by linking them to characteristics used to navigate through the tree. Some of these symptoms may well be causes if confirmed or corroborated by developers and testers involved. In the context of the current analysis, there are essentially two ways to use the classification trees:

- *Passive tracking and occasional correction:* The classification trees can be used persistently over time to track problems, to identify certain high-risk or abnormal patterns of defect impact and associated symptoms, to guide additional causal analysis, and to derive appropriate remedial actions.

- *Active identification and control of product quality:* This use relies on externally identified targets of product quality and the identification of symptoms by classification trees. For example, if usability represents the primary concern for certain products, further analysis of usability-dominant subsets of defects needs to be done to actively identify and act upon corrective and preventive actions.

Many intricate links between data attributes can only be understood by the people with product-specific knowledge. Effective usage of modeling results requires close collaboration between the people from quality and process organizations and people intimately involved with the product development, testing, and data collection.

21.6 CONCLUDING REMARKS

Because of the highly uneven distribution of defects in software systems, there is a great need for effective risk identification techniques so that high-defect modules or software components can be identified and characterized for effective defect removal and quality improvement. The survey of different risk identification techniques presented in this chapter brings together information from diverse sources to offer a common starting point for software quality professionals and software engineering students. The comparison of techniques can help them choose appropriate techniques for their individual applications.

The tree-based modeling (TBM) technique was found to possess various desirable properties as an effective risk identification technique and is therefore highly recommended for various practical applications. Another example of the effective use of TBM for effective reliability risk identification and product reliability improvement is presented in Chapter 22. In addition, tree-based modeling can handle categorical data or combined categorical and numerical data seamlessly — a unique advantage among all the risk identification techniques covered in this chapter. Therefore, as a general recommendation, tree-based models should be considered in many situations for risk identification and quality improvement initiatives, either as the primary technique or to be integrated with other techniques to achieve the common goal of focused remedial actions on the identified problematic areas for effective quality improvement.

Besides the risk identification techniques based on empirical data we described in this chapter, there are various other techniques for risk identification, analysis, and management (Boehm, 1991; Charette, 1989). For example, software prototyping or rapid software prototyping can be used in software development or evolution to proactively identify and address various risks or potential problems (Luqi, 1989; Tanik and Yeh, 1989). Quantitative risk analyses based statistical decision theory (Pratt et al., 1965) can also be adapted to work with software prototypes to make management decisions based on related risk analysis (Cárdenas-García et al., 1992; Cárdenas-García and Zelkowitz, 1991). Risk identification also play a very important role in the spiral development process (Boehm, 1988) in assessing the project risk and initiating the next development spiral.

Problems

21.1   What is the primary motivation for risk identification?

21.2   Have you heard of the 80:20 rule before reading this book? If so, in what context? If not, do you think it applies to many situations that you are familiar with? Give some specific examples.

21.3   Most of the risk identifications we described in this chapter are about defects. Can you list some other risks related to software projects from both the internal/development view and the external/user view?

21.4   Are traditional statistical techniques commonly used in analyzing software defect and other data from your organization? What about some of the newer techniques covered in Section 21.3? If not, do you think that some of them can be applied?

21.5   Principal component analysis is often used as a data transformation techniques in various software engineering studies. Compare the relative merits and drawbacks of this use and the use of other data transformations (for example, log-transformation we mentioned in Section 21.2).

21.6   Besides artificial neuron networks, various learning algorithms and artificial intelligence techniques have also found valuable applications in software engineering and other application domains. Do you know of some such applications or can you find some such examples in software engineering/quality literature? (*Hint*: Pay special attentions to genetic programming, expert and decision support systems, pattern matching, heuristic algorithms.)

21.7   What are the similarities and differences between decision trees and tree-based models?

21.8   In Selby and Porter (1988), the first known application of tree-based models in software engineering, the trees has fixed partitions (either a 4-way or an 8-way partition). What are the relative advantages and disadvantages of this model and the binary partitions supported by S-PLUS?

21.9   Trace through the tree-based modeling algorithm in Figure 21.3, and explain how a tree like that in Figure 21.4 can be obtained.

21.10   Compare the relative advantages and disadvantages between tree-based modeling and optimal set reduction.

21.11   We didn't explicitly compare the applicability to different application environments and different types of data, although several of the criteria are related to applicability. Can you perform a formal applicability comparison?

21.12   Besides using tree-based models to perform multi-way analysis for ODC data, what other analysis or modeling techniques can your suggest?

CHAPTER 22

SOFTWARE RELIABILITY ENGINEERING

This chapter introduces the general topic of software reliability engineering (SRE) (Musa et al., 1987; Malaiya and Srimani, 1990; Lyu, 1995a) and illustrates its applications through examples for several large software products developed in the IBM Software Solutions Toronto Laboratory (Tian et al., 1995; Tian and Palma, 1997; Tian, 1998; Tian and Palma, 1998; Tian, 1999). The specific topics include:

- After a brief introduction to SRE in Section 22.1, the general testing environment for large software systems is characterized and matched against SRE assumptions in Section 22.2.

- Two types of existing models, input domain reliability models (IDRMs) and software reliability growth models (SRGMs), are introduced and adapted to work in practical applications in Section 22.3 and Section 22.4, respectively.

- A new integrated modeling technique, tree-based reliability modeling (TBRM), is introduced to analyze diverse measurement data and improve reliability in Section 22.5.

- Some implementation issues and software tool support for SRE are discussed in Section 22.6.

22.1 SRE: BASIC CONCEPTS AND GENERAL APPROACHES

As mentioned in our general discussion about quality and quality attributes in Chapter 2, one important aspect of software quality is *reliability*. Reliability can be defined as the probability of a software system to perform its specified functions correctly over a long period of time or for different input sets under the usage environments similar to that of its target customers (Goel, 1985; Musa et al., 1987; Tian, 1995). Software reliability engineering (SRE) is the branch of software engineering that studies the issues related to the measurement, modeling, and improvement of software reliability. Two general approaches are commonly used to analyze reliability:

- *Time domain approach*: The failure arrival process is viewed as a stochastic process and analyzed using various software reliability growth models (SRGMs) to assess current reliability, to predict future reliability, to serve as an exit criterion to stop testing, or to estimate time or resources needed to reach a reliability target. Many SRGMs have been proposed and used in various practical applications (Goel, 1985; Lyu, 1995a; Musa et al., 1987).

- *Input domain approach*: Input domain reliability models (IDRMs) are used to analyze input states and failure data, providing valuable information relating input states to reliability. Many IDRMs have been proposed and used to estimate reliability (Brown and Lipow, 1975; Nelson, 1978; Ramamoorthy and Bastani, 1982), typically as a weighted ratio between input states that result in successful executions over the total sampled input states, based on the common assumption of repeated random sampling without error fixing.

In this chapter, we characterize the typical testing environment for large software systems, select appropriate measurements to assess product reliability using IDRMs and SRGMs, and use tree-based reliability models (TBRMs) (Tian, 1995) to analyze the combined time and input domain data for reliability improvement. Implementation and software tool support issues are also discussed.

22.2 LARGE SOFTWARE SYSTEMS AND RELIABILITY ANALYSES

In a series of recent studies (Tian et al., 1995; Tian and Palma, 1997; Tian, 1998; Tian and Palma, 1998; Tian, 1999), the reliability of several software systems developed in the IBM Software Solutions Toronto Laboratory were analyzed. The size of these systems range from several hundred thousand to several million lines of source code. They share many of the common characteristics of large software systems, and therefore are used in this chapter to illustrate the use of software reliability engineering under similar environments.

Characterizing a typical system testing environment

For many large software systems, system testing is mainly used to assess the overall quality from a customer's perspective, and is executed in an environment that attempts to resemble the actual usage environment by target customers. Because of the large product size and the lack of precise customer usage information due to the large user population and diverse usage environments, a *scenario-based* testing strategy is often used: The test scenarios roughly describe customer usage situations, based on existing product information or customer surveys. These scenarios are generally grouped into scenario classes according to high-level functionalities. Actual test cases are derived from these scenarios. Each observation of a failure generally triggers related test runs to locate the faults and additional test runs to verify the fixes. Typically large numbers of test cases are run, with hundreds or even thousands of failures being observed during system testing for such large software systems, which provides large amounts of data for statistical modeling.

Scenario-based testing for large software systems can be characterized by the mixture of structured (centered around the framework of scenario classes), clustered (focused on locating faults and verifying fixes), and randomized testing. This environment has a strong effect on the choice of reliability measurements and models.

Satisfiability of general assumptions for SRE

The following general assumptions (**A1** through **A4**) made by SRGMs and IDRMs (Goel, 1985) have to be matched against this testing environment before appropriate models can be selected and used for reliability analysis:

- **Assumption A1.** *The software usage resembles that of its target customers,* or the testing follows operational profiles (OPs) we described in Chapters 8 and 10.

  Although precise OPs were not available for these products, the test scenarios roughly describe customer usage situations and the scenario distribution across scenario classes roughly corresponds to customer usage frequencies. Therefore, this assumption is generally satisfied.

- **Assumption A2.** *Failure intervals or observations are independent,* which implies randomized testing.

  Despite the individual dependencies due to structured testing according to scenarios, testing is generally conducted by different testers in parallel, interleaving in some arbitrary fashion. And, despite short-term dependencies among clusters of test runs used to locate faults and verify fixes, there is no long-term dependency among test runs used to deal with different failures. Therefore, random testing can be approximated by scenario-based testing.

- **Assumption A3.** *Probability of failure in SRGMs is a function of the number of faults existing in the software system,* which implies a homogeneous distribution of faults.

  Although faults are generally distributed unevenly across components in large software systems, this distribution evens out as testing progresses if risk identification and management techniques can be used to focus on problematic areas for remedial actions early in testing (Section 22.5). Consequently, SRGMs can be used late in testing for reliability analyses.

- **Assumption A4.** *Time is used as the basis to define failure rates in SRGMs,* which requires that appropriate time measurement be selected from the following two categories:

  - *Usage-independent time measurement* which marks failure instances but ignores software usage information. Calendar time and wall-clock time fall into this category.

  - *Usage-dependent time measurement* that counts only the time when software is used. Such measurements include: 1) *test run count,* where each test run represents a well defined unit of software usage linked to some user-oriented operations (Tian et al., 1995), 2) *execution time* (Musa et al., 1987), and 3)

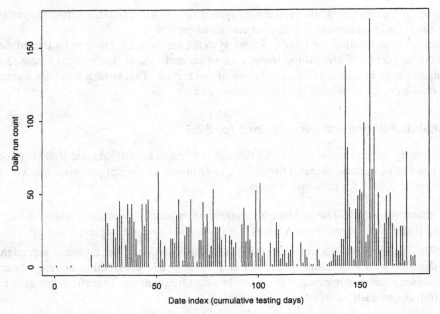

Figure 22.1   Measured runs (per day) for products D

detailed task measurement, generically referred to as *transactions* (Tian and Palma, 1997).

Usage-independent time measurements are generally unsuitable for reliability analyses for large software systems, because of the large variations in software usage and test activities typified by the test run count per testing day for product D (Tian, 1995) and transactions per run for product E (Tian and Palma, 1997) plotted in Figure 22.1 and Figure 22.2, respectively. Such variations are caused by shifting focuses during testing, partial dependencies in test scenarios, staffing level fluctuations, etc. Therefore, appropriate usage-dependent time measurement needs to be used with SRGMs.

To summarize, appropriate reliability measurements and models can be selected to analyze the reliability of large software systems under scenario-based testing.

22.3   RELIABILITY SNAPSHOTS USING IDRMS

In the input domain reliability analysis, the reliability of a software system is defined to be the probability of failure-free operation for specific input states. Therefore, the key to reliability measurement in the input domain reliability modeling is both failure and input state measurement. The latter captures the information of precise input state for the software systems, which can be related to testing results by using various input domain reliability models (IDRMs).

IDRMs generally use data from repeated random sampling to analyze product reliability. When used for data at different stages of testing, they can provide a series of reliability snapshots. Therefore, they can be used directly for current reliability assessment and as an exit criterion for stop testing.

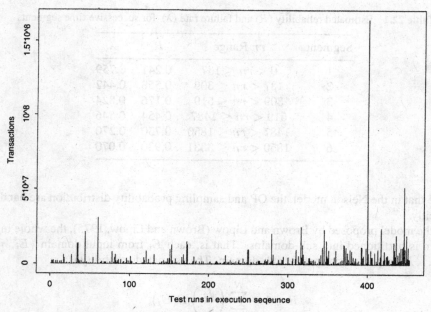

Figure 22.2   Measured transactions (per run) for products E

The successive reliability snapshots above can also help us analyze reliability change over time. Similarly, when we apply IDRMs to different areas or product components, they can help us analyze reliability variations and identify high-risk (low-reliability) areas for focused reliability improvement. These novel usages of IDRMs will be explored further in Section 22.5.

Some commonly used IDRMs

In Nelson's input domain reliability model (Nelson, 1978), an unbiased estimation of reliability $\hat{R}$ is the ratio between input states that result in successful executions over the total sampled input states. $\hat{R}$ can be derived from observations of running the software for a sample of n inputs according to the following setup:

- The n inputs are randomly selected from the set $\{E_i : i = 1, 2, \ldots, N\}$, where each E_i is a set of data values needed to make a run.

- Sampling probability is according to the probability vector $\{P_i : i = 1, 2, \ldots, N\}$, where P_i is the probability that E_i is sampled. This probability vector defines the operational profile (OP).

- If the number of failures is f, then the estimated reliability $\hat{R}$ is:

$$\hat{R} = 1 - r = 1 - \frac{f}{n} = \frac{n - f}{n},$$

where r is the failure rate. The estimated reliability $\hat{R}$ for a given input set equals to the number of successes over the total number of runs.

Table 22.1 Estimated reliability ($\hat{R}$) and failure rate ($\hat{\lambda}$) for successive time segments

Segment	rn Range	$\hat{R}_i$	$\hat{\lambda}_i$
1	$0 < rn \leq 137$	0.241	0.759
2	$137 < rn \leq 309$	0.558	0.442
3	$309 < rn \leq 519$	0.176	0.824
4	$519 < rn \leq 1487$	0.454	0.546
5	$1487 < rn \leq 1850$	0.730	0.270
6	$1850 < rn \leq 3331$	0.930	0.070

Notice that in the Nelson model, the OP and sampling probability distribution are handled implicitly.

In the model proposed by Brown and Lipow (Brown and Lipow, 1975), the whole input domain is partitioned into sub-domains. That is, each E_i from input domain $\{E_i,\ i = 1, 2, \ldots, N\}$ represents a specific sub-domain. The estimated reliability is:

$$\hat{R} = 1 - \sum_{j=1}^{N} \left(\frac{f_j}{n_j}\right) P(E_j),$$

where n_j is the number of runs sampled from sub-domain E_j, f_j is the number of failures observed out of n_j runs, and $P(E_j)$ explicitly defines the probability that inputs in sub-domain E_j are used in actual customer operational environment. This model adjusts for the different usage frequencies between the testing environment (as reflected by n_i as a proportion of all test runs) and the customer usage environment (as captured in $P(E_i)$). Therefore, it is more widely applicable than the Nelson model. When there is an exact match between the two frequencies (that is, $P(E_i) = n_i / \sum_{j=1}^{N} n_j$), the Brown-Lipow model reduces to the Nelson model.

IDRMs applications and related analyses

Table 22.1 gives several different reliability snapshots by applying the Nelson model to data in different time segments indexed by the run number rn in the overall test execution sequence for an IBM product during its testing process, showing both the estimated reliability ($\hat{R}$) and failure rate ($\hat{\lambda}$) for each segment. Notice that these estimated reliabilities vary considerably, but following a general trend of later segments being more likely to be associated with higher reliability than earlier ones. This reliability change (or growth) can be analyzed by using SRGMs, such as in Section 22.4. In addition, data associated with these segments can be treated as grouped input data to SRGMs to produce more stable reliability assessments and predictions (Tian, 2002).

On the other hand, for normal operational usage where no observed defect is immediately fixed, the Nelson estimate of reliability is more like to be more stable. For example, applying the Nelson model (Nelson, 1978) to daily data of web errors (= failures) and web hits (= number of sampled input) for the SMU/SEAS web site described in Chapter 20, we can obtain the daily reliability snapshots or related daily failure rates based on data extracted from both the access and error logs. Table 22.2 gives the range (min to max), the mean, and the standard deviation (std.dev), for these daily error rates. We also include the daily error counts for comparison. Because these rates and error counts have different magnitudes, we

Table 22.2   Daily error rate (or failure rate) for SMU/SEAS

Daily Error Rate	min	max	mean	std.dev	rse
errors/hits	0.0287	0.0466	0.0379	0.00480	0.126
errors/day	501	1582	1101	312	0.283

use the relative standard error, or *rse*, defined as: $rse = std.dev / mean$, to compare their relative spread in Table 22.2. These daily error rates fall into tighter spread than daily error counts, which indicates that they provide more consistent and stable reliability estimates than counting the daily errors alone.

In both the Nelson model and the Brown-Lipow model described above, as well as other IDRMs (Thayer et al., 1978), one common assumption is repeated random sampling without error fixing. Therefore, one of the primary use of IDRMs is as the product release criterion based on results from acceptance testing.

However, in practical testing environments before the final stage of acceptance testing, whenever a failure is observed, appropriate actions are taken to identify, locate, and remove the underlying faults that have caused the failure. The reliability is changed due to defect removals. To assess the reliability at this point, another batch of runs needs to be executed, and the defect fixing problem arises again. A small subset of runs towards the end of testing can be used as a biased estimate of reliability. In general, the smaller the sampling window, the less bias there is. However, the confidence levels of the estimation are severely compromised because of the smaller sample size. This situation points to the need of using relevant time domain information to strengthen IDRMs, such as in the tree-based reliability models (Tian, 1995) using both time and input domain information discussed in Section 22.5.

Realizing the impracticality of failure detection without fixing during software development, many researchers focus instead on maximizing the product coverage of test suites. The implicit assumptions here are twofold: 1) all detected defects will be removed, and 2) higher coverage leads to higher reliability. Consequently, the focus of this approach is not on the reliability assessment, but rather on increasing the various coverage measures that can be defined and gathered, and maximizing testing effectiveness defined accordingly (Weyuker and Jeng, 1991; Tsoukalas et al., 1993). An alternative way of using coverage information in reliability modeling is to weigh time intervals by the coverage analysis results for individual test runs (Chen et al., 2001), based on the assumption that only test runs that cover new territories are more likely to trigger failures.

22.4   LONGER-TERM RELIABILITY ANALYSES USING SRGMS

Many software reliability growth models (SRGMs) have been proposed and used to analyze reliability growth through software testing and related defect removal. We next define reliability in the time domain, describe several commonly used such SRGMs, and illustrate their use in assessing reliability and reliability growth.

In the time domain approach, the reliability of a software system is defined to be the probability of its failure-free operations for a specific duration under a specific environment (Musa et al., 1987; Malaiya and Srimani, 1990; Lyu, 1995a). Reliability is usually characterized by hazard and reliability functions. The hazard function (or hazard rate) $z(t)$ is defined as:

$$z(t)\Delta t = P\{t < T < t + \Delta t \mid T > t\},$$

where T marks the failure time, P is the probability function, and $z(t)\Delta t$ gives the probability of failure in time interval $(t, t + \Delta t)$, given that the system has not failed before t. The reliability function $R(t)$ is defined as:

$$R(t) = e^{-\int_0^t z(x)dx},$$

which gives the probability of failure free operations in the time interval $(0, t)$. MTBF (mean time between failure) is commonly used as a measure of reliability for its intuitiveness. MTBF can be calculated as:

$$\text{MTBF} = \int_0^\infty R(x)dx.$$

In practical applications, comparing to other reliability measures, the measure MTBF is easy to interpret and directly meaningful to customers as well as software managers, developers, and testers.

Various measurement data are necessary for model fitting and usage. There are three key elements to time domain reliability measurement: failure, time, and usage environment. The key to failure measurement is consistency in failure definition and data interpretation. The environment is generally assumed to be similar to the actual customer usage environment, so that the analysis results can be directly extrapolated to the likelihood of in-field product failures (Musa, 1998). For time measurement, the basic requirement is that actual usage amount or intensity is reflected. Therefore, if we do not have constant usage intensity over calendar date or wall-clock time, some usage-dependent time measurements are needed, which are generally harder and more expensive to obtain.

Some commonly used SRGMs

De-eutrophication models link failure probability to the number of defects remaining in the current system in a functional form, thus capturing reliability growth (or de-eutrophication) in testing as a result of defect observations and removals. In the Jelinski-Moranda model (Jelinski and Moranda, 1972), one of the earliest and most widely used models, chance of failure for unit time is *proportional* to the number of defects remaining in the current system. That is, the hazard rate z_i for the i-th failure is:

$$z_i = \phi(N - (i - 1)),$$

where N is the total number of defects at the beginning of testing (that is, before discovering the first failure), and ϕ a proportionality constant for the model. The hazard rate between successive failure observations remains constant, and the discovery and removal of each defect contribute the same to the hazard rate reduction. Therefore, the failure rates over successive failures form a step function of time, with uniform downward steps at corresponding failure observations.

The failure arrivals can also be viewed as a stochastic process and analyzed accordingly (Karlin and Taylor, 1975). The most commonly used such process is the non-homogeneous Poisson process (NHPP), with the number of failures $X(t)$ for a given time interval $(0, t)$ prescribed by the probability $P[X(t) = n]$ as:

$$P[X(t) = n] = \frac{(m(t))^n e^{-m(t)}}{n!},$$

where $m(t)$ is the *mean function*, and the failure rate $\lambda(t)$ (used in place of $z(t)$ in such situations) is the derivative of $m(t)$, that is, $\lambda(t) = m'(t)$. Different choices of the mean function $m(t)$ can be used to model different failure arrival patterns. One of the earliest and most wide used NHPP model is the *Goel-Okumoto model*, also known as the exponential model, (Goel and Okumoto, 1979) with

$$m(t) = N(1 - e^{-bt}),$$

where N (estimated total defects) and b are constant. Another NHPP model commonly used in industry is the S-Shaped model (Yamada et al., 1983) with

$$m(t) = N(1 - (1 + bt)e^{-bt}).$$

This model allows for a cumulative failure arrival pattern with a slow start, a steep middle part, and a more saturated late part.

Also popular in software reliability engineering are the two execution time model by Musa et al. (1987). The basic Musa model (Musa, 1975) is essentially the same as Jelinski-Moranda model, but with the emphasis of using CPU-execution time as the time measurement. This model also includes a predictive element, enabling the user of this model to estimate model parameters from product and process characteristics even before actual failures are observed. Logarithmic execution time model by Musa and Okumoto (1984) is a variation of NHPP model with

$$m(\tau) = \frac{1}{\theta} \log (\lambda_0 \theta \tau + 1),$$

where τ measures CPU-execution time, λ_0 is the initial failure intensity, and θ is a model parameter. Both these models have been used successfully in various telecommunication systems (Musa et al., 1987), and are often used together to bound the reliability predictions from above (basic Musa) and below (Musa-Okumoto).

SRGMs application examples

Using SRGMs, product reliability at a given time can be estimated by the slope of the fitted SRGMs, and overall reliability change (or reliability *growth* due to failure observations and fault removals) can be characterized by the slope change from the beginning of testing to the current time.

Figure 22.3 plots the failure arrivals against cumulative test runs for product D, and shows the fitted Goel-Okumoto and S-Shaped SRGMs (labeled GO and S). Various other SRGMs were also fitted, but were omitted in Figure 22.3 because they provide similar results. With such plots, flatter curves indicate slower failure arrivals and higher product reliability. These assessments can be quantified by the current failure rate and MTBF (mean-time-between-failures) derivable from fitted SRGMs, such as shown in Figure 22.3. Future reliability as well as time or resources to reach a reliability target can also be predicted from these models by extrapolating fitted curves into the future. These results and related studies of other products or systems (Tian et al., 1995; Tian, 1995; Tian and Palma, 1997; Tian et al., 2004) point to several important conclusions, including:

- *Many uses of test run counts*: Test run data over time can be easily collected (Section 22.6), consistently used to track testing progress, and can lead to accurate reliability assessments with SRGMs if runs are homogeneous, such as for product D plotted in Figure 22.3.

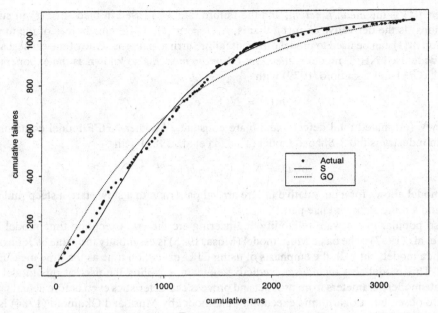

Figure 22.3   SRGMs for test run indexed failures for product D

- *Limited applicability of execution time*: For large software systems studied here, because many test runs involve little execution and much setup and manual operations, SRGMs fitted to execution time data do not perform well.

- *Using transactions*: When run homogeneity cannot be assured, detailed usage measurements, such as measured by transactions, can be used effectively for reliability analyses with SRGMs. An example of this was given in Figure 19.4 (Chapter 19).

To summarize, SRGMs can be used effectively to assess current reliability, to predict future reliability and time/resources to reach given reliability targets, when consistent failure measurement and appropriate time measurements are used.

22.5   TBRMS FOR RELIABILITY ANALYSIS AND IMPROVEMENT

SRGMs offer overall reliability assessments and predictions for software products, but provide little information on how to improve reliability. Therefore, we need alternative models and analysis techniques, such as tree-based reliability models (TBRMs), to identify and correct problems for effective reliability improvement. In an earlier study (Tian et al., 1995), noticeable reliability variations across different sub-groups of test scenarios or testing sub-phases were observed. Such input domain information can be used in conjunction with time domain information for problem identification and reliability improvement.

In IDRMs, the reliability of a software system is the probability of failure-free operation for a set of input states randomly sampled according to its OP, as described above. In Nelson's IDRM described earlier, an unbiased estimate of reliability $(\hat{R})$ is the ratio between input states that result in successful executions over the total sampled input states. IDRMs can be easily extended to model reliability for data subsets, to analyze reliability variations, to identify problematic areas, and to guide remedial actions for reliability improvement. Much of the *input* and *timing* information can be used to partition the runs into different subsets. However, to handle the large number of possible partitions and the mixed numerical timing data and categorical input state data, an appropriate analysis method with automated tool support is required. To fulfill these needs, a statistical analysis technique called tree-based modeling described in Chapter 21 can be used, as described below.

22.5.1 Constructing and using TBRMs

In tree-based models, modeling results are represented in tree structures, where each node represents a set of data and each edge from its parent node represents a property or condition for data associated with the node. The data used in such models consist of multiple attributes, with one attribute identified as the *response* variable and several other attributes identified as *predictor* variables. The data is recursively partitioned into smaller subsets by selecting a split condition defined on a predictor variable to minimize the difference between the predicted response values and the observed response values. A binary variant of recursive partitioning, summarized in Figure 21.3 in the previous chapter, is used in this chapter. The use of such models in reliability analyses that integrate both time and input domain data leads to the tree-based reliability models or TBRMs (Tian, 1995).

In TBRMs, each run is treated as a data point, the result indicator r_{ij} ($r_{ij} = 1$ if the j-th run of subset i is a success, $r_{ij} = 0$ otherwise) as the response variable, and the timing and input state information as the predictor variables. Let there be n_i runs with f_i failures for subset i. The predicted result s_i for subset i according to Step 4 of Figure 21.3 is:

$$s_i = \frac{1}{n_i} \sum_{j=1}^{n_i} r_{ij} = \frac{n_i - f_i}{n_i} = \hat{R}_i,$$

which is exactly the estimated reliability $\hat{R}_i$ by the Nelson model restricted to a subset of runs.

When the success rate is measured in units other than runs, the above TBRM need to be modified accordingly. Let t_{ij} be the transactions (or execution time) for run number j in subset i, then the individual success rate s_{ij} for that run is $s_{ij} = r_{ij}/t_{ij}$. The overall success rate s_i for subset i is the total number of successes S_i divided by the total transactions T_i. When the individual failure rates were weighed by the corresponding individual transactions (an option available in S-PLUS (StatSci, 1993), with modified Step 4 of Figure 21.3), we have:

$$s_i = \frac{\sum_{j=1}^{n_i} t_{ij} s_{ij}}{\sum_{j=1}^{n_i} t_j} = \frac{\sum_{j=1}^{n_i} r_{ij}}{\sum_{j=1}^{n_i} t_j} = \frac{S_i}{T_i} = \hat{R}_i.$$

Therefore, the success rate s_i for each subset i and the partition selection for both variations of the TBRMs can be automatically handled by S-PLUS.

Each node in a TBRM gives the estimated reliability for a specific subset of runs characterized by the series of split conditions from tree root to the current node, linking estimated reliability to input state or timing predictors. The selected partitions and associated split conditions are local optimums according to the selection criterion in Figure 21.3. For an interior node, if an input state variable is selected to partition the data set, it indicates that the product is more reliable in handling certain subsets of input states than others. This information can be used to identify problematic areas for focused remedial actions. On the other hand, if a time predictor is selected to partition the data set, it indicates that reliability change over time is predominant. The partition distinguishes one cluster of runs of higher estimated reliability from another one of lower reliability, separated by a cutoff time. Primary usages of TBRMs include:

- *Identifying problematic areas for focused remedial actions.* Subsets of runs with exceptionally low reliability can be easily identified in TBRMs and characterized by the split conditions leading to the corresponding tree nodes. The identification of such problematic areas represents opportunities for cost effective reliability improvement through focused remedial actions.

- *Monitoring reliability change and enhancing existing exit criteria.* The progression of TBRMs over time helps us track reliability progress and reliability distribution across different subsets of runs. A product should exit from testing only if it achieves uniformly high quality across different functions and components, as typified by TBRMs with major partitions defined on time variables, with later runs demonstrating higher reliability than earlier ones.

22.5.2 TBRM Applications

TBRMs have been used in several large software products developed in the IBM Software Solutions Toronto Laboratory, including products D and E discussed earlier. The data for product D in the subsequent example include several attributes:

- Timing: *date* (calendar *year, month, day*), *tday* (testing day), *et* (execution time).

- Input state: *SC* (scenario class), *SN* (scenario number), *log* (corresponding to a sub-product with a separate test log) and *tester*;

- Test *result*.

The tree in Figure 22.4, covering data at approximately the halfway point of testing for a sub-product in product D, represents typical results in the earlier part of testing. Here, the most important factor linked to the estimated reliability is the test scenario information (*SC* and *SN*), which indicates that different parts or function groups are of different quality. From this tree some subsets with very low success rates can be easily identified: the leftmost node, and the center node with $s = 0.143 \land n = 7$. Appropriate remedial actions were taken to detect and remove related faults.

In contrast, the tree in Figure 22.5, covering the whole testing phase for the same sub-product, represents typical results toward the end of testing. The time information has become a major factor linked to success rate, and all the subsets associated with low success rates are associated with early runs. The primary split at the root indicates that later test runs ($tday > 37.5$) have much higher success rate (0.846) than earlier ones (0.526 for $tday < 37.5$).

The final TBRM for the whole product was shown in Figure 19.5 (Chapter 19), which shares some of the common characteristics for late trees. In particular, tree nodes associated with late runs have substantially lower failure rate than early ones. As demonstrated by this example, a series of conscious decisions can be made throughout testing to focus on problematic areas for reliability improvement with the use of TBRMs, leading to products exiting testing with uniformly high quality.

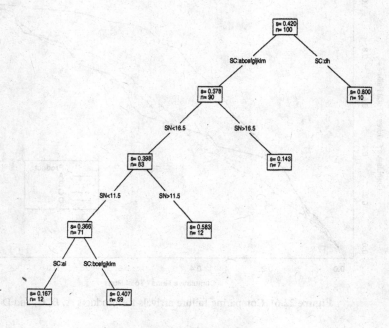

Figure 22.4   TBRM1 for product D

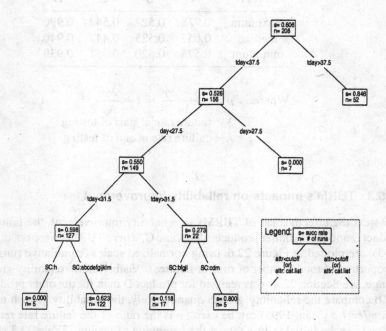

Figure 22.5   TBRM2 for product D

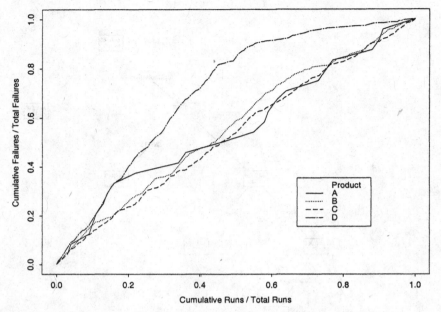

Figure 22.6   Comparing failure arrivals for products A, B, C, and D

Table 22.3   Comparing purification levels for products A, B, C, and D

| Purification | Product | | | |
Level ρ	A	B	C	D
maximum	0.715	0.527	0.542	0.990
median	0.653	0.525	0.447	0.940
minimum	0.578	0.520	0.351	0.939

Where: $\rho = \dfrac{\lambda_0 - \lambda_T}{\lambda_0} = 1 - \dfrac{\lambda_T}{\lambda_0}$

λ_0: failure rate at start of testing

λ_T: failure rate at end of testing

22.5.3   TBRM's impacts on reliability improvement

To assess the effectiveness of TBRMs in reliability improvement, the failure arrivals for product D and three similar products (A, B, and C, where TBRMs were not used (Tian et al., 1995)) are plotted in Figure 22.6, using normalized scales (cumulative runs or failures as a proportion of total number of runs or failures). Visibly more reliability growth (or slope change, see Section 22.4) was realized for product D than for the other products.

To compare the reliability growth quantitatively, the reliability growth measure *purification level* ρ (Tian, 1995) can be used. ρ is the ratio of the failure rate reduction during testing over the initial failure rate at the beginning of testing. Table 22.3 shows ρ values estimated by different fitted SRGMs, with the maximum, minimum, and median estimates shown, for the four products. In product D, where TBRMs were actively used, there is a much stronger reliability growth as captured in the purification level ρ than in the earlier products.

22.6 IMPLEMENTATION AND SOFTWARE TOOL SUPPORT

The implementation of the above approach to reliability analysis and improvement involves close collaboration between quality analysts and relevant test and development teams in defining measurements, gathering data, building TBRMs and SRGMs, and performing remedial actions. Weekly meetings were held to ensure timeliness and usefulness of analysis results in addressing project problems. Analyzing product reliability using SRGMs and TBRMs requires good understanding of the analysis techniques and familiarity with various software tools. This, in turn, requires the involvement of some dedicated quality analysts in the beginning, and the gradually maturation of the technology and its eventual transfer to the test and development teams.

An effective implementation of this strategy also calls for automated support for data collection, analysis, and result presentation. Among the various tools that can be adapted and used, there is no single tool that satisfies all the needs, and it is too costly to construct a comprehensive tool to satisfy all these needs. Consequently, a collection of loosely integrated tools were used to work together toward the common goals (Tian et al., 1997): Existing tools were adapted to support some individual needs, and special purpose tools were constructed where no appropriate tool existed. This approach can be considered an adaptation of the general tool support strategy we outlined in Chapter 18 to support SRE.

For reliability analysis and improvement, failure, timing and input information associated with individual test runs needs to be captured. In many large software development organizations, failure and test case information is routinely collected and tracked during software development and testing, using various configuration management and defect tracking tools. With minor modifications, failure, input state, and test run count can be easily captured using these tools. Execution time information can be captured by independent system monitors that record the utilization of system resources during testing. Transactions need to be captured using specifically designed data collection tools (Tian et al., 2004) or application program interfaces (APIs) (Tian and Palma, 1997).

The collected data need to be screened for errors and noise to ensure data consistency. They often need to be transformed into different forms for different analyses. Support for visualization and presentation of measurement data and analysis results was also needed, including:

- *Progress tracking*: Plots of testing effort (days, runs, execution time and transactions), and failures over calendar time can be used for progress tracking and schedule management.

- *Visualizing reliability growth*: Failure arrivals can be plotted against different measurements of time, such as in Figure 22.6, to examine reliability growth.

- *Presenting modeling result*: Modeling results can be presented in graphical forms like in Figure 22.3 for SRGMs or in Figure 22.5 for TBRMs.

The above functions are supported by the extended S-PLUS facilities and additional utility programs implemented in C and AWK by the quality analyst and other project personnel.

As mentioned in Section 22.5, the above TBRMs are supported by S-PLUS. Various SRGMs can also be easily implemented in S-PLUS by fitting the built-in nonlinear models to observed failures indexed by test runs, execution time or transactions. For example, the fitted models presented in Figure 22.3 were produced by S-PLUS. Existing reliability modeling tools, such as SMERFS (Farr and Smith, 1991), were used to fit other SRGMs, with the help of the utility programs mentioned above to make these tools more accessible and usable.

To summarize, an integrated implementation and support strategy for software reliability measurement and improvement is both feasible and effective, as demonstrated by the successful application of this approach in several large commercial software products developed in the IBM Software Solutions Toronto Laboratory. Careful planning for the implementations that minimize disruption to existing development process can help the reception and technology transfer. To accommodate the diverse data sources, and to support different analyses and usages of the analysis results, a comprehensive suite of software tools can be used. The tools can be integrated to work together by observing common data content and format rules, using common tools for multiple purposes, and using utility programs specifically constructed for tool integration.

22.7 SRE: SUMMARY AND PERSPECTIVES

Analysis and improvement of software reliability are of great practical importance to software development organizations and software users. Testing environment and software system characteristics have to be analyzed and matched against model assumptions to ensure that proper measurements and models are selected. As demonstrated in this chapter, properly selected measurement data can be fitted to SRGMs for reliability assessment. The TBRMs provide both reliability assessment and effective reliability improvement, combining the ability to provide overall reliability assessment by SRGMs and the ability to associate product reliability to input states in IDRMs.

Appropriate infrastructure and tool support are essential for industrial applications. The implementation described in this chapters has proved to be practical and effective in several large software products developed in the IBM Software Solutions Toronto Laboratory.

Current research and future development of software reliability engineering concentrate on several areas, including:

- *New application domains:* Traditionally, SRE has be used successfully in various large software systems such as telecommunication and commercial software systems, which are generally classified as *medium-reliable* systems in Chapter 19. One direction is to combine SRE with various safety analysis, assurance and improvement techniques (Leveson, 1995) to work for safety-critical systems. The other direction is to adapt SRE to work for mass-market, low-cost software, which can be restarted easily without incurring much damage if failures occur, and where other quality concerns, such as usability and maintainability, may be more important. Some systems, such as web-based applications, cover a whole spectrum of concerns and variety of systems both in size and in functionality (Kallepalli and Tian, 2001; Tian et al., 2004). These new application domains require additional research to adopt and mature SRE for effective applications to ensure and improve reliability for such systems.

- *Early reliability prediction and improvement:* One of the most severe drawbacks of traditional SRE is its late applicability, although TBRMs described in this chapter pushed it earlier to the early part of system testing. However, much of the quality assurance activities that can be applied in earlier phases of development, such as inspection and formal verification, are not typically used with SRE. Again, certain adaptations and customizations are necessary to allow us to predict and improve product reliability based on data from these early activities (Tian, 1999).

- *Reliability composition and maximization:* Another trend in software engineering is the component-based software engineering, or CBSE, where software systems are assembled from reusable components instead of developed from scratch. This new paradigm also calls for appropriate adaptation of SRE, so that component reliability can be assessed, and the whole system can be assembled to maximize overall system reliability based on the different system architecture and interconnections among the components. Component OPs (Hamlet et al., 2001) can also be developed to ensure component reliability, which is of critical importance to CBSE.

- *Testing-reliability relation*: Some investigations focus on the relationship between different types of testing and reliability (Duran and Ntafos, 1984; Hamlet and Taylor, 1990; Tsoukalas et al., 1993; Frankl et al., 1998). A good understanding of this relationship would provide a means to assess product reliability earlier during software development based on testing techniques used, time, structure, coverage, etc. (Horgan and Mathur, 1995; Chen et al., 2001; Malaiya et al., 2002), before statistical testing based on operational profiles (OPs) can be used on the whole system.

The above effort should help us apply SRE effectively to a wider variety of products, with product reliability measured early and improved continuously throughout the software development process to meet and exceed our customers' quality expectations.

Problems

22.1 Among the quality measures, defect count, defect density, reliability, and safety, which one is more meaningful to customers and users? Why?

22.2 Can you still estimate your system reliability if coverage-based testing instead of OP-based statistical testing is used?

22.3 Characterize the software testing environment in your organization, and answer the question: Is software reliability analysis and modeling applicable to your environment?

22.4 Among the existing SRGMs and IDRMs, the simplest models are typically the most commonly used ones. Explain why.

22.5 When there is a mismatch between your reliability model and your testing and defect data, what would you do? Change the model? Transform or change the data? Or do something else?

22.6 Software reliability engineering is both an active area of research and an area with great potentials for practical applications. What do you think is the potential for its application in the web-based applications and software, or other emerging market?

BIBLIOGRAPHY

Aldemir, T., Siu., N., Mosleh, A., Cacciabue, C., and Goktepe, P. G. (1994). *Reliability and Safety Assessment of Dynamic Process Systems*. NATO ASI Series. Springer-Verlag, New York.

Allen, F. E. and Cocke, J. (1972). Graph theoretic constructs for program control flow analysis. Technical Report RC3923, IBM T. J. Watson Research Center.

Avižienis, A. A. (1995). The methodology of N-version programming. In Lyu, M. R., editor, *Software Fault Tolerance*, pp. 23–46. John Wiley & Sons, Inc., New York.

Avritzer, A. and Weyuker, E. J. (1995). The automatic generation of load test suites and the assessment of the resulting software. *IEEE Trans. on Software Engineering*, 21(9):705–716.

Bachiochi, D. J., Berstene, M. C., Chouinard, E. F., Conlan, N. M., Danchak, M. M., Furey, T., Neligon, C. A., and Way, D. (1997). Usability studies and designing navigational aids for the World Wide Web. *Computer Networks and ISDN Systems*, 29(8-13):1489–1496.

Basili, V. R. (1995). The experience factory and its relationship to other quality approaches. In Zelkowitz, M. V., editor, *Advances in Computers, Vol. 41*, pp. 65–82. Academic Press, San Diego, CA.

Basili, V. R. and Mills, H. D. (1982). Understanding and documenting programs. *IEEE Trans. on Software Engineering*, 8(3):270–283.

Basili, V. R. and Rombach, H. D. (1988). The TAME project: Towards improvement-oriented software environments. *IEEE Trans. on Software Engineering*, 14(6):758–773.

Basili, V. R., Zelkowitz, M. V., McGarry, F. E., Page, J., Waligora, S., and Pajerski, R. (1995). SEL's software process-improvement program. *IEEE Software*, 12(6):83–87.

Beck, K. (1999). *Extreme Programming Explained: Embrace Change*. Addison-Wesley, Reading, MA.

Beck, K. (2003). *Test-Driven Development*. Addison-Wesley, Reading, MA.

Behlandorf, B. (1996). *Running a Perfect Web Site with Apache, 2nd Ed.* MacMillan Computer Publishing, New York.

Beizer, B. (1990). *Software Testing Techniques, 2nd Ed.* International Thomson Computer Press, Boston.

Beizer, B. (1995). *Black-Box Testing: Techniques for Functional Testing of Software and Systems*. John Wiley & Sons, Inc., New York.

Beizer, B. (1998). Software is different. *Software Quality Professional*, 1(1):44–54.

Bhandari, I., Halliday, M., Tarver, E., Brown, D., Chaar, J., and Chillarege, R. (1993). A case study of software process improvement during development. *IEEE Trans. on Software Engineering*, 19(12):1157–1170.

Biffl, S. and Halling, M. (2003). Investigating the defect detection effectiveness and cost benefit of nominal inspection teams. *IEEE Trans. on Software Engineering*, 29(5):385–397.

Binder, R. V. (2000). *Testing Object Oriented Systems, Models, Patterns, and Tools*. Addison-Wesley, Reading, MA.

Bisant, D. B. and Lyle, J. R. (1989). A two-person inspection method to improve programming productivity. *IEEE Trans. on Software Engineering*, 15(10):1294–1304.

Black, R. (2004). *Critical Testing Processes*. Addison-Wesley, Reading, MA.

Blum, B. I. (1992). *Software Engineering: A Holistic View*. Oxford University Press, New York.

Boehm, B. and Basili, V. R. (2001). Software defect reduction top 10 list. *IEEE Computer*, 34(1):135–137.

Boehm, B. W. (1981). *Software Engineering Economics*. Prentice-Hall, Englewood Cliffs, NJ.

Boehm, B. W. (1988). A spiral model of software development and enhancement. *IEEE Computer*, 21:61–72.

Boehm, B. W. (1991). Software risk management: Principles and practices. *IEEE Software*, 8(1):32–41.

Bowers, N. (1996). Weblint: Quality assurance for the World-Wide Web. *Computer Networks and ISDN Systems*, 28(7-11):1283–1290.

Briand, L. C., Basili, V. R., and Hetmanski, C. J. (1993). Developing interpretable models with optimal set reduction for identifying high-risk software components. *IEEE Trans. on Software Engineering*, 19(11):1028–1044.

Briand, L. C., Bunse, C., and Daly, J. W. (2001). A controlled experiment for evaluating quality guidelines on the maintainability of object-oriented designs. *IEEE Trans. on Software Engineering*, 27(6):513–530.

Brooks, F. P. (1987). No silver bullet, essence and accidents of software engineering. *IEEE Computer*, 20(4):10–19.

Brooks, F. P. (1995). *The Mythical Man-Month: Essays on Software Engineering, Anniversary Edition*. Addison-Wesley, Reading, MA.

Brown, J. R. and Lipow, M. (1975). Testing for software reliability. In *Proc. Int. Conf. Reliable Software*, pp. 518–527, Los Angeles.

Burnstein, I. (2003). *Practical Software Testing*. Springer-Verlag, New York.

Buss, E. and Henshaw, J. (1992). Experiences in program understanding. Technical Report TR-74.105, IBM PRGS Toronto Laboratory.

Card, D. N. and Glass, R. L. (1990). *Measuring Software Design Quality*. Prentice-Hall, Englewood Cliffs, NJ.

Cárdenas-García, S. R., Tian, J., and Zelkowitz, M. V. (1992). An application of decision theory for the evaluation of software prototypes. *Journal of Systems and Software*, 19(1):27–39.

Cárdenas-García, S. R. and Zelkowitz, M. V. (1991). A management tool for evaluation of software designs. *IEEE Trans. on Software Engineering*, 17(9):961–971.

Chaar, J., Halliday, M., Bhandari, I., and Chillarege, R. (1993). In-process evaluation for software inspection and test. *IEEE Trans. on Software Engineering*, 19(11):1055–1070.

Charette, R. (1989). *Software Engineering Risk Analysis and Management*. McGraw-Hill, New York.

Chen, M. H., Lyu, M. R., and Wong, W. E. (2001). Effect of code coverage on software reliability measurement. *IEEE Trans. on Reliability*, 50(2):165–170.

Chillarege, R., Bhandari, I., Chaar, J., Halliday, M., Moebus, D., Ray, B., and Wong, M.-Y. (1992). Orthogonal defect classification — a concept for in-process measurements. *IEEE Trans. on Software Engineering*, 18(11):943–956.

Chow, T. S. (1978). Testing software design modeled by finite-state machines. *IEEE Trans. on Software Engineering*, 4(3):178–187.

Chruscielski, K. and Tian, J. (1997). An operational profile for the cartridge support software. In *Proc. 8th Int. Symp. on Software Reliability Engineering*, pp. 203–212.

Clark, L. A. and Pregibon, D. (1993). Tree based models. In Chambers, J. M. and Hastie, T. J., editors, *Statistical Models in S*, chapter 9, pp. 377–419. Chapman & Hall, London.

Clarke, L. A. (1976). A system to generate test data and symbolically execute programs. *IEEE Trans. on Software Engineering*, 2(3):215–222.

Clarke, L. A., Hassel, J., and Richardson, D. J. (1982). A close look at domain testing. *IEEE Trans. on Software Engineering*, 8:380–390.

Cohen, E. I. (1978). *A Finite Domain-Testing Strategy for Computer Program Testing.* Ph.D. thesis, Ohio State University.

Denning, P. J. (1992). What is software quality? *Communications of the ACM*, 35(1):13–15.

Deo, N. (1974). *Graph Theory with Applications to Engineering and Computer Science.* Prentice-Hall, Englewood Cliffs, NJ.

Dijkstra, E. W. (1968). Go To statement considered harmful. *Communications of the ACM*, 11(3):147–148.

Dijkstra, E. W. (1975). Guarded commands, nondeterminacy, and formal derivation of programs. *Communications of the ACM*, 18(8):453–457. EWD472.

Dromey, R. G. (1995). A model for software product quality. *IEEE Trans. on Software Engineering*, 13(2):146–162.

Dromey, R. G. (1996). Cornering the chimera. *IEEE Software*, 13(1):33–43.

Dugan, J. B. (1995). Software system analysis using fault trees. In Lyu, M. R., editor, *Handbook of Software Reliability Engineering*, pp. 615–659. McGraw-Hill, New York.

Dunsmore, A., Roper, M., and Wood, M. (2003a). The development and evaluation of three diverse techniques for object-oriented code inspection. *IEEE Trans. on Software Engineering*, 29(8):677–686.

Dunsmore, A., Roper, M., and Wood, M. (2003b). Practical code inspection techniques for object-oriented systems: An experimental comparison. *IEEE Software*, 20(4):21–29.

Duran, J. W. and Ntafos, S. C. (1984). An evaluation of random testing. *IEEE Trans. on Software Engineering*, SE-10(4):438–444.

Fagan, M. E. (1976). Design and code inspections to reduce errors in program development. *IBM Systems Journal*, 3:182–211.

Farr, W. J. and Smith, O. D. (1991). Statistical modeling and estimation of reliability functions for software (SMERFS) users guide. Technical Report NSWC TR 84-373, Revision 2, Naval Surface Warfare Center.

Fenton, N. and Pfleeger, S. L. (1996). *Software Metrics: A Rigorous and Practical Approach, 2nd Edition.* PWS Publishing, Boston.

Frankl, P. G., Hamlet, R. G., Littlewood, B., and Strigini, L. (1998). Evaluating testing methods by delivered reliability. *IEEE Trans. on Software Engineering*, 24(8):586–601.

Frankl, P. G. and Weyuker, E. J. (2000). Testing software to detect and reduce risk. *Journal of Systems and Software*, 53(3):275–286.

Fromme, B. (1998). Web software testing: Challenges and solutions. In *InterWorks'98*.

Garg, V. K. (1999). *IS-95 CDMA & CDMA 2000: Cellular/PCS Systems Implementation*. Prentice-Hall, Englewood Cliffs, NJ.

Gerhart, S. A., Craigen, D., and Ralston, T. (1994). Experience with formal methods in critical systems. *IEEE Software*, 11(1):20–28.

Ghezzi, C., Jazayeri, M., and Mandrioli, D. (2003). *Fundamentals of Software Engineering, 2nd Edition*. Prentice-Hall, Englewood Cliffs, NJ.

Gilb, T. and Graham, D. (1993). *Software Inspection*. Addison-Wesley Longman, London.

Goel, A. L. (1985). Software reliability models: Assumptions, limitations, and applicability. *IEEE Trans. on Software Engineering*, 11(12):1411–1423.

Goel, A. L. and Okumoto, K. (1979). A time dependent error detection rate model for software reliability and other performance measures. *IEEE Trans. on Reliability*, 28(3):206–211.

Goodenough, J. B. and Gerhart, S. A. (1975). Toward a theory of test data selection. *IEEE Trans. on Software Engineering*, 1:156–173.

Gries, D. (1987). *The Science of Programming*. Springer-Verlag, New York.

Guttag, J. V., Horowitz, E., and Musser, D. R. (1978). Abstract data types and software validation. *Communications of the ACM*, 21(12).

Hamlet, D., Mason, D., and Woit, D. (2001). Theory of software reliability based on components. In *Proc. 23rd Int. Conf. on Software Engineering*, pp. 361–370, Toronto.

Hamlet, D. and Taylor, R. (1990). Partition testing does not inspire confidence. *IEEE Trans. on Software Engineering*, 16(12):1402–1411.

Hamlet, R. G. (1977). Testing programs with the aid of a compiler. *IEEE Trans. on Software Engineering*, 3:279–290.

Hatton, L. (1998). Does OO sync with how we think? *IEEE Software*, 15(3):46–54.

Henley, E. J. and Kumamoto, H. (1981). *Reliability Engineering and Risk Assessment*. Prentice-Hall, Englewood Cliffs, NJ.

Hoare, C. A. R. (1969). An axiomatic basis for computer programming. *Communications of the ACM*, 12(10):576–580.

Holmes, J. S. (2003). Identifying code-inspection improvements using statistical black belt techniques. *Software Quality Professional*, 6(1):4–14.

Horgan, J. R. and Mathur, A. P. (1995). Software testing and reliability. In Lyu, M. R., editor, *Handbook of Software Reliability Engineering*, pp. 531–566. McGraw-Hill, New York.

Howden, W. E. (1976). Reliability of the path analysis testing strategy. *IEEE Trans. on Software Engineering*, 2(3):208–215.

Howden, W. E. (1980). Functional testing. *IEEE Trans. on Software Engineering*, SE-6(2):162–169.

Howden, W. E. (1982). Weak mutation testing and completeness of test sets. *IEEE Trans. on Software Engineering*, SE-8:371–379.

Humphrey, W. (1998). The software quality profile. *Software Quality Professional*, 1(1):8–18.

Humphrey, W. S. (1989). *Managing the Software Process*. Addison-Wesley, Reading, MA.

Humphrey, W. S. (1995). *A Discipline for Software Engineering*. Addison-Wesley, Reading, MA.

Huo, Q., Zhu, H., and Greenwood, S. (2003). A multi-agent software environment for testing web-based applications. In *Proc. 27th Int. Computer Software and Applications Conf.*, pp. 210–215, Dallas, TX.

IBM (1991). *Programming Process Architecture, Version 2.1*. IBM.

IEEE (1990). *IEEE Standard Glossary of Software Engineering Terminology*. IEEE STD 610.12-1990.

ISO (2001). *ISO/IEC 9126-1:2001 Software Engineering – Product Quality – Part 1: Quality Model*. ISO.

Jain, A. K., Mao, J., and Mohiuddin, K. M. (1996). Artificial neural networks: A tutorial. *IEEE Computer*, 29(3):31–44.

Jelinski, Z. and Moranda, P. L. (1972). Software reliability research. In Freiberger, W., editor, *Statistical Computer Performance Evaluation*, pp. 365–484. Academic Press, New York.

Jeng, B. and Weyuker, E. J. (1994). A simplified domain-testing strategy. *ACM Trans. on Software Engineering and Methodology*, 3(3):254–270.

Kallepalli, C. and Tian, J. (2001). Measuring and modeling usage and reliability for statistical web testing. *IEEE Trans. on Software Engineering*, 27(11):1023–1036.

Kan, S. H. (2002). *Metrics and Models in Software Quality Engineering, 2/e*. Addison-Wesley, Reading, MA.

Kaner, C., Falk, J., and Nguyen, H. Q. (1999). *Testing Computer Software*. John Wiley & Sons, Inc., New York.

Karlin, S. and Taylor, H. M. (1975). *A First Course in Stochastic Processes, 2nd Ed*. Academic Press, New York.

Khoshgoftaar, T. M., Allen, E. B., Kalaichelvan, K. S., and Goel, N. (1996). Early quality prediction: A case study in telecommunications. *IEEE Software*, 13(1):65–71.

Khoshgoftaar, T. M. and Szabo, R. M. (1996). Using neural networks to predict software faults during testing. *IEEE Trans. on Reliability*, 45(3):456–462.

King, S., Hammond, J., Chapman, R., and Pryor, A. (2000). Is proof more cost-effective than testing. *IEEE Trans. on Software Engineering*, 26(8):675–686.

Kitchenham, B. and Pfleeger, S. L. (1996). Software quality: The elusive target. *IEEE Software*, 13(1):12–21.

Knight, J. C. and Myers, E. A. (1992). An improved inspection technique. *Communications of the ACM*, 36(11):51–61.

Knuth, D. E. (1973). *The Art of Computer Programming*. Addison-Wesley, Reading, MA.

Koru, A. G. and Tian, J. (2003). An empirical comparison and characterization of high defect and high complexity modules. *Journal of Systems and Software*, 67(3):153–163.

Koru, A. G. and Tian, J. (2004). Defect handling in medium and large open source software projects. *IEEE Software*, 21(4):54–61.

Krishnan, M. S. and Kellner, M. I. (1999). Measuring process consistency: Implications for reducing software defects. *IEEE Trans. on Software Engineering*, 25(6):800–815.

Kung, D. C., Hsia, P., and Gao, J. (1998). *Testing Object-Oriented Software*. IEEE Computer Society Press, Los Alamitos, CA.

Kuvaja, P., Simila, J., Krzanik, L., Bicego, A., Koch, G., and Saukonen, S. (1994). *Software Process Assessment and Improvement: the BOOTSTRAP Approach*. Blackwell Publishers, Oxford, UK.

Leveson, N. G. (1995). *Safeware: System Safety and Computers*. Addison-Wesley, Reading, MA.

Li, Z. and Tian, J. (2003). Analyzing web logs to identify common errors and improve web reliability. In *Proc. IADIS International Conference on e-Society*, pp. 235–242, Lisbon, Portugal.

Lu, P. and Tian, J. (1993a). Applying software reliability engineering in large-scale software development. In *Proc. 3rd Int. Conf. on Software Quality*, pp. 323–330, Lake Tahoe, NV.

Lu, P. and Tian, J. (1993b). Software reliability engineering experience in the IBM Toronto Laboratory. In *Proc. IBM Software Engineering ITL Conf.*, pp. 459–467, Toronto.

Luqi (1989). Software evolution through rapid prototyping. *IEEE Computer*, pp. 13–25.

Lutz, R. R. and Mikulski, I. C. (2004). Ongoing requirements discovery in high-integrity systems. *IEEE Software*, 21(2):19–25.

Lyu, M. R., editor (1995a). *Handbook of Software Reliability Engineering*. McGraw-Hill, New York.

Lyu, M. R., editor (1995b). *Software Fault Tolerance*. John Wiley & Sons, Inc., New York.

Lyu, M. R. and Avižienis, A. A. (1992). Assuring design diversity in N-version software: A design paradigm for N-version programming. In Meyer, J. F. and Schlichting, R. D., editors, *Dependable Computing for Critical Applications 2*. Springer-Verlag, New York.

Ma, L. and Tian, J. (2003). Analyzing errors and referral pairs to characterize common problems and improve web reliability. In *Proc. 3rd International Conference on Web Engineering*, pp. 314–323, Oviedo, Spain.

Mackenzie, D. (1994). Computer-related accidental death: An empirical exploration. *Science and Public Policy*, pp. 233–248.

Maddux, R. (1985). *A study of program structure, Ph.D. dissertation*. Ph.D. thesis, University of Waterloo.

Malaiya, Y. K., Li, M. N., Bieman, J. M., and Karcich, R. (2002). Software reliability growth with test coverage. *IEEE Trans. on Reliability*, 51(4):420–426.

Malaiya, Y. K. and Srimani, P. K. (1990). *Software Reliability Models: Theoretical Developments, Evaluation & Applications*. IEEE Computer Society Press, Los Alamitos, CA.

DeMillo, R. A., McCracken, W. M., Martin, R. J., and Passafiume, J. F. (1987). *Software Testing and Evaluation*. Benjamin/Cummings, Menlo Park, CA.

McAllister, D. F. and Vouk, M. A. (1995). Fault-tolerant software reliability engineering. In Lyu, M. R., editor, *Handbook of Software Reliability Engineering*, pp. 567–614. McGraw-Hill, New York.

McCabe, T. J. (1976). A complexity measure. *IEEE Trans. on Software Engineering*, 2(6):308–320.

Mealy, G. H. (1955). A method for synthesizing sequential circuits. *Bell System Technical Journal*, 34:1045–1079.

Miller, E. (2000). *The Website Quality Challenge*. Software Research Inc., San Francisco, CA.

Miller, E. F. and Howden, W. E. (1981). *Tutorial: Software Testing and Validation Techniques, 2nd Ed.* IEEE Computer Society.

Mills, H. D. (1972). On the statistical validation of computer programs. Technical Report 72-6015, IBM Federal Syst. Div.

Mills, H. D., Basili, V. R., Gannon, J. D., and Hamlet, R. G. (1987a). *Principles of Computer Programming: A Mathematical Approach*. Alan and Bacon, Inc., Boston.

Mills, H. D., Dyer, M., and Linger, R. C. (1987b). Cleanroom software engineering. *IEEE Software*, 4(5):19–24.

Moore, E. F. (1956). Gedanken experiments on sequential machines. *Automata Studies. Annals of Mathematical Studies #34*.

Munson, J. C. and Khoshgoftaar, T. M. (1992). The detection of fault-prone programs. *IEEE Trans. on Software Engineering*, 18(5):423–433.

Musa, J. D. (1975). A theory of software reliability and its application. *IEEE Trans. on Software Engineering*, 1(3):312–327.

Musa, J. D. (1993). Operational profiles in software reliability engineering. *IEEE Software*, 10(2):14–32.

Musa, J. D. (1998). *Software Reliability Engineering*. McGraw-Hill, New York.

Musa, J. D. and Everett, W. W. (1990). Software-reliability engineering: Technology for the 1990s. *IEEE Software*, 7(6):36–43.

Musa, J. D., Iannino, A., and Okumoto, K. (1987). *Software Reliability: Measurement, Prediction, Application*. McGraw-Hill, New York.

Musa, J. D. and Okumoto, K. (1984). A logarithmic Poisson execution time model for software reliability measurement. In *Proc. 7th Int. Conf. on Software Engineering*, pp. 230–238, Orlando, FL.

Myers, G. J. (1979). *The Art of Software Testing*. John Wiley & Sons, Inc., New York.

Nelson, E. (1978). Estimating software reliability from test data. *Microelectronics and Reliability*, 17(1):67–73.

Offutt, J. (2002). Quality attributes of web applications. *IEEE Software*, 19(2):25–32.

Oivo, M. and Basili, V. R. (1992). Representing software engineering models: The TAME goal oriented approach. *IEEE Trans. on Software Engineering*, 18(10):886–898.

Parnas, D. L. (1972). On the criteria to be used in decomposing systems into modules. *Communications of the ACM*, 15(12):1053–1058.

Parnas, D. L. and Madey, J. (1995). Functional documentation for computer systems. *Sci. Comput. Program*, 25(1):41–61.

Parnas, D. L. and Weiss, D. M. (1985). Active design reviews: Principles and practices. In *Proc. 8th Int. Conf. on Software Engineering*, pp. 215–222. IEEE Computer Society Press.

Paulk, M., Weber, C. V., Garcia, S. M., Chrissis, M. B., and Bush, M. W. (1993). Key practices of the capability maturity model, version 1.1. Technical Report CMU/SEI-93-TR-24, DTIC Number ADA263432, Software Engineering Institute.

Paulk, M. C., Weber, C. V., Curtis, B., and Chrissis, M. B. (1995). *The Capability Maturity Model: Guidelines for Improving the Software Process*. Addison-Wesley, Reading, MA.

Peterson, J. L. (1981). *Petri Net Theory and the Modeling of Systems*. Prentice-Hall, Englewood Cliffs, NJ.

Pfleeger, S. L. and Hatton, L. (1997). Investigating the influence of formal methods. *IEEE Computer*, 30(2):33–43.

Pfleeger, S. L., Hatton, L., and Howell, C. C. (2002). *Solid Software*. Prentice-Hall, Upper Saddle River, NJ.

Porter, A. A. and Johnson, P. M. (1997). Assessing software review meetings: Results of a comparative analysis of two experimental studies. *IEEE Trans. on Software Engineering*, 23(3):129–145.

Porter, A. A. and Selby, R. W. (1990). Empirically guided software development using metric-based classification trees. *IEEE Software*, 7(2):46–54.

Porter, A. A., Siy, H., and Votta, L. G. (1996). A review of software inspections. In Zelkowitz, M. V., editor, *Advances in Computers, Vol. 42*, pp. 39–76. Academic Press, San Diego, CA.

Porter, A. A. and Votta, L. G. (1997). What makes inspections work. *IEEE Software*, 14(5):99–102.

Prahalad, C. K. and Krishnan, M. S. (1999). The new meaning of quality in the information age. *Harvard Business Review*, 77(5):109–118.

Pratt, J. W., Raiffa, H., and Schlaifer, R. (1965). *Introduction to Statistical Decision Theory*. McGraw-Hill, New York.

Pratt, T. W. and Zelkowitz, M. V. (2001). *Programming Languages: Design and Implementation*. Prentice-Hall, Upper Saddle River, NJ.

Prechelt, L. (2000). An empirical comparison of seven programming languages. *IEEE Computer*, 33(10):23–29.

Putnam, L. H. (1978). A general empirical solution to the macro software sizing and estimation problem. *IEEE Trans. on Software Engineering*, pp. 345–361.

Ramamoorthy, C. V. and Bastani, F. B. (1982). Software reliability: Status and perspectives. *IEEE Trans. on Software Engineering*, 8(4):359–371.

Raymond, E. S. (1999). *The Cathedral and the Bazaar: Musings on Linux and Open Source by an Accidental Revolutionary*. O'Reilly and Associates, Sebastopol, CA.

Reichheld Jr., F. F. and Sasser, W. E. (1990). Zero defections: Quality comes to services. *Harvard Business Review*, 68(5):105–111.

Rosenblum, D. S. and Weyuker, E. J. (1997). Using coverage information to predict the cost-effectiveness of regression testing strategies. *IEEE Trans. on Software Engineering*, 23(3):146–156.

Rothermel, G. and Harrold, M. J. (1996). Analyzing regression test selection techniques. *IEEE Trans. on Software Engineering*, 22(8):529–551.

Seaman, C. B. and Basili, V. R. (1997). Communication and organization in software development: An empirical study. *IBM Systems Journal*, 36.

Seaman, C. B. and Basili, V. R. (1998). Communication and organization: An empirical study of discussion in inspection meetings. *IEEE Trans. on Software Engineering*, 24(7):559–572.

Selby, R. W., Basili, V. R., and Baker, F. T. (1987). Cleanroom software development: An empirical evaluation. *IEEE Trans. on Software Engineering*, SE-13(9):1027–1037.

Selby, R. W. and Porter, A. A. (1988). Learning from examples: Generation and evaluation of decision trees for software resource analysis. *IEEE Trans. on Software Engineering*, 14(12):1743–1757.

Shneiderman, B. (1977). Measuring computer program quality and comprehension. *Int. J. of Man-Machine Studies*, 9.

Shneiderman, B. (1980). *Software Psychology*. Winthrop Publishers, Cambridge, MA.

Spiliopoulou, M. (2000). Web usage mining for web site evaluation. *Communications of the ACM*, 43(8):127–134.

StatSci (1993). *S-PLUS Programmer's Manual, Version 3.2*. StatSci, A Division of Math-Soft, Inc., Seattle, WA.

Tai, K.-C. (1984). A program complexity metric based on data flow information in control graphs. In *7th Int. Conf. on Software Engineering*, pp. 239–248, Orlando, FL.

Tanik, M. M. and Yeh, R. T. (1989). Rapid prototyping in software development. *IEEE Computer*, 22:9–10.

Thayer, R., Lipow, M., and Nelson, E. (1978). *Software Reliability*. North-Holland, New York.

TIA/EIA (1994). *Mobile Station-Base Station Compatibility Standard for Dual Mode Wideband Spread Spectrum Cellular System, Version 0.04*. TIA/EIA/IS-95-A.

Tian, J. (1995). Integrating time domain and input domain analyses of software reliability using tree-based models. *IEEE Trans. on Software Engineering*, 21(12):945–958.

Tian, J. (1996). An integrated approach to test tracking and analysis. *Journal of Systems and Software*, 35(2):127–140.

Tian, J. (1998). Reliability measurement, analysis, and improvement for large software systems. In Zelkowitz, M. V., editor, *Advances in Computers, Vol. 46: The Engineering of Large Systems*, chapter 4, pp. 159–235. Academic Press, San Diego, CA.

Tian, J. (1999). Measurement and continuous improvement of software reliability throughout software life-cycle. *Journal of Systems and Software*, 47(2-3):189–195.

Tian, J. (2000). Risk identification techniques for defect reduction and quality improvement. *Software Quality Professional*, 2(2):32–41.

Tian, J. (2001). Quality assurance alternatives and techniques: A defect-based survey and analysis. *Software Quality Professional*, 3(3):6–18.

Tian, J. (2002). Better reliability assessment and prediction through data clustering. *IEEE Trans. on Software Engineering*, 28(10):997–1007.

Tian, J. (2004). Quality-evaluation models and measurements. *IEEE Software*, 21(3):84–91.

Tian, J. and Henshaw, J. (1994). Tree-based defect analysis in testing. In *Proc. 4th Int. Conf. on Software Quality*, McLean, VA.

Tian, J. and Lin, E. (1998). Unified Markov models for software testing, performance evaluation, and reliability analysis. In *4th ISSAT International Conference on Reliability and Quality in Design*, Seattle, WA.

Tian, J., Lu, P., and Palma, J. (1995). Test execution based reliability measurement and modeling for large commercial software. *IEEE Trans. on Software Engineering*, 21(5):405–414.

Tian, J., Ma, L., Li, Z., and Koru, A. G. (2003). A hierarchical strategy for testing web-based applications and ensuring their reliability. In *Proc. 27th Int. Computer Software and Applications Conf. (1st IEEE Workshop on Web-based Systems and Applications)*, pp. 702–707, Dallas, TX.

Tian, J. and Nguyen, A. (1999). Statistical web testing and reliability analysis. In *Proc. 9th Int. Conf. on Software Quality*, pp. 263–274, Cambridge, MA.

Tian, J., Nguyen, A., Allen, C., and Appan, R. (2001). Experience with identifying and characterizing problem prone modules in telecommunication software systems. *Journal of Systems and Software*, 57(3):207–215.

Tian, J. and Palma, J. (1997). Test workload measurement and reliability analysis for large commercial software systems. *Annals of Software Engineering*, 4:201–222.

Tian, J. and Palma, J. (1998). Analyzing and improving reliability: A tree based approach. *IEEE Software*, 15(2):97–104.

Tian, J., Rudraraju, S., and Li, Z. (2004). Evaluating web software reliability based on workload and failure data extracted from server logs. *IEEE Trans. on Software Engineering*, 30(11):754–769.

Tian, J. and Troster, J. (1998). A comparison of measurement and defect characteristics of new and legacy software systems. *Journal of Systems and Software*, 44(2):135–146.

Tian, J., Troster, J., and Palma, J. (1997). Tool support for software measurement, analysis, and improvement. *Journal of Systems and Software*, 39(2):165–178.

Trivedi, K. S. (2001). *Probability and Statistics with Reliability, Queuing, and Computer Science Applications, 2nd Edition*. John Wiley & Sons, Inc., New York.

Troster, J. and Tian, J. (1995). Measurement and defect modeling for a legacy software system. *Annals of Software Engineering*, 1:95–118.

Troster, J. and Tian, J. (1996). Exploratory analysis tools for tree-based models in software measurement and analysis. In *Proc. 4th Int'l Symp. on Assessment of Software Tools*, pp. 7–17, Toronto.

Tsoukalas, M. Z., Duran, J. W., and Ntafos, S. C. (1993). On some reliability estimation problems in random and partition testing. *IEEE Trans. on Software Engineering*, 19(7):687–697.

van Solingen, R. and Berghout, E. (1999). *The Goal/Question/Metric Method: A Practical Method for Quality Improvement of Software Development*. McGraw-Hill, New York.

Vatanasombut, B., Stylianou, A. C., and Igbaria, M. (2004). How to retain online customers. *Communications of the ACM*, 47(6):65–69.

Venables, W. N. and Ripley, B. D. (1994). *Modern Applied Statistics with S-Plus*. Springer-Verlag, New York.

Vixie, P. (1999). *Open Sources: Voices from the Open Source Revolution*, chapter Software Engineering, pp. 91–100. O'Reilly & Associates, Inc, Sebastopol, CA.

Voas, J. (1998). *Software Fault Injection - Inoculating Programs Against Errors*. Wiley Computer Publishing, New York.

Voas, J. M. (1999). Certifying software for high-assurance environments. *IEEE Software*, 16(4):48–54.

Voas, J. M. (2000). Developing a usage-based software certification process. *IEEE Computer*, 16(8):32–37.

von Mayrhauser, A. (1990). *Software Engineering: Methods and Management*. Academic Press, San Diego, CA.

Wallace, D. R., Ippolito, L. M., and Cuthill, B. (1996). *Reference Information for the Software Verification and Validation Process*. NIST Special Publication 500-234.

Weiser, M. D. (1984). Program slicing. *IEEE Trans. on Software Engineering*, 10:352–357.

Weyuker, E. J. (1998). Testing component-based software: A cautionary tale. *IEEE Software*, 15(5):54–59.

Weyuker, E. J. and Jeng, B. (1991). Analyzing partition test strategies. *IEEE Trans. on Software Engineering*, 17(7):703–711.

Weyuker, E. J., Ostrand, T. J., Brophy, J., and Prasad, R. (2000). Clearing a career path for software testers. *IEEE Software*, 17(2):76–82.

White, L. J. and Cohen, E. I. (1980). A domain strategy for computer program testing. *IEEE Trans. on Software Engineering*, 6:247–257.

Whittaker, J. A. (2001). Software's invisible users. *IEEE Software*, 18(3):84–88.

Whittaker, J. A. and Poore, J. H. (1993). Markov analysis of software specifications. *ACM Trans. on Software Engineering and Methodology*, 2(1):93–106.

Whittaker, J. A. and Thomason, M. G. (1994). A Markov chain model for statistical software testing. *IEEE Trans. on Software Engineering*, 20(10):812–824.

Wiener, R. (1998). Watch your language! *IEEE Software*, 15(3):55–56.

Wirth, N. (1995). A plea for lean software. *IEEE Computer*, 28(2):64–68.

Yamada, S., Ohba, M., and Osaki, S. (1983). S-shaped reliability growth modeling for software error detection. *IEEE Trans. on Reliability*, 32(5):475–478.

Yih, S. and Tian, J. (1998). Developing and checking prescriptive specifications for safety improvement. *Microprocessors and Microsystems*, 21(10):587–594.

Zelkowitz, M. V. (1988). Resource utilization during software development. *Journal of Systems and Software*, 8:331–336.

Zelkowitz, M. V. (1993). Role of verification in the software specification process. In Yovits, M. C., editor, *Advances in Computers, Vol. 36*, pp. 43–109. Academic Press, San Diego, CA.

Zhao, L. and Elbaum, S. (2003). Quality assurance under the open source development model. *Journal of Systems and Software*, 66(1):65–75.

INDEX

Printed in the United States
by Bookmasters

Printed in the United States
By Bookmasters